The Cultural Feast

The Cultural Feast

An Introduction to Food and Society

Carol A. Bryant
Anita Courtney
Barbara A. Markesbery
Kathleen M. DeWalt

West Publishing Company
St. Paul   New York   Los Angeles   San Francisco

Copyediting: Sonsie Carbonara Conroy

Cover and text design: Biblio Book Design

Composition: Rolin Graphics

Artwork: Rolin Graphics and Wayne Clark

Index: Jo-Anne Naples, Naples Editing Service

Cover photograph: Produce for sale at weekly market in Chia, Colombia, 1981 by Paul N. Patmore

Photo Credits

4, 67, 92, 142, 188, 204, 236, 370, 412 James Lindenberger; **34, 326, 378, 432** Agency for International Development (AID); **40** William Midness; **74** Paul N. Patmore; **100, 148** Billie DeWalt; **196** UN/John Isaac; **242** USDA/Bill Marr; **242** UNICEF/Davico; **278** UNICEF/Wolff; **284** NASA; **332** United Nations/FAO/Benaissa; **424** LaVerne M. Dutton.

COPYRIGHT© 1985 By WEST PUBLISHING CO.
610 Opperman Drive
P.O. Box 64526
St. Paul, MN 55164–0526

Printed in the United States of America

95 94   8 7 6 5 4 3
Library of Congress Cataloging in Publication Data
Main entry under title:

The Cultural feast.

   Bibliography: p.
   Includes index.
   1. Food.   2. Food habits.   3. Food supply.   4. Diet.
I. Bryant, Carol A., 1948–
TX353.C85   1985   363.8   84-25638
ISBN 0-314-85222-0

∞

About the Authors

Carol Bryant, Ph.D., M.S., received her training in applied anthropology from the University of Kentucky. First interested in psychological anthropology, she developed a mental health unit for Puerto Ricans at the University of Miami School of Medicine, before returning to Kentucky to complete her Ph.D. in anthropology, 1978, and her M.S. in clinical nutrition. Currently she is Deputy Commissioner for Nutrition and Health Education at the Lexington-Fayette County Health Department and Adjunct Assistant Professor of Anthropology at the University of Kentucky.

Anita Courtney received her Bachelor of Science degree in nutrition from the University of Kentucky in 1978. Since then, she has worked at the Lexington-Fayette County Health Department, first, as a community nutritionist and more recently as supervisor of the Nutrition Section.

Barbara Abram Markesbery, R.D., graduated in Dietetics from Iowa State University in 1958. While a therapeutic dietitian in a community hospital, she earned her R.D. In 1974 she joined the Lexington-Fayette County Health Department and continues as a community nutritionist with emphasis in nutrition education and promotion.

Kathleen Musante DeWalt, M.S., Ph.D., received her B.A., M.S. (1976) and Ph.D. (1979) in anthropology at the University of Connecticut. During her undergraduate years she began to study the effects of agricultural change on diet, which took her to Temascalcingo, Mexico in 1970. She returned there for a year's study in 1973, and again in 1977 for four months to finish field work for her Ph.D.

She joined the faculty of the College of Medicine at the University of Kentucky in the Department of Behavioral Science in 1978 where she is presently an Associate Professor.

A Note on the Photographic Research

In developing *A Cultural Feast,* we wanted to illustrate concepts difficult to articulate verbally, to focus attention on particularly significant points of information, to suggest other topics related to the text,
and to increase the esthetic quality—the readability—of the book.
Underlying these "tasks" was something more heartfelt: a desire to
communicate that the study of nutritional anthropology is more than
simply an accumulation of data, but also an experience of individuals
and their relationship to their most primary resource, food. The actual
process of developing the photographic portion of the book involved
many steps and a sustained effort. We searched many sources and reviewed literally hundreds of photographs. Many we had taken specifically when we could not find "just the right one". We hope we have
succeeded in visually portraying the larger world that many of us are
not fortunate enough to experience first hand.

James H. Lindenberger

Contents

Preface   ix

Introduction   1

Part I

Chapter 1   Diet and human evolution: Are we what they ate?   4

Highlight 1–1   No milk please! The story of lactase deficiency   34

Chapter 2   Food in historical perspective: Three dietary revolutions   40

Highlight 2–1   Vegetarianism: An old solution to a new problem   66

Chapter 3   Eating is a cultural affair   75

Highlight 3–1   Culture and body image   92

Part II

Chapter 4   Food technologies: How people get their food   101

Highlight 4-1   Food processing: Nutrients lost and found   142

Chapter 5   Food in social context   148

Highlight 5–1   U.S. federal food programs

Highlight 5–2   Hold the grits!: Regional and ethnic food
                 practices   196

Chapter 6   World view, religion and health beliefs:
                 The ideological basis of food
                 practices   204

Highlight 6–1   Nutrition education: Bridging the
                 communication gap   236

Part III

Chapter 7   The world food supply: Enough for
                 all   242

Highlight 7–1   The Green Revolution: Production
                 benefits and social costs   279

Chapter 8   The world food crisis and resource
                 distribution   284

Highlight 8–1   "As if people mattered": Appropriate
                 technology   326

Part IV

Chapter 9   Understanding dietary change   332

Highlight 9–1   Diet counseling: Helping people stick
                 with it   370

Chapter 10   Nutrition programs and strategies   378

Highlight 10–1   Program planning   412

Highlight 10–2   Helping mothers to breastfeed:
                 Program strategies in the United
                 States   424

Highlight 10–3   The ethics of directed change   432

Preface

The nutritional and social sciences have been engaged in a long-standing investigation of the fascinating and complex topic of food. Scientific advances concerning nutrient needs and how to meet them, combined with new approaches to culture, social change, and dietary behavior now help provide better health for more people than ever before. While this provides some measure of hope, the challenge of implementing appropriate and adequate diets remains.

Many people in developed countries suffer from diseases of over-nutrition, while staggering numbers of people in less developed countries end each day without enough to eat, many dying of starvation. The solutions, to understate the obvious, are difficult, and require from many disciplines continuing scientific inquiry and the application of the knowledge and skills already known.

As a team of anthropologists and nutritionists, we have attempted to blend this knowledge from various disciplines, with a goal of communicating three major points: that the relationships between people, their culture and society, and their food are complex; an awareness that food issues are global, as well as some actions that can and are being taken; and how combining nutritional and social science skills can increase success in helping people meet their nutrient needs.

In writing this book, many people provided invaluable assistance and guidance. Among those whose impact was most significant are Sara Quandt, Jake Gibbs, Tom Dillehay, Joseph Willet, Trudy Marshall, Ann Joseph, Pat Woodruff, John VanWilligen and Billie DeWalt, who read and commented on portions of the manuscript. We wish to make special mention of Karen Thompson for serving as primary research assistant, spending countless hours in confirming details and tracking down obscure references, and of Fran Turley, our very good friend and manuscript assistant, who typed more drafts of this manuscript than we care to remember, as well as Alice Alexander, Cynthia Gentry and Ann Scott for assisting with the typing.

We also wish to thank Ann Stasch, Jodee Dorsey, William Alex McIntosh, Antoinette Brown, Marjorie Cho Sue, Kathryn Kolasa, Randy Kandel, and Gretel Pelto, for reviewing various drafts of the manuscript and helping focus the content of this book.

Pat Britower and Marianna Pasqualis Politi at the Pan American World Health Organization, Dorothy Staats at USDA, Mary Felder and Clyde McNair at the Agency for International Development, and Yvonne Simmons and Ned Gilhooly at UNICEF all provided much help in researching the photographs used.

Henry and Jean Bryant and Angus and Judy Williams allowed us to escape to their mountain homes where the bulk of the manuscript was produced. We would also like to thank the editorial staff of West Publishing, particularly Gary Woodruff, Pamela Rost and Phyllis Cahoon for their guidance and patience during the development of the book and, finally, Jim Lindenberger, for his guidance in the research and development of the photographic content of the book.

We dedicate this book to those dearest to us, whose belief and love made all the difference:

Henry and Jean Bryant
Edwina and James Courtney
Bill, Susanne, Kendall and Allison Markesbery
David and Marguerite Abram
Billie, Saara, and Garreth DeWalt

Introduction

With nutrition knowledge expanding at a seemingly explosive rate during this century, human nutrition and diet have become popular topics throughout the U.S. and Canada. Yet even the most well-informed consumer is left with many puzzling questions. Consider, for example, the following:

> After years of being told to drink large amounts of milk for strong teeth and bones, meat to grow healthy, and liver for its rich iron content, nutritionists now advise moderation in consuming these same foods.

> A West African tribe, faced with food shortages, threw away North American relief shipments of powdered milk, claiming it was food of the evil spirits.

> The Chinese of Hunan Province savor live, wriggling shrimp, the Scottish enjoy their haggis made of "a cow's lung, intestines, pancreas, liver and heart, seasoned with onions, beef suet, and oatmeal, all cooked together in a sheep's stomach" (Farb and Armelagos 1980:165), and the natives of the Gilbert Islands delight in their tradition of sucking eyes from fish heads—practices that would startle most North Americans.

> Each year the U.S. government pays farmers to leave their fields fallow, and food industries discard 27 million tons of safe, nutritious, but cosmetically imperfect foods at the same time that 15 to 30 million children starve to death (Crittenden 1981:10).

> Although almost every magazine on today's newsstands features articles on methods to promote health through good nutrition, many people are unable to control their weight; lower their consumption of fat, cholesterol, sugar, and salt; or make other recommended dietary changes.

This book is organized to provide answers to these and other questions facing today's consumer. In Chapters 1 and 2, we look at our genetic heritage and its implications for modern human dietary practices. In an exploration of human evolution from the earliest hominids through the rise of modern Homo sapiens, we note humans' ability to inhabit an ever-widening range of environments through cultural as well as physiological and genetic adaptations. Then, as we move into historic times, we focus on three cultural revolutions—agricultural, industrial, and scientific—and their impact on human food practices.

Chapters 3, 4, 5, and 6 are concerned with modern human populations and how they use culture to adapt to the physical, social, and supernatural environment. Culture—a society's knowledge, traditions, beliefs, and values—is shown to exert a major influence on food practices, including what is considered edible and nonedible, how groups select certain items to make up their diet, and how they prepare and distribute food. In our analysis of technology—a society's tools, techniques, and traditions for obtaining food and shelter and adapting to other aspects of the physical environment—we compare five major strategies used to obtain food: foraging, horticulture, agriculture, pastoralism, and industrialized agriculture. Next we look at social organization—the cultural traditions people develop to guide their interactions with one another and organize themselves in order to achieve common goals. Food practices are shown to be tied to social organization in many ways. Food is used to build and maintain social, economic, and political relationships; food is linked with gender, age, social class, and ethnicity; and it is used as a symbol of prestige. In our discussion of ideology, we focus on the impact that world view, religion, and health beliefs have on dietary practices.

The world food situation is the subject of Chapters 7 and 8. First, we discuss factors affecting food production and our ability to feed the world's growing population. This is followed by a look at the politics of world hunger and the distribution of food supplies between rich and poor nations.

The final section, Chapters 9 and 10, focuses on dietary change and factors that influence the process of change. People's willingness to accept new ideas and modify their dietary practices is shown to be influenced by certain characteristics of the change or modification itself, as well as the attributes of both those advocating the change and potential adopters or consumers. Next we review major program strategies and techniques for improving diet practices and nutritional status in our own and other societies. Finally, our exploration of human food practices and dietary change concludes with a discussion of the ethics of nutrition intervention. It is our hope that an understanding of the cultural context in which food habits persist and change will assist readers to proceed responsibly and effectively as they take on the exciting nutrition challenges of our times.

1

Diet and human evolution: Are we what they ate?

You may be clothed in the latest fashions, and your car may be the latest model out of Detroit, but the body you live in is that of a caveman or cavewoman. You have come a long way from the cave dwellers in many ways: in language skills, in the arts, in medicine, and especially in the use of machinery. But in the ways your body handles food, bacteria, toxins, and air pollutants, there have been few, if any, changes. You now have essentially the same body and brain your ancestors had 12,000 years ago.

(Hamilton and Whitney 1982:5)

As humankind moves into the twenty-first century, we find ourselves in a precarious situation. Living in bodies evolved for life as tropical hunters and gatherers, we face entirely new environmental challenges: acid rain, hazardous waste dumps, pesticides, herbicides, and foods containing additives, antibiotics, artificial colorings, and a host of other compounds completely new to the human body. In developed countries, we are adapting to diets high in calories, cholesterol and saturated fats, while the poor who live in underdeveloped countries face critical shortages of protein and calories.

On this evolutionary journey, we also find that the threats from disease are changing. Infectious diseases pose less of a problem than they did for our ancestors, but cancer, diabetes, heart disease, and stroke are on the rise in developed countries. Vitamin deficiencies and protein/calorie malnutrition continue to plague our Third World neighbors. Because so many of these new "killer" diseases have been linked to changing dietary habits, the study of human nutrition has become increasingly important in recent years. More and more consumers are asking: What should I eat to stay healthy? Is my body designed to be carnivorous or herbivorous? Is it safe to feed my children hamburgers from the fast food chain or should I stick to foods I prepare myself? Is all the concern about food additives justified or an unnecessary worry in a world already fraught with anxiety?

In a search for answers to these questions, scientists have turned to many sources: controlled animal studies, epidemiological research contrasting diets in western and nonwestern societies, and a variety of other human studies. Biological anthropologists offer another valuable perspective: how the human diet has evolved. Their knowledge of the almost inperceptibly slow process by which the human body and diet have developed is derived from analyses of the fossils of human ancestors, observations of feeding behaviors of living primates, and studies of the dietary habits of foragers—people who live much like our recent ancestors did during the last 300,000 years of our evolution. These data give us important insights into our nutritional needs and limitations. For example, information derived from all three sources suggests that our bodies are designed to be omnivorous; that is, we can digest both plant and animal material, and probably are healthiest when our diets contain both types of food.

An understanding of human evolution gives us an important perspective of how our bodies have developed and the possible history and function of human nutrition. Therefore, we begin this chapter with a discussion of the processes by which humans adapt to their environment through behavioral, physiological, and genetic changes. Then we will examine the major stages in human evolution and their nutritional significance for modern peoples.

epidemiology
The study of the origin, nature, and distribution of diseases

biolological anthropologists
Scientists who study the animal origins and biological nature of humankind and the biological variations of human populations

foragers
People who obtain their food by gathering plants and hunting (see Chapter 4 for a discussion of the foraging way of life)

The human species occupies a more widespread range of environments than any other Primate Species, extending from the northern arctic to humid tropical forests and arid desert zone, living at altitudes from sea level to over 5000 meters above sea level. The range of climatic conditions to which human populations are exposed today nearly corresponds with the total variation present on this planet; ancestors of living populations must have experienced an ever wider variety of climatic conditions as weather and atmospheric conditions fluctuated during the course of human prehistory and evolution.

(Underwood 1979:160)

Adaptation

To understand our amazing success as a species, it helps to look at how humans adapt to their environments. Beneficial adaptational responses represent solutions to challenges posed by the environment: what to eat, how to protect oneself from hazards, and, for humans, how to fill psychosocial needs such as those for love and a sense of purpose. Both individual organisms, as well as entire populations, can be said to adapt. "As an individual's survival is enhanced, so is his potential for reproduction. And increased reproductive potential enhances the survival of the individual's group" (Johnston 1982:56).

Humans adapt to their environments through behavioral, physiological and genetic responses. A change in our environment may activate all three types of responses, but the rates at which we adapt behaviorally, physiologically, and genetically are quite different. Imagine for a minute that the earth suddenly grew much much colder. Your first reaction would be behavioral: you might put on a jacket, turn up the thermostat, and cancel your picnic plans. Behavioral responses such as these are the most rapid way to adapt to environmental pressures. But if these behavioral adaptations proved insufficient to keep you warm, shivering would then begin, your metabolic rate would rise, and peripheral blood vessels would constrict to conserve heat loss. These physiological adaptations might protect you and most of your friends from the cold. However, if the climatic disturbance persisted, genetic adaptation would reinforce, and perhaps replace, the behavioral and physiological responses. Individuals with traits that allowed them to adapt to cold temperatures, such as excessive body fat or elevated metabolic rates, would be healthier and produce more offspring than those without these adaptive traits. If these attributes were genetically transmitted, the next generation and each one after that would contain a higher proportion of people with these adaptive features. As the population evolved, people might become so well adapted genetically that they could enjoy the outdoors without jackets or metabolic changes.

Figure 1.1

Natural Selection. Darwin's early studies involved observation of finches on the Galapagos Islands. He noted important similarities and differences in beaks, body forms, and plumage that supported his views of natural selection.

Behavioral adaptation

As we have just seen, behavior offers people the quickest and most flexible means of responding to environmental pressures. Behavioral responses include *individual* behavior (that which is unique to you) and *cultural* behavior (that which is learned, patterned, and shared with other members of your social group).

Culture is an important mechanism by which humans modify the environment and create new conditions as they adapt to the pressures around them. Health beliefs and medical practices, for example, act as a buffer between you and disease. As medicine becomes more effective, our reproductive potential and general well-being are enhanced. This is called *cultural adaptation.*

Throughout much of human evolution and into contemporary times, the ability to create culture has been humanity's most important adaptive tool. For example, it is through cultural adaptation that people have been able to colonize regions with harsh environmental conditions (Frisancho 1981:3). When faced with environmental challenges, we develop weapons—not fangs or claws—to defend ourselves from predators; we build houses and make clothes—rather than grow fur—to protect ourselves from the elements. This means that, unlike other animals that adapt genetically through natural selection, we can adjust our cultural response quickly to changing environmental demands. Various finches on the Galapago Islands, for example, have developed different kinds of beaks depending on the kind of foods they eat. This evolutionary process took many generations. Humans, on the other hand, have not developed different kinds of mouths based on the types of foods they eat. Rather we have adapted *culturally* by using our superior intelligence to develop technologies for obtaining and preparing various foods.

This ability to adapt culturally gives humans a tremendous advantage over other species, many of which have become extinct in the face of rapid environmental change. In fact, as we shall see, culture has proven to be so advantageous that one of the major evolutionary processes operating on our primate ancestors was selection for the capacity to create culture in the form of bigger brains, increased intelligence, and other anatomical changes that enabled humans to develop language.

While culture continues to be our major adaptive mechanism, culture and technology also create stressful conditions that require new adaptive responses. For example, "A modification of one environmental condition may result in the change of another . . . . Advances in the medical sciences have successfully reduced infant and adult mortality to the extent that the world population is growing at an explosive rate, and unless the world food resources are increased (and distribution systems altered) the twenty-first century will witness a world famine" (Fisancho 1981:3–4).

Physiological adaptation

Health and survival depend upon our ability to adjust to external changes and maintain a stable internal environment. In humans, as in many other animals, the blood, lymph, and other body fluids must be maintained within relatively narrow limits for the cells, tissues, and organs to function properly. When the body is unable to maintain this internal balance, the individual sickens and eventually dies.

Physiological adaptation involves biochemical, anatomical, and other morphological characteristics that allow us to maintain a stable internal environment in a wide range of external environmental conditions.

This adaptability comes from the body's ability to respond physiologically through a variety of buffering mechanisms and other adaptive features. To appreciate this physiological adaptability more fully, let's look at how the body maintains a stable internal environment even when the amount of nutrients consumed changes. Many vitamins and minerals can be consumed in amounts larger than needed, because your body can break down the excess amounts and excrete the byproducts in urine, sweat, and other bodily secretions, keeping the nutrients from reaching toxic levels. Also, when your diet contains a smaller amount of vitamins and minerals than needed, your body has several mechanisms that enable it to adapt by absorbing and processing them more efficiently. Take calcium as an example.

Calcium plays several critical roles in the body: maintenance of strong bones and teeth, viable cell membranes, and strong, flexible collagen fibers that hold the skin together. Calcium also is critical for muscle relaxation, heart regulation, and transmission of nerve impulses, as well as serving as a catalyst in several biochemical reactions such as blood clotting. Because calcium is so vital to good health, your body has developed several systems to maintain the proper level (about 10mg/100ml) in your blood. The first of these involves blood proteins that bind extra calcium circulating in the bloodstream. As dietary calcium levels drop, these proteins release their calcium, making it available for use.

Another regulatory mechanism is absorption by intestinal cells. With the help of vitamin D, a calcium-binding protein is produced that controls how much of the mineral is absorbed. Because of this physiological response, a woman may take up almost twice as much calcium from the same diet when she is pregnant as when she is not.

In a similar fashion, children absorb about 50 to 60 percent of the calcium they consume; adults, whose bones and teeth are already formed and therefore need less, absorb only 30 percent.

The calcium stored in bones and teeth offers the body a third way to maintain proper calcium balance. When the diet contains sufficient calcium to meet the body's needs, calcium stores build; when dietary levels fall, the stores are mobilized and used by the body.

A final defense against calcium imbalance is found in the kidneys, where the amount of calcium excreted is regulated to match dietary levels with the body's needs (Whitney and Hamilton 1981:424–5).

Your body's ability to regulate calcium, like other nutrients, is limited. Chronically low intakes will eventually deplete stored calcium and deficiency diseases such as osteoporosis will develop. While excessive amounts of dietary calcium do not seem to create a problem, consumption of large quantities of some vitamins and minerals can overload the body's regulatory systems and create toxic reactions. Within limits, then, the body's elaborate metabolic system allows people to adapt physiologically to a wide range of short-term and long-term dietary fluctuations.

Another interesting illustration of physiological adaptability involves human growth and body size. For many years, average body size has increased in most human populations. Most likely you and the majority of your friends are somewhat taller than your parents and other members of their generation. This is believed to be the result of improved nutritional status and medical care. It also reflects an important adaptative characteristic ability to respond to limited food resources through growth retardation and the reduction of body size. That is, when protein and calories are in short supply, children respond by slowing their growth rate and terminating growth before achieving their full genetically programmed adult size. Because they are smaller, these people require less protein, calories, and other nutrients and are better able to survive in the face of limited food resources. Compare, for instance, the caloric requirements of the average male in Colombia, where the population has adapted to limited food supplies through reduced body size, and the average male in North America, where food supplies are more abundant. Clearly, the Columbian requires far less food to perform the same activities than his larger North American counterpart (Stini 1975:22). This adaptive response is important for entire populations, as well as individual survival, because reductions in body size and caloric requirements "relax the pressure on food resources available to each individual and thereby allow a larger number of individuals to coexist," thus reducing the group's likelihood of extinction (Stini 1975:20).

Table 1.1 Comparison of Caloric Requirements of Males of Mean Body Weight in United States and Colombia.	United States	Heliconia, Colombia
Mean body weight (kilograms)	70	60
Caloric costs (kilocalories)		
Resting (8 hours)	570	480
Sedentary activity (6 hours)	492	266
Light labor (8 hours)	1,527	1,123
Moderate labor (2 hours)	654	482
Total	3,243	2,351

Source: From William A. Stini, "Adaptive Strategies of Human Populations Under Nutritional Stress," in Elizabeth Watts, Frances E. Johnston, Gabriel W. Lasker (eds), *Biosocial Interrelations in Population Adaptation,* The Hague: Mouton Publishers, p. 21.

Genetic adaptation

When an environmental pressure continues for a long period of time, as when major climatic changes occur or when populations move into new areas, behavioral and physiological responses are reinforced by genetic adaptation. For example, when nutritional stress is severe or prolonged, cultural and physiological responses often are insufficient to protect all members of a population from disease and death. Even with slowed growth rates and reduced body size, many people sucumb to protein/calorie malnutrition. When some people in a population have inherited traits that enable them to adapt to the nutritional stress and they produce more offspring than other people without this trait, the stage is set for genetic adaptation.

The driving force of genetic adaptation is *natural selection.* Natural selection is the process of eliminating deleterious traits and transmitting advantageous ones to succeeding generations. As was shown earlier, individuals within a group may vary from one another. Some may carry a trait that enables them to more efficiently utilize food or other resources, ward off predators, resist disease, or meet other environmental challenges more effectively than those who do not have this trait. Because of their advantage, the individuals who have the more efficient adaptive trait produce more offspring than others. If the trait is genetically transmitted, subsequent generations will have a higher proportion of individuals who carry the adaptive trait than the previous one. In this way, adaptive traits replace maladaptive ones and the population becomes better suited to its environment (Ritenbaugh 1978:112).

Natural selection can be an incredibly slow process. In a species such as *Homo sapiens,* which has a long life span and a late reproductive age (generations are separated by about 20 years), thousands of years are required for adaptation to occur through genetic change. Selective forces are slowed further in human populations because of their physiological and cultural adaptiveness; individuals are able to adapt to many short- and long-term environmental disturbances without loss of health or fertility, and therefore experience relatively few genetic changes at the populational level. For example, as we shall see in Chapter 2, Mexicans whose food supply is typically low in calcium have not adapted genetically, but physiologically (by absorbing calcium more efficiently) and behaviorally (by processing cornmeal in a way that increases the calcium content).

Natural selection and genetic adaptation are the basis for evolutionary change. Therefore, when using an evolutionary perspective to study human diets, it is important to keep in mind that natural selection acts only upon genetic traits that affect the individual's survival or reproductive success. Dietary patterns bring about evolutionary change when they affect functioning, fertility, gestation, lactation, and/or mortality.

> Nutritional stress may reduce fertility by retarding growth rates and slowing or preventing sexual maturation; reducing the ovulation rate . . . reducing sperm count, motility, and longevity; causing resorption of the fetus(es); causing lactational failure; or increasing the risks of infant death from various causes associated with low birth weight.
>
> *(Gaulin and Konner 1977:4)*

Because food selection is so critical to health and reproduction, many behavioral aspects of feeding have a genetic basis and are responsive to the selective forces of evolution. Taste and smell, for instance, enable the individual to reject poisonous items and consume more nutritionally suitable foods. A preference for sweet substances is shared by many animals, presumably because sweet foods, high in calories and typically nonpoisonous, made good choices during a long period in our evolutionary development.

As a population or species becomes specialized to a particular environment, it may at the same time become less suited to different environmental conditions. Traits adaptive in one place and time may be maladaptive in another. With the development of highly concentrated sugar sources, the sweet tooth that once proved so adaptive is now the bane of many obese people. For our ancestors, a metabolic system highly efficient in using calories for energy and the ability to store excess energy in the liver and fatty tissue was clearly advantageous. It freed them from the need to eat constantly throughout the day, as most animals must do, and allowed them to survive temporary food shortages. While highly adaptive for animals faced with an unreliable food supply, these same metabolic traits produce obesity and its associated diseases in people who have abundant supplies of calorie-rich foods and little opportunity to exercise. Thus, an elegant solution for one set of environmental conditions is not always well suited for another.

Interaction of cultural, physiological, and genetic responses

In today's struggle to cope with environmental change, all three mechanisms—behavioral, physiological, and genetic adaptation—work together. These adjustments are complex and often difficult to sort out. Culture, for example, enables us to meet many new challenges, but in doing so sometimes creates new problems requiring additional adaptive responses. The use of salt provides a good illustration. As early as Egyptian times, and perhaps much before, humans learned to salt meat and fish as a way of preventing spoilage: salting and pickling enable human societies to adapt to unreliable food supplies by preserving valued foods. These cultural practices, while adaptive, have created a new environmental challenge: diets high in sodium. With salt and other sodium-containing compounds now readily available, their use has increased dramatically. The average American consumes about 4 to 8 grams of sodium each day, an amount significantly higher than the provisional Recommended Dietary Allowance (RDA) of only 1.1 to 3.3 grams. Although the human body is able to adapt physiologically to high sodium intakes by increasing water consumption and urinary excretion, many believe a chronically high sodium content can overstress the body's regulatory mechanisms and cause high blood pressure in some people. For some people with hypertension, large amounts of sodium contribute to the progression of the disease. Thus, the cultural solution to one environmental problem, food spoilage, has created a new condition—high sodium intake, which in turn requires a new adaptive response.

An example that shows how genetic adaptations can interact with dietary practices comes from the Mediterranean, where people are faced with the life-threatening disease, malaria. The high incidence of malaria in the Mediterranean region is accompanied by the presence of a disorder rare in other parts of the world.

inborn error of metabolism
An inherited disorder caused by a defective gene or genes, usually for a specific enzyme

Glucose–6–Phosphate Dehydrogenase (G6PD) deficiency, the lack of a red blood cell enzyme, is an inborn error in metabolism. Those who have inherited this deficiency are resistant to malaria because their red blood cells are less hospitable to the growth of the malaria-producing parasite than normal red blood cells that contain G6PD. Scientists have concluded, therefore, that the high frequency of G6PD deficiency in this area of the world is the result of natural selection and represents a genetic adaptation to malaria.

Dietary practices interact with this genetic adaptation in an interesting way. People with G6PD deficiency are highly sensitive to fava beans, a crop widely cultivated throughout the region. Fava consumption produces a serious anemia called favism in some G6PD deficient people (particularly children) by destroying their red blood cells. The reaction to fava bean consumption may appear anywhere from a few hours up to several days after the consumption of the beans. In modern times, with the use of transfusion therapy, the mortality rate is about 1 in 12 cases. In the past, before transfusions were available to abate the crisis, it was probably much higher.

Thus, as is so often the case, one adaptation (G6PD deficiency) creates a new environmental challenge (favism), and thus the need for another adaptive response. One cultural response to favism has been the development of elaborate practices and beliefs surrounding the fava bean. Drying, soaking, and removing the skins are among the many cooking and processing techniques used to decrease the bean's toxicity and lower the risks of favism. Taboos held by some groups prohibit fava consumption among children and pregnant women, and folk remedies have been developed to treat favism, many of which are pharmacologically sound.

Despite these cultural adjustments, favism still takes a heavy toll on human populations, and scientists have wondered why Mediterranean peoples have not substituted a safer bean for the potentially dangerous fava. Investigations of the agricultural and nutritional advantages of the beans cultivated in the region show that favas produce large yields in a variety of environmental circumstances. However, their protein values are lower than the kidney beans and chickpeas also cultivated in this area. Scientists have concluded, therefore, that

> While their agricultural potential is quite significant and therefore cannot be ignored, their nutritional value is not high enough to argue for their continued consumption in those regions where these other legume substitutes are available. This is not to imply that populations select from available foods in view of relative nutrient composition. Instead, we suggest that, because the nutritional value of fava beans is not markedly

higher than that of other indigenous legumes, their consumption cannot be expected to have enhanced the survival potential
among the populations in question. Continued use must, then,
be ascribed to other factors.

(Katz and Schall 1979:461)

Subsequent investigations into this evolutionary paradox have
shown that fava consumption does indeed offer humans another important selective advantage, one that has nothing to do with the
bean's nutritional value. Scientists first noticed that people with
G6PD deficiency reacted to antimalarial drugs in much the same
way that they reacted to fava beans. This led them to examine the
chemical composition of the antimalarial drugs and fava beans.
Comparison revealed that both contained several compounds believed to produce anemia in G6PD deficient individuals—
compounds believed to have antimalarial properties. Fava beans,
then, may contain antimalarial properties that offer people without
G6PD deficiency valuable protection against the disease. It is this
protection that gives fava beans their adaptive value, and accounts
for their continued use by Mediterranean peoples (Katz and Schall
1979:473).

In sum, humans adapt to an ever-changing environment through
cultural and physiological responses. When environmental changes
affect individual health and/or fertility, affected people are less
likely to reproduce and pass on their genes. Those carrying the advantageous trait(s) will contribute more offspring to the succeeding generations. Thus, the genes for these advantageous traits increase within the population, thereby enabling it to adapt through
genetic changes. In the next section we examine the interaction of
cultural, physiological, and genetic adaptations made during our
evolutionary emergence as a species.

As we examine our evolutionary legacy and what it means for
health and diet in today's world, a word of caution is in order. It is
tempting to argue that any feeding practice, or food, differing significantly from those present during our evolutionary development is
likely to be harmful. After all, changes such as an increased intake
of white sugar and the use of artificial food substances have occurred so rapidly that the human body has not had time to adapt
them through natural selection.

Yet, we cannot conclude automatically that just because a diet
practice is new, it is necessarily bad. The human body is able to digest an amazingly wide range of foods with no apparent harm. And
although it is reassuring to know that a particular type of diet sustained our ancestors for millenia, we cannot be sure that a more recent modification is necessarily any better or any worse. Other types

of research that provide quicker feedback are needed to decide the risks associated with new dietary practices.

Caution should be exercised in using an evolutionary explanation of dietary practices for other reasons as well. Because most diseases strike the elderly and therefore do not affect reproductive outcome, natural selection does not have a direct impact on the frequency of these diseases in future generations. Also, because today's environmental stresses are quite different than those of the past, today's dietary needs may also be different. For example, because there are now more potentially carcinogenic substances in our environment and our diet, it may be wise for us to eat more foods high in carotene than we once needed. Dark green and bright orange vegetables such as broccoli, greens, carrots, and sweet potatoes are high in carotene, which some research suggest has anticarcinogenic properties (Ames 1983, National Research Council 1982). Likewise, because most people are taller than previous generations, nutrient needs may be greater: calcium, for instance, may be needed in larger quantities during childhood to support growth of a larger skeleton.

carcinogen
Cancer-promoting substance

Lessons from human evolution

As animals, humans share some traits in common with all creatures descended from the first single-celled animal that appeared about 1 billion years ago. Because we share a common ancestry with other animals, we also share certain biological and nutritional features that developed during our primordial beginnings. One of these characteristics is the dependence on external sources, rather than internal synthesis, for many of the carbon compounds needed to sustain life. These compounds—amino acids, carbohydrates, and fats, as well as vitamins and minerals—are called *essential nutrients* because they must be obtained from the diet for growth and maintenance of tissues. In contrast to plants, which can make all 20 of the amino acids found in their proteins, animals depend upon external sources for about half of these. Humans need at least 45 and maybe as many as 50 essential nutrients (Scrimshaw and Young 1980:52).

primordial
The first in order of appearance in the growth or development of an organism

Evolutionary biologists believe that the earliest forms of life, simple bacterium-like organisms, were capable of manufacturing all the compounds they needed from mineral salts, carbon, and water. Occasionally, however, through normal, randomly occurring mutations, life forms appeared that lacked those manufacturing capabilities. Whenever needed nutrients were available in the external environment, such mutations did not prove fatal and were passed on to succeeding generations.

Focus 1-1

Primate nutrient needs

We have just seen how humans are similar to other living primates because of shared evolutionary pressures and genetic adaptations. Another interesting feature with nutritional significance is our inability to manufacture vitamin C. Most animals produce their own vitamin C by combining chemicals already present in the body. Only humans, most other primates, and a few other animals do not have this ability and therefore must consume a diet containing sufficient quantities of the vitamin. Evolutionists hypothesize that the inability to manufacture vitamin C resulted from a mutation that occurred millions of years ago. This mutation altered the enzyme that catalyzed the final step in the production of ascorbic acid from glucose. Linus Pauling believes that this mutation was advantageous because it freed glucose for use as energy. The mutation did not prove lethal because the mutant primate's diet of green leaves and other vegetables provided abundant quantities of the nutrient (a gorilla consumes about four to five grams of vitamin C a day) and was transmitted selectively to its descendants (Schrimshaw and Young 1980:52; Vander 1981:104).

Some scientists hypothesize that natural selection actually favored these mutations because they eliminated "unnecessary" biochemical reactions in already "busy" cells (Scrimshaw and Young 1980:51). Over time, then, animals evolved that relied more and more on the environment for nutrients and less and less on internal synthesis.

Our primate heritage

People are primates. As primates, we are members of a group of rather diverse animals characterized by a set of physical and behavioral traits that distinguish us from other animals.

Primates became primates, that is, they developed special distinguishing traits, because of their adaptation to an arboreal (tree-dwelling) existence. Life in the tree tops presented the earliest primates with many challenges. Those best equipped for climbing and

mutation
An alteration in the genetic material. If a mutation occurs in a sex cell (sperm or ovum), the change will be passed on to the next generation. Such mutations are rare—only 5 to 100 for every 1 million sex cells. Mutations that alter peoples' genes after birth (and do not occur in sex cells) have no evolutionary impact

17

jumping from branch to branch were selected over the less skilled aerial acrobats. The need to collect fruits, insects, and small animals also encouraged selection of good eye-hand coordination and the ability to grasp with well-coordinated movements.

Some of the major primate adaptations to the environmental pressures of life in the tree tops that have also contributed to human nature and feeding patterns are summarized below (Clark 1959, Harris 1980).

tactile pads
Areas on finger tips that are sensitive to touch

opposable thumbs
Thumbs that can be pressed against the fingers to grasp or clutch objects

1. Hands and feet are designed to clutch and grasp. The fingers and toes are moveable; flattened nails and highly sensitive tactile pads have replaced sharp claws. These features, and particularly opposable thumbs, enable primates to grasp and carry food.

2. Arms rotate, flex, and extend easily. This trait also enables primates to pick leaves, throw sticks or spears, and travel adeptly through the tropical forest.

3. Vision is highly developed. Primate eyes are large and located toward the front of the head instead of the sides. This produces stereoscopic vision—the ability to gauge distances—which is important for swinging through the trees while foraging or hunting game.

4. Social behavior is complex and cooperative. "Most primates spend their lives as members of groups . . . . These groups cooperate in finding food and in defending themselves against predators. Group life is facilitated among primates by relatively complex communication systems consisting of signals which indicate the presence of food, danger, sexual interest, and other vital matters" (Harris 1980:23).

5. The brain is large and intelligence is highly developed.

> The arboreal environment, with its wind-blown, rain-spattered and light-dappled foliage, requires constant monitoring and interpretation. The exploratory manuevers of the arms and fingers and their capacity for bringing objects close to the eyes for inspection also need complex neural circuits. But most demanding of all is the high level of social interaction. It is no accident that the primates are among the "brainiest" as well as the most social of the mammals . . . . It is also no coincidence that human beings, the brainiest of the primates, are also the most social of the primates. Our intelligence is above all an evolutionary consequence of our extreme sociality.
>
> *(Harris 1980:23)*

Hominoid

Monkey

Tarsier

Lemur/loris

Tree shrew

Figure 1.2
The primate order.

Primate dietary adaptations

Until recently, people were believed to have distinctively different
diet habits from other primates. Our closest relatives, the great apes,
gorillas, chimpanzees and orangutans, were once believed to be
nonaggressive vegetarians lacking both the tools and social cohesiveness needed to hunt. In contrast, the human hunter was depicted as an aggressive, meat-eating predator who evolved from a
killer ape millions of years ago. We also were distinguished from the
gentle great apes by a propensity to share food, the ability to make
as well as use tools, and the capacity to create language and culture.

More recent observations of primates in their natural habitats have muddied these distinctions, creating a new and different picture of our primate cousins. First, the great apes are not vegetarians, but omnivorous. The bulk of their diet is derived from leaves, shoots, flowers, buds, fruits and berries, grains, seeds, husks, pods, nuts, seeds and grasses, vine stems, and even barks and resins (Teleki 1981:305). This vegetarian mainstay often includes several hundred floral species. The surprising news that apes are also meat eaters first came in the 1960's from Jane Goodall's observations of chimpanzees in Tanzania's Gombe National Park. Since that time intensive research has been conducted on chimps and orangutans in Africa and Borneo. Chimps, in particular, have been found to have an amazingly omnivorous diet. They eat just about everything available in their environment—ants, termites, caterpillars, cocoons, birds and their eggs, and small mammals (Johnston 1982:168). This omnivorousness gives apes and humans the ability to adapt to a variety of environmental conditions by allowing them to live off a wide range of foods.

Perhaps even more surprising is evidence that some primates seem to prefer meat and will eat large quantities of it when available. One example comes from a study of baboons in Botswana. When the grasshopper populations expanded and infested certain trees, baboons in the area changed from their usual vegetarian fare to one based largely on insects. One troop spent 72 percent of its time collecting and consuming the insects; while troops nearby which did not have access to the increased grasshopper population continued to exist almost solely on plants (Harding and Teleki 1981). Chimpanzees also are known to spend a significant portion of their feeding time hunting small animals and collecting insects (Teleki 1981).

Figure 1.3

Chimpanzee termiting.
(Geza Teleki)

A second important finding to emerge from primate studies concerns predatory or hunting behavior. Chimpanzees, baboons, and other primates now are known to frequently attack and kill small mammals. Among baboons, 47 small animals kills were documented during only 1,032 hours of observation. Also, a primatologist, Teleki (1981:314), observed over 162 animal kills in his 13 year study of chimpanzees in Gombe National Park. He estimates that as much as 10 percent of the chimpanzees' feeding time may be devoted to hunting mammals. He also notes that most hunting is done by males, while collection of ants and other insects is primarily a female activity (Teleki 1981:327–328).

More important than the frequency with which primates hunt game is the fact that they sometimes hunt cooperatively. At one time this type of social cooperation was considered characteristic of humans only. Again, Jane Goodall was among the first to provide a different picture of the apes. Goodall observed a group of chimps chasing small monkeys through the tree tops, capturing and then eating them. Of special interest was the fact that some of the chimps gave chase while others moved ahead to cut off the monkeys' retreat. In other instances, as many as nine chimps have been seen working in a coordinated manner, positioning and repositioning themselves to maintain an enclosure, sometimes for an hour or more (Teleki 1981:332).

These findings suggest that both omnivorousness and a taste for meat may have their roots in our primate heritage. However, we also should note that while our cousins, the nonhuman primates, share our preference for meat, they do not have the same opportunities to express it: monkeys and apes are relatively poor hunters, and animals are less readily available as their prey. In comparison with Western humans, who derive as much as 40 to 50 percent of their calories from meat, insects and animals probably make up less than 5 percent of most chimpanzees' diets (Busse 1977:908). (Because meat intake is difficult to assess in wild primates, these estimates should be viewed cautiously.) Thus, while it may be reassuring to know that meat consumption has a foundation in our primate past, we should not expect that our primate bodies are equipped to handle large quantities of meat on a regular basis (Brody 1981:437).

Finally, the distinctions between apes and humans based on food sharing, tool production and the capacity to create culture are now being challenged. While important differences certainly exist in the degree to which these traits are expressed, it appears as if the foundation for much of our cultural and social nature was laid millions of years ago as part of our primate legacy.

Reconstructing hominid evolution

The evolutionary divergence between humans and the great apes occurred between 8 and 4 million years ago. A set of interrelated genetic and cultural adaptations occurred that gave rise to hominids, the zoological family made up humans and their immediate ancestors.

Data sources In reconstructing our hominid ancestors' diets, anthropologists must rely on an incomplete record. Stone tools and bones of large vertebrate animals associated with hunting are much sturdier and more likely to be unearthed at archeological sites than vegetable remains, baskets, or wooden tools. For this reason evidence of meat consumption is overreported, while plant collection and consumption is underemphasized. Fortunately, other methods have been developed to generate information on hominid diets.

For early hominids, much dietary evidence comes from studies of fossil teeth. Certain morphological features, for example, are associated with the types of foods consumed. Teeth of carnivores are

carnivore
Flesh-eating animal; an animal that needs meat to survive

Focus 1-2

Hominid diets:
Were we meant to be meat eaters?

Evidence from several sources suggests that while hominids did not evolve as exclusively herbivorous, neither did they develop as flesh-eating carnivores. Rather, hominids have some features of both herbivores and carnivores, and on balance several characteristics suggest a heavily vegetarian diet. The first set of evidence comes from studies of fossil teeth.

Morphologically, hominid teeth appear to be designed for an omnivorous diet: our front teeth are large and sharp and good for biting, our canines are small, our molars are flat with thick enamel crowns good for chewing gritty and fibrous plant foods, and our jaws are mobile for grinding. Preliminary evidence from scanning electron microscopy also suggest that our ancestors ate more plant than animal food (Walker, Hoeck, Perez: 1978).

The digestive tract of humans provides a third set of clues to our early diet. The human digestive tract, while lacking the double stomach of totally herbivorous ruminants like cows, bears even less resemblance to that of carnivores. Our intestines are long and highly convoluted, allowing us to digest substances such as high-fiber plant foods that take a long time to be broken down and absorbed.

But whether they are of plant or animal origin, foods take a long time to pass through the human tract. This leaves meat residues in the body for far longer than they remain in carnivores. Such prolonged contact may be related to the high rates of colon cancer found in people who eat diets high in meat. Also, the large amount of saturated fat and cholesterol in meat may result in accumulations of cancer-producing chemicals in the gut.

carnassials
The last promolar and first lower molar in carnivores

designed for killing prey, cutting, and tearing flesh. The front teeth are long, strong, and pointed (fangs) to stab and hold flesh. Their carnassials, premolars, and molars are also large; designed for cutting, they are able to slice through flesh like a pair of shears. As a result, the jaw moves very little from side to side, limiting carnivores' ability to grind food.

Herbivores, by contrast, have small canines and sharp cutting incisors in front for biting off mouthfuls of food. Their molars have flat surfaces, well-suited for grinding and crushing. In addition, the jaws of herbivores move easily from side to side, enabling them to thoroughly chew the fibrous vegetable foods they live on. Thorough chewing greatly enhances the digestibility of plant foods.

Another method, scanning electron microscopy, is used to examine the wear patterns on fossil teeth. Plant foods leave distinctive scratch patterns useful in determining the types of food consumed. Unfortunately, the last items eaten before the animal dies tends to leave the most obvious markings. However, when samples from large numbers of animals representing various feeding sites and seasons are studied, microwear analysis gives a general picture of the animals' diets (Mann 1981:15).

For our more recent ancestors, another source of information for reconstructing diet patterns and nutritional status is the analysis of human fecal remains. In some instances, human feces deposited in caves or other dry places have fossilized and remained undisturbed for centuries. These feces are called coprolites. When analyzed, human coprolites provide archaeologists with evidence regarding the dietary patterns, food preparation methods, and seasonal activities of prehistoric populations. This technique is now widely used. Coprolites from settlements dating to as early as 300,000 years ago have been analyzed.

Coprolite analysis Coprolite analysis involves several steps. First, the source of the coprolites must be identified. To accomplish this, the specimen is immersed in a dilute solution of trisodium phosphate. When coprolites of human origin are immersed, the resulting fluid turns dark brown or black, while specimens from other animals produce fluids with different characteristic colors. The contents of coprolites are then analyzed by passing the sample through mesh screens to trap solid residues for analysis with a microscope. The remaining liquid is centrifuged in order to collect small objects such as pollen grains and plant crystals.

centrifuging
Rotation in a machine in order to separate, by centrifugal force, substances having different densities

Analysis of coprolites helps in identifying foods in the diet, how food was prepared, and seasonal occupation of a specific location. Materials that resist digestion, and therefore are found in coprolites, include seeds, fish and reptile scales, and bones of small mammals, fishes and reptiles. Although large animal bones are not likely to be ingested, indigestible hairs may adhere to meat and be swallowed. Such materials often make it possible to identify the particular species of animals and plants eaten.

The condition of seed fragments also may offer clues about food preparation methods. Crushed seeds may suggest pounding while seeds that have been split probably were rolled back and forth on a stone *metate*. Charred seeds suggest roasting, and whole seeds may suggest that they were ingested as part of a fruit. For example, seeds of chili peppers, tomatoes, berries, and squashes are common in coprolites from Central America.

Pollen grains also resist digestion and can help in identifying plant species. The pollen may have come from plant blossoms that were eaten. For instance, a study by V.M. Bryant, Jr. and G. Williams-Dean (1976) found pollen grains in coprolites from an archaeological site in southwestern Texas that come from the blossoms of agave, sotol, and yucca. It is unclear whether the blossoms were chewed for their nectar, used for brewing tea, or for making salads (or used for all three purposes). Small quantities of windborn pollens also may have been ingested accidentally from drinking water or simply inhaled and swallowed. Even such accidentally ingested pollens provide useful information, however; because pollen is associated with a particular season, it indicates the time of year a site was characteristically occupied and provide background information on seasonal variations in food-getting activities of prehistoric populations.

Human skeletal analysis When studying early human populations, another rich source of information comes from analyses of human skeletal remains. Dental caries and periodontal diseases are easily observed, for example, and may indicate nutritional stress, high-carbohydrate diets, and/or vitamin C deficiency (Brown 1981:410). Radiography (X rays) of bones reveals small lines made by increased mineral density. These lines are formed when growth is temporarily stopped by disease and malnutrition during childhood or adolescence. Analyses of mineral composition of bones also provide valuable dietary information. Levels of certain minerals—calcium, fluoride, strontium, zinc as well as many others—are directly related to the amounts of minerals consumed. Strontium, for instance, is found in larger concentrations in plants than in animal flesh, and therefore its presence has been used to identify carnivores, omnivores, and herbivores. Strontium analyses have been performed on earlier hominid bones as well. However, until more is known about the exchange of chemicals between buried bones and the surrounding soils, paleontologists are reluctant to use bone mineral analysis in reconstructing early hominid diets.

The results of radiographic and chemical analyses must be used cautiously, however. Many types of diseases and nutritional problems can affect bones and teeth in a similar fashion, making it difficult to determine the exact cause. For this and other reasons, information from a variety of techniques should be combined along with assessments of the mortality (death) and morbidity (illness) rates

paleontologist
A scientist who studies the ancient life on earth, usually by studying fossils of plants or animals

for an entire population in order to properly reconstruct its dietary patterns (Brown 1981).

Retracing human evolution

Although the precise reasons for hominids divergence from the great apes is unknown, several scenarios have been proposed. In the remainder of this chapter we summarize some of the more widely accepted theories in an attempt to understand how humans and their dietary patterns have evolved.

The emergence of australopithecines When tropical forests began to dry up as a result of worldwide climatic changes, some primates ventured out into the surrounding grasslands. Probably these were the most omnivorous, social, and intelligent of the primates, carrying traits that proved highly adaptive in their search for food in the new environment.

The grasslands, however, posed many new selective pressures. For instance, life on the ground brought advantages for primates who could walk upright on two legs, leaving their hands free to collect food and perform other activities. As a result, more upright posture and bipedalism (the ability to walk and run on two legs) evolved.

By 4.0 to 3.75 million B.P., the first hominid, *Australopithecus,* had emerged in Africa. Footprints and skeletal remains from this period suggest that the australopithecines were fully bipedal and had powerful hands capable of precise manipulations. "The cheek teeth are relatively large and are capped with a thick enamel, probably an adaptation to chewing large quantities of fruits, seeds, pods, roots and tubers some of which may have been quite tough." (Pilbeam 1984:94)

Thus far, no stone tools have been found with australopithecine remains. Most likely, however, they used tools made from stems, wood, and/or unaltered stones to collect and prepare food (much like chimpanzees do today). Such tools would leave no trace 4 million years later (Pilbeam 1984:95).

We also can be fairly certain that our australopithecine ancestors who lived between 4.0 and 1.5 million B.P. were omnivorous; gathered roots, fruits, berries, nuts and other vegetable matter; collected insects, molluscs, and eggs; captured small animals; and hunted large game. Fish and aquatic reptiles also have been found in sites dating back to 1 to 2 million years. Known as a foraging or hunting and gathering subsistence mode (see Chapter 4 for a detailed discussion), this lifestyle provided our ancestors with a largely vegetarian diet supplemented by smaller amounts of animal products (Gaulin and Konner 1977:70–71; Nelson and Jurmain 1979:261).

B.P.—Before Present
This notation has largely replaced B.C.—Before Christ—when referring to periods occurring long ago. To translate B.P. into B.C., subtract 2000 years.

Homo erectus About 1.5 million years ago a more advanced hominid—*Homo erectus*—emerged. Although debates continue about the transition between *Australopithecus,* other early hominids, and *Homo erectus,* all agree that *Homo erectus* was the first widely distributed hominid species. Archeological remains of *Homo erectus* cover three continents—Africa, Asia and Europe—and span the period from 1.5 million to 300,000 years ago.

Homo erectus, compared to earlier hominids was relatively tall and robust (about 5 feet), big-brained and had a small face and cheek teeth. *Homo erectus* also was advanced in several aspects of culture, remaining, of course, quite primitive by modern human standards. Tools were crude, all-purpose instruments such as stone hand axes that allowed *Homo erectus* to break soil and roots, hack off tree limbs, and dismember game. Smaller stone flakes probably were used for "trimming wood, cutting meat and sinew, and scraping hides" (Harris 1980:73) Other archaeological evidence includes a wooden lance with a tip that may have been hardened by fire, stone cleavers, scrapers and choppers. Fire was used in hunting, tool-making, and most likely cooking, by at least 500,000 B.P. (Stahl 1984).

Clothing was also certainly worn by *Homo erectus* in the cold regions of Europe. Everywhere there is evidence of a well-organized, cooperative social life. Some of the most detailed illustrations of how *Homo erectus* lived and ate come from three European archeological sites dating back some 300,000 years.

stone flakes
Byproducts of the manufacture of large stone tools, such as hand axes that have very sharp edges; flakes can be used as tools themselves.

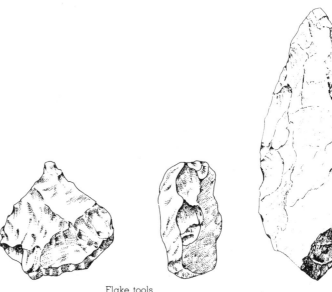

Figure 1.4
Homo erectus' tools. Homo erectus relied heavily upon stone tools such as handaxes and stone flakes.

Flake tools

Biface (handaxe)

The Terra Amata site at Nice, France, was a seasonal camp occupied periodically from late spring to early summer and fall. A sheltered cove located on the edge of the Mediterranean Sea, the camp offered water and a place to gather seafood, hunt, and make a few tools before departing for another spot. Tools, food refuse, coprolites, and pollen, as well as other archeological evidence, have been interpreted by Henry deLumley (1969:45) to give us this picture of how these hominids may have occupied themselves during their stay at Terra Amata:

> The evidence shows that they gathered a little seafood, manufactured stone tools and hunted in the nearby countryside. The animal bones unearthed at Terra Amata include the remains of birds, turtles and at least eight species of mammals. Although the visitors did not ignore small game such as rabbits and rodents, the majority of the bones represent larger animals. They are, in order of their abundance, the stag *Cervus elaphus,* the extinct elephant *Elephas meridionalis,* the wild boar *(Sus scrofa),* the ibex *(Capra ibex)*, Merk's rhinoceros *(Dicerothinus merki)* and finally the wild ox *Bos primigenius.* Although the hunters showed a preference for big game, they generally selected as prey not the adults but the young of each species, doubtless because they were easier to bring down.
>
> The visitors did not systematically exploit the food resources available in the Mediterranean. Nevertheless, they were not entirely ignorant of seafood. A few shells of oysters, mussels and limpets at the site show that they gathered shellfish; fishbones and fish vertebrae indicate that on occasion the hunters also fished.

The Torralba and Ambrona sites in Northern Spain were hunting and butchering stations where elephants, horses, cattle and other large mammals were butchered before being carried away, probably to a nearby living camp. Based on the large number of animals killed close to each other, the lack of traps, stockpiles of stones, charred objects that may have been firebrands, and the presence of only one flimsy spear, archeologists believe that the animals were driven by fire into a swamp or marsh where they became mired and were stoned to death. The amount of meat produced at these sites is impressive. During a single period that the site was occupied, approximately 30,000 pounds of meat was provided by the animals killed. At five pounds per person, this would represent 6000 days of meat rations. For this group, then, meat must have comprised a significant portion of the diet, at least on a periodic basis.

The type of hunting activity depicted at these sites most definitely required advance planning and highly developed communication (language). Likewise, butchering and distribution of the meat suggests that *Homo erectus* had a rather sophisticated social organization that provided a system for sharing and cooperating as a group (Freeman 1975:679–682).

Compared to the early hominid *Australopithecus, Homo erectus* represents major evolutionary advancements in culture, social organization, and language proficiency.

How do we account for the dramatic evolutionary advances made between the australopithecines who lived 3.75 million years ago and *Homo erectus* at 300,000 b.p. This period, like other phases in human evolution, is best viewed as a series of continuous, mutually reinforcing changes that enabled our ancestors to adapt to their environment. These genetic and cultural changes increased our ancestors' abilities to get food and adapt to other environmental stresses. We have already seen, for instance, the advantages bipedalism and a more upright posture had for hominids in their search for food in the grasslands. Other adaptations made during the time of australopithecines and *Homo erectus* (as well as more recent periods of human evolution) involve food-getting, tool production, dentition, brain size, and the capacity for culture.

Hominids living on the ground had fewer plant resources and more game available than primates inhabiting trees in tropical forests. As hunting skills became of increased value, improved tool production and more elaborate forms of social cooperation evolved. Tool use and tool production favored improved motor coordination and more sophisticated conceptual skills, both of which came with larger brains. A larger brain, in turn, meant a greater capacity to think and develop culture, improve tool-making and create greater social cohesiveness. Both tool use and social cooperation are advantageous in gathering and hunting food. As meat consumption increased along with improved hunting skills, the massive molars required to grind fibrous foods became less beneficial and smaller cheek teeth evolved.

Other links between biology and culture involve bipedalism, brain size, infant and childhood dependency, social organization, and cultural capacity. As full bipedalism developed, a rather narrow pelvic base was needed to support the body and permit leg rotation. At the same time, increased brain size required a wider pelvis opening for the birth of larger-brained babies. A compromise between these opposing forces appears to have been struck in the birth of immature infants whose heads could pass through a relatively small pelvis. Immaturity at birth, however, necessitated an extended period of infancy and childhood dependency. Prolonged childhood dependency provided an opportunity to teach offspring the cultural traditions of the group. And this, along with bigger brains, further enhanced language proficiency, social cohesiveness, and cultural complexity. Finally, an increased reliance on culture and social cooperation led to better planning, division of labor between the sexes, improved tool production, and more efficient hunting. As we shall see below, each of these developments greatly enhanced our ancestors' ability to obtain meat as well as plant foods and thus enhanced their nutritional status. These traits proved highly advantageous and have continued to develop in a mutually reinforcing way until the present (Kottak 1982:131).

Homo sapiens   *Homo erectus'* evolutionary development into *Homo sapiens* was gradual, spanning the period from 1.5 million to 250,000 years ago. Successive advances and retreats of glaciers imposed environmental stresses on *Homo erectus,* who adapted biologically through natural selection and culturally through learning and innovation (Johnston 1982:296). Although many of the changes—increased brain size and enhanced intellectual capabilities, more sophisticated tools and more complex forms of social organization—have continued until the present, most paleontologists mark the transition to early *Homo sapiens* at 250,000 B.P. and the appearance of modern *Homo sapiens* at 35,000 B.P.

The culture of early *Homo sapiens* was similar in many ways to that of *Homo erectus.* With the "Ice Age still at hand, large, cold-adapted mammals were common and, as a result, hunting continued to play an important role" (Johnston 1982:300). The major advances made by early *Homo sapiens* include a more sophisticated tool kit with extensive use of hand axes and stone flakes, development of clothing and shelter able to resist subfreezing cold (which allowed early humans to expand into northern regions), and burial of the dead along with flowers, food, tools, and other ritual objects indicative of a belief in an afterlife.

By about 30,000 B.P. the transition to modern *Homo sapien* was complete, occurring in Africa, Europe and Asia. Everywhere culture proved to be an increasingly important source of adaptive innovations. And everywhere humans were selected largely for their cultural adaptiveness, language proficiency and the ability to cooperate in groups.

Debates continue to rage over the relationship between various archeological finds representing this period. "All agree, however, that by 35,000 years ago, there was only one species of hominid left in the world . . ." (Harris 1980:86). *Homo sapiens,* with the species' superior intelligence and sophisticated cultural methods of dealing with environmental stresses, proved to be both highly adaptive and highly prolific. The population soon expanded into three new continents: Australia, North America, and South America. One of the cultural advancements associated with this final step in human evolution was the development of new and more sophisticated tools and weapons, including the bow and arrow, spear throwers, pins and awls, needles with eyes, spoons, engraving tools, axes, stone saws, antler hammers, shovels, and pestles and grinding slabs.

awl
A pointed instrument used to pierce small holes into leather or wood

pestle
Tool used to mix substances, usually in a mortar

Focus 1-3

Adaptations in modern populations

In some areas behavioral developments have been accompanied by physiological and genetic responses, and have helped early humans to adapt to their new environments. Eskimos, for example, have several physiological mechanisms that enable them to endure the Arctic cold. One such adaptation is "nonshivering thermogenesis," a chemical response in brown fatty tissue that enables adults to elevate their metabolism 25 percent over normal levels. While all human infants have this ability, apparently it is retained into adulthood in people native to cold areas (Moran 1982:119).

For a while, Eskimos also were believed to have many other unique morphological and metabolic adaptations, such as the ability to consume large quantities of fat without developing cardiovascular disease. More recently, however, the genetic basis for this extraordinary metabolic ability has been questioned. It now appears that the low incidence of cardiovascular disease is due to the Eskimos' diet. Even though they eat large quantities of fat, most of it is polyunsaturated. Sea mammals and other wild game hunted by Eskimos contain little saturated fat. Also, their high-fat diet may contain another protective feature: the polyunsaturated fatty acid eicosapentenoic acid (EPA). EPA has been shown to alter blood chemistry (reducing the amounts of cholesterol and triglycerides) in ways that have potential therapeutic value for people with cardiovascular disease (Woodcock 1984; Saynor, et al. 1984).*

---

*Fish oil containing EPA significantly reduced plasma triglyceride levels and whole blood viscosity in 19 patients with arterial disease (Woodcock 1984) and reduced triglyceride levels, VLDL and LDL levels, and bleeding times while increasing HDL levels in 92 patients with heart disease or hyperlipidemia (Saynor et al. 1984).

Cave art, carvings on tool handles and other objects suggestive of religion or magic, lamps, and many other innovations also appear (Lenski 1970:154–6). Other developments involved hunting patterns, the use and control of fire, the use of clothing, new settlement patterns, large population sizes, and ritual activity (Pilbeam 1984:96).

The cultural and genetic changes that occurred during this final step in human evolution greatly increased humans' abilities to obtain food from a greater variety of environments. Improved tools and cooking methods enabled people to prepare their food with greater efficiency and variety. Cooking breaks down cellulose and starch, making fibrous vegetables more readily digestible; increases the availability of nutrients in high-fiber foods; and detoxifies many dangerous chemicals and toxic microorganisms in plants and animals (Stahl 1984).

Although humans everywhere continued to practice a basic hunting and gathering existence up until 10,000 B.P., as they moved into new areas some groups developed specialized cultural adaptations to the new environmental pressures they encountered. Along coastal areas, fish, shellfish, and other marine life were hunted and foraged. Areas abundant in large game animals were populated by peoples largely dependent on hunting, while in other areas foraging continued to provide a largely vegetarian diet.

As we approach modern times, the archaeological record abounds with evidence of culture's increasing importance as an adaptive tool. The efficiency with which people hunted and collected food improved as evidenced by increasingly elaborate tool kits and more complex social arrangements. People developed better means of collecting, storing, and transporting food and the work required to feed themselves decreased. Food supplies also became more reliable, and with less work and improved health, populations grew. By the year 10,000 B.P. almost every corner of the earth was populated with a remarkably intelligent creature, one that relied more and more heavily on cultural achievements to adapt to environmental stresses. The stage was set for a major cultural revolution in how people obtained their food.

Summary

- The human species occupies a broader range of environments than any other primate. This amazing success is the result of our ability to adapt behaviorally, physiologically, and genetically to environmental stresses.

- Behavioral adaptation includes individual as well as cultural responses. Physiological adaptation involves changes in biochemical, anatomical, and other morphological characteristics that allow us to maintain a stable internal environment in a wide range of external conditions. When some people in a population have inherited traits that enable them to adapt to environmental and therefore, produce more offspring than those without this trait, genetic adaptation may occur.

- People are primates; sharing special distinguishing traits that developed as an adaption to a tree-dwelling existence. Primates are omnivores. The bulk of their diet is derived from plant food, supplemented by smaller quantities of animal products; primarily insects, birds, and small mammals.

- By 4.0 to 3.75 million years B.P., the first hominid—Australopithecus—had emerged in Africa. Australopithecines were fully bipedal and almost certainly were omnivores who gathered roots, fruits, berries, nuts, and other plant foods; collected insects, molluscs, and eggs; and captured small animals and hunted large game.

- *Homo erectus,* a big-brained hominid, lived between 1.5 million and 300,000 years B.P. *Homo erectus* was relatively advanced in several aspects of culture: tool use and production, control of fire (by about 500,000 B.P.), cooperative hunting, and use of clothing. In addition to providing large amounts of meat, cooperative hunting demanded advance planning, highly developed communications, and a rather sophisticated social organization.

- *Homo erectus'* evolutionary development into *Homo sapiens* was gradual, spanning the period from 1 million to 250,000 years ago.

- During *Homo erectus'* evolutionary development into early *Homo sapiens* and then into modern *Homo sapiens,* culture proved to be an increasingly important source of adaptation. Natural selection operated to preserve and increase intelligence, language proficiency, tool manufacturing capabilities, and ability to cooperate in groups, all of which greatly enhanced *Homo sapiens'* effectiveness in obtaining and preparing food.

- With their sophisticated cultural methods of dealing with environmental stresses, *Homo sapiens* proved highly adaptive and highly prolific. The population grew rapidly, so that by 10,000 B.P. modern humans inhabited almost every corner of the earth.

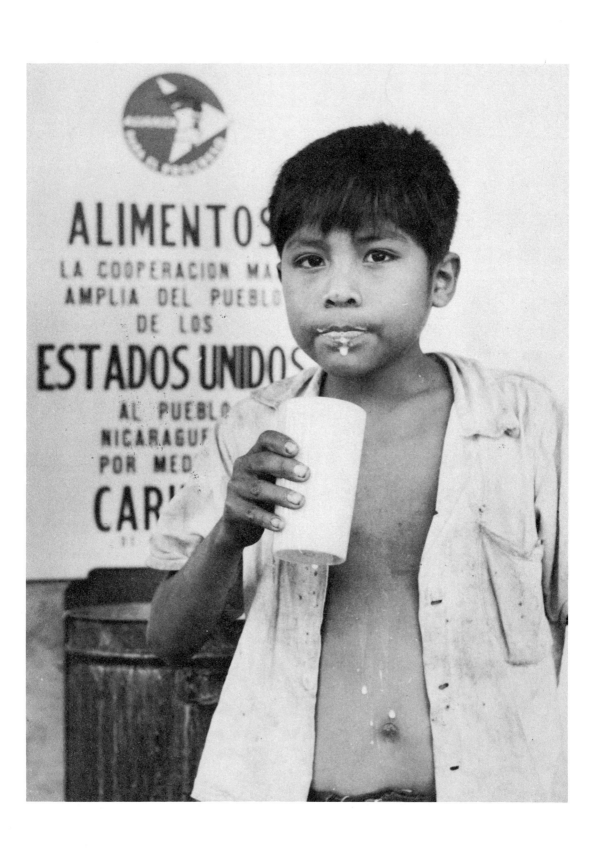

Highlight 1-1 No milk please: The story of lactase deficiency

Probably the best known genetic adaptation to dietary factors is the variation in different human populations' ability to digest milk. Contrary to the advertising jingle, it is not true that "everybody needs milk." In fact, among most peoples, milk consumption creates severe discomfort in adults.

A main ingredient of milk is the sugar, *lactose,* which the body digests by the enzyme, *lactase.* Many people are lactase-deficient, and because they cannot digest lactose, milk ferments in the large intestine, causing gas, flatulence, intestinal pain, and sometimes cramps, and even vomiting (Simoons 1983:214).

In all human populations, infants and young children can digest milk—an obvious necessity to any young mammal. However, as most children get older they produce less and less lactase, and by age 5 or 6 most are lactase deficient. This condition is also known as lactose intolerance.

For years, scientists were unaware of the prevalence of lactase deficiency throughout the world. They were perplexed by the strong preference for milk in some societies and the equally strong aversion to it in others. Because milk is a relatively inexpensive source of calories, protein, calcium, and other essential nutrients, many people assumed that everyone would want to drink it. When relief agencies in the U.S., Canada and other nations donated shipments of powdered milk to developing countries, they were surprised by the response: the people of Colombia and Guatemala used it as whitewash, the Indonesians took it as a laxative, the Kanuri of West Africa believed it was a food of evil spirits, and many groups simply threw it away (Farb and Armelagos 1980:187). Where the milk was consumed, it often produced illness in the very people the relief agencies had hoped to help (Nelson and Jurmain 1979).

Some scientists attempted to explain this widespread aversion to milk as the result of some societies' reluctance to take up the strange practice of keeping animals for the milk they produce and then drinking it. As Simoons (1983:211–12), a pioneer in the study of lactase deficiency, points out:

That explanation did and still does make sense, for, when asked, nonmilking persons would point out that manipulating the udder of an animal was indeed strange procedure. They also noticed that the end product of milking was a white animal secretion, a substance that, when consumed, could make a person ill. It was suspected that such an illness was psychosomatic in origin, an understandably strong reaction to an alien and somewhat revolting food.

The view that milk aversion is due to beliefs alone was dispelled in the late 1960s, however. At that time, Simoons (1970 and 1971) began assembling data on the history and geographical distribution of dairying and milk consumption throughout Asia and Africa. These findings were then compared to the distribution of high and low prevalences of lactase deficiency among the world's peoples. Societies that have traditionally practiced dairying and milk consumption were found to have a low prevalence of lactase deficiency, while those who never relied heavily on domestic animals and who avoided milk had high frequencies of deficiency.

Some medical researchers believed the strong relationship between milk consumption and lactase deficiency resulted from milk's ability to induce lactase activity. They argued that if a person, even one from a nondairying group, drank milk from infancy onward, she would retain the ability to make lactase and digest milk. When efforts to induce significant lactase activity by giving infants and adults large quantities of milk failed, it became clear that a person's ability to digest milk is under genetic control (Simoons 1983:214).

But why have some groups inherited a genetic trait that allows them to digest milk as adults, making them different from most of humanity and other land mammals? One of the best explanations points to the advantage derived from milk consumption. According to this hypothesis, all early foraging populations were lactase-deficient. About 10,000 years ago, humans began to domesticate animals, raising them for meat and hides. Domesticated animals offered another resource: milk. However, to take advantage of this new food, people had to be able to produce lactase throughout adulthood (Johnston 1982:339). At some unknown point in time, a mutation occurred that enabled humans to produce the enzyme lactase and digest milk as adults. In societies that made use of domesticated animals, individuals with this trait for lactose tolerance had an advantage in being better nourished than those who could not make use of the new nutrition resource. As dairying practices developed in some societies, lactose-tolerant individuals survived in greater numbers and gave birth to more offspring who also inherited the same advantage. Through natural selection, the frequency of the genetic trait for lactose tolerance increased in dairying societies until the majority of people were

able to digest milk throughout adulthood (McCracken 1971; Farb and Armelagos 1980:188).

In northern European regions, where a cloud cover limits sunlight for much of the year, another advantage also may have been operating. Because of the lack of sunlight, people have difficulty in producing the vitamin D essential for intestinal absorption of calcium. Calcium absorption also is facilitated when lactose is present and being digested. Therefore, people who drink milk had a major advantage: the increased ability to absorb calcium (which prevents rickets) (Flatz and Rothawe 1973). Meanwhile, in nondairying groups, lactose-tolerant people did not have the same advantages and the frequency of the mutant trait did not increase proportionally.

In the United States today, lactose-tolerant people may fare better because they are able to take advantage of a nutrient-dense food that is widely promoted through the Basic Four Food Groups system and federally subsidized food programs. On the other hand, the consumption of large amounts of dairy products also may be linked to atherosclerosis and heart disease, among the major causes of death in this country. One wonders, then, the extent to which lactase deficiency is an advantage or disadvantage in the U.S. today.

Nutritional applications

Health care providers should be aware that approximately two-thirds of the world's population is lactase-deficient after early childhood. Seventy to 80 percent of American blacks, 80 to 100 percent of Asian-Americans, and large proportions of American Indians, Jews, and Middle Easterners are lactase-deficient. In contrast, white, non-Jewish persons of European descent have a very low prevalence of deficiency: 6 to 20 percent (Simoons 1983:213; Nelson and Jurmain 1979:459; Johnston 1982:339; Newcomer and McGill 1984:43).

Lactose intolerance, often used as a synonym for lactase deficiency, refers to how a person responds symptomatically to milk consumption. The range of tolerance for lactose is extremely wide in lactase-deficient people. For some, intestinal symptoms develop after a single glass of milk; for others, problems do not result until considerably more is consumed. Most lactase-deficient people have no trouble with small amounts such as the few teaspoons that might be added to a cup of coffee. Most people with lactase deficiency learn to recognize the amount of milk they can tolerate and either reduce or completely eliminate milk consumption (Newcomer and McGill 1984:43; Mann and Mann 1983:12).

Because some milk products contain little lactose, they can be digested by lactase-deficient people. Fermentation, for instance, lowers the lactose content of fresh milk (from 6.6 to 2.6 percent) while leaving many other nutrients unchanged. Naturally fermented yogurt can be absorbed far better, creating less flatulence and diarrhea than regular milk. Some commercially available yogurts, however, contain levels of lactose that are only slightly lower than milk and may be poorly tolerated by lactase-deficient people (Kolars et al. 1984). Other fermented milk products include buttermilk, sour cream, and acidophilus milk.

Fermented milk products have been used for centuries in some lactase-deficient populations. Yogurt, for example, is popular among people of the Middle East and many other groups. The use of fermented milk products explains why some South African tribes and other groups are cattle herders and milk consumers, despite a high prevalence of lactase deficiency (Segal et al. 1983).

When working with lactase-deficient groups, health care providers also can make use of naturally fermented milk products. Buttermilk, for instance, is often popular among many people. For people who do not like the taste of soured milk products, there is sweet acidophilus milk, which tastes much like regular milk and contains less lactose. [Although the acidophilus bacteria added to this milk will break down lactose when it is warmed in the human digestive tract, some lactase-deficient people do not tolerate it well and therefore it should be used carefully until proven safe (Newcomer et al. 1983)].

Another method shown to permit symptom-free milk consumption in people sensitive to lactose involves the addition of the enzyme lactase to milk at home. The enzyme is marketed in liquid form as the product Lact-Aid. Four or five drops of the liquid enzyme are added to a quart of milk two to four hours before drinking. About 70 percent of the lactose is broken down, giving the milk a very sweet taste. Lact-Aid can be purchased in many health food stores and pharmacies. Recently, another low-lactose milk powder (LLM) has been developed that contains 86 percent less lactose than regular skim milk powder. The lactose in the LLM is replaced by malto-dextrin, which has the same sweetening effect as lactose. Nutrition, taste, and price compare favorably with regular milk powder.

Not all people who cannot tolerate milk are unable to digest lactose sugar. Some have an allergy to one or more of the proteins in cow's milk. These people are not able to tolerate the lactose-reduced milk products mentioned above.

There are also many nondairy milks. For millenia, the Chinese and Japanese have used a milk made from soybeans. Soy milk is a thick, heavy milk which, though different from animal milk, is quite tasty. This milk can be made into soy cheese, or tofu, which is becoming quite popular in the U.S.

The American Indians of the Southeast made milk from ground hickory nuts. In the Middle East, a milk is made from sesame seeds. Perhaps one of the most delicious nondairy milk is almond milk. This can be prepared by liquifying one cup of raw almonds, one quart of water, and one tablespoon each of honey and oil in a blender. The milk is best strained and is suitable for the many uses to which other milk is put. Similar milks can be made from cashews and coconuts. Such a milk made from coconut is used in South Indian cooking, where it is added to various curried vegetables to give them a rich flavor.

While lactase deficiency is of concern to all health care professionals, it is particularly important for nutritionists working in the Women, Infant and Children (WIC) Program, school lunch cafeterias, and other feeding programs that distribute milk products. Because these programs serve blacks and other populations with high rates of lactase deficiency, professionals need to consider alternate foods and menus for those who cannot tolerate milk. For instance, WIC nutritionists are allowed to modify the types and amounts of foods offered to lactating women. Lactase-deficient mothers can be advised to use fermented milk products,

Lact-Aid, aged cheeses containing little lactose, and other nondairy milk substitutes. School lunch programs and food programs for the elderly can plan dairy-free menus or offer acceptable substitutes for lactase-deficient people.

Because milk is an excellent source of calcium, lactase-deficient people should be sure to consume sufficient quantities of this essential nutrient. In addition to fermented milk products, and sweet acidophilus milk, calcium can be obtained in small amounts from mustard, turnip, and dandelion greens; kale; broccoli; bok choy; okra; rutabagas; molasses; almonds; sardines and salmon with bones; and corn tortillas that have been treated with lime (See Chapter 1 for a discussion of how the body adapts to lowered intakes of calcium).

Finally, because few people have been medically diagnosed as lactase-deficient, health care professionals should be aware of the more subtle evidence of milk intolerance. Commonly, clients explain that milk gives them gas, or they just don't like it or never drink it. If this person is from a population with a high prevalence of lactase deficiency, the professional should proceed cautiously before promoting milk consumption.

2

Food in historical perspective: Three dietary revolutions

If you are among the millions of North Americans who have a garden plot, you no doubt appreciate the joys of producing your own food. You may be less aware, however, of the revolutionary impact agriculture has had on our entire way of life. For, as we shall see in this chapter, the domestication of plants and animals is one of three major cultural revolutions people have undergone in how they adapt to their physical and social environments. Along with the industrial and scientific revolutions, the agricultural revolution has radically altered our eating habits, paving the way for modern life as we know it today.

About 12,000 years ago, a dramatic change in the way humans acquired their food began to unfold. In the Middle East, subSaharan Africa, Southeast Asia, China, and Central and South America, people gradually shifted from food collection (foraging) to food production. Although the transition took thousands of years (it was more of an evolutionary than a revolutionary process), we consider this a major cultural revolution because of its dramatic impact on how humans interact with their environment.

As we saw in Chapter 1, before the advent of agriculture most people lived in small groups and roamed from place to place in

The terms foraging *and* hunting and gathering *will be used interchangeably throughout this book to describe roaming in search of wild plants and animals for food.*

In a few areas of the New and Old Worlds, foraging groups living on river banks and in coastal areas with access to ample shellfish and plant foods were able to develop sedentary lifestyles.

search of food. In general, populations were kept small because most areas were not lush enough to feed large groups for long. Migratory lifestyles were necessary because as vegetation was depleted and animal populations dwindled, groups were forced to move to new places. As people learned to domesticate plants and animals, the food supply became more stable and abundant, allowing humans to settle into villages and increase their population. The establishment of large sedentary villages, made possible by agriculture, had dramatic effects on many other aspects of culture and provides the foundation for modern civilization.

The crucial feature of the agricultural revolution was domestication or control over plant and animal reproduction. Domestication involved the transformation of wild species into domesticated species that flourished under human manipulation. By breeding only those species with desirable characteristics (flavor, yield, ease of cultivation), people were able to improve their crops and animal stock.

During domestication, many plants and animals lost the characteristics that had once allowed them to propagate in the wild. The wild ancestor of modern corn, for example, did not have a husk and therefore could disperse its seeds by shattering its ear when ripe. Domesticated corn has lost this ability and must rely on humans to harvest and husk the ears in order to reproduce.

Many questions about how, why, and where plants and animals were domesticated remain unanswered. It probably started simply enough as people noticed that plants spring up from seeds tossed on the ground. Young animals that were captured alive may have been brought to the home base and became quite tame as they grew dependent on the people who tethered or caged them. It is thought that women were responsible for much of the development of agriculture, as they stayed by the campsites and cared for the young, while men roamed in search of food. Thus, women were in a position to observe the growth of plants from seeds and care for captured animals.

We know that people switched very slowly from harvesting wild species to planting selected varieties. At first, the cultivated varieties served only as supplements to the wild plants and animals they consumed. Through time, people grew increasingly dependent on cultivated plants and animals until agriculture produced the vast majority of foods eaten (Kottak 1982:162).

Development of agriculture in the Tehuacan Valley

To illustrate how people shifted from foraging for food to food production, we will describe the agricultural revolution that occurred in the central highlands of Mexico. We have selected this region because extensive archeological research has been carried out there, giving us a relatively good understanding of the domestication process.

Archeological data from human occupations in the New World begins perhaps as early as 25,000 years ago when the first people crossed the Bering Strait. Most likely these hunters and gatherers followed large game animals into the new lands, completely unaware that they had crossed into a new continent. As these early bands spread throughout North and South America, they adapted to the diversity of specific environments they encountered. Along coastal and riverine areas, fish, shellfish, and other aquatic resources were foraged. Throughout much of the Americas, mastodons, mammoth, big-horn bison, camels, tapirs, and other large mammals lived in great abundance and supported big game hunting societies. As these animals become extinct, about 11,000 B.P., seed collection and smaller game become more important. In several regions of Central and South America, groups began to domesticate plants and animals. Eventually, agriculture spread to most societies in the Americas.

In Central America, the transition from foraging to domestication of plants and animals began between 7,000 B.P. and 10,000 B.P. Caves in the Tehuacan Valley were inhabited for thousands of years and offer us a rare view of the dietary changes accompanying the shift from foraging to agriculture. Because of the extreme dryness in the caves, remains of many foods and human feces were preserved. The dried feces, coprolites, contained parts of a number of plants, including setaria (a kind of millet), cactus, century plant leaves, squash, gourds, and chili peppers, as well as pieces of charred snail shells, bones from mice, lizards, snakes and birds, feathers, and fragments of shells. (See Chapter 1 for a discussion of coprolites.) At another Mexican site, coprolites contained bits of uncooked grasshoppers and the shells of snails that had been eaten raw. Analysis of these archeological finds suggest that the people living in the Tehuacan Valley 10,000 years ago obtained all of their food from hunting and gathering. Their diet contained a mix of animals and foraged plants, including the wild ancestors of domesticated squash, avocadoes, corn and beans.

The first evidence for cultivated plants comes about 7,000 years B.P. At this time we find cultivated varieties of squash, corn, bottle gourds, a variety of beans, a fruit called *zapote*, domesticated chilies, avocado, setaria, and amaranth. Diets still contained a large proportion of wild plants, but meat consumption had dropped considerably.

Over the next 7,000 years, the Tehuacan inhabitants relied more and more heavily upon cultivated crops, until about the time of Christ, when domesticated plants made up almost their entire diet. Wild plants and animals, the domesticated turkey, and a small

Bering Strait
The 56-mile-wide portion of the North Pacific Ocean that separates Asia (U.S.S.R.) from North America (Alaska). At certain times in its geological past, it has been dry land.

riverine
located or situated on the banks of a river

mastodon
a primitive elephant-like mammal, now extinct

century plant
A plant used for food, fiber, and ornament. The leaves can be roasted and eaten to make a mildly alcoholic drink called pulque. It is so named because of the mistaken notion that the plant only blooms one in 100 years

tapir
a large mammal having short stout limbs and a long snout

Figure 2.1
The amaranth plant. Amaranth is a grain producing plant with bright red flowers. Once a staple food in Mexico, it fell into obscurity when Cortez banned its cultivation in 1519 due to its mystical association. Currently some agriculturalists are trying to revive interest in this ancient crop because of its high protein content and drought resistance.

hairless dog (the only animals originally domesticated in Mexico) contributed only a small portion to their nutrient intake. Finally, the Mexican diet became even more narrowly focused, with corn, beans, and squash serving as its core (DeWalt: 1983).

This rich archeological account of people living in one area over thousands of years demonstrates the slow transition with which they changed from a foraging to an agricultural existence. The gradual way in which the production of food developed may be due, in part, to the nutritional risks inherent in an agricultural way of life. Diets of hunters and gatherers include a wide variety of plants and animals, and therefore tend to be nutritionally well-balanced. Agriculturalists, on the other hand, typically rely on a limited number of cultivated crops. If these crops do not contain an adequate balance of nutrients necessary for survival, as is often the case, other wild foods must be used as supplements.

In Mexico, full dependence on agriculture had to wait until a group of foods were domesticated that could sustain human populations as adequately as the more traditional diet obtained through foraging. Not until corn, beans, and squash were combined did agriculture adequately meet the protein, energy, and vitamin needs of humans.

Corn does not provide sufficient protein to sustain life. As a staple, it is deficient in lysine and tryptophan, two amino acids that must be present to make up the complete protein essential in human diets. However, when corn is combined with beans (a good source of lysine and tryptophan), together they provide a high-quality protein mixture capable of supporting human populations. Squash seeds also make a good protein calorie supplement to a corn diet.

Corn and beans were not domesticated at the same time and place in all parts of the New World. Archeological evidence compiled by Kent Flannery (1971) reveals that wild deer, rabbits, waterfowl, and insects occupied an important dietary role in parts of Central America even after the cultivation of corn appeared. Not until cultivated beans and corn diffused into the same areas did hunting give way to a complete agricultural way of life (Kaplan 1971).

Methods used to prepare corn also may have influenced the rate at which people became fully dependent on agriculture. In this instance, niacin (a B vitamin) proved to be the limiting factor. Corn contains a fair amount of this essential nutrient, but 97 to 98 percent of it is bound as niacytin (Kodicek 1962), making it biologically unavailable to humans. Niacin is an important substance in human energy utilization and deficient intake of niacin leads to the condition known as pellagra. Pellagra, a disease characterized by the "four D's"—diarrhea, dementia, dermatitis and death—was common among corn-dependent people of the Southern U.S., the

Focus 2-1

A protein primer

Amino Acids are the building blocks of protein. Human tissue contains 22 different amino acids. Of the 22 amino acids, 13 can be made by the body; the other 9 must be obtained from the foods we eat and are called essential amino acids (EAAs). Our bodies must have all 9 EAAs for maximum protein use.

Protein is found in a variety of foods: meat, fish, dairy products, eggs, beans, grains, and vegetables. But all proteins are not created equal. Animal foods contain all 9 EAAs and are easily utilized by the body. Most plant foods, however, contain limited amounts of one or two amino acids. For this reason, single-item diets, such as those comprised almost solely of corn or yams, can lead to protein deficiency.

But if a diet contains several different plant foods, protein deficiency does not occur. The reason for this is that some plant foods have generous amounts of amino acids that others are lacking. If combined, the strengths of one plant food can complement the weaknesses of another and together they make a high quality protein. This is called protein complementation. Figure 2.2 illustrates this concept.

Plant food can be divided into three broad groups based on EAAs strengths and weaknesses. The groups are (1) whole grains (wheat,

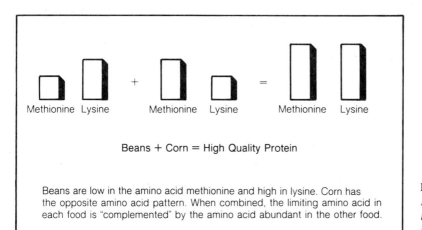

Methionine Lysine + Methionine Lysine = Methionine Lysine

Beans + Corn = High Quality Protein

Beans are low in the amino acid methionine and high in lysine. Corn has the opposite amino acid pattern. When combined, the limiting amino acid in each food is "complemented" by the amino acid abundant in the other food.

Figure 2.2
Protein complementation: Bar graphs showing amino acid content of beans and corn

rye, barley, rice, corn, etc.); (2) legumes (beans, peas), nuts, and seeds; and (3) vegetables. Vegetables and the legume group generally compensate for the EAAs underrepresented in the grain group. Even within groups, the proteins often complement each other to some extent, since all foods have a slightly different collection of amino acids. For example, legumes complement the protein of nuts and seeds. Dairy products, eggs, and meats can improve the protein efficiency of any of the groups.

Interestingly, before scientists discovered the need for essential amino acids, complementary protein combinations evolved spontaneously as the basis of many cuisines. Examples include Chinese soy products and rice; African sorghum or millet and cowpeas; lentil curry and rice from India; Italian pasta and beans *(pasta e fagioli);* and soup beans and corn bread from the Southern United States.

Mediterranean, and Africa until earlier in this century when the cause of the problem was discovered and niacin supplementation became common. While still common in some areas, pellagra has not been a problem in Mexico and Central America (May and McClellan 1972).

Central Americans are protected from this debilitating disease by their traditional methods of preparing corn for use as tortillas. Throughout Mesoamerica, corn is processed by heating the grain in a solution that contains an alkali. In Central Mexico, lime is added to the cooking water; while in some other areas, ashes are used. The corn-lime-water mixture is cooked, and, after heating, the product (*nixtamal*) is allowed to stand, usually overnight. The liquid is poured off and the *nixtamal* is washed and ground into a dough (*masa*). Formerly, the grinding was done in a stone quern (*metate*) with a grind stone called a *mano*. Today, the grinding is usually done at a commercial mill, where the customer is charged for the amount of *nixtamal* that has been ground. The *masa* is patted or pressed into thin cakes and baked on a clay or iron griddle into *tortillas*.

Soaking corn in a heated alkaline solution for a sufficient length of time releases all of the bound niacin. Kodicek and Wilson (1959) found that 100 percent of the niacin in corn tortillas became biologically available after the treatment procedures outlined above had been followed.

Lime treatment of corn also significantly increases its calcium content. Untreated ground corn contains about 25 mg. of calcium per 100 grams while an equal amount of tortilla has about 140 mg. of calcium. This calcium undoubtedly comes from the lime used in making the *nixtamal*.

alkali
a compound capable of neutralizing acids

quern
a small hand mill used for grinding grain

The cooking of maize, another name for corn, in an alkaline solution also affects its amino acid pattern (the ratio of essential amino acids). Bressani and Scrimshaw (1958) report that while the overall protein content was lowered after lime treatment, changes in specific amino acids varied. For example, 21.0 percent of the leucine, 18.7 percent of the arginine, 12.5 percent of the cystine, and 11.7 percent of the histidine were lost, in contrast to only 5.3 percent of the lysine. The proportionally large loss of leucine in corn after lime treatment changes the ratio of isoleucine to leucine, making it more usable by the human body (Bressani and Scrimshaw 1958).

Looking at ethnographic data, Katz et al.(1974)found that most Central American groups that rely on corn as a dietary staple use some kind of alkali treatment process in preparing corn for human consumption. In those cultural groups that had no alkali treatment, corn made up a minor part of the diet and was heavily supplemented with either game and/or other vegetable foods that would supply the deficient nutrients.

ethnography
the descriptive study of contemporary cultures

It seems reasonable to hypothesize, then, that reliance on corn as a major staple may have been delayed in the Tehuacan Valley until an alkali treatment process was developed.

Archeological evidence needed to test this hypothesis is difficult to find. Tools used to grind corn, *metates*, date back to 5,000 B.P., before corn became the major dietary staple. However, this does not tell us whether or not lime or ashes were used in processing the corn. By 3,000 B.P. tortillas were being baked on clay griddles called *comales* (MacNeish 1967). But clear evidence of limesoaking pots do not appear until about 2100 B.P. (Katz et al. 1974).

The archeological record of the shift from hunting and gathering to agriculture in Tehuacan Valley illustrates two points. First, the transition took thousands of years. Even after people learned to cultivate crops, they continued to forage for wild plants and animals. Second, full dependence on agriculture may have been delayed until the food system could be adjusted to provide adequate nutrition. In Mexico, the combination of crops and the development of food processing methods may have been necessary before people could give up a foraging way of life.

Nutritional consequences of the agricultural revolution

Most human societies have made the shift from foraging to domestication. Only a few groups, now living in marginal areas of the world that are not suitable for agriculture, still live as our ancestors once did. (These contemporary hunters and gatherers will be discussed in more detail in Chapter 4.)

The agricultural revolution has had a profound impact on human dietary practices and nutritional status. As we have already seen, hunters and gatherers generally consume a diet comprised of a wide variety of small animals, insects, tubers, seeds, berries, nuts, fruits, and other vegetables. Besides ensuring an adequate supply of essential nutrients, this diversity helps guarantee survival during climatic disturbances that affect the availability of any particular type of food. Times of food scarcity certainly exist, but famine is a relatively infrequent occurrence (and chronic malnutrition, even rarer) among hunters and gatherers.

With the advent of agriculture, the picture changes. Dependency on a small number of cultivated crops or domesticated animals increases the risk of widespread famine. A less diversified diet makes it far harder to achieve an adequate balance of essential nutrients, especially protein and certain vitamins. Vitamin deficiency diseases are especially problematic in grain-dependent communities.

Claire Cassidy (1980) has attempted to assess the nutritional impact of the introduction of agriculture on pre-Columbian native Americans by examining the skeletal remains of two precontact villages in Kentucky. The older village, Indian Knoll, was inhabited by foragers about 5,000 years ago. The more recent site, Hardin Village, was inhabited by agriculturalists about 1,000 years ago.

Remains of food refuse at each site suggest very different diets. At Indian Knoll, large quantities of river mussels and snails were consumed. Other meat sources included deer, small mammals, wild turkey, box turtle, fish, and occasionally dogs. The archeological remains of wild plants were incomplete, but similar sites contain hickory nuts, walnuts, acorns, elderberry, persimmons, sunflower seeds, and other wild berries (Cassidy 1980:124). The agriculturalists at Hardin Village relied primarily on cultivated corn, beans, and squash. These were supplemented with deer, eel, small mammals, wild turkey, box turtle, and wild plants.

For a discussion of methods used to analyze human skeletal remains, see Chapter 1.

Cassidy examined 296 skeletons from Hardin Village and 285 skeletons from Indian Knoll. She summarizes the data on health derived from careful analyses of the bones and teeth below:

1. Life expectancies for both sexes at all ages were lower at Hardin Village than at Indian Knoll.

2. Infant mortality was higher at Hardin Village.

3. Iron-deficiency anemia of sufficient duration to cause bone changes was absent at Indian Knoll, but present at Hardin Village, where 50 percent of cases occurred in children under age five.

4. Growth arrest episodes at Indian Knoll were periodic and more often of short duration and were possibly due to food shortage in late winter; those at Hardin Village occurred randomly and were

more often of long duration, probably indicative of disease as a causative agent.

5. More children suffered infections at Hardin Village than at Indian Knoll.

6. The syndrome of periosteal inflammation was more common at Hardin Village than at Indian Knoll.

7. Tooth decay was rampant at Hardin Village and led to early abscessing and tooth loss; decay was unusual at Indian Knoll and abscessing occurred later in life because of severe wear to the teeth. The differences in tooth wear rate and caries rate are very likely attributable to dietary differences between the two groups.

(Cassidy 1980:138)

Cassidy concludes, therefore, that the agricultural Hardin Villagers were less healthy than the Indian Knollers, who lived by hunting and gathering. In Cassidy's opinion, most of the health conditions were related to dietary factors, especially the lack of animal protein in the agriculturalists' diet.

Despite a higher incidence of malnutrition and disease in the agricultural population, domestication of plants and animals was associated with population growth. Hardin Village, like millions of agricultural communities, increased significantly, growing from 100 to 300 people over a 150 year period. Thus, while overall health was poorer, food production allowed a much larger population to live together than could be sustained by the previous way of life (Cassidy 1980:140).

Social and political consequences of the agricultural revolution

The domestication of plants and animals brought more fundamental changes in culture and social organization than humans had experienced in all the preceding millions of years of their evolution. As we have just seen, farming and animal husbandry provided sufficient food for population growth and the establishment of large, sedentary villages; with this development came the opportunity for increased social interaction. Agriculture also fostered trade with people in other ecological zones. Because agricultural societies are sedentary, their members cannot move about in search of varied food resources but rather must trade with neighboring groups.

The surpluses generated by agriculture meant that for the first time in history not everyone had to be involved in food-getting activities. People began to master ceramics, bronze casting, brickmaking, masonry and other skills. Surplus food and goods were sold in centralized market places and the rise of a merchant class led to the accumulation of private property.

As population density increased, competition for limited water, land, and other basic resources occurred. The task of organizing the production, distribution, and trade of goods and the defense of groups was gradually taken over by a political/religious/military hierarchy which led, in turn, to the rise of states and empires.

This was quite different than the way of life of foragers, who had no specialized laborers and held all possessions in common. Foragers had no class system and, of course, no organized government. But as the agricultural revolution progressed, people became divided for the first time into rich and poor, rulers and ruled, priests, warriors, and artisans.

The social stratification that occurred with the development of settled agriculture changed humans' patterns from homogenous ones, where everyone who lived in the same area ate similar foods, to heterogeneous diets, where food patterns of a region varied considerably between people of different rank or status. In ancient Greece, for instance, aristocrats ate more meat and a wider variety of foods than the poor, who ate little more than coarse bread. As a result, skeletons of ancient Greek aristocrats were found to be three inches taller than those of the common folk (Gordon 1983:18).

By the end of the fifteenth century, the advent of agriculture had brought cities and complex political systems to most parts of the world. Trade networks linked many areas of the world and the age of exploration, which would greatly expand these networks, was about to begin. As we shall see below, food played an interesting role in the political developments of this era.

The search for spices

"One half teaspoon pepper, one teaspoon cumin, one-fourth teaspoon celery seed . . ." As twentieth-century cooks measure seasonings into a soup pot, they rarely give thought to the impact these spices have had on the course of history. While spices are a pleasing addition to some dishes, they hardly seem to be a matter worthy of global concern. But in the fifteenth century, spices were so highly valued that the quest for them stimulated the discovery of new lands and brought nations into keen competition.

Why this passion for spices? There are several reasons: spices preserved foods and disguised the flavor of bad food, they were used as status symbols, they acted as currency, they were believed to be a cure for many diseases, and were even thought to improve sexual functioning. That's quite a list of credentials!

Europe's desire for spices was frustrated by the high cost of bringing them out of the East. To establish a more direct route, two barriers had to be overcome: a political one (the Ottoman Turks would not let anyone travel their lands to look for spices), and a geographical one (Africa). No one knew how far south Africa stretched, because no one in recent times had sailed around it. Anyone that could bypass the established land routes and the expensive Ottoman and Italian middlemen by sailing straight to the Spice Islands and buying directly from Indian producers would have a profitable business indeed.

Marco Polo was the first of many spice-seeking explorers. He came home to Venice from China with tantalizing descriptions of ginger, nutmeg, pepper, and cloves. Geographical observations and calculations of the Portuguese governor, Henry the Navigator, enabled early seafarers to travel to West Africa for cargoes of pepper. While Bartholomew Dias navigated his way around the Cape of Good Hope in search of an eastward passage to India, another Portuguese, Pedro de Covilihao, made his way overland to Calicut on India's west coast.

And, of course, there was Columbus. King Ferdinand and Queen Isabella of Spain financed Columbus's trip westward in hopes that a direct route to the Spice Islands would be discovered and be a boon to the royal treasury. In 1492, Columbus reached the Americas (though he maintained until his dying day that he had not discovered a new continent but islands off the coast of Asia) and returned home just about empty-handed. Undaunted, he made further trips to the "Indies" only to bring back pineapples that wouldn't grow in European soil and a form of pepper (actually the pimento) that surely must have been disappointing to the voyages' financers who expected the real thing. Though Columbus did not bring the variety and volume of spices the Queen had hoped for, he did change the course of history by discovering new lands.

The goal of finding a sea route to the Spice Islands was realized in 1498 when Vasco da Gama, following the route marked out by Dias, cast anchor on the west coast of India. The Indian king of Calicut refused to exchange his spices for the glass beads and woolen cloth da Gama had brought to barter with, but the King did accept gold and silver. Da Gama's disappointment in having to pay cash for spices was alleviated by the high price he got for them when he returned to Lisbon.

Within 25 years, the European nations were dissatisfied with the Portuguese monopoly of spices just as they had been earlier when the trade had been controlled by the Turks and Italians. But gradually the Dutch, and then others, began to whittle away at the Portuguese position.

The English entered the competition by forming their own East India company in hopes of driving down the cost of pepper. The English didn't succeed in breaking the Dutch hold on the spice trade, but the rivalry that developed played an important role in the new political alignments of that century and spurred the race to colonize new countries.

The exchange of food between the old and new worlds

Although the New World produced few of the spices that helped to spur the overseas voyages of discovery, it did contribute many new foods to the Old World diet. For various reasons not all the foods known to native Americans were to enjoy widespread acceptance. In some cases, the foods simply weren't exportable or wouldn't grow well in alien soil. In others, they affected a group's cultural sensibilities in such a way that it wouldn't accept them.

The story of European settlers colonizing the Americas illustrates how the diets of different cultures occupying the same land are affected by contact with each other. The exchange of foodstuffs between the colonists and the natives altered dietary patterns radically; changes came slowly, however, and were not always welcomed.

In the early 1600s, English colonists settled the northeastern coast of the U.S., bringing with them the gastronomic tastes of the British Isles. The colonists had come to a land of plenty. Their new home was well-stocked with fish and game, a variety of crops cultivated by the natives, as well as wild mushrooms, cherries, nuts, and berries. Why, then, did the new arrivals nearly starve?

First, the colonists did not have much experience making their way in the wilderness. The situation called for hard work and endurance. Most of the Puritans and Pilgrims were middle class merchants, tradespeople, artisans, or landowners who managed properties worked by hired laborers. Poor timing (the Pilgrims arrived in the cold month of December) and little knowledge of farming, fishing, or hunting accounted for many of their initial difficulties in obtaining food.

The colonists' survival also was jeopardized by their reluctance to accept new foods available in America. The settlers relied upon shipments sent from England rather than collecting fish and other foods that were in abundant local supply. When shipments failed to bring sufficient quantities of food, the colonists began to adopt some of the staples in the native Indian diet. And faced with eating the alien grain, corn, or starve, they ate corn.

As you might expect, people are much more likely to accept new foods if they are similar in some way to foods that they are already familiar with. For this reason, two important Indian vegetables—beans and squash—made their way into the diets of the colonists. The Indian bean looked much like the European broad bean and was accepted readily. Squash was adopted too, for though there were no true squashes in Europe, there were edible plants that resembled them.

A well-known example of the use of native foods by colonists is that of Thanksgiving Day, which originated in the festivities held by the Plymouth Colony in December of 1621. On this historic day, about 90 native Americans shared a bountiful meal with the Pilgrims, who were grateful for the end of a difficult year, a successful harvest, and the Indians' help in learning how to secure food in the new land. The native fruits and vegetables, wild turkeys, and pumpkin pies that filled the tables at that first thanksgiving feast became the traditional foods for the day and are still enjoyed as Americans celebrate the holiday over 350 years later.

Though the colonists were becoming more open-minded about indigenous foods, they were also working hard to import and develop their beloved European foods: apples, apricots, pears, and a variety of vegetables and beans. The native Americans were quite receptive to these unfamiliar foods. In a short time after their introduction, apple, peach, apricot, and pear trees were grown by many native Americans. Vegetables from the Old World were assimilated smoothly into the native bill of fare, partly because they looked similar to Indian foods. Lettuce and cabbage resembled the greens so prevalent in the native American diet. Lentils were accepted as another kind of bean, while onions, turnips, and beets looked somewhat like indigenous tubers.

The introduction of domestic animals by the Europeans was also accepted and added to the Indians' predominately vegetable-based diet. The first cows came to Florida about 1550, and for the first time native Americans had access to milk and beef. Domesticated sheep and pigs also were adopted by some tribes.

The industrial revolution

Industrialization, the introduction of factories and the organization of people and machines into large-scale enterprises, was the next major change in the ways people adapted to their physical and social environments. The industrial revolution brought dramatic changes in the way people earned their livelihood, the conditions of their material existence, and the pattern of their daily lives. Not since the agricultural revolution had people so drastically changed how they related to the world around them. The agricultural revolution brought fields, farms, and villages into existence; the industrial revolution gave birth to factories and densely populated industrialized cities. These changes also strongly affected dietary patterns in the new urban centers.

Britain, the first nation to experience large-scale industrialization, began its revolution in the late eighteenth century. During the nineteenth century, other European countries and the U.S. changed dramatically as well. Throughout history, new discoveries had always stimulated other discoveries and developments, but this process, for the most part, had been slow. What is so striking about the industrial age was the speed of change: Each technological advancement seemed to set off a landslide of others.

Enclosure

In Britain, the industrial revolution was closely related to the changes people made in farming and livestock breeding during the eighteenth century. These changes came about when large landowners sought to make farming a more efficient production. Up until this time, a system of commonly owned lands, open fields, and semicollective methods of farming that allowed animals to roam freely was used. Although equitable, the system was less than efficient. As early as 1523, in the first textbook on farming, called *Husbandry,* the use of enclosed fields was recommended.

To improve production and increase profits, British landowners lobbyed for the Acts of Enclosure in Parliament, permitting them to enclose tracts of land with fences. When these laws were enacted, large areas were brought under more efficient cultivation. However, the Enclosure Movement also displaced many small landowners and poor people, who were forced to seek employment in the new manufacturing cities. This influx of people provided much of the surplus labor necessary for the industrial revolution to gain momentum.

Food and the industrial revolution

The pace of industrialization and urbanization varied from country to country, but eventually new towns were developed all over the European and North American continents to house the mass of people who flocked from rural areas in search of factory jobs.

A radical transformation occurred in people's occupations and their physical environment as hordes of people left small villages and farming to work as wage laborers in large crowded cities. Conditions in the industrialized towns were often deplorable. Bad housing and poor sanitation were combined with dehumanizing working conditions. After a long, hard day in a noisy, dark, and stifling factory, the working class went home to overcrowded slums. Cooking facilitie   1, the water supply was often contaminated by sewage and the sewage systems themselves were barely functional. Paradoxically, workers who left the countryside for higher wages in the city barely made enough money to feed themselves.

Hundreds of thousands of people died from disease and malnutrition. As students of nutrition know, the two go hand in hand, as an inadequate diet lowers the body's resistance to infection — and an inadequate diet it was. A typical meal for the British working class consisted of tea and boiled potatoes, occasionally supplemented with bits of bacon. Bread, cheese, and porridge were also common foods. A survey taken in London during the 1840s showed that in one working class district, bread was the only solid food given to children in 17 out of 21 meals in a week. As you might expect, vitamin deficiencies were widespread.

Industrialization influenced not only what people ate but also when and where they ate it. Agrarian Europeans had traditionally eaten two meals a day, a large meal at noon after a strenuous morning in the fields and a lighter meal at the end of the work day in the late afternoon. Industrialization introduced a new rhythm to the work day. Since people now worked ten to twelve hours a day, they consumed breakfast to provide enough energy for the first half of the day. Lunch, previously food served during a two- to three-hour break in the middle of the day, was shorter, less caloric, and eaten at the factory so the worker could get back to the machines as soon as possible. After a long day at the factory, workers went home and consumed a third meal.

While the working class struggled to survive in the first part of the eighteenth century, the middle classes of industrial England increased in number and power. They included bankers, merchants, shippers, lawyers, and clergymen. Unlike factory workers, they were not forced to eat the food that was cheapest but were able to exercise some choice. Their diets included meats, butter, cheese, a finer bread, and occasional fruits and vegetables.

The richest of all, the royalty, exercised an even wider choice. The elaborate menu of a dinner given by Britian's Prince Regent in 1817 included 4 soups; 4 fish dishes (including eel, lobster, trout, and turbot); 36 main dishes; 8 elaborate display pieces, some made with pastries, with names such as "the ruins of Antioch" and "the Chinese hermitage"; and 32 side dishes including truffles, pineapple cream, oysters, and liqueur-flavored jelly (Tannahill 1973).

The emergence of national cuisines

As people migrated into cities during the late eighteenth century, regional cuisines developed based on the popular cooking styles of the major urban centers. Mass production of foods and advertising elevated some of these urban food styles into national cuisines. For example, the pasta of Milan, Turin, and Rome expanded into an Italian national cuisine; while Parisian bread, butter-based cooking, and red wine became a French national cuisine. English fish and chips emerged, as did American hot dogs, canned beans, and white bread. By the end of the nineteenth century, most major countries had their own national cuisines; foods that immediately struck visitors as characteristic. The association of certain dishes with nationalities reflected the emergence of the nation-state in the political life of the Western world in the nineteenth century. (Gordon 1983:23)

Transportation, refrigeration, and canning

By 1850 it was becoming clear that the ever-increasing numbers of laborers needed to be supplied with more abundant, cheaper food. If not, they would be unable to continue to supply the labor needed for the new industrialized economy. This situation, first recognized in England, was soon noticed in other European countries and the U.S. as well. People worked to find solutions to the existing food problems. Technological advancements in transportation, refrigeration, and food processing improved the diet of the working class considerably by making food cheaper, expanding the variety of foods available, and keeping them fresher longer.

Transportation Before the industrial revolution, most people in the United States and Europe had access to locally grown fresh foods. This changed, however; as cities expanded it became harder and harder to provide food to urban dwellers who now lived miles from where their food was produced.

Land transport was limited in that only small amounts of food and other products could be hauled by oxen or horses over narrow bumpy roads. The construction of canals greatly improved the situation in some areas, and food prices declined. In the U.S., flour, which had sold for $16 a barrel in coastal cities, dropped as low as $4 when the Erie Canal was opened in 1825. Not only did the building of canals promote the exchange of goods, it also encouraged agriculture by giving farmers access to urban markets.

With the development of the steamboat and railroads in the 1820s; transportation and food became even cheaper. The railroad not only improved people's diet by increasing the number of foods available, but it improved the quality of the foods as well. Foods arrived at their destinations fresher, and thus they were more nutritious. In London, meat had been transported on the hoof — often traveling long distances to reach the slaughterhouse. The long hike developed the cows' muscles, producing stringy, tough meat. Cattle transported by train were not only tastier, but cheaper, because they lost less weight on the journey from pasture to slaughterhouse. Pork improved too. Before the advent of the locomotive, pigs had been bred partly for their ability to walk to market. Now that this was no longer necessary, breeders could focus on developing stock that produced rich meat. (See "The Story of Beef, Chapter 4.)

Refrigeration   One of the early solutions to keep food fresh in hot weather was the icehouse. Ice was cut from a nearby frozen pond and stored in the icehouse, often lasting through much of the summer.

In the 1830s, machines that made ice were patented. Many houses built in the U.S. in the mid 1800s and the early 1900s featured a small porch built outside so that the iceman could deposit the machine-made ice into an icebox when no one was home. Each household would leave a note indicating the amount needed. The iceman would slide a block of the specified size onto a thick rubber apron and deposit it into the icebox. A Boston family buying ice in this fashion in 1855 paid $2.00 a month for the delivery of 15 pounds of ice a day (Root and de Rochemont 1976). Mechanical refrigeration was patented as early as 1834; however, it was almost a century before the refrigerator would become a common household appliance.

The combination of improved refrigeration and faster transportation greatly expanded available foodstuffs around the world. Beef preserved by refrigeration was shipped from the United States to Great Britain; bananas from the West Indies could now be shipped to Europe; and other fruits, vegetables, dairy products, and eggs

Figure 2.3
1920s Milwaukee iceman (Courtesy of John van Willigen)

were distributed throughout the United States and Europe. Vitamin deficiencies and incidences of food poisoning decreased dramatically as a result of this expanded and well-preserved food supply. But, as we shall see in Chapter 4, a food supply produced far from home is not without its problems.

Canning Although foods have been processed by salting, fermentation, and other methods for many thousands of years, modern food processing began in 1809 when Nicholas Appert invented vacuum-packed, airtight glass bottles for foods. For his invention, Appert won a prize (2000 francs) from Napoleon, who needed a supply of unspoilable foods for his armies. Napoleon kept this process a French monopoly by treating it as a military secret until the same principle was discovered by others.

The next step, using tin cans in place of breakable glass bottles, started in England. By 1818, a canning factory was turning out corned and boiled beef, carrots, vegetable soup, and veal. Though canned food was cheap and convenient, it did not get high marks for taste. Canned meat, for instance, was described as coarse, stringy, fatty, and generally unappetizing. Safety posed another problem. During the initial stages of the canning industry, sterilization processes were poorly understood. Often the larger cans of meat were contaminated. Later, standardization of temperatures and processing times made canned food a safer product. By the end of the nineteenth century, canned foods were providing industrialized populations with a diversity of fruits, vegetables, and meats not previously obtainable. As with refrigeration and improved transportation systems, advances in the food processing industry helped offset some of the negative impact of the industrial revolution on laborers' diets.

While technology advanced in leaps and bounds in Europe and North America, industrialization moved at a snail's pace in other countries. In order to continue to expand industrialization, Europe and America tried to find overseas markets for their products. Thus the nineteenth century pursuit for empire was in part a search for overseas markets. In order for Western nations to maintain their own markets, industrial development in overseas countries was retarded —in part by denying colonial subjects the technical and managerial skills necessary for industrialization. As a result, large sections of Africa and Asia remained hundreds of years behind Western countries in terms of economic growth.

As "progress" swept the United States, Europe, and later Japan, other nations lagged increasingly behind. By the close of the nineteenth century the social, economic, and dietary distinctions between "developed" and "underdeveloped" countries were undeniably clear. (The relationship between the developed and underdeveloped worlds and its consequences for diet and disease in the modern world is discussed in greater detail in Chapters 7 and 8.)

The scientific revolution

The seventeenth and eighteenth centuries brought with them yet another major cultural revolution. Copernicius, Kepler, and Galileo challenged religious dogma in search of physical laws that governed the universe. With Newton and the discovery of the law of universal gravitation, the Age of Enlightenment was born. Quantitative natural science, based on the combination of experiment and reason, triumphed over the mysticism and metaphysics of previous eras. The scientific revolution has led us to our current level of knowledge about human nutrition and enabled us to exert an unprecedented control over our food supply, health, and physical well-being.

Adulteration

By the nineteenth century, industrialized countries were extremely science-conscious. One of the first substantial impacts of science on food came when scientists brought popular foods into their laboratories and found, much to the manufacturers' chagrin, that they contained many questionable ingredients. Investigators discovered, for example, that commercial breads were laden with alum, poisonous salts of copper and lead gave candies their bright colors, and cheeses were laced with hemlock to add a more appealing orange color.

alum
potassium aluminum sulfate, used as an astringent and to produce vomiting

hemlock
a poisonous herb

When Dr. Harvey Wiley, chief of the Bureau of Chemistry of the United States Department of Agriculture (USDA), conducted experiments in the early 1900s demonstrating that some food additives were dangerous to health, food manufacturers attempted to have him removed from office. Although they were not successful, Wiley later resigned in frustration.

Wiley's reports made little impression on the public or on federal legislation. Some consumers had a difficult time believing that their favorite foods were dangerous when labels and advertisements promised otherwise. The dramatization needed to alert the public to the dangers of adulteration came in 1906 with the publication of Upton Sinclair's book, *The Jungle*. Sinclair's book described in graphic detail Chicago's meat packing plants as filthy, rat-infested buildings where spoiled meat was chemically treated and handled by tubercular workers. The book, read widely throughout America, created a public protest. Under the spur of aroused public opinion, the U.S. Congress passed two measures to protect consumers. One arranged for regular meat inspection services; the other established the Pure Food and Drug Act of 1906, designed to prevent the "manufacture, sale, or transportation of adulterated, misbranded, poisonous or deleterious foods, drugs, medicines and liquors" (Robinson and Lawler 1977:274).

Food preservation

Food preservation also owes much to scientific discoveries. The work of Appert, Pasteur, and Koch has had a tremendous impact on the safety and availability of foods. Before their discoveries, many foods (milk in particular) were heavily contaminated with microorganisms. The food system served as a vehicle for typhoid, dysentery, tuberculosis, and other diseases. Pasteurization was the first scientific breakthrough in food processing, making milk, for example, a much safer product.

Scientific developments in food processing have been a mixed blessing. Consider condensed milk. When used during the American Civil War, canned condensed milk provided a safe supply of nutrients that soldiers could carry with them. Later, however, some manufacturers began making cheaper brands from skimmed rather than whole milk. The condensed skim milk lacked the fat-soluble Vitamins A and D. Because it was cheaper, consumption of the skimmed product rapidly increased, especially among infants and children. When it was realized that infants and children raised on this milk characteristically developed rickets, British legislation ruled that condensed skim milk must carry a label clearly stating it was skimmed and not suitable for feeding infants and children. Unfortunately, the mandatory labeling did not have the desired effect. A report published 17 years later revealed that many poorer families continued to use it because of its low cost, and many consumers believed that the labels' warning—"Machine Skimmed"—meant it was a technologically superior, not a nutritionally inferior, product.

The story of white bread illustrates a common problem encountered with food processing: the removal of nutrients. In 1840, a new method of milling flour was invented, using iron rollers to process grain more rapidly and give flour a more consistent quality. The old mills removed the bran from the wheat kernel, but not the germ. Although some nutrients and fiber were lost when the bran was removed, much remained in the germ, making flour a relatively nutritious food. In contrast, the new mills removed both germ and bran. This delighted the millers, bakers, and shopkeepers because the white flour did not become rancid as quickly as wheat flour containing the oil of the germ. Whiter flour also appealed to some consumers who liked the lighter baked products it yielded.

pasteurization
partial sterilization of a substance at a high temperature for a short time to destroy objectional micoorganisms without significantly changing the chemical makeup of the product

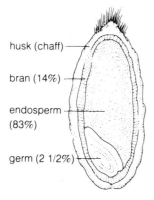

husk (chaff)

bran (14%)

endosperm (83%)

germ (2 1/2%)

Figure 2.4
Whole wheat kernel. The whole wheat kernel has three parts: the endosperm, the bran, and the germ. Most of the vitamins, minerals, and fiber are found in the bran and germ. Because whole wheat flour is ground from the whole wheat kernel, it is rich in vitamins and minerals. New milling techniques, developed in 1840, removed both the bran and germ from the whole wheat kernel, leading to widespread vitamin deficiencies in Southeast Asia.

Because a somewhat varied diet was available in industrialized countries, the removal of B vitamins from flour did not create a dramatic widespread nutrition problem. The missing vitamins were supplied by other foods. But in Southeast Asia and other places where a more limited variety of foods was available, the introduction of the new milling process had a swift and corrosive effect on the health of the people. There, the new mills were used to process rice, the dietary staple. As with flour, the new milling process removed most of the essential B vitamins. As people switched to polished rice, beriberi—the Vitamin B_1 deficiency disease that affects the nerves, heart, and digestive tract—swept through the population. Dutch rulers became so concerned about the number of deaths occurring in their East Indies colonies that they dispatched a research team to determine what could be done about the incidence of beriberi. The findings of this investigation led to one of the greatest scientific discoveries in the history of nutrition: the identification of vitamins.

The discovery of vitamins

It had long been known that different foods had positive and negative effects on health, but it wasn't until the late 1800s that scientists began to identify the fundamental components of food. The story is an interesting one. For two years, the Dutch researchers concentrated on the possibility that beriberi was an infectious disease. It was 1886, only a short time after Pasteur's discoveries had astounded the world, and it was only natural that the researchers should think in terms of microbes and infection. Scientific workers often deplore the limited amount of funds available for research, but for Dr. Christian Eijkman, it turned out to be a blessing in disguise. The hospital at which he was studying had such limited funds that the experimental hens had to be fed with leftovers from the ward kitchen. Eijkman observed that the hens fed on the polished rice diet developed a curious inability to walk and exhibited other symptoms similar to beriberi. At first he thought they had become infected by the "beriberi germ," but then he noticed that the hens recovered promptly when fed rice bran. This information was soon applied to humans, and hundreds of patients who had dragged themselves into the Buitenzorg beriberi hospital on swollen legs were able to walk out only a short time later, fully recovered.

It was not until 1901 that Eijkman identified the importance of the rice germ itself, and even then neither he nor the scientific world realized the significance of his discovery. It was an entire decade later before the word "vitamin" was coined to refer to this new category of food components so essential to health and survival.

Throughout the twentieth century, technological know-how and scientific knowledge have increased steadily in all industrialized nations. These cultural changes have made possible the production of the most abundant, reliable food supply ever known to humankind.

The industrial and scientific revolutions have also created new environmental conditions to which we must now respond. The abundance and convenience of the food supply in industrialized countries has led to perhaps dangerously high intakes of refined carbohydrates, salt, cholesterol, and saturated fats, while dietary fiber consumption has dropped. Little physical exertion is required to obtain this abundant supply of calorically dense foods. It is not surprising, then, that obesity, cardiovascular disease, and diabetes are major killers among humans who evolved for millions of years as hunters and gatherers.

Modern-day adaptations

In the last 30 years, science and technology have produced yet another potential environmental problem: a food supply containing a large menu of chemical compounds never before ingested by humans. We know little of these chemicals' effects upon liver function, nervous tissues, the immunological system, fetal development, or biochemical genetics (Gaulin & Konner 1977:71).

The questions we must ask ourselves today are: how are we adapting to these new environmental stresses, and what will these adaptations bring for life tomorrow? There is no doubt that we are responding to dietary changes on all three levels: genetically, physiologically, and behaviorally. Genetically, this is evident in the different rates of fertility, morbidity, and mortality found among people in industrialized and nonindustrialized nations. We cannot predict the direction nor rate of genetic changes brought about by natural selection, but we do know that humankind is still undergoing biological evolution (Vander 1981:57).

Physiologically, the picture is much clearer. "States of health and disease are expressions of the success or failure experienced by the organism in its efforts to respond adaptively to environmental challenges" (Dubos 1980:xvii). The fact that industrialized societies have achieved record lows in infant mortality rates and enjoy a long life expectancy attests to our physiological adaptability, while recent warnings against fetal alcohol syndrome, the teratogenic effects of thalidomide, the potential carcinogenic effects of food additives such as nitrites, and the ever-growing number of occupational hazards remind us that our physiological adaptability also has limits—limits that are being exceeded by our modern, industrialized way of life.

teratogenic
tending to cause
malformations

Focus 2-2

Obesity in modern industrialized societies: have we outgrown our genes?

If genetic adjustments take hundreds of generations to unfold, how do they keep pace with an environment that changes as rapidly as that found in modern industrialized societies? Unfortunately, they don't. Many dietary practices are simply too new for our bodies to have adapted genetically. This does not mean that all dietary changes are necessarily bad just because they are new. After all, as we have already seen, our bodies are amazingly adaptable and respond both physiologically and behaviorally to many environmental stresses.

Nevertheless, there is evidence that our bodies, prepared by several millions of years of natural selection that operated when humans obtained their food as foragers, are not designed for many aspects of the modern industrial lifestyle. In stark contrast to the forager mode, the industrial lifestyle provides a continuous supply of calories, little motivation to exercise, a relative lack of fiber, and a preponderance of refined carbohydrate, saturated fats, and cholesterol (Gaulin and Konner 1977:73). This lifestyle, in turn, has been associated with an increased prevalence of obesity, diabetes, hypertension, and cardiovascular disease.

Perhaps the best illustration of modernization's effects on our health status come from societies that have emerged rapidly from a traditional to a more industrialized way of life and diet. For example, among many North American Indian tribes, obesity and diabetes were extremely rare prior to 1940. But as these peoples shifted from an agricultural to a more industrial lifestyle and replaced their traditional diet with one abundant in refined carbohydrates and calories, obesity and diabetes became epidemic. While rates are still low in a few North American tribes, obesity and diabetes are now exceedingly common in many groups. The most extreme rates are found among the Pima of Arizona and the Cherokee of North Carolina, where as many as 84 percent of the Indians over 35 years of age are diabetic (West 1977:33).

Other populations (Polynesians, Micronesians, and the Aborigines of Australia) also have experienced dramatic rises in obesity, cardiovascular disease, hypertension, and diabetes as they have entered the modern era (Fitzpatrick-Nietschman 1983).

Rx for a modern lifestyle

The diet and exercise plan now recommended by most nutrition experts, as well as the U.S. and Canadian governments, calls for a return to diets high in complex carbohydrates and dietary fiber and low in fat, saturated fat, cholesterol, and simple carbohydrates, as well as salt. Increased exercise and reduced calorie intake also is recommended for maintenance of ideal weight.

Dietary Guidelines for Americans

- Eat a variety of foods
- Maintain ideal weight
- Avoid too much fat, saturated fat, and cholestrol
- Eat foods with adequate starch and fiber
- Avoid too much sugar
- Avoid too much sodium
- If you drink alcohol, do so in moderation

U.S. Department of Agriculture

Interestingly, this plan closely resembles the diet and exercise patterns believed to be practiced by our hominid ancestors and early humans who foraged for food during our evolution into modern *Homo sapiens.*

Behaviorally, we are trying numerous adaptive strategies. In the U.S., for example, many chemicals (such cyclamates, DDT, red dye No. 2, EDB, and dioxin) are restricted by governmental agencies. Also an increasingly large number of us are making changes in our personal consumption patterns, switching to organically grown vegetables or passing up most of the highly processed convenience foods that now stock supermarket shelves.

While it is difficult to predict the direction in which these changes will take us, we do know that culture offers us the most rapid and flexible way to adapt to an ever-changing environment. In the next chapter we will explore the concept of culture and its potential for helping us deal with the nutritional challenges facing us today.

Summary

- Our diets have changed dramatically through history. We have gone from foraging wild foods in the wilderness to shopping in supermarkets for items such as frozen dinners and produce grown thousands of miles away. The chain of events that occurred between these two dramatically different ways of securing food can be divided into three major revolutions: agricultural, industrial, and scientific.

- About 12,000 years ago, a change in the way humans got their food began to unfold as people gradually shifted from food collection to food production. Nutritional status was affected as people switched from eating a wide variety of foraged foods to a small number of domesticated plants and animals. The additional life expectancy and increase in population that are associated with agriculture are at the basis of modern civilization.

- During the fifteenth century, the search for spices stimulated the discovery of new lands. As new lands were discovered, the exchange of foods between countries led to diversified diets.

- During the eighteenth and nineteenth centuries, the industrial revolution gave birth to factories and industrialized cities. The nutritional status changed for the worse initially as people moved from farms into overcrowded cities. Technological advancements in transportation, refrigeration, and food processing gradually improved diets by making food cheaper, expanding the variety of foods available, and keeping them fresher longer.

- The scientific revolution of the nineteenth and twentieth centuries has led us to our current level of knowledge about human nutrition and enabled us to exert an unprecedented control over our food supply, health, and physical well-being. Scientific developments in food processing have had both good and bad effects on the food supply. While the discovery of pasteurization increased the safety of food, the milling of grains led to widespread vitamin deficiencies in some parts of the world. The discovery of vitamins paved the way to a new understanding of food and its effect on health.

Highlight 2-1 Vegetarianism: An old solution to a new problem

One way Americans are reducing the health risks associated with a modern lifestyle is through the use of vegetarian diets somewhat similar to those of our foraging ancestors. Once considered an eccentric practice, vegetarianism is now the subject of much scientific research, as well as many popular books and articles.

Because the high fiber/low fat content of most vegetarian diets is linked to decreased rates of heart disease, cancer, and obesity, some vegetarian diets have gained growing acceptance among health providers as well. Also, while recommendations published in government reports (U.S. Dietary Guidelines, National Academy of Science's "Diet, Nutrition and Cancer," and Nutrition Canada) do not specifically suggest a *vegetarian* diet, they recommend dietary steps that take the consumer in that direction with a decreased consumption of animal products and an increased intake of plant foods.

The main dietary factors affecting heart disease are saturated fat and cholesterol (derived primarily from animal foods), which can clog blood vessels with fatty deposits and make heart disease more likely. Vegetarians may be protected from heart disease by limiting animal foods and replacing them with high-fiber foods such as beans, oats, and carrots, which have been shown to lower cholesterol levels in the blood (Jenkins, 1981).

Limiting fat may limit a vegetarian's chances of developing cancer as well. Although the mechanism(s) by which a high fat intake relates to cancer are not clear, people who eat high-fat diets are at greater risk for developing the disease (Hamilton and Whitney 1982:142). In addition, increased fiber intake stimulates intestinal contents to move along quickly, limiting the amount of time carcinogens are in contact with the colon. Recently, fruits and vegetables high in beta carotene, such as cantaloupe, broccoli, sweet potatoes, and orange squash, have been shown to provide protection against cancer. Also, vegetarians may be less likely to be obese than meat eaters. In one study, young vegetarians in Boston weighed an average of 33 pounds less than a meat-eating comparison group (Ames 1983).

In addition to health benefits, people practice vegetarianism for a variety of other reasons as well. Trappist Monks, Seventh Day Adventists, Krishna devotees, and Mennonites are among the religious groups that advocate a vegetarian diet. Disapproval of inhumane treatment of animals and personal taste are two other reasons people avoid meat.

Recently, environmental considerations have drawn many people to vegetarianism. They reason that meat consumption is ecologically wasteful because grain is fed to animals (See "The Story of Beef" in Chapter 4) rather than directly to people. Depending on the type of animal, between three and sixteen pounds of grain are required to produce one pound of edible meat. Therefore, more protein would be available if these plant sources were eaten directly by people instead of pigs, cattle, and chickens.

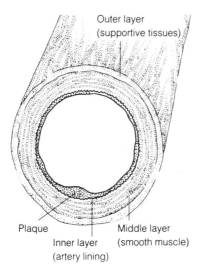
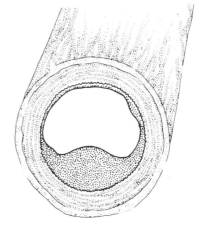

Outer layer
(supportive tissues)

Plaque

Inner layer
(artery lining)

Middle layer
(smooth muscle)

An artery (section) with plaque just
beginning to form. Plaques can
easily appear in a person as young
as 15.

The same artery, years later,
half blocked by plaque.

Figure HL2.1

*Atherosclerosis: healthy artery versus artery blocked by
plaque. Diets high in fat and cholesterol are linked to the
development of atherosclerosis. (Whitney and Hamilton,* Understanding Nutrition, *third edition, St. Paul: West Publishing Company,
1984, p. 110.)*

Applications for nutritionists

Because of the increased popularity of vegetarianism, nutritionists may find that they
are now working with more clients following these types of diets. For this reason, the
various forms of vegetarianism and guidelines for assessing their nutritional adequacy
are discussed below.

There are several different types of vegetarian diets. Strict vegetarians (*vegans*) exclude all animal products from their diets.
Lacto-vegetarians consume milk but no
eggs or meat, while *ovo-lacto-vegetarians*
eat eggs and milk but avoid meat. Even
within these classifications there is a wide
variety of vegetarian dietary practices. Some

people eat fish but no meat; others eat poultry but no red meat; and while most have
diets low in fat, some vegetarians eat such
large amounts of dairy products that the fat
content of their diet is close to that of avid
meat eaters. Others call themselves "part-
time vegetarians" and rely predominately on
plant food but eat meat occasionally. Because of this diversity, the knowledge that a
person is vegetarian explains little about his
or her diet. Further questioning is needed to
learn important specifics.

The wide variation in vegetarian diets
also makes it important to assess each diet
individually. In evaluating the nutritional
content of vegetarian diets, six nutrients are
considered: protein, vitamin B-12, vitamin D,
calcium, zinc, and iron.

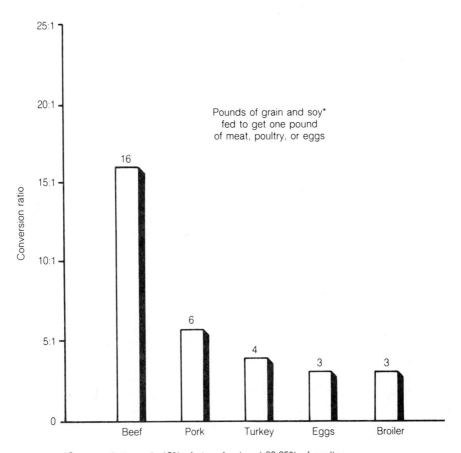

*Soy constitutes only 12% of steer feed and 20-25% of poultry.

Figure HL2.2
Though cows can convert grass into protein, and hogs can thrive on waste products, most cattle and hogs in the U.S. today are fed large amounts of grain and soybean products that produce larger animals with fattier meat. As you can see, cattle are particularly inefficient in converting grain and soy to meat. (U.S. Department of Agriculture, Economic Research Service, Beltsville, Maryland.)

Protein

Many people mistakenly think that the major failing of vegetarian diets is their limited protein content. However, in assessing the protein content in a vegetarian diet three things need to be considered. First, most Americans consume twice as much protein as they need. (The RDA for protein is 46 grams for women and 56 grams for men.) Second, the protein in milk and eggs is more efficiently used than that in meat and fish. And third, plant foods, though usually low in one or more essential amino acids (EAAs), can contribute high-quality protein if correctly combined in the diet (See "Protein Primer" in Chapter 2).

Although ovo-lacto-vegetarians have no difficulty getting adequate protein, strict vegans must be sure to consume a wide variety of plant foods each day. Because legumes (beans, peas, lentils, etc.) are necessary for balancing grain and vegetable protein, they are a staple in the vegan diet.

Vitamin B-12

Vitamin B-12 requirements also are met easily in a meatless diet that contains milk and eggs. The RDA for adults is 3 μg (micrograms). One cup of milk and one egg each contain 1 μg of B-12; one cup of cottage cheese contains 2.5 μg.

However, because vitamin B-12 is found almost exclusively in animal products, vegan diets may be lacking in this nutrient. Small amounts of B-12 are found in nutritional yeast and fermented soy products such as miso and tempeh, two items popular in macrobiotic diets. If there is no source of vitamin B-12 in the diet, a vitamin supplement is necessary.

Vitamin D

Vegetarians that do not eat dairy products can obtain vitamin D by using fortified margarine and soy milk, and also by exposing their skin to sunlight.

Calcium

Milk-drinking vegetarians have no problem getting sufficient dietary calcium. On the other hand, this nutrient may create problems for vegans who must get this nutrient in small amounts from a wide variety of foods such as blackstrap molasses, greens (collard, mustard, and kale), tortillas, almonds, and hard water. Calcium supplements are another option for strict vegetarians.

As discussed in Chapter 1, several factors affect the body's ability to use calcium. Of particular interest to vegetarians is the relationship between calcium and protein. Excessive protein decreases the efficiency of calcium utilization. This is thought to be a factor in osteoporosis, the brittle bone condition so prevalent in older women. Once thought to result from a deficiency of calcium, osteoporosis is now associated with an excessive protein intake as well (Margen et al. 1974). Calcium absorption is also decreased by excessive fat, which binds with calcium in the intestines and forms insoluble soaps. Thus the low fat and protein intakes of many vegetarians may allow them to absorb calcium more efficiently.

Zinc

Zinc is an important nutrient for vegetarians to consider because it easily may be marginal in a meatless diet. Though grains and legumes contain zinc, they are also high in phytic acid, a compound that binds zinc and other minerals in the intestines and reduces their absorption. It seems, however, that people who eat large amounts of grains and legumes adjust through increased production of the enzyme phytase, which breaks down phytic acid in the intestine (Bitar and Reinbold 1972). The process of leavening bread also destroys some phytic acid. As a result, the zinc in yeast bread is more available than that in unleavened bread. Zinc supplements are an option for vegetarians.

Iron

Iron obtained from meat is more easily absorbed than the iron in plant foods. But because a major factor governing absorption is the body's need for iron, vegetarians may use the iron in their diet much more efficiently, enabling then to obtain the amounts needed. Also vegetarians can improve the iron content of their diet by including foods such as beans, whole grains, greens, and dried fruits, which are rich in this nutrient. They also can enhance their iron intake by consuming a vitamin C source with these foods to enhance absorption or by using cast-iron cookware that can increase the iron content of acidic foods such as spaghetti sauce as much as 29 times (Moore 1973).

Infants need animal protein

Despite the foregoing evidence that adults can live healthfully on a vegan diet, infants and young children need animal protein to grow properly. A baby can develop normally on an ovo-lacto-vegetarian diet but may suffer growth retardation when raised on a strict vegan diet.

A postscript for meat eaters

You don't have to become a total vegetarian to derive many of the benefits of a vegetarian diet. By cutting back on meat several times a week and taking up the slack with more vegetable foods, the fat content of the diet will decrease while the fiber content increases, bringing the diet closer to the vegetarian prescription for health.

Table HL2.1   Four Food Groups for a Meatless Diet: A Daily Guide

Grains, Legumes, Nuts, and Seeds

Six servings or more. Include several slices of yeast-raised, whole-grain bread, a serving of beans, and a few nuts or seeds.

Vegetables

Three servings or more. Include one or more servings of dark leafy greens, like romaine, spinach, or chard.

Milk and Eggs

Two or more glasses of fresh milk for adults, three or more for children. (Children under nine use smaller glasses.) Other dairy products or an egg may be used to meet part of the milk requirement. Eggs are optional—up to four per week.

Fruit

One to four pieces. Include a raw source of vitamin C, like citrus fruits, strawberries, or cantaloupe.

Reprinted by permission from *Laurel's Kitchen: A Handbook for Vegetarian Cookery and Nutrition* by Laurel Robertson, Carol Flinders, and Bronwen Godfrey, copyright© 1976, Nilgiri Press, Petaluma, CA.

Table HL2.2 Four Food Groups for the Vegan

BALANCING PROTEIN		Men	Women
For the vegan, the four food groups and their proportions are determined by the formula for vegan protein balance:	60% from grains	33 g	28 g
	35% from legumes	20	16
	5% from leafy greens	3	2
	Total protein RDA	56 g	46 g

Grains

33 grams grain protein for men; 28 grams for women. Include 4 slices of bread, 3 to 5 servings of grain, and 1 serving of nuts or seeds every day.

EXAMPLE:

	Protein(g)	Calories
1 cup oatmeal	5	132
1 cup brown rice	5	232
½ cup cracked wheat	3	108
¼ cup sesame meal	4	130
2 slices commercial whole wheat bread	5	122
2 slices Rye Bread	11	244
	33	968

Legumes

20 grams legume protein for men; 16 for women. Include ⅓ cup beans and 2 cups fortified soybean milk OR

1¼ cups beans plus other sources of vitamin B-12 and calcium every day.

EXAMPLE:

	Protein(g)	Calories
2 cups soy milk	15	312
⅓ cup navy beans	5	75
	20	387

Vegetables

4 or more servings of good-quality vegetables every day (3 grams of protein). Include 2 substantial servings of dark leafy greens for calcium and riboflavin.

Fruit

1 to 4 servings a day. Include a raw source of vitamin C.

LIMITED NUTRIENTS & GOOD SOURCES

Vitamin B-12   Two cups fortified soy milk, fortified nutritional yeast, or a vitamin pill

Calcium   Fortified soy milk, leafy greens without oxalates, sunflower seeds, unhulled sesame seeds, blackstrap molasses

Riboflavin   Beans, green leaves, certain nuts, nutritional yeast, wheat germ

Reprinted by permission from *Laurel's Kitchen: A Handbook for Vegetarian Cookery and Nutrition* by Laurel Robertson, Carol Flinders, and Bronwen Godfrey, copyright© 1976, Nilgiri Press, Petaluma, CA.

3

Eating is a
cultural affair

If you have traveled to other countries, you probably have noticed that foods considered a delicacy in one society may provoke amusement or disgust in another. For instance, as a North American, you may not share the Iranian's taste for a chutney made from fruits allowed to rot in a spicy sauce. And when encountering puppy hams and suckling pigs featured in Chinese cuisine, you may fail to appreciate the careful breeding that has gone into making these delicacies. You also may have been surprised to learn that natives from the Gilbert Islands are equally startled at the idea of eating eggs, and some Brazilian Indians react similarly to milk. To them, the milk of other animals is an excretory secretion as distasteful as urine or feces.

Differences in what is considered edible and the notions associated with food are well illustrated by various reactions to *entomophagy*—insect-eating. Europeans arriving in the New World were shocked by the sight of Indians eating "large fat spiders, white worms that breed in rotten wood and other decayed objects" (Columbus 1959). This aversion to insect-eating is not widespread though. In fact, from ancient times to the present, insects have been

chutney
A condiment that is made
with fruits and sometimes
added raisins, nuts, on-
ions and seasoned with
spices.

!Kung Bushmen
The exclamation point (!)
is placed before Kung to
denote that the "K" is pronounced with a clicking
sound.

a valuable nutritional resource, as well as a taste treat, for most of
humankind.

Insects far outnumber any other animal on earth, both in the
number of species and the number of individuals. There are many
groups that capitalize on this fact and use insects as a nutritious addition to their diet. Insects are calorically rich and contain protein,
fat, carbohydrate, water, vitamins, and minerals. By eating an average of 150 ants per day, the !Kung Bushman, modern-day foragers in
Africa's Kalahari Desert, enhance their diet with 60 grams of protein, 118 mg. of calcium, 48 mg. of iron, 142 mg. of copper, and
220 mg. of phosphorus, as well as vitamins B-1 (thiamine) and B-2
(riboflavin) (Hetzel 1978:41).

People also eat insects for enjoyment. To Australian Bushmen,
sugar ants are a delicacy. The ants' abdomen is swollen with nectar,
providing sweetness followed by the sharp astringent taste of formic
acid. Among the Japanese, the smell of frying silk worm larvae
brings back memories of working in silk factories. Like the Japanese,
most societies prefer the larger bugs cooked (beetles are shelled,
fried, and mixed with sugar to make a sauce; grasshoppers are
roasted with soya sauce), but smaller varieties may be eaten raw. In
some places, lice and fleas are eaten immediately while delousing
friends or relatives. Although most peoples are quite selective about
the *types* of insects they eat, some societies consume just about anything they catch. The complete absence of insects in European and
North American diets is unique.

European and North Americans are not alone, however, in their
decision not to use many potentially nutritious resources in the environment. Although *Homo sapiens* as a species has eaten just about
everything physiologically possible—including a wide range of poisonous plants, clay, blood, urine, feces, raw as well as rotted
meat, dried cowhide, and each other—no group has used *all* available nutritious substances for food (Foster and Anderson 1978:265).
Everywhere people have overlooked valuable resources, failed to
develop technologies to raise nutritious plants and animals, and rejected items for ideological reasons. Even hunters and gatherers living in harsh environments exercise discrimination in choosing what
they will eat. The !Kung Bushmen, for example, derive 90 percent
of their vegetable diet from only 23 of the 85 available edible species. Of the 223 local species of animals known to the Bushmen, 54
species are classified as edible and of these, only 17 species are
hunted on a regular basis.

How do groups choose what items will make up their diet?

Diets are influenced by a composite of biological, environmental,
and cultural factors. First and foremost, a successful diet must be

compatible with human biological needs: it must provide enough energy and essential nutrients for the group's members to live and reproduce. If it doesn't, the society will eventually die out. Physiological limitations restrict all diets: no human is able to digest cellulose or avoid toxic reactions caused by eating certain poisonous plants. Allergies and digestive intolerances further limit the diets of some people. As we have already seen, some individuals are lactase deficient (they lack the enzyme necessary to digest the sugar in milk) and experience gastrointestinal distress if they eat milk products containing lactose.

See Highlight 1-1, "No Milk Please! The Story of Lactase Deficiency."

Food choices are influenced also by environmental factors, since people can eat only what is available. Many people still rely primarily on foods produced close to home. However, just about all societies have established trade networks with other groups and obtain some foods produced outside their homeland. Today, food availability for most people is influenced by a complex set of technological, economic, and political factors. Improved transportation, refrigeration, and food processing make it technologically feasible to ship food just about anywhere on the earth. Access to food, however, varies tremendously within and between nations. The ways societies organize themselves economically (e.g., the class structure) and politically (e.g., capitalism versus Communism), greatly influences who has the financial resources needed to purchase foods available in local markets. Sometimes governments may exert other controls over food supplies. Each year the Soviet government, for example, determines how much of its grain will be set aside as cattle feed, directly influencing the availability of beef in the U.S.S.R. Government policies affect international trade as well. Consider the impact of U.S.—U.S.S.R. grain deals on both the Soviet consumer's access to beef and the price of bread in the United States. (We look more closely at the impact of international trade laws, oil prices, and political relations between nations on world food supplies in Chapters 7 and 8.)

Biology and environmental factors are only part of what determines human food choices. Our diets are also a reflection of what we consider acceptable as food. Several groups living in the same environment, with the same nutritional resources at hand, may select remarkably different items to make up their diet. This is because the groups have different traditions and practices regarding what and how foods should be obtained, prepared and eaten. *Culture* is the term used to describe the knowledge, beliefs, values, and practices that a group has learned and shared through generations.

Culture has a pervasive influence on human diet. As we have just seen, it influences what a person defines as edible. By defining "food," culture influences which of the biologically compatible substances available in the environment will be eaten. Americans, for example, have decided that insects are not culturally acceptable as food, regardless of their nutritional value and abundance. "There are many nutritious items highly esteemed by the members of other cultures, and known to us, that we do not define as edible: horses, dogs, small birds such as larks and warblers, frogs, salamanders, sea urchins, octopus, seaweed, acorns, armadillos, rattlesnakes . . . and the Mexican 'flying bedbug', the *jamil*. The list could be extended many times over and it is possible, in fact, that a nutritionally acceptable diet could be constructed of 'foods' that most Americans never eat" (Foster and Anderson 1978:265).

Members of a social group also share many ideas about how foods should be prepared. Most North Americans believe that meat should be both fresh and cooked. Yet some societies prefer their meat raw and many like it "high," or slightly spoiled. Rotten fish, carefully buried between layers of grass and fish eggs, is savored by some tribes of the Northwest Coast of North America; the Miskito and Sumer Indians of Central America eat bird eggs that are practically rotten; Polar Eskimos eat decayed birds, feathers and all; and the Lepcho prefer their meat high but not maggoty (Gillian 1972:80). Raw fish and meats such as Peruvian *ceviche,* Japanese *sashimi* and Russian steak tartare are less unusual to us than rotted foods, but still appear only rarely on our dinner tables.

ceviche
Marinated raw seafood

sashimi
Thinly sliced raw fish

steak tartare
Finely ground beef steak mixed with egg yolk and spices and served raw

Cultural factors also interact with biological and environmental demands to influence our appetites: how often and when during the 24–hour cycle we will eat. Four meals a day is standard in a number of European societies; three is typical in North America; two are found among the Tiv of Nigeria, who eat at dawn and dusk; and a single meal is eaten at irregular times depending on the work schedule by the Bemba of Central Africa and the Tupinamba of Brazil. Among some hunters and gatherers there are no meals as such, just continuous snacking throughout the working hours.

Taste preferences are also a combined product of cultural and biological factors. We all share the physiological ability to distinguish between sweet, salty, sour, and bitter, but preferences for different tastes vary considerably between cultural groups. For example, many Mexicans prefer hot and spicy foods which most Americans consider to be too "strong." Of course, taste preferences vary quite a bit within cultural groups as well. For example, two children raised in the same family may have very different likes and dislikes.

Because culture has such a pervasive influence on our diets, we will devote the remainder of this chapter to an exploration of the concept of culture and the importance of a cultural perspective for the study of human dietary habits.

In our exploration of the cultural context of human diet and change, we draw upon examples from a wide variety of societies, past and present. In some examples, the customs and beliefs we describe are not practiced in their traditional form today. In a few instances, the practices, and even the society, may no longer exist. Whenever possible, we attempt to alert the reader to this by noting briefly how food practices and other cultural traits have changed. However, because we do not always know the extent or nature of change experienced by some societies, we refer to these societies and their customs as "traditional" and/or note the period when the observations were made, either as part of the text or as references noted at the end of the passage.

Some definitions

Culture refers to the knowledge, traditions, beliefs, and values that are developed, learned, and shared by members of a society.

Subculture refers to the knowledge, traditions, beliefs, and values shared by members of a subgroup within a society. Ethnic groups, socioeconomic classes, age groups, and even families, share some ideas that set them apart from other subgroups.

Society refers to a group of people interacting in a common territory who share a sense of unity and a common culture. This enables them to meet the basic conditions needed for social life. The term *society* refers to a group of people; while *culture* describes their *design for living*.

It is also helpful to distinguish between a particular culture and culture in general. A culture refers to the complete way of living shared by members of a *specific identifiable group*. Culture, without the modifier "a," is used in a more general way to describe the practices that guide human behavior without reference to a specific group. Thus, we can talk of the capacity for culture, in general, or discuss aspects of the !Kung Bushman culture, in particular.

Culture as an adaptation to the environment

Culture enables people to meet the challenges posed by their physical, social, and supernatural environments. As an adaptive mechanism, culture can be divided into three major sections: *technology, social organization* and *ideology*.

Technology refers to the knowledge, practices, and tools a group has developed to help them adapt to the physical environment and meet the basic biological needs for subsistence, shelter, and protection from natural enemies. Technology includes the

Technology, social organization, and ideology, as they relate to food and nutrition, will be discussed in Chapters 4, 5, and 6.

practices a society has for producing food and other goods; distributing resources; constructing houses, clothes, and tools; and transporting people and goods.

Social Organization refers to the practices a group has developed to regulate social life. Social organization deals with the way humans organize themselves to achieve common goals. This includes ways of organizing marriage, reproduction, familial relationships, and friends, creating political alliances, and the maintenance of law and order. In addition to the notions groups have about how the social group *ought* to be structured, social organization can refer to how it is *actually* structured. Thus, we may speak of a culturally-shared definition of the "American nuclear family" as two parents and their children, and at the same time describe the increasing proportion of single-parent households.

Ideology, the third adaptive mechanism of culture, refers to shared beliefs and values that enable humans to adjust to the supernatural and metaphysical environment. Everywhere people ask questions about the meaning of life, death, and the future. Our ideologies attempt to provide answers to these questions. They help define our relationship with the supernatural and they justify our particular way of life. Religion, folklore, art, music, literature, and philosophy are all aspects of ideology.

In many cases, the cultural solutions groups devise are quite successful: When people started to use ice to keep foods cold, the number of food-borne illnesses was significantly reduced. Some cultural solutions, however, are maladaptive. The use of the insecticide DDT on crops is a good example. Intended to improve crop yield, DDT accumulated in ecosystems and had toxic effects on animals and people.

metaphysical
Relating to a reality beyond what is perceived by the senses

How culture is learned

Like all people, you are born with the potential to learn any culture, regardless of your genetic background. Anthropologist Clyde Kluckholn (1968:25) describes a young man he met in New York

> who did not speak a word of English and was obviously bewildered by American ways. By "blood" he was as American as you or I, for his parents had gone from Indiana to China as missionaries. Orphaned in infancy, he was reared by a young Chinese family in a remote village. All who met him found him more Chinese than American. The facts of his blue eyes and light hair were less impressive than a Chinese style of gait, Chinese arm and hand movements, Chinese facial expressions and Chinese modes of thought. The biological heritage was American, but the cultural training had been Chinese. He returned to China.

The process by which we learn the beliefs, attitudes, behavioral standards, and even body movements of a society is called *encultu- ration*. In all societies, the family is the major vehicle for training the young to fit into society. But as many parents know, it is not al- ways easy to induce children to conform to social conventions. Par- ents rely on formal instruction, subtle and not-so-subtle rewards and punishments, and modeling correct behavior to educate children in traditional ways of thinking and behaving.

Industrialized societies have formal institutions—schools— to enculturate their children. This formal schooling is combined with informal teaching and modeling by relatives, friends, and the media as a way to motivate people to adopt the society's values and goals. Many positive characteristics such as pride in oneself, loving others, and sharing may be encouraged in this way. Unfortunately, sexism, classism, and scorn for minorities are sometimes taught to the young as well.

Because much of our enculturation took place early in life and the culture we learned is shared by almost by everyone around us, certain behaviors appear automatic or instinctual rather than cultur- ally patterned. Many of the assumptions we learned to make about how the world works and what we were taught to value in life are unconsciously accepted as "just human nature" or as the correct way of looking at things. Most of us are not aware that these conventional understandings are a product of our culture: one distinctive view among many. For example, many Americans would agree that com- petition is a human instinct, and it is just natural for people who play and work together to compete. A look at some other societies shows us that competition isn't "just human nature." The Samai of Malaysia, for instance, exhibit no competition when playing or working together. In fact, competition actually is looked down upon.

The enculturation process is not exactly the same for all persons within the same society. We have not all been exposed to the same ideas. Members of one ethnic group, for example, may learn very different dietary practices than those of another. Values and goals between various segments that make up a society also may be quite different, and may create tension or even open conflict. The civil rights movement, antinuclear protests, women's liberation, and French Canadians' efforts to secede from English-speaking Canadi- ans are recent examples from the North American continent.

People often question some aspects of their culture, and a cul- ture is not replicated perfectly as it is passed on to new members. We forget some ideas and decide to reject or ignore other informa- tion. For instance, you probably do not rely solely on family tradi- tions and your parents' cooking practices when making a meal. Most likely you practice some traditional ideas but reject others. While you probably use some family recipes, you might also clip recipes from a magazine, try exotic fruits and vegetables available at the local supermarket, and swap advice about vitamin and mineral supplements with friends.

In many societies, new ideas are being adopted at such a rapid rate that we sometimes speak of a "generation gap": the ideas held by the younger generation often differ from those held by their elders. To some extent, when rapid change occurs there is a break in the passage of information from one generation to another (Harris 1980:110). The changes in infant feeding practices in industrialized countries in the last 40 years provide a good example of this. After World War II, many mothers stopped the traditional practice of breastfeeding and began using infant formulas to feed their children. When these bottlefed children became mothers in the 1970s and 1980s, many chose to breastfeed. Lactation is not always easy and many of the new mothers found that they needed advice; but, unlike women in other times and places, their traditional source of information, their own mothers, had not experienced breastfeeding and so the chain of information had been broken. To compensate, the La Leche League, nutritionists, and nurses stepped in to reintroduce the lost information.

Culture as a guide for behavior

Culture has been likened to a mental map. As members of society, each of us uses this map to help us decide how to act and how to interpret what other people do. Because most people in society have a similar map, people's behavior is fairly consistent and predictable, enabling society to function smoothly.

The mental map that we call culture is made of *norms, beliefs, values,* and other conceptions about what should take place. *Norms* refer to principles, rules or standards for behavior — they are people's conception of what should occur in a given situation. People in each society make choices from a wide range of possible alternatives about how to behave. Schwartz and Ewald (1968:187) offer a good example of this in their comparison of several societies' norms for how male friends should greet each other after a few weeks separation.

> Such behavior probably takes hundreds of forms in the world at large, but in a given culture the alternatives are few. Latins will most commonly shake hands. . . . Two Barabaig males (eastern Africa) will clasp hands much as it is done in the United States, then shift the grip to the thumb, and then back to the handclasp, all in rapid succession. . . . Among a neighboring group, men were observed to spit into each other's right hand . . . Each pattern of behavior constitutes a cultural rule, a cultural choice among conceivable alternatives. By our definition, each represents a culture norm.

La Leche League (*La Leche* is *The Milk* in Spanish). An international organization founded in the U.S. in 1956 by seven women who wanted to make breastfeeding easier and more enjoyable for mothers and children. The organization offers information and encouragement to those who want to breastfeed through mother-to-mother support groups. The Information Services Department of LLL also provides information to health care professionals. LLL is currently active in 40 countries and has contact with over 100,000 mothers per month.

Throughout history, many people have questioned cultural norms and acted differently. Currently in North America, some men have rejected the traditional firm handshake as the only appropriate greeting for male friends and choose to hug each other instead.

In the dietary realm, there are many norms for how to prepare, cook, and serve food. In an urban commune in North Carolina, the household of 18 people follows many norms regarding food: Meat is prohibited, foods are cooked only in cast iron cookware (aluminum cookware is prohibited), the person assigned to cook for the week serves food, and when the meal is over, each person washes his or her own plate and utensils. Their neighbors just three doors down expect meat at every meal and usually delegate the cooking to the mother and oldest son, while the two youngest sons usually do the dishes.

Even the most intimate bodily functions are influenced by culture. "Of all the regulations relating to table manners through the ages, that against breaking wind (or passing gas) has had the longest life. Surviving texts are not always specific about which aspects of the subject they are discussing . . . but it is clear that while a delicate burp has usually been acceptable in most societies, the audible release of digestive gases from the nether regions most certainly has not" (Tannahill 1973:231).

Cultures allow several choices in deciding how a specific situation should be handled. For example, we have a wide range of options for what is acceptable to serve to dinner guests: hamburgers, tacos, lasagne, barbecued chicken; almost any food we eat. However, it would be unusual for North Americans to serve dessert first or to offer hot oatmeal as an appetizer.

In addition to norms, members of a society share *beliefs*. Beliefs are conceptions of reality and propositions about how the universe works. Each society has a set of beliefs about food and conceptions about how it affects the human body. Southeast Asian peasants avoid

Figure 3.1
North American male greetings (Lindenberger)

Hare Krishna Devotees
Members of a religious
sect — The International
Society for Krishna Con-
sciousness — which is
based on ancient Hindu
philosophy

fish because they believe it will give them worms; the Australian
Bushmen won't kill animals they believed to be ancestoral spirits;
Hare Krishna devotees shun meat because they believe it is dirty;
and North Americans encourage their children to drink milk because it is seen as having special properties that promote health and
strength.

Cultures are also made up of *values:* conceptions of what is desirable and undesirable; what is good and bad. As we acquire our society's values, we begin to react with approval and disapproval toward certain situations. In a society that values honesty and
generosity, people who display these traits are admired. Those who
do not, meet with some form of disapproval.

Values such as North American concepts of democracy and freedom have an integrating, unifying effect; giving meaning to broad
areas of life. Values are expressed in literature, art, religion, and
other cultural institutions, including health practices. The value
placed on youthfulness is seen in North Americans' obsession with
youth and youthful figures. Norge Jerome (1970:230), a nutritional
anthropologist who has studied how values in contemporary North
American society influence food habits, tell us: "Beauty, vigor and
vitality are sold and encouraged in most areas of daily life including
food consumption or the lack thereof. Food and nutrient (vitamin)
consumption . . . are designed for the retention or the recapture of
youth and vitality." To the Chinese, who hold their elders in great
esteem and value the wisdom and maturity of old age, these American food habits valued because of their association with youth
might seem strange indeed. (See Chapter 6 for a more detailed discussion of how North American values influence food practices.)

Culture is expressed through behavior and artifacts

artifact
Anything produced or
modified by people

We have said that culture is comprised of norms, beliefs, values, and
broader conceptions about life. Because these are concepts or ideas,
they are not directly observable. We can observe, however, the ways
in which culture is expressed in people's behavior and in the tools
and other artifacts they use. Archaeologists reconstruct the way ancient societies built homes from postholes and other artifacts. *Ethnographers,* anthropologists who compare and analyze cultures,
infer norms and beliefs from how people act as well as from the explanations people give for their behavior. When people respond to
a given situation in a repetitive, patterned way, they are likely to be
following shared norms for how to act. By observing a group of people, ethnographers can begin to notice behavioral patterns and by
talking with people, they are able to uncover the traditions that
guide individuals' behavior.

Take, for example, the case of the ethnographer observing a hypothetical tribe. She notices that men usually eat the food prepared

by their wives but that they occasionally dine with their sisters. Her curiosity piqued, she begins to record when the men eat with their sisters. After several months, a pattern is discovered: Most men dine with their wives for 25 consecutive days and then eat with their sisters for the next 5 or 6 days. A few men, mostly older ones, deviate from this pattern and dine only with their wives. The regularity of this behavior leads the ethnographer to believe that the tribe's people are following a norm of some type. When she discusses her observations with them, her suspicions are confirmed. The tribe believes that women have magical powers when menstruating and that men may be harmed if they eat food prepared by menstruating women. When a man's wife is menstruating, he dines with a sister or other female relative whose food is not potentially harmful to him. Older men, whose wives are postmenopausal, eat at home throughout the month.

In this instance, the tribe's behavioral pattern corresponds closely with their normative pattern. In other words, they act according to their beliefs. But people do not always do what they believe they should. Some Catholics eat meat on Fridays during Lent, some Mormons drink coffee or tea, and some nutritionists eat the sugary desserts they advise others to avoid. Because behavioral patterns frequently vary from normative patterns, nutritionists must be careful to distinguish between what clients say they should eat and what they actually eat.

Culture as a functionally integrated system

Norms, beliefs, and values do not develop haphazardly. Groups choose cultural traits that are compatible with other traits comprising the cultural whole. Traits are chosen that fit and that reinforce the overall cultural system. Soviet-style farming collectives, for instance, would be unlikely to succeed in highly individualistic society such as Canada or the United States; and the introduction of steak sauce into a Hindu society in which most people do not eat beef would make little sense. Cultures, then, are best viewed as loosely integrated systems of norms, beliefs, and values. When we refer to culture as an integrated system, we are saying that all parts have a special relationship to the whole.

Food serves many functions—economic, political, recreational, social, aesthetic, religious, ceremonial, magical, legal and medical. Consider, for example, the variety of ways food functions in your life. Like many North Americans you may use food as gifts, host dinner parties to improve business relations, share meals with relatives in order to build kinship ties, or cook special meals for aesthetic or creative gratification. Observance of food prohibitions or other special practices may allow you to express religious beliefs or prevent illness.

Sometimes health care providers' immersion in the scientific aspects of nutrition diverts their attention from the important role food plays in social life. Health care professionals need to remember that food is more than just something to eat; it has social as well as nutritional functions. Sometimes when health workers advise a person to replace one food with another, they don't stop to consider how this will alter its social significance. The client, unwilling to sacrifice the social benefit associated with the food, may reject the professionals' scientifically correct advice. The trick, then, is to change diets in such a way that the social function of the food is left intact.

Awareness of the many functions food plays in people's lives helped one nutritionist work successfully with a 53-year-old woman suffering from severe heart disease. This woman ate many foods high in calories, cholesterol, and saturated fat each Wednesday night at a church potluck supper. Recognizing that the church supper was not just a place to eat, but that it fulfilled important social functions as well, the nutritionist did not recommend that the client stop going to the suppers. Instead, he worked with her to find ways to make the occasion less devastating to her diet. As a result, the woman decided to eat light throughout the day so that she could afford to eat a little extra at the suppers; she also began bringing tasty, low-calorie dishes to the potlucks and encouraged her friends to do the same. In this way, she was able to enjoy the social benefits of the potlucks without jeopardizing her health.

Despite the functional linkages between cultural traits, no system is in perfect harmony. All societies experience some degree of strain between inconsistent parts. This is especially true where societies undergo rapid change. Nutrition controversies, for example, are a regular feature in our current magazines and newspapers. Recently, the United States Department of Agriculture and the U.S. Department of Health and Human Services issued a set of "Dietary Guidelines for Americans". The recommendations were hardly revolutionary; basically the guidelines recommended a decrease in fat, particularly saturated fat, cholesterol, refined sugar, salt, alcohol, and overall caloric intake while increasing complex carbohydrates and fiber. Yet the meat, dairy, and egg industries, whose foods were implicated, protested loudly. The debate over this and many other nutrition issues continues as we attempt to strike some compromise between inconsistent dietary beliefs and values. (See Chapter Five for further discussion of political lobbying by industries.)

Intracultural variations

Before ending our discussion of culture, we would like to emphasize the need to recognize forces that create intracultural variation; that is, the cultural differences that exist within a social group.

These influential factors include socioeconomic status, household size, occupation, age, and ethnicity, as well as a host of other situational variables. No doubt your own diet habits differ from those of your friends and relatives, particularly during stressful periods or when daily routines are disrupted.

Even within subcultures, we find important dietary differences. Puerto Ricans in Dade County, Florida, for example, practice a variety of infant feeding practices. Methods selected to feed infants depend on many noncultural variables: the length of time spent in the United States, the location of the mother's mother, the husband's attitudes toward different feeding methods (especially breast-feeding), and access to information about infant feeding from friends and health care providers (Bryant 1978).

We certainly cannot assume uniformity in the dietary practices of Puerto Ricans or members of any subcultural group. As Gretel Pelto (1981:54) points out:

> In practically all studies comparing different ethnic or socio-economic groups, broad sociocultural variables have accounted for only a small part of the total variance. We are aware of this problem closer to home. We know that our peers exhibit differences in their health, food behavior, and relationships to health care agencies, despite general similarities in occupation, education, and income.

In other words, *culture,* while a powerful conceptual tool, cannot explain all of the interesting diversity in human dietary practices today.

Ethnocentrism and cultural relativity

Our cultural heritage is so much a part of our way of thinking that we sometimes find it difficult to look at our own actions or those of others objectively. We may accept our own way of life and value system as natural, good, beautiful, or important, while puzzling over the strangeness of other societies' lifestyles. The uncritical acceptance of one's own value system and lifestyle as the most appropriate is called *ethnocentrism.* Using an ethnocentric point of view, American nutritionists, for example, may view the absence of dairy products in the diet of Mexican Americans critically, seeing it as an indication of a low calcium intake, and forgetting the fact that corn treated with lime in the production of tortillas provides significant amounts of this essential nutrient. Because of Americans' heavy reliance on animal products, some of us have a tendency to view the vegetarian diet with skepticism, wondering if it can provide adequate protein. We have already discussed entomophagy, or insect-eating, a practice that North Americans find repugnant but that many groups of people rely on for survival. Some groups find it most convenient to eat from a common pot using the fingers and hands as implements. Many North Americans view this as unsanitary or primitive and are devoted to the use of metal or, in a pinch, plastic utensils for conveying their food from their own individual plates to their mouths.

The danger of ethnocentrism lies in a failure to view alternative practices as viable alternatives with potentially equal or even superior value in some situations. For over a century, ethnocentrism prevented Western medical practitioners from appreciating the benefits of acupuncture, acupressure and other Chinese medical practices. (See Chapter Six for a discussion of health beliefs and practices.)

The reverse of ethnocentrism is a viewpoint known as *cultural relativism*. According to this viewpoint,

> The standards of rightness and wrongness (values) and of usage and effectiveness (customs) are relative to the given culture of which they are a part. In its most extreme form, it holds that every custom is valid in terms of its own cultural setting. In practical terms, it means that anthropologists learn to suspend judgment, to strive to understand what goes on from the point of view of the people being studied, that is, to achieve empathy, for the sake of humanistic perception and scientific accuracy.

(Hoebel and Frost 1976:23)

Cultural relativity offers us an objective way of analyzing and comparing cultural differences. It enables us to focus on the function and meanings a custom has in another society, detached from our own values and beliefs. We can study, for example, the functions of cultural practices such as warfare, Hindu deification of the cow, or polygamy even though they run counter to our personal ethics and values. Cultural relativity does not imply that just because a cultural group behaves in a certain way, we should accept it as morally correct. We can recognize the economic advantages herders gain by having multiple wives and yet still find polygamy unacceptable. Nor does cultural relativity imply that we should reject our own lifestyle and adopt the cultural ways of other societies. We may challenge certain attitudes or practices such as racism or imperialism in our own as well as other cultures, without sacrificing the objectivity afforded by a culturally relativistic perspective.

By pointing out the conflicts between a narrow ethnocentric point of view and a culturally relativistic point of view, we wish to impress upon students the need to approach new situations and people with an open mind, one that looks objectively at new situations and examines critically the implicit assumptions with which they approach the world. Throughout this and other chapters we will emphasize the need to view food and health-related practices as functional units of a wider cultural context, as well as to recognize the adaptive nature of certain food practices. At the same time we will critically examine situations in which a range of interventions can result in improvement.

Implications for health care professionals

Students of health and nutrition no doubt recognize the need to understand how people choose and prepare the foods that make up their diet, and how to use this understanding to help them improve people's nutritional status. Health professionals learn quickly that human dietary behavior is complex and attempts to change it, more often than not, will be resisted, resented or ignored (Fauthauer 1960).

We believe than an understanding of the concept of culture can be useful to nutritionists. First, by recognizing the pervasive influence culture has over all aspects of human behavior, we are less likely to make the common mistake of assuming that people are empty vessels into which we pour the truth. Being sensitive to the norms, beliefs, and assumptions people make about food and recognizing the need to introduce advice in ways that are compatible with their culture will result in more effective dietary changes. For example, nutrition educators who assume that their task is to tell people "the facts" about nutrition will soon find that little change takes place. A more effective strategy is to package information in such a way that it fits into the clients' way of life. At a meeting with a group of working mothers, a nutritionist began by asking them their concerns about feeding their children. When she learned that their major problems were lack of time and money, she abandoned her prepared lecture notes and led a discussion of ways to prepare nutritious foods cheaply and quickly. The meeting proved effective in changing some of the mothers' practices because it was compatible with their needs and interests.

Second, recognition that much of culture is implicit can prevent health care providers from assuming that other people's way of life is just like theirs. With this perspective in mind, a nurse found that the way in which she ate her meals was very different from that of many of the clients she encountered. In her family, meals were served three times a day with everyone gathered around the table. Had she assumed that everyone ate this way, her nutrition counseling would have been less effective with many of her clients. By listening, she found that in some families, a meal, as such, was rarely eaten. Instead, family members snacked throughout the day. If she had distributed copies of menus for breakfast, lunch, and dinner to these clients, the information would have been of little use. A more effective strategy proved to be a discussion of nutritious snacks and ways to be sure nutrient needs were being met.

Third, appreciation of culture as an adaptive, functionally related system enables health care professionals to understand an important problem inherent in making dietary change: modification of one cultural trait will often bring about concomitant changes in related traits. When these ties are not anticipated, resistance and sometimes negative effects may occur as the system achieves a new internal balance. Take, for example, the failure of the Eighteenth Amendment, which prohibited the sale of liquor in the United States. Reformers originally promoted the amendment as a means of abolishing the saloons used by political ward bosses to amass support for their corrupt political machines and uplifting the lower classes they felt were morally corrupted by drink. Unfortunately, lawmakers, administrators, and reformers mistakenly viewed the sale and consumption of liquor as an isolated custom rather than as part of an integrated cultural system. When they abolished the legal sale of liquor they were unprepared for the widespread repercussions created in family life, politics, law enforcement, and the economy. As hoped, blue-collar workers consumed less alcohol because they couldn't afford bootleg prices; however, the middle and upper classes began to support unlicensed saloons ("speakeasies") where homemade brews such as "bathtub gin" were sold. In fact, prohibition caused a major economic shift.

bootleg
To produce or sell alcohol illegally

Because alcohol could still be produced for medical, industrial, and sacramental (religious) purposes, these industries expanded, with approximately one-third reaching bootleg channels at the expense of previous manufacturers. Wine making also prospered with the creation of a "harmless grape jelly" that could be converted to wine simply by adding water. Smuggling, another illicit source of alcohol, played a crucial role in the expansion of the Canadian liquor industry and contributed to the economic growth of other countries as well. Another unanticipated consequence of Prohibition was increased drinking among young members of the middle class and newly liberated women. Largely because it was something disapproved of by society, drinking bootleg booze and visiting a speakeasy became for many a way of flaunting convention and an expression of independence. A final and more tragic, unanticipated consequence of Prohibition was its impact on entrepreneurial crime in the United States. The emergence of bootlegging gangs, the consolidation of organized crime, the resulting gangland violence, and the general public's open contempt for the law finally led to the passage of the Twenty-First Amendment and reinstitution of legal liquor sales (Nelli 1976).

Finally, the use of cultural relativism encourages us to look with an objective interest at norms and customs of other groups. We are less likely, for instance, to respond with amazement, disgust, or intolerance at other people's eating habits. While we may not be interested in consuming the diet of other groups, we are better able to understand why people eat differently in other social groups. A nutritionist that appears to be critical of a client's diet—something that is very personal—rarely gains the rapport needed to educate the client. Even practices we find morally objectionable can be changed more effectively if we first learn the reasons they came about and identify their functional relationship to other parts of the culture.

Summary

- Societies differ in what foods they define as edible and inedible, tasteful and distasteful.

- Foods considered delicacies in one society may not be considered edible in another. Differences in food choices can be traced to cultural factors, as well as biological and environment factors.

- Culture refers to the knowledge, traditions, beliefs, and values that are developed, learned, and shared by members of a society.

- People develop culture to adapt to their environment. The *technology* a group develops enables them to adapt to the physical environment; *social organization* refers to the customs that organize social life; and *ideology* describes a group's philosophy about the meaning of life.

- Shared norms, beliefs, and values are part of a group's culture. Culture is manifest in behavior and artifacts.

- Culture is a functionally integrated system. Food, for example, fulfills many needs other than nourishment. It serves economic, social, aesthetic, and religious functions as well.

- While culture is a useful concept for describing a group in general terms, there is much intracultural variation. People from the same culture may have very different diets.

- The unexamined acceptance of one's own lifestyle and value system as the most appropriate is called *ethnocentrism*. The reverse of ethnocentrism is *cultural relativism,* a viewpoint that encourages approaching new situations and people with an open mind.

Highlight 3-1   Culture and body image

A nutritionist was recently invited to give a talk at a midwestern women's college dormitory. After showing a film that focused on improving the quality of one's diet by eating fewer processed foods and more fresh foods, the nutritionist fielded questions from the audience. She quickly noticed a common theme:

- "Does whole wheat bread have fewer calories than white bread?"
- "Do vitamin pills cause you to gain weight?"
- "Do grapefruits burn fat?"
- "Does skipping breakfast cause you to be less hungry throughout the day?"
- "How long can you fast without damaging your health?"

Question after question focused on how to become thin. Interestingly, the questions were being asked by thin women. As the group continued talking, the nutritionist became impressed by the amount of time and energy these women devoted to maintaining their slim figures. Many exercised for as much as two hours each day; women on different floors competed to see which floor could lose the most weight collectively; some sold the Cambridge Diet to their peers while others went on five-day fasts together.*

This event is just one example of a much larger phenomenon: slenderness has become a major preoccupation for many North Americans. The diet industry is now a multimillion-dollar business as millions of people turn to diet pills, diet sodas and other weight-reducing potions in their quest for thinness. Diet and exercise books occupy several slots on the New York Times best seller list almost every week. Exercise spas and weight loss clubs are booming in Canada and the U.S., and a significant portion of the population is investing large amounts of time, energy, and money (as well as enduring considerable discomfort) to achieve the ideal physique.

Beauty is in the culture of the beholder

Definitions of the ideal body size and shape vary from one culture to another. As we have just seen, many North Americans consider a slim figure both attractive and healthy. In addition, many fat people face discrimination from employers and others who unfairly assume that they are lazy, messy, and lack character or self-restraint. As for an ideal body type, "we don't have to look far to see the image of the slim, attractive female as portrayed throughout the popular culture. Motion picture stars, television personalities, women in advertisements and

*The Cambridge Diet consists of a flavored powder designed to be mixed with water and consumed three times a day in place of food. Many questions have been raised about the safety of this weight reduction regime (Newark and Williamson, 1983).

fashion models, all reflect the definition of the beautiful female as the one who is thin" (Goldblat, Moore and Stunkard, 1965). Men, too, are depicted as slim; however, extreme thinness is usually avoided because of its association with the "97-pound-weakling" image.

North Americans are not the only people who have possessed a desire to be thin. The Cretans reportedly had a drug that allowed them to eat all they wanted, yet remain slender. The Spartans, as well as the Athenians, were sticklers about fat. In the sixteenth century, some people swallowed sand in order to irritate their stomachs, thus limiting their food intake.

In contrast to these notions, obesity is the ideal body image for many cultures. Fat is often viewed as a symbol of wealth and the luxury of inactivity and overeating, as well as a sign of good health. In one African culture, for example, brides-to-be go through a fattening process and are secluded in special houses to overeat for several weeks and up to a year, depending on their wealth. When women emerge from the huts, their bodies laden with extra fat, they are considered quite beautiful. Traditionally the Samoans of Polynesia also placed a high value on obesity as a sign of high social status. This is illustrated by one Samoan's response to an American visitor's question about the village leader, "Can't you see he is a chief? See how big he is!" (Connelly and Hanna, 1978).

*While fairly high body weights remain the standard in many Polynesian areas, migrants to the U.S. are adopting North American norms and now see obesity as a sign of unhealthiness.

Figure HL3.1
Samoan beauty (Chris Ware)

In the past, European societies also admired the obese. A trip to the art museum reminds us that many Renaissance artists chose obese subjects to depict beauty. In Reuben's eyes, cellulite was beautiful!

Cultural differences in body imagery are often appreciated by North Americans who travel to societies where a plumper standard is in vogue. While living in a Peruvian village, one author (then twelve pounds heavier than recommended by the Metropolitan Life Insurance weight-for-height tables) was barraged with attempts to fatten her up. In addition to their concern over her health and financial situation, the Peruvians expressed their fear that she would be unable to attract a husband unless she gained weight. To them she appeared sickly and unattractive.

Cultural definitions of ideal body types also change through time. Compare, for example, notions of female attractiveness in the U.S. during this century. During the 1920s, the flapper's lean, flat-chested, angular look was all the rage. Thirty years later, this was replaced with the softer, rounder shape depicted by Marilyn Monroe and other more voluptuous figures. By the 1980s, the slim, toned shape of Jane Fonda has become the fashion. Thus it appears that body images, much like hemlines, change cyclically, making us question how long North Americans' current obsession with thinness will last and when a plumper figure will again be idealized.

Body image and health

In some cases, cultural images of ideal body size and the methods used to achieve them have serious health consequences. In fact, research has shown that both very thin and very fat people have increased morbidity and mortality. Obesity, for instance, has been shown to increase the risk of heart attacks, strokes, diabetes, hypertension, and

other problems. The hazards facing underweight people are not as well-documented but include greater risks from infectious diseases such as tuberculosis.

Other health problems can result from culturally prescribed means of achieving the ideal shape. The conversion of the female figure into an hourglass shape with a corset, popular in the late 1800s, scratched the flesh, displaced internal organs, and interfered with eating and digestion. Today some men take hormones with potentially carcinogenic or other adverse health consequences in an attempt to build bigger muscles. The physical and emotional consequences of chronic dieting are considerable. Irritability, poor concentration, depression, apathy, fatigue, and social isolation have all been associated with prolonged calorie restriction (Keys et al., 1950).

Anorexia nervosa, self-induced starvation, and *bulimia,* a disorder characterized by gorging followed by purging (vomiting and/or use of laxatives), are serious problems associated with the current quest for thinness in North America. Among girls 16 to 18 years old, as many as one in every hundred may suffer from anorexia nervosa, and figures may be even higher for young women in the middle and upper socioeconomic classes. Bulimia is even more common, with 19 percent of the students at one college admitting to purging (R.T. Harris 1983:800).

The health consequences of both anorexia nervosa and bulimia are extreme. The anorexic may lose 25 percent or more of her normal body weight—not only fat, but muscle as well. At this point the signs of chronic starvation appear: menses stop, a covering of soft hair appears on the skin, the heart rate slows, and the individual feels cold even in warm surroundings. The mental trauma the anorexic undergoes is said to be tortuous. One in five anorexics die from the disorder.

People with bulimia may consume up to 5000 calories in an hour or two, then induce vomiting; repeating the behavior as often as four times a day. Victims commonly develop severe tooth decay from destruction of the tooth enamel by acidic vomitus. Other side effects include a constant sore throat, esophogeal inflammation, swollen glands near the cheeks, liver, heart, and kidney damage; dehydration, and stomach rupture.

Applications for nutritionists

Health care providers frequently are requested to assist people in achieving their ideal weight. Their success requires an understanding of both the medical and cultural definitions of the term "ideal weight," as well as the ability to reconcile the differences between them.

Medically, ideal weight is usually determined in terms of height, as given in the Metropolitan Life Insurance tables or other indexes. Because the relative amounts of fat, lean (muscle) tissue, and bone size vary greatly from person to person, ideal weights are given as ranges. For a 5'4" woman with a medium frame, the best weights range between 124 and 138 pounds. Even so, many experts challenge the reliability of these tables and suggest that the concept of "ideal weight" be made more flexible (Knapp, 1983). They point out that health hazards only are associated with extreme overweight and underweight (20 percent over or under the ideal range), and therefore, efforts should focus on these people rather than those whose weights deviate only minimally from the ideal.

This flexibility in medical definitions of ideal or acceptable weights gives the health care professional an opportunity to adapt his or her recommendations to the client's cultural notions of body size. For example,

Figure HL3.2
Every body is different. Television, movies, and magazines may make it seem that all women are tall and thin, and all men are "all muscle." But the fact is—every body is different.
(Chris Ware)

when working with people who value fatness, the professional can recommend weights that fall at the upper end of the range. Both groups can be made aware that a range, rather than a specific weight, will allow them to maintain good health.

An understanding of cultural ideas about body weights can be useful in other ways as well. In addition to recognizing a group's definitions of ideal weight or size, professionals can benefit from an appreciation of the significance associated with thinness and fatness. For example, one author studied cultural variations in how mother's view infant body size. She found important differences between ethnic groups (as well as within each group) in the size deemed most desirable. Most Puerto Ricans and Cubans selected a plumper body, while the majority

Table HL3.1   1983 Metropolitan Height and Weight Tables

Men					Women				
Hight		Small Frame	Medium Frame	Large Frame	Height		Small Frame	Medium Frame	Large Frame
Feet	Inches				Feet	Inches			
5	2	128–134	131–141	138–150	4	10	102–111	109–121	118–131
5	3	130–136	133–143	140–153	4	11	103–113	111–123	120–134
5	4	132–138	135–145	142–156	5	0	104–115	113–126	122–137
5	5	134–140	137–148	144–160	5	1	106–118	115–129	125–140
5	6	136–142	139–151	146–164	5	2	108–121	118–132	128–143
5	7	138–145	142–154	149–168	5	3	111–124	121–135	131–147
5	8	140–148	145–157	152–172	5	4	114–127	124–138	134–151
5	9	142–151	148–160	155–176	5	5	117–130	127–141	137–155
5	10	144–154	151–163	158–180	5	6	120–133	130–144	140–159
5	11	146–157	154–166	161–184	5	7	123–136	133–147	143–163
6	0	149–160	157–170	164–188	5	8	126–139	136–150	146–167
6	1	152–164	160–174	168–192	5	9	129–142	139–153	149–170
6	2	155–168	164–178	172–197	5	10	132–145	142–156	152–173
6	3	158–172	167–182	176–202	5	11	135–148	145–159	155–176
6	4	162–176	171–187	181–207	6	10	138–151	148–162	158–179

Source: Reproduced with permission of Metropolitan Life Insurance Company. Source of basic data: *1979 Build Study,* Society of Actuaries and Association of Life Insurance Medical Directors of America, 1980.

Weights at Ages 25–29 based on lowest mortality. Weights in pounds according to frame (in indoor clothing weighing 5 pounds for men or 3 pounds for women, shoes with 1-inch heels.)

of Anglos chose a thinner figure as ideal for infants. Moreover, interviews showed that many Cubans, Puerto Ricans, and some Anglos viewed fatness as a sign of attractiveness, wealth, and quality of maternal care as well as health. Thus, even if a mother was convinced that a thin body was healthy, other concerns might interfere with her willingness to control her baby's weight.

A rather humorous example of how cultural meanings associated with fatness affects people's receptivity to professional advice comes from a small African village.

There the villagers value fatness as a sign of wealth, and many women—rich and poor alike—are obese. Concerned about the health consequences of obesity, health educators launched an advertising campaign to alert women to the benefits of weight loss. A poster was designed to teach women that they would feel more energetic and healthy if they lost weight. The poster showed a thin, energetic woman dusting a table next to a fat women sitting listlessly on a couch. After displaying the poster throughout the community, an evaluation was conducted.

The results illustrated the importance of understanding cultural conceptions of body images: many villagers had believed the poster showed a rich woman relaxing on a couch while a maid cleaned her house!

Concern for body image is equally important when working with North Americans and other societies that value thinness. Health care professionals in these settings need to be careful not to add to the the barrage of media messages portraying an ultra-thin figure as the only way to be attractive and healthy. Particularly when working with groups prone to anorexia nervosa and bulimia, the idea should be promoted that health can be maintained within a range of weights and a variety of sizes and shapes is acceptable.

Methods have been designed for quantifying cultural ideals of beauty and obesity. One test utilizes a series of photographs of persons which have been systematically varied by means of an anamorphic lens to produce images that are both thinner and heavier than the original one (Massara and Stunkard, 1979). Respondents then are asked to sort the photographs according to categories.

Here is your chance to take the test. After completing it, compare your answers with those selected by classmates.

1. Which body size would you prefer to have?

2. Which body size do you think is most healthy?

3. Which body size do you think is most attractive?

4. Which body size do you prefer in people of the opposite sex?

5. Which body size do you prefer in persons of the same sex?

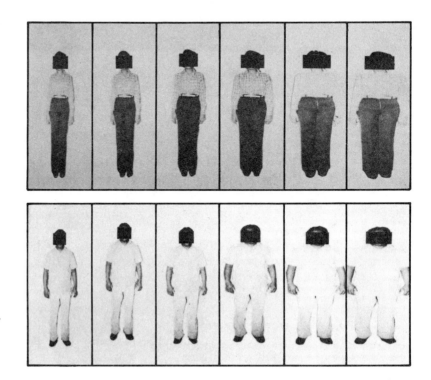

Figure HL3.3

Body imagery (Emily B. Massara and Albert J. Stunkard, International Journal of Obesity *1979 (3), pp. 149–52.)*

4

Food technologies: How people get their food

The next time you go into a supermarket, take a few moments to consider the technological achievements behind today's food system. As you hunt and gather fresh fruit and vegetables from the produce section, notice the amazing abundance before you. Oranges, grapes, tomatoes, corn, and broccoli, most foods, in fact, are now available all year. Just 40 years ago, the same items were missing from the grocer's shelves during much of the year. Today, modern transportation not only enables you to eat your favorite produce in winter, but brings you many new and exotic foods: California artichokes, Australian kiwi fruit, avocados and mangoes from Florida, and the tropical papaya and plantain. Access to foods from such a diversity of regions is unprecedented in human history: it may make it necessary to ask your produce specialist for advice in preparing, or even identifying, the store's newest selections. Consider also how this produce reaches your supermarket. The transportation system that makes this abundance possible is not without its costs. In fact, over 500 million gallons of gasoline are used annually to move fresh vegetables and produce to market; 1,300 million gallons are needed to move manufactured food products from processors to warehouses and supermarkets.

As you leave the produce section and push your cart down the aisles, past the meat and dairy compartments, stop again—this time to appreciate the tremendous variety of food products from which you may chose. Your supermarket has well over 10,000 different items stacked on its shelves, 40 percent of which were not there just ten years ago. Ask yourself how these new products are made. Can you, for example, name the major ingredients in Cool Whip, give the formula for 7-Up, or explain how Grape Nuts and Bugles are processed? If you are among the vast majority of North Americans who were not raised on the farm, you may also recall the first time you realized that hamburger meat, drumsticks, and pork chops came from those lovable animals pictured in your storybooks.

When your shopping is finished and you line up at the checkout counter, stop to compare your experience in getting food with that of people in other places and times. There are several striking differences. First, unlike the vast majority of people to inhabit the earth, you are probably not directly involved in collecting, hunting, or raising your own food. Because farmers in industrialized societies can produce enough food to feed 35 to 50 people, you are free to pursue other occupational interests, investing only a small proportion of your time and money for food.

A second difference is your access to a food supply set apart from all others by its remarkable quality, quantity, safety, and convenience. Whether you are in New York City or Carmel, California, you are likely to find a similar selection of breakfast cereals, canned vegetables and juices, and meat and dairy products. When you purchase a carton of strawberry yogurt you expect to get a product flavored in a consistent way and free from the risk of food poisoning.

Finally, because you are not directly involved in food production and you have access to such a predictable food supply, it may often appear as if modern industrialized societies have achieved technological mastery over the environment. When eating tropical fruits during winter, it is sometimes hard to recognize how environmental conditions influence your diet and health. Even the economic effects of droughts, untimely frosts, and other climatical disasters are cushioned by government price policies. Nevertheless, warnings of vanishing topsoil, acid rain, shrinking farmlands, and the danger of pesticides should remind you that our culture, too, is struggling to achieve a harmonious balance between its technology and the environment.

This chapter is about how people adapt culturally to the challenges posed by the physical environment. Every society has developed tools and techniques for obtaining food, clothing, shelter, transportation, and protection from natural predators. We refer to this part of culture as *technology*.

At the core of each culture's technology is food-getting, or subsistence activities. A society that lacks effective methods for obtaining food or other energy resources cannot survive. Subsistence activities are cultural because they are shared and take place in an organized, systematic manner based on decisions the group has made about the use and distribution of food and energy. People do not simply go out and hunt, plant, raise animals, build irrigation channels and terraces, or establish factories as if they were independent workers. Subsistence activities, and the distribution of the resultant food and wealth, requires that group decisions be made about the directions hunters will take in pursuit of animals, how land will be divided, which fields will be cultivated, where factories will be built, and who will work in them.

Because the provision of an adequate food supply is imperative to survival, a society's subsistence activities are intricately tied to other aspects of its culture. In fact, when societies are grouped according to the type of food-getting techniques employed, those falling into the same subsistence categories often share many similar social organizational (how groups organize themselves), and ideological features (religious and philosophical beliefs) as well.

Five major types of subsistence systems, their characteristic social organization, and ideological features, as well as their consequences for diet and health, are described below. As with any attempt to group societies into categories, we must overlook many important differences between the societies grouped together in order to focus on the outstanding characteristics shared within each category. Keeping this in mind, we nevertheless find it useful to compare societies by how they obtain their food: foraging, pastoralism, horticulture, intensive agriculture, and industrialized agriculture.

Foraging

Foraging, or hunting and gathering, is a subsistence technology that relies almost totally on human energy and simple tools to collect wild plants and kill free roaming animals. It is the system that was followed by all prehuman and human groups until 10,000 years ago. Today there are only about 70 groups in which more than 75 percent of the food comes from the gathering of wild plants, the hunting of wild animals, and fishing. These groups are found in marginal lands not suitable for agriculture in the desert fringes of Australia, Southern Africa, and North America; in the forests of Asia,

South America, and Central Africa; and in the frozen wastelands of Siberia, and the Arctic.

Foragers live in small groups that move frequently in their search for food; that is, they are nomadic. While there is a good deal of variation in the size of foraging groups, population density rarely exceeds one person per square mile. The exact size of a group and its density appear constrained by the resources available and the nomadic lifestyle. The average population density for contemporary hunters and gatherers is about one person for every 20 square miles. In harsh environments, camps may be limited to two or three families that move frequently within a large area. In more lush surroundings, especially near rivers or other sources of fish, 50 to 100 families may reside in camps for much of the year.

Until recently, foragers were believed to live on the brink of starvation, working long hours each day to eke out a meager existence. Anthropological studies have shown that quite the contrary is true for all but a few groups living in extremely harsh regions such as the Arctic. The vast majority of foraging tribes enjoy good nutritional status and leisurely work schedules. The !Kung Bushmen, studied in great detail by Richard Lee (1968), offer a good example. Typically, the !Kung woman collects enough food in two days to feed her entire family for a week. The rest of her time is spent cooking, fetching wood, embroidering, dancing, storytelling, resting, and visiting with friends. This steady mixture between work and leisure varies little throughout the year. The man's schedule is more uneven. Hunting may occupy an entire week followed by several leisurely weeks. As with the woman, two or three days of hunting produce enough food for the entire week. Even the most avid hunter in the tribe studied by Lee only worked 32 hours per week.

Figure 4.1
*Carrying her child, a
!Kung woman gathers.
(Courtesy of Jon Yellen)*

Social, political, and ideological features

In foraging groups, labor is divided according to age and sex. Young children assist their mothers in gathering food and young boys also hunt small animals. Women collect most of the vegetable matter and men do the hunting. Because plants are in great abundance and easy to collect, women usually contribute a much larger proportion of the diet than men, often a two to three times greater volume of food. Meat comprises only 20 to 40 percent of the calories, but is more highly valued than vegetables (Harlan 1975:8).

All members of foraging societies are food-producers. Children learn early to collect plants and small animals, although they are not expected to contribute regularly to the food supply until they are older. All men hunt game and all women gather plant foods. There are no other specialized occupations.

Most hunters and gatherers place a high value on generosity and sharing. Because no single hunter has consistent success and meat spoils quickly without refrigeration, sharing ensures that most people in the camp gets an adequate supply of protein. Typically, the culture includes customs regulating how large game animals are distributed among family members, hunting parties, and visitors (Marshall 1976:297–99). The value placed on generosity and the regular exchange of food also strengthens ties within the group, enhancing cooperation and social cohesiveness.

The words of Nisa, a !Kung woman, have been recorded by Marjorie Shostak (1981:88). About the value of sharing food, Nisa says:

> When we were living in the bush, some people gave and others stinged. But there were always enough people around who shared, people who liked one another, who were happy living together, and who didn't fight. And even if one person did stinge, the other person would just get up and yell about it, whether it was meat or anything else, 'What's doing this to you not giving us meat?'

> When I was growing up, receiving food made my heart happy. There really wasn't anything, other than stingy people, that made me unhappy. I didn't like people who wouldn't give a little of what they had.

The basic unit of social organization in foraging societies is the band, a small group of people related by real or fictional kinship ties. Members are expected to marry outside the band and usually live with either the husband's or wife's parents. There are no recognized social groups outside of the family—no clubs, no classes or other stratifications within the group. In most societies, one of the elderly males is recognized as the band's headman. But, this is neither a full-time nor formal position. The headman has no legitimate power and cannot enforce his opinions.

In most hunting and gathering societies, hunting is the focus of religious belief and ritual. Supernatural favor is sought to attract game and increase the hunter's chance of success. For example, during the whale-hunting season, the Eskimo hunter carries out rituals, wears special amulets that give him good luck, and adheres to special taboos such as the avoidance of raw meat.

amulet
A charm often inscribed with a symbol to bring the wearer good luck

Diet and health

The diet of most foragers is comprised largely of vegetable matter, typically 60 to 80 percent by weight. Meat is consumed less regularly than plant food, contributing 20 to 30 percent of calories to

Focus 4-1

Modern-day foragers in the Western world

> Why spend your weekend spraying expensive weed killers on your lawn—control crabgrass by eating it instead! Most lawn and garden weeds are edible; thistles, dandelions, crabgrass— all are worth the forager's attention.
>
> *(Gibbons and Tucker 1979:23)*

It is stated elsewhere in this book that no society uses all of the food sources available in the environment. You may wonder why anyone would *want* to eat crabgrass or any other weed, for that matter. Well-known contemporary American foragers such as the late Euell Gibbons have described the benefits of using these foraged foods. Foraging experts point out that many wild plants are nutritious and can provide alternate sources for vitamins and minerals. For example, dandelions can be used in salads and have more vitamin A, calcium, and iron than the garden lettuce they could replace (Harris 1973:9).

Such plants have provided emergency food for people lost or isolated without other food supplies, and they have been used by soldiers during times of war. They are accessible in many environments; edible wild plants can "be found in field and forest, gardens, lawns and waste piles, roadsides, swamps and brooks" (B.C. Harris 1973:9).

Another attraction of wild plants is that they do not have to be cultivated or purchased. As one forager states, when gathering wild plants, "nature is the farmer and . . . nothing is ever due at any checkout counter" (Angier 1974:23).

Some Western foragers view wild food gathering as a way of dealing with today's ecological problems. Foraging encourages people to learn more about their environment. It also discourages wastage because foragers usually collect only the amount needed for immediate consumption. As noted by Gibbons and Tucker (1979:iii), foraging has brought a renewed optimism to our view of nature:

> In 1962, the same year in which Rachel Carson's monumental *Silent Spring* was released, Euell Gibbons' first book, *Stalking*

the Wild Asparagus, was also published . . . . His writing cele-
brated the bounty and resiliency of nature at a time when most
of us were crying doom and destruction (Gibbons and Tucker
1979:iii).

Finally, foragers note that food gathering is pleasurable and puts
them in touch with nature. It can be viewed simply as "a very enjoyable outdoor sport" (Gibbons and Tucker 1979:i).

A number of handbooks and field guides are now available to
help the western forager identify, gather, and prepare edible wild
plants. Commonly used wild plants include watercress as well as
dandelion leaves, milkweed shoots, Burdock stems, and fruits such
as blueberries and crabapples. The recommended uses for wild
plants are numerous and varied. For example, in using wild grasses
for food, the seeds may be ground into meal (Crabgrass and Cock-
spur grass) or the leaves may be chopped for preparing a tea (sweet
vernal grass). Purslane, lambsquarters, mallow and amaranth are
often considered worthless garden weeds, but B. C. Harris suggests
that they provide "tangy salad greens, and novel pot herbs and
whole wheat flour substitutes" (B. C. Harris 1973:19). Wild plants
are also suggested for use as coffee substitutes and for teas, for fla-
voring homemade vinegars, for canning, blended and used in salad
dressings, and in the form of juices and powdered food
supplements.

It is important to emphasize that all of the handbooks are based
on one rule-of-thumb: never eat a wild plant you cannot identify. Because some plants are poisonous, it is essential to distinguish edible
plants from other plants. In addition, the part of the plant to be used,
the appropriate season for its use, and methods of preparation are all
information needed by a modern forager.

---

the diet. Groups living in the Arctic rely almost exclusively on hunting. Animal products contribute as much as 90 percent of the calories to their diet. This diet contains more than enough protein, but,
in order for essential vitamins and minerals to be obtained, the entire animal (entrails, organs, etc.) must be consumed. Some vegetable foods are provided through the consumption of the stomach
contents of grazing animals such as caribou.

Nutritional surveys of contemporary hunters and gatherers
show them to be generally free from severe protein-calorie malnutrition, scurvy, rickets, or vitamin B deficiency diseases. In two studies, bitot spots, indicative of vitamin A deficiency, were noted in a
small percentage of children. Although evidence of severe deficiency is rare among most hunter and gatherers, loss of subcutaneous fat during leaner times of the year has been noted, suggesting

caribou
A large antlered deer

scurvy
A disease caused by vita-
min C deficiency, marked
by bleeding gums and im-
proper healing

rickets
A disease caused by cal-
cium or vitamin D defi-
ciency that causes mal-
formed bones in children

that the amount of energy available at those times is not optimal. Some Eskimos who live traditionally experience severe food shortages during the harsh winter months. It has been reported that old or unhealthy members of the community have left the camp and wandered off to the ice floes to die in order to take some of the pressure off the community created by the limited food supply.

The children of some foragers who have left hunting and gathering as a way of life and settled with agriculturalists have been shown to grow taller and heavier than the children of those living traditionally. This suggests that energy intake, overall, may be somewhat restricted. However, as has been noted by Fredrick Dunn (1968) and others, foragers rarely experience the periodic times of famine and starvation that can accompany crop failure among agriculturalists. The wide variety of the wild diet means that few specific nutrient deficiencies are found. Also, as noted by Dunn (1968) and Black (1974), the small size of the foraging group protects them from many of the infectious diseases that plague people living in more crowded conditions. For example, illnesses such as measles, mumps, polio, influenza, and even the common cold, require a more dense population to spread. In modern times, such diseases have been introduced into small isolated communities by outsiders. The result is that all community members get the disease quickly, but once there are no more susceptible people the disease dies out until it is reintroduced by an outsider again.

parasite
An organism living in or on another organism

Because foragers are nomadic or seminomadic, they usually move away from their waste. This means that they have less contact with sources of parasite infection. Therefore, the number or parasites in the intestines tends to be low. Other parasitic and infectious diseases, such as those transmitted by insects and other hosts, including sleeping sickness, typhus, and tetanus may be major afflictions.

Without modern medical care, there is a high mortality rate and fewer children reach adulthood. Children and adults are healthier, however, than in many peasant agricultural communities.

The chronic diseases we see in more modern societies are rare in these simple societies. This is partly because fewer people reach the ages at which these illnesses occur. Also, the active lifestyle and low fat content of many foragers' diets help protect them from cardiovascular disease.

In sum, the foraging mode of subsistence has proven to be a successful adaptation to a wide range of environments. Although now restricted mainly to marginal areas of the world, hunters and gatherers generally enjoy an adequate diet, good nutritional status, and good health.

At the present time, few, if any completely independent foraging groups remain. Most have some contact with settled, technologically more complex groups. For some, steel tools have replaced stone, bone, and wooden tools. Most !Kung, for example spend some time working for their agriculturalist neighbors, using the cash they have earned to purchase foods. The Pigmies of the Iturie forest of Zaire, Africa have traded meat for agricultural products with their neighbors for centuries. In competition for land and resources with more complex societies, the technologically simpler foragers are at a disadvantage.

Horticulture

Horticulture is a nonmechanized system that relies solely on human labor to cultivate plants in small garden plots. It is characterized by its reliance on human energy and a limited inventory of simple tools. Digging sticks and hoes are used rather than plows; neither irrigation nor terracing is employed. In traditional horticultural groups, food production is intended for home consumption rather than commercial sale and each farmer has control over his own production, and there is little interdependence between groups. Horticulture is still practiced by a large number of people throughout the world. In Southeast Asia, for instance, one third of the total land area used for agriculture is cultivated with this type of subsistence technology (Jerome et al. 1980).

terracing
Cutting into hillsides to form contoured terraces for planting, thus preventing soil erosion

Today, few horticulturists are independent. Many people using the simple techniques associated with horticulture are peasant farmers producing crops for sale as well as home consumption. In Central America, farmers cultivating hillsides with only their own labor and a machete or digging stick look out over mechanized agriculture being practiced in the valley below.

In most areas, horticulture is practiced as "slash-and burn" agriculture. The trees and bushes covering a small garden plot are cleared and burned and the ashes are left on the ground to fertilize the soil. After the plot has been cultivated for a year or longer (depending on climate, soil type, etc.), a new plot is cleared and the old one allowed to lie fallow until the soil has rejuvenated. This prevents soil exhaustion and enables many horticulturists to live in sedentary villages (Kottak 1982).

lie fallow
Allowing land that is usually cultivated to remain unplanted for a growing season

The shifting of garden plots in and out of cultivation means that at any one time a great amount of potential garden land is not in cultivation. The environment surrounding a village is more "natural" than that around intensive agricultural villages; wild plants and animals are still available for use as food. The "wild" and "tamed" parts of the environment are close to one another.

Horticulture demands relatively little investment of labor to produce an adequate diet. Among sago palm farmers in New Guinea, one day of work is sufficient to produce food that will meet 85 percent of the family's caloric needs for four or five days (Jerome et al.

taro
An edible starchy tuber-
ous plant

1980). In a similar study of another group, the New Guinea Tsembaga, Rappaport (1968) found that only 380 hours per year per food producer were needed to grow enough taro, yams, and other crops to meet caloric needs. Horticultural tasks have a seasonal rhythm requiring large inputs of labor at planting and harvesting times, interspersed with more leisurely periods at other times of the year.

Social, political, and ideological features

As in foraging societies, labor is divided according to sex. Men clear the brush, fence off the land, care for large domesticated animals, and defend the villages from outsiders. They also help with the harvesting. Women are usually responsible for cultivating, planting, weeding, most of the harvesting, raising small animals, and preparing food.

Horticulturists, unlike foragers, may claim exclusive rights over land. Garden plots are owned by individual families or kinship units and people are expected to recognize the rights of the owner to the food produced in her plot. The increased value of land places emphasis on territorial protection and warfare.

Most horticulturists produce large enough food supplies to store for future needs and trade for luxury items with other groups. Because they are able to produce surpluses, horticulturists often place great value on the accumulation of private wealth, thus creating differences beween families.

The families with the most possessions frequently command the most respect and have the greatest influence in the community; however, this gap is not large enough to create major inequalities in control over resources or lead to the formation of social classes.

Another feature of horticultural societies is the increased complexity of social organization. Because most settlements are sedentary, relationships between households are close and long-lasting. In addition to the family group that shares a common household, larger kin groupings are recognized. In most societies, people are organized into groups that trace their descent from a common ancestor. A leader of the descent group, typically a male, is expected to settle disputes and make decisions on behalf of the group's members.

Political organization varies depending largely on the size, density, and permanence of villages. The leader or headman's power may be relatively weak, based primarily on respect and persuasion, or he may have formal authority and considerable power. Typically the headman has acquired more wealth than members of the society and is selected for personal attributes such as generosity, eloquence, bravery, or supernatural powers, as well as wealth. In some horticultural societies the headman has the obligation and authority to regulate conflict and enforce rules. More commonly, however, he lacks the right to issue orders and must persuade people to take his advice. Headmanship in horticultural societies is not a full-time occupation. Headmen are neither relieved of their farming tasks, nor supported through taxes and tributes, although they do enjoy some special privileges not found in hunting and gathering societies (such as the use of special insignia or clothing).

Much of the religious or ritual activities of horticulturists is aimed at improving food supplies. Fertility rites and other cultural artifacts are associated with horticultural societies dating back to the agricultural revolution 10,000 years ago.

Diet and health

Horticulturists rely primarily on cultivated plants for food, with the products of hunting and fishing used to supplement the diet. Wild berries, honey, and insects, along with some wild vegetables, are also collected and provide needed vitamins and minerals.

Horticultural societies that consume a wide variety of wild and domesticated plants and animals enjoy a well-balanced diet. The Tsembaga, for example, combine 36 species of domesticated and wild plants with domesticated pigs and small wild animals. Many horticulturists' diets (like the prehistoric horticulturists at Hardin Village described in Chapter 2) rely primarily on one or two crops that are high in carbohydrate and low in protein. Crops such as yams, sweet potatoes, plantain, and manioc are the dietary mainstay of many horticulturists. Because their diet contains minimal amounts of protein and sometimes other nutrients as well, and "... because they have more of their eggs in one basket, they live a more precarious nutritional existence" (Pelto and Pelto 1976:4) than hunters and gatherers. In particular, they are susceptible to widespread protein malnutrition and are more vulnerable to starvation when crops fail. Kwashiorkor, beriberi, and other deficiency diseases are commonly found in societies that rely upon a single grain crop as a major dietary staple.

For some horticultural groups, such as the Northern Kayapo who still live independently in Brazil's Amazon rain forest, fertile land is readily available for gardening and the uncultivated forest provides a wide variety of wild plants and animal resources for food. The Kayapo cultivate sweet potatoes, manioc, and bananas, all crops high in starch and low in protein. These cultivated staples, along with some cultivated papaya, provide about 50 percent of the diet. The other 50 percent comes from the meat of wild animals such as tapir, jungle cats, peccary (wild pig), pacca and agouti (large rodents), birds, fish, and wild plants (including the protein-rich Brazil nut). Nutritional studies of the Kayapo show them to be well-nourished and healthy.

plantain
A starchy fruit that looks somewhat like a banana but is green in color; it is a staple food in some tropical areas

manioc
A starchy edible plant

kwashiorkor
Severe malnutrition in infants caused by a diet high in carbohydrate and low in protein

beriberi
A disease caused by the deficiency of vitamin B_1 (thiamin), and marked by changes in the nerves and digestive system, and heart degeneration

Horticulturists' health is also affected by their pattern of living in permanent or semipermanent villages. Villages provide new breeding places for many forms of disease. Domesticated animals such as cattle, pigs, and fowl can transmit anthrax, Q Fever (a tick-borne disease), brucellosis, tuberculosis, and intestinal infections such as salmonella and ascaris. Horticulturists in some regions also face increased threats from typhus and malaria when clearing new ground for cultivation.

> Livingston (1958) has impressively illustrated the relationship between the spread of agriculture, malaria, and sickle-cell anemia. As the west African agriculturalists expanded into the forest and destroyed the trees in the preparation of ground for cultivation, they encroached on the environment of the pongids [apes]. The pongids which were the primary host of [malaria] carried by the [mosquito] were exterminated or forced further into the forest. The mosquitos quickly transferred to the hominids for their meals. Livingston points out that agricultural activity, which provides new breeding areas for mosquitos and provides a large population for the mosquitos to feed, led to malaria becoming an endemic disease.
>
> *(Armelagos and Dewey 1970:41)*

endemic
Belonging to or native to a particular region

Pastoralism

Pastoralism is a set of technologies that extracts food and other forms of energy from large herds of domesticated animals. Predominantly found in the Near East and Africa, pastoralism is a cultural adaptation to semiarid, open country where the land will support ruminant animals but not agriculture (Goldschmit 1968). By specializing in animal husbandry, pastoralists are able to exploit harsh environments that cannot be irrigated and are too dry to support other modes of subsistence.

ruminant animals
Animals that have multichambered stomachs and so are able to digest grass and other plants that are indigestible by humans.

Pastoralism developed as a distinct way of life in the Old World, Africa, Asia and Europe. Five different zones of pastoralism, relying on different types and mixes of animals have been noted (Gaisford 1978). In the desert and semidesert regions of the Sahara, East Africa, Arabia, Iran, and Baluchistan, the camel is best adapted to herding. Cattle are also well-suited to the grasslands of central Africa, while sheep and goats are kept on the desert's fringes. In the more temperate mountains and valleys of southwest Asia and the Mediterranean, sheep are herded. Mongolian nomads have traditionally herded horses in central Asia, and have also raised Bactrian camels, sheep, goats, and cattle. In the sub-Arctic tundra of northern Europe and Asia, only the reindeer can be herded.

Because they must move from place to place to keep their grazing animals well-fed, some degree of nomadism is involved in this
lifestyle. Fully nomadic pastoralists do not occupy permanent
dwellings; they do not practice agriculture nor depend on hunting
and gathering for food. Seminomadic pastoralists differ in that part
of the group, usually women and children, set up seasonal settlements near water and cultivate crops (Jerome et al. 1980).

Often pastoralists depend upon neighboring agriculturalists for
grain and other produce. Regional arrangements are established for
trade and collective defense. Because pastoralists are mobile and
can steal the agriculturalists' grain surpluses, they can force neighbors to acknowledge them as overlords. The Mongols and Arabs are
two examples of pastoralists who gained control over huge civiliza-
tions (Harris 1972).

Even today, the reluctance of pastoralists to observe laws and
national boundaries has resulted in efforts to settle them.
Pastoralists are being driven from their lands and relocated on sedentary ranches by encroaching agricultural technologies that have
acquired the ability to cultivate arid terrains (Jerome et al. 1980).
In some areas, improved water and fodder supplies have allowed
pastoral nomads to settle while maintaining pastoralism as a way of
life.

fodder
Feed for domestic
animals

Social, political, and ideological features

Labor among the pastoralists is divided according to sex. Adult
women in seminomadic groups usually stay in camps to look after
the children and collect and cultivate crops, while men and older
children tend the herds. When the pastoral way of life is fully nomadic, women and children accompany the men. The major social
correlates associated with pastoralism have been outlined by Walter
Goldschmidt (1968):

- Because of their mobility, pastoralists own few tools or material objects.

- Pastoralists are usually considered militaristic, frequently
  raiding neighbors' food supplies and fighting to protect their
  herds.

- Pastoral societies are frequently organized into male-
  dominated groups. When a woman marries, she usually leaves
  her family to join her husband's group.

- In pastoral societies, inheritance of wealth, like descent, is
  passed down through male lines.

- There is little or no concept of land ownership in pastoral
  cultures.

- Because water is scarce, the pastoralists travel throughout the year depending upon the availability of water. Often several months are spent camped near watering holes.

Diet and health

The pastoralists' diet is based on renewable animal products: milk, milk products, and blood. Meat is eaten on a limited basis because the animals' milk and blood are more valuable than their meat. Only old or sick animals are slaughtered.

Drinking the blood of live animals is extremely practical in nomadic groups. Blood is naturally stored and will not spoil as long as the animal remains alive. In their sweep across the Steppes, the Mongols relied on the blood of their horses as a major food source. Horses may be bled about once every ten days with no ill effect. Blood may be obtained by thrusting a sharpened hollow needle or other instrument into a blood vessel in the animal's neck and catching the blood that is released. In some pastoralist societies, milk products are the primary foods. Among the Khurgiz of Afghanistan, milk from yaks is used in a variety of ways. Yogurt, cheese, and ghee (clarified butter) enable these people to preserve milk as well as enjoy it in a variety of forms. Finally, some societies rely on a combination of blood and milk products. The Masai of Africa, for example, mix the blood and milk of their cattle and drink them together.

Although pastoralists have been characterized as relying exclusively on animal products, pastoral groups eat some vegetable foods

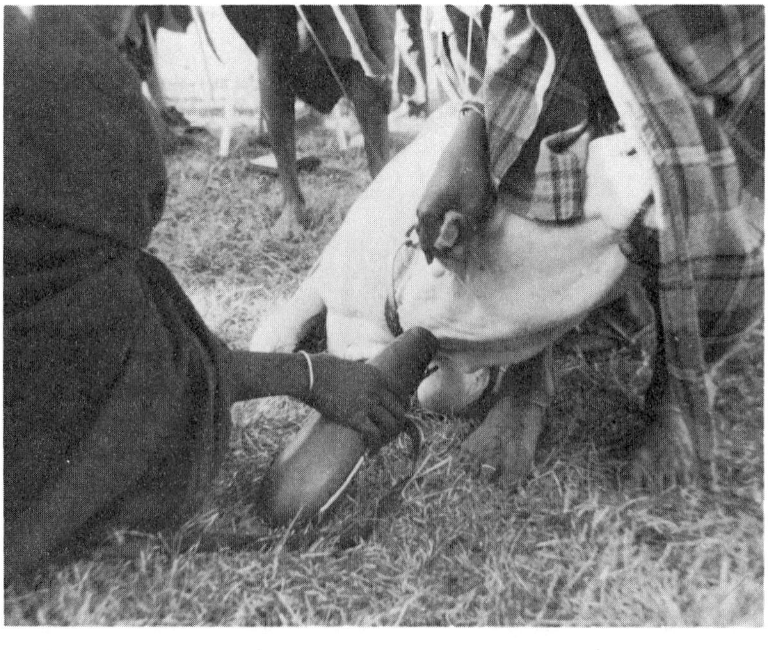

Steppes
A vast plain devoid of forest cover, located in Russia

yak
A large, long-haired ox

Figure 4.2
Masai herders collecting blood from the neck of their cattle
(David Imbrogno)

—primarily grains—as well. Frequently they trade animal products such as milk and cheese for grains; when this fails they may raid the grain fields of neighboring agriculturalists (Harris 1980).

In recent years, attention has been directed toward the health of pastoralist groups, most notably the Masai. Their heavy reliance on blood and whole milk makes their diet high in saturated fat and cholesterol, both of which have been implicated in the development of atherosclerosis ("hardening of the arteries") and coronary heart disease. The Masai, however, seem to have little or no heart disease. In an attempt to understand this phenomenon, Mann, et al. (1971) examined the hearts and aortas from 50 deceased Masai. Although none of the hearts showed any signs of myocardial infarction, the amount of atherosclerosis present was equal to that of Americans of comparable ages. The saving factor appeared to be that the blood vessels of the Masai were far larger than those of the Westeners. In fact, the blood vessels of the Masai were large enough that the atherosclerosis that was present did not affect their functioning. Mann attributed the increased size of their blood vessels to the Masai's extensive exercise.

myocardial infarction
Dead heart tissue caused by obstruction of blood circulation

Intensive agriculture

Agriculture is a form of plant cultivation that requires intensive labor and land use. Unlike horticultural systems, animal and mechanical labor supplement human labor. Irrigation, terracing, and manure or other fertilizers may be used so that land may be cultivated continuously. Hoes, plows pulled by draft animals, and the large inputs of human labor needed to maintain irrigation systems and to care for animals sets this subsistence mode apart from horticulture.[1] The increased labor investments of agriculturalists are rewarded by the long-term yields gained from the land. Unlike horticulturists, who must allow their fields to lie fallow, intensive agriculturalists can produce one or two crops a year for many consecutive years. This, in turn, allows populations to form more dense, permanent settlements around their fields.

Social, political, and ideological features

The maintenance of irrigation and terracing systems requires organized labor. Farmers must work together to build irrigation channels

---

[1] Many societies' subsistence systems include features of both horticulture and agriculture. Kottak (1982) suggests viewing cultivators as falling on a continuum between horticulture and agriculture rather than grouping them into separate categories.

Figure 4.3
Peasant agriculturalists using draft animals. Peasant agriculturalists employ more sophisticated technology in cultivating crops and livestock than their "cousin" horticulturalists. This results, among other things, in higher yields, and encourages a more stratified society.
(AID)

and regulate the water supply. Life in large, permanent villages requires cooperative social relations among community members. Agricultural societies often have the following social organizational features:

- Specialized occupations, with some individuals performing skilled tasks such as engineering and tool making and repair.

- Significant differences between the rich and poor; society is stratified into social classes.

- Formalized political and legal systems to protect land rights, protect irrigation systems, and resolve conflicts.

As we noted in Chapter 2, the development of intensive agriculture about 5000 B.P. is associated with the rise of complex political and religious systems. Because intensive agriculture enhances population growth and frees a portion of the population to pursue nonagricultural specialties, an elite class can rise to power. With this ruling class comes the development of an elitist ideology: some segments of society are seen as inherently more valuable than others. As the elite gain greater control over the rest of society, cities and complex political forms known as states come into existence.

Today these states are organized into nations tied together by international laws and trade agreements. Yet most nation-states still are organized into a ruling elite, most of whom live in urban centers, and a much larger group of rural agriculturalists. Thus, with the exception of a few isolated economically independent societies, today's agriculturalists live in regular contact with market towns and cities. They participate in the social and political and religious life of the nations in which they are found and are dependent on the nation's markets as outlets for their surplus crops. Agriculturalists who make up part of a larger economic and political unit are referred to as *peasants*.

Modern peasant societies

Peasants are rural cultivators who raise crops and livestock primarily for household consumption, not as a business enterprise. They also produce some cash crops and enough surplus to support the urban elite. Peasants use their surpluses to pay tax or rent and buy necessities and luxury items produced outside their communities. Thus, unlike traditional or independent horticulturists who distribute their surpluses to members within their own group, peasants are linked through trade and other economic exchanges to an elite or wealthy group outside the community. Typically, the elite use peasants' surpluses to enhance their own standard of living. This link between peasants and the elite is a key factor distinguishing peasants from more autonomous agriculturalists. It also is essential in understanding the peasants' lifestyle and the social inequities that exist between them and the larger society (Jerome et al. 1980).

The crops grown by peasant agriculturalists to sell for cash often end up on the international market. Small agriculturalists in Northern Mexico produce vegetables and fruits that appear on the tables of North Americans. In many areas, commercial agriculturalists produce crops for export while peasant agriculturalists produce the basic grains that feed the people of the area.

Peasant agriculturalists are characteristically small farmers. Frequently they farm less than three acres; rarely more than twelve. Most rely on hand labor and simple tools—the hoe, machete, cutlass (a short sword with a curved blade), and axe. Some use larger machines such as plows pulled by animals or humans to aid in planting, cultivating, and harvesting. Little fertilizer or chemicals are used. Women provide over half the labor on small farms—in planting, cultivating, and postharvest food processing. In some regions of Africa, women do most or all of the farm labor; almost everywhere they do all the cooking. In addition, women usually transport produce to rural markets where they work as small vendors. Older children often assist with agricultural duties or collection of wild foods. Practically the entire family must work to obtain food needed to sustain its members.

Figure 4.4
Family plowing.
Sometimes agricultural
peasants cannot afford
draft animals. In this Ko-
rean community, eco-
nomic progress is slow,
and agricultural neces-
sity occasionally re-
quires this woman to
hitch herself to the plow.
(AID)

This form of agriculture is referred to as subsistence agriculture because the farmer's main interest is in raising food for his or her family. It also is known as traditional agriculture because of the dependence on traditional farming practices handed down for many generations. Specific practices vary from one society to another, and even between regions. Usually, however, the methods and systems used are well-adapted to the environment. In some areas of the tropics, for example, land is used to grow crops for several seasons and then allowed to lie fallow for long periods of time; fruit trees may be planted if lengthy fallow periods are required to replenish the soil for crop cultivation.

Other methods used to get optimal use of the land include mixed cropping and intercropping. With mixed cropping, several plant species are grown together in the same field. Individual plants can be positioned in the plot to yield maximum growth for each species. Intercropping is similar: two or more crops are planted in rows side by side. Several crops can use sunlight, soil nutrients, and water more effectively than one. Plants with leaves on different levels enable a small, rapidly growing crop to temporarily use empty spaces between larger, slower growing plants. Also, crops with varying root lengths can more effectively intercept water as it percolates down through the soil. In this way, nutrients can be absorbed that would otherwise dissolve and wash below the roots and erosion is reduced. If legumes or other nitrogen-fixing crops are planted, nitrogen is made available for other plants as well. Finally, diseases and pests are minimized with mixed cropping by making it harder for a fungus or pest affecting one species to reach other plants of the same type in the field.

Because the various crops sharing one field often are not planted or harvested at the same time, most work must be done manually. For the small farmer this is not a major drawback, however, because the plot is small; labor is readily available; and machines for planting, cultivation, and harvesting are beyond his or her financial reach anyway.

Nicholson and Nicholson (1979) describe an example of mixed cropping in Tanzania. Coffee, beans, bananas, corn, and meat are produced together on the slopes of Mt. Kilimanjaro. Banana trees are positioned so that they provide shade for the coffee trees. Beans, a nitrogen-fixing crop, are planted near the coffee trees wherever sufficient sunlight is available. Beans and bananas provide food. The banana leaves and stalks are fed to cattle, who in turn provide manure to fertilize the bananas and coffee. When the farm is large enough, corn and other crops also are grown for food.

This is not to say that all small farmers live harmoniously with the land or produce enough to feed their families well. Population pressures and increased production of exportable crops, combined with destructive agricultural practices, have thrown traditional land/human relationships out of balance in many parts of the world. Increased population pressure, for instance, has forced some farmers in the tropical rain forest to shorten the period during which land is allowed to lie fallow. Subsoil is eroded when it is overcultivated and land productivity declines. Flooding may result from the soil's inability to hold water, further damaging the subsoil. Overcropping in fragile ecosystems such as the Sahelian area is contributing to the process of desertification. In fact, the desert is expanding in parts of the Sudan at the rate of six to seven kilometers per year due to overuse of the land.

Soil erosion and declining fertility has placed many peasant groups in nutritional jeopardy. The Bapedi, a Bantu-speaking group in the northeastern Transvaal, South Africa, traditionally ate a diet that was based on thick porridges made from maize corn, sorghum, or millet. Traditionally, the stiff boiled porridge was rolled into balls and dipped into a gravy or relish made from meat or vegetables. Loss of soil fertility and erosion and overhunting of game means that the ingredients for the nutritionally important supplementary relishes and gravies are less available. The result is that the use of these dishes has declined and so has the nutritional adequacy of the Bapedi diet (Waldmann 1980).

The transition to market economies

Today, most peasant societies are experiencing a shift from subsistence food crops to cash crops and a cash economy. Rather than raising

jute
A plant that produces glossy fiber used in making burlap and twine

most of the food they eat, peasants now grow tobacco, jute, cotton, sugar, or other crops that are sold for cash. The cash is then used to buy foods. This shift is accompanied by serious nutritional problems. As Jerome, et al. explain (1980:32):

> Often, the most fertile land is used for the cash crop (coffee, peanuts, cotton, cocoa), thus lowering the production capacity of the land under food cultivation. The shift to a cash economy also means that a large part, if not the majority of food is purchased instead of produced. The high cost of protein rich foods often makes them prohibitive, thereby forcing people into an affordable high carbohydrate diet, which is often much less nutritious than the original peasant diet.

One example of the nutritional consequences of the transition to cash crops comes from Gross and Underwood's study (1971) of a Brazilian community as it shifted from cattle raising and agriculture to sisal production. (Sisal is a plant cultivated for the fiber in its large leaves, which is made into rope.) Before the introduction of sisal as a cash crop, the chief crops were manioc, corn, and beans, supplemented with beef. Except during drought years, many households raising these foods approached self-sufficiency in their food production. But with the opportunity to earn increased income as cash wages, many agriculturalists shifted their attention to the production of sisal.

Unfortunately, the peasants' profit-making expectations were not realized. Sisal plants take about four years to mature. While the immature plants occupied the agriculturalists' fields, the new sisal growers were forced into the labor market to make money to support their families. Most men worked in sisal processing plants in laborious jobs requiring expenditures of large amounts of calories. Even after the sisal plants matured, most men continued to work in these processing plants because deflated sisal prices did not give them sufficient profit to survive.

As a result of this new subsistence mode, the social inequities between the small number of factory owners and managers and the large number of sisal farmers and part-time laborers increased. Diets improved for the wealthier segment, but not for the rest of the community. Laborers' wages, even when combined with sisal profits, were inadequate to offset the increased food needed to cover the large expenditure of calories required to work in the sisal factories. The caloric cost of sustaining the strenuous activity of the laborer proved so great that "the only way in which the workers' energy requirement could be satisfied was to deprive the dependent nonproductive members of the household of needed food" (Gross and Underwood 1971:733). Men ate more, while women and children ate less. This example is not unique. In a similar case in Mexico studied by Hernandez, et al. (1974), thirteen years of agricultural development resulted in a 600 percent increase in production among small farmers. At the same time the population doubled. The crops grown changed somewhat. While corn production increased at about the same rate as the population, bean production did not keep pace with population growth. The greatest increases in crop production came in coffee, cocoa, sugar, and bananas: all export crops. Over this time the diets of townspeople (representing merchants and middlemen) improved, while the diets of the rural cultivators who experienced the tremendous increase in production remained about the same. About 22.5 percent of children under five years of age showed moderate to severe malnutrition. It seems that the unequal status of peasant producers in relation to the wealthier merchants means that peasants are denied access to the fruits of their agricultural labor.

There are, in fact, numerous examples of peasant farmers who abandon subsistence crops for cash crops, either on their own or as a result of pressure from outside. In many instances, the economic benefits of this shift are not seen by the farmer, who must use his or her cash to buy a diet that is less nutritious than the one previously produced.

Industrialized agriculture

In industrialized societies, agriculture is a large-scale business enterprise requiring large amounts of capital and energy. Jerome, et al. (1980) characterize industrialized agriculture as "a commercial venture that incorporates a wide range of knowledge and skills in agricultural science and business to achieve high productivity." Industrialized agriculture refers to the fact that human and animal labor is replaced by machinery using fossil fuel as an energy source. Food systems in industrialized societies are technologically complex, with several components making up the chain from field to table (Katz and Goodwin 1980:140):

- *Food sources*—farmers, ranchers, and fishermen

- *Farm marketing*—people who assemble, buy, sell, or handle farm products, including retail outlets (supermarkets, grocery stores, restaurants, and vending machines)

- *Food processing*—people employed in canning, freezing, refining, and manufacturing food products

- *Transportation*—truck drivers, train and flight crews, and

Figure 4.5
*Agribusiness in the
United States.
(USDA/Doug Wilson)*

- *Scientific research*—researchers at USDA, food companies, many state universities

Industrialized agriculture exists alongside more technologically simple agriculture in some developing countries, but for an in-depth examination of industrialized agriculture, we look at the food system in the U.S., one of the most industrialized systems. When you think of a modern American farm, what comes to mind? Checkered fields of corn, oats, hay, and clover . . . chickens scrambling for food in the backyard . . . cattle grazing in the fields, and horses in their stalls? Today few farms resemble these traditional conceptions. Rather, they are likely to produce only one or perhaps two crops. Cattle are fed grain in crowded pens and draft horses have been replaced with tractors, some equipped with front wheels that reach seven feet in height and air conditioned cabs. Chicken farms consist of long buildings that house thousands of birds in small cages. Their food and water are delivered, and their eggs and waste are removed, by conveyor belts.

Industrialized agriculture in the U.S. and elsewhere relies predominantly on monoculture. Monoculture is the practice of growing one crop within a given land area. In some places, such as the American corn belt, entire regions are planted in genetically identical varieties. As Nicholson and Nicholson (1979:54–55) explain, this "genetic uniformity means that every plant in a field is essentially identical to every other plant and responds in the same way to the environment. The farmer can then plant seed of a corn hybrid

Figure 4.6
*A modern chicken
farm.   Rows of laying
cages in the round.
(USDA/McKinney)*

which was specifically developed to give high yields within his geographic location. This is advantageous because hours of daylight, average daily temperature, and total days suitable for growth and maturation of the crop can differ greatly between geographic regions."

Genetic uniformity typically is associated with the use of mechanical equipment and chemicals. Because the crop can be bred to produce fruit that will form at the same place on the plant and that is firm enough to be handled mechanically, a machine operated by one or two people can be used to harvest the crop. Planting, cultivating, and fertilizing also can be done mechanically, often by a single person.

Chemical fertilizers are another key feature of the agricultural systems of developed nations. Chemical fertilizers contain phosphorus, potassium, nitrogen, or some combination of these. Other minor nutrients may also be added. Soil is especially vulnerable to nitrogen depletion. Unless crops that contain nitrogen-fixing bacteria (e.g., clover, alfalfa, soybeans) are planted to replenish the soil, its natural fertility drops. With the development of chemical processes that synthesize atmospheric nitrogen into inorganic compounds, it has been possible to greatly boost soil fertility and crop yields.

Other practices associated with industrialized agriculture are multiple cropping (planting more than one crop on the same land in the same year); the use of chemical pesticides and herbicides to control insects, weeds, and other pests; and irrigation to provide controlled amounts of water to a crop throughout the growing season.

One of the most outstanding features of the U.S. farm is its production efficiency. It is recognized throughout the world for its efficiency and ability to increase crop yields while keeping inputs relatively constant. In fact, productivity, the output or yield obtained from all inputs (fertilizer, seed, etc.), has risen over 130 percent since 1920; in just one decade (1970 to 1979) productivity increased 16.7 percent. Actual gains in farm productivity depend on how efficiency is defined. As Rawlins (1980:43) explains:

> There are many different ways to measure farm efficiency, and the degree of efficiency depends on the type of measurement used. One of the most common indicators used is the number of persons supplied by the average farm worker. Presently, the average farm worker supplies over 55 persons with food and fiber, compared with only 20 in 1955 and 15 in 1945. The ratio of total farm output to farm inputs may also be used as an indicator of efficiency. Overall output per unit of input has increased over 20 percent since 1960. Also, output per labor-hour for farm workers has increased much faster than that of nonfarm workers since 1969. The result of this amazing productivity is the reliable, abundance of the United States food supply.

The family farm continues to be the basic production unit of industrialized farming. These farms vary, however, in their size and profit-making potential. Many farmers, especially those with small land holdings, produce less income and must rely on off-farm jobs for themselves or family members to supplement the farming income. Larger farmers do much better and account for most of the nation's agricultural production. In 1975, for example, less than 4 percent of the farms had sales of $100,000 or more; these accounted for almost half of total farm sales. On the lower end of the scale, about 25 percent of the farms sold less than $2500 worth of farm products, accounting for only 1 percent of farm sales (Rawlins 1980:39).

The optimal acreage and the amount of capital and labor needed for a profitable operation differ both by crop and geographical area. John Walsh (1975:532) explains:

> In the corn belt one man, equipped with the proper machinery, can handle virtually all the work necessary to farm 600 to 800 acres of corn. He will need help from his family and one or two hired workers only at the busiest time. If the farmer fattens hogs or cattle in the same region, not so much land is required. Hogs, for example, can be profitable raised on 300 to 400 acres of land planted in corn or soybeans for feed.

In general, however, small farmers do not have sufficient land or capital to withstand inflation (e.g., increased costs of fertilizer, seeds, and pesticides) and wide fluctuations in crop prices. Over the last 60 years, the average farm size has tripled from 150 to 450 acres as smaller farmers sell out to larger, more profitable operators. Between 1950 and 1970, over 100,000 small farms were lost each year, nearly 2000 per week (Cornucopia Project 1981).

Large corporations also have entered the farming scene. For the most part, however, their operations are concentrated in particular food industries such as feedlots (where cattle are fattened, slaughtered and processed) and citrus fruit operations. More significant is

Table 4.1 Farm sales in 1975		
Sales Classes	**Share of Total Farm**	**Share of Receipts**
100,000 and up	3.9	46.8
40,000–00,000	12.1	23.7
20,000–39,000	20.1	18.8
10,000–19,000	11.6	5.6
5,000– 9,999	9.1	2.2
2,500– 4,999	17.3	2.0
less than 2,500	25.9	.9

Agricultural Outlook, Research Service, A0–16, USDA: 1976.

the corporation's role as a service industry to the family farm. Corporations provide farmers with the inputs (machinery, fertilizers, pesticides, animal biologicals) and absorb the outputs by purchasing, processing, and marketing their crops. In some instances, they contract with farmers for crops at negotiated prices. This protects farmers against a drop in prices and allows them to plan more effectively; it also prevents them from reaping rewards when prices rise (Walsh 1975).

The United States' food supply is also the product of technological achievements in food processing, manufacturing, and transportation. Every culture has its own way of processing and preparing foods. However, in the United States food technology has become big business: "The fourth largest industrial user of energy, the employer of about one-seventh of the working population is a complex network with its parts spanning the globe. (It's no wonder that few of us know where our food comes from, how it gets to us or what processes it passes through on the way.)" (Katz and Goodwin 1980:149).

North Americans have a love-hate relationship with food technology. Throughout Canada and the United States, people appreciate the convenience and abundance of their food supply but condemn its impact on their social and physical environments. (For more information on the controversy surrounding food technology see Highlight 4–1.)

> Thanks to technology, consumers have more food available than ever before. They pay comparatively less for it than they did twenty-five years ago. The price includes all the built-in 'maid-service' features in our modern food supply—frozen foods, baked products, and other processed foods . . . . However, the convenience of highly processed food is purchased at the expense of valuable nutrients and home-cooked flavors. Natural texture, taste and aroma are replaced with artificial color, flavor, and even a smell to simulate natural food. Preservatives are added to extend shelf life.
>
> *(Meyerhoff and Tobias 1980:1828)*

The food industry's corner on the North American market has grown explosively over the last ten years. With women entering the labor force, less time is available for menu planning and preparation of home cooked meals. At the same time, women's earnings allow them to buy more processed foods. These same factors have led to the rise of another component in industrialized nations' food systems: the "away-from-home food market." This market consists of restaurants, cafeterias, fast food chains, taverns, clubs, hotels and motels, trains, boats, planes, vending machines, and all other facilities that sell food. According to figures published by the USDA, total expenditures for meals and snacks eaten away from home were $77.3 billion in 1977. This represents 26 cents of each dollar spent on food in the United States. Approximately one-fifth of those sales take place in fast food franchises (O'Rourke 1981:3–8). Increased travel, smaller households, and women's increased participation in the work force is expected to contribute to the continued success of these restaurants. Already, most towns in the United States have the familiar Golden Arches of McDonalds, Burger King, Kentucky Fried Chicken, Ponderosa Steak House, and Long John Silver's Seafood Shops. Conveniently located near shopping centers, theaters, and busy thoroughfares, these restaurants offer a standardized, predictable menu at moderate prices. The menu also reflects the very features of the developed nations' diet which are under attack: foods high in fat, cholesterol, salt, sugar, and preservatives. This concerns many nutritionists because of the increasing reliance on these fast foods: 40 percent of all meals consumed in the United States are now eaten away from home.

Industrialized agricultural technology appears at first glance to represent a major advance in people's mastery over nature. Never before has humankind produced such high yields per farmer or controlled such a wealth of knowledge about plant and animal domestication and the preservation of foods. Modern technology allows us to grow food in areas once considered uncultivatable and synthesize completely new food products.

Despite these achievements, many scientists are concerned. As with all technologies, new practices affect the environment and create new environmental conditions that require even newer technological responses. Industrialized agriculture creates stress on soils, water supplies, flora, and fauna. Unlike subsistence technologies, the effects of industrialized agriculture are not confined to the immediate environment. Demands for gasoline to run tractors and for oil to produce fertilizers have contributed to oil shortages and price increases felt around the world. North Americans complain about high prices at the gas pump while Latin American peasants find that they can no longer afford the fertilizer made from natural gas that helps make their farms profitable. Some scientists fear that industrialized agricultural techniques, combined with other technological advances of Western societies, may jeopardize the environment to such an extent that humans may be working themselves out of existence. Others claim that the environment is not in grave danger (at least not yet) and advocate the spread of industrialized agricultural techniques throughout the world. In either case, energy shortages, smog alerts in major cities, and contaminated rivers and lakes have made members of industrialized societies aware of the ongoing struggle to adapt to the physical environment.

Energy

If you count calories, you no doubt are aware of the energy you get from eating food. But how often do you consider the amount of energy that went into producing it? You may be surprised to learn that in the U.S. it takes nine kilocalories of energy to produce just one

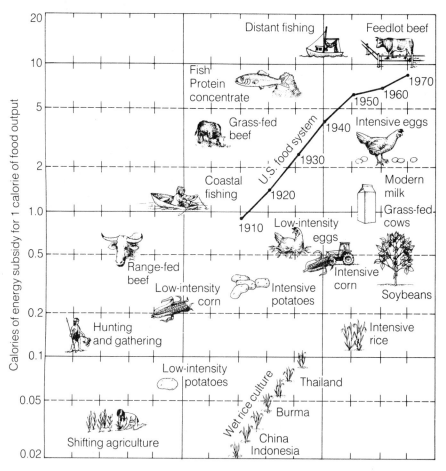

Figure 4.7
Energy subsidies for various food crops. The energy history of the United States food system is shown for comparison.
(Adapted with permission from Steinhart, J. S. and C. E. Steinhart,
Science:*184, 307-317, Figure 19, April 1974. Copyright© 1974 by the*
American Association for the Advancement of Science.)

kilocalorie of food. You may also be surprised to learn that this is a much less efficient energy ratio than food produced in non-industrialized societies, or even in the United States 20 years ago (Steinhart and Steinhart 1978).

Why does it take so much energy to produce our food? First, industrialized agriculture is highly mechanized and farm machines use large amounts of gasoline. Second, chemical fertilizers are made from natural gas, and the production of pesticides also requires fossil fuels. Third, food processing is a major consumer of natural gas as well as petroleum products. And fourth, the transportation of food from farms and processors to warehouse retailers consumes millions of gallons of gasoline and diesel fuel. Finally, retailers, especially fast food restaurants, are significant consumers of energy. One study estimated that the equivalent of 12.7 million tons of coal was used in 1971 by McDonald's hamburger franchises alone (Perelman 1976:76). When the fuel bills of all components in the food system are totaled, the agricultural industry is responsible for 10 to 20 percent of the nation's energy consumption (Rawlins 1980).

This reliance on nonrenewable energy resources creates serious problems for farmers who must pay higher prices. It also has national and international significance as we attempt to decrease our dependence on foreign oil and avoid future energy shortages.

Soils

A problem that is not unique to industrialized agriculture, but nevertheless important for today's society, is soil erosion. Most soils have the capacity to regenerate between two and five tons of topsoil per acre annually. "If erosion does not exceed the rate of regeneration, the soil resource is maintained. Most soils, therefore, incur some erosion without significant adverse impacts. A soil tolerance loss of five tons per acre has come to be accepted as the threshold at which erosion becomes excessive. When this standard is applied to the available information on erosion soil loss, the problem seems to be relatively concentrated; that is, the most severe erosion occurs on a small proportion of the acreage" (Knutson et al. 1983:331).

Most erosion reaches excessive proportions on croplands, particularly those used to grow cotton and sorghum. Rangelands and pastures experience considerably less erosion. The recent expansion of U.S. agriculture into foreign markets, resulting in higher prices, has encouraged many farmers to plant crops year after year and from "fence to fence—frequently at the expense of shelter belts and windbreaks" (Knutson et al. 1983:331). The 1970s and 1980s, therefore have brought increased rates of soil erosion and new concerns for soil conservationists.

rill

A small brook

Table 4.2   Combined sheet, rill, and wind erosion
on land used in the United States for row crops
and small grains (including fallow), 1977.

Rate of erosion (tons/acres)	Acres (millions)	Percent of total	Excess erosion (millions)	Percent of total
0–4.9	203.2	60.2	0	0
5–9.9	67.2	19.9	133.5	8.5
10–14.9	25.0	7.4	180.4	11.4
15–19.9	13.2	3.9	162.1	10.3
20–24.9	7.6	2.2	131.3	8.3
25–over	21.3	6.4	967.7	61.5
Total	337.5	100.0	1574.9	100.0

Clayton Ogg and Arnold Miller, *Minimizing Erosion on
Cultivated Land: Concentration of Erosion Problems and the
Effectiveness of Conservation Practices,* Washington, D.C.,
USDA: 1981.

Water

For many years, water was taken for granted and treated as an unlimited resource. But as irrigation uses expanded from surface to ground supplies, water supplies dropped and fears of water shortages have spread throughout much of the country (Knutson et al. 1983). In addition, many surface water sources have become polluted with chemical fertilizers, pesticides, and topsoil. Lake Erie and the rivers feeding into it contain startling amounts of phosphates, acids, oils, and other agricultural, mining, and industrial pollutants. Once a major source of freshwater fish, today Lake Erie supports only a few fishing operators. Lake Michigan and the other Great Lakes also appear to be following a similar fate (Franke and Franke 1975). It is hoped that recent governmental efforts to revive these freshwater lakes will be successful, fostering more effective water conservation policies.

People

Industrialized agriculture has its social costs, too. The decline in the number of farms and people employed on farms and the expansion of corporations into many segments of the food system have raised questions about the potential survival of the family farm. Fluctuating inflation presents a unique problem to farmers because they cannot adequately adjust their crop prices to meet the new cost of inputs. When crop prices drop, cash flow becomes an acute problem and many farmers are forced to seek supplemental jobs or face bankruptcy.

Small farm closures and mechanization that displaces human labor force people to migrate to urban areas in search of employment. When the nonfarming sector cannot absorb them, problems arise. "The transition or movement of people out of agriculture is often extremely painful, imposing a severe burden on those who are displaced . . . " (Knutson et al. 1983:169).

Alternatives

Many consumers, dissatisfied with the high environmental, economic, social, and health costs incurred by industrialized food systems, are developing alternative strategies. Included among these are organic farming techniques, systems to increase sales of locally grown foods, food co-ops and buying clubs, and personal dietary changes.

Organic or sustainable farming

One of the most popular alternatives available to help solve some of these problems is organic or sustainable farming. A report on organic farming published by the United States Department of Agriculture (USDA) in 1980 suggests that many farmers can, and perhaps should, adopt organic farming practices—combining them with conventional practices as necessary. The study team responsible for the report was impressed by the ability of organic farmers to "control weeds in crops through timely tillage and cultivation, delayed planting and crop rotations, with little or no use of herbicides" (United States Department of Agriculture 1980).

Many farmers have greatly reduced or eliminated their reliance on chemical fertilizers with the use of organic techniques. This is done by planting hybrid crops that are less dependent on fertilizer, rotating the growth of legumes that return nutrients to the soil, and using animal manure and crop residues to enrich soils. Also, some small farmers are replacing monoculture with the more traditional practice of diversified farming. A farmer may grow corn, oats, hay, clover, a family garden of vegetables and fruit trees, and raise cows, chickens, and pigs. Such a system creates a healthy ecosystem and allows for recycling of wastes.

Local food systems

A popular alternative to supermarkets is the farmers' market. Many towns have recently formed or revitalized farmers' markets. Fairgrounds, public squares, parking lots, and closed-off streets provide space where farmers can sell their locally grown food directly to consumers. In 1976, the New York City Council on the Environment began a small program to help preserve the few farms in the area and provide consumers with locally-grown fresh fruits and vegetables. Since then, the program has grown to 15 weekly farmers' markets where more than 50 farmers sell produce to 20,000 New Yorkers.

As an outgrowth of this project, the Council recently initiated a farm survival program to expand their efforts to help local farms. This project works to improve regional marketing channels, dealing with issues such as land preservation, zoning legislation, and small farmers' tax problems.

In 1980, Rodale Press began the *Cornucopia Project* with the goal of making a systematic, state-by-state study of America's food system and developing strategies for creating a food system that avoids some of the problems of our present one. One of the major recommendations of the Cornucopia Project is to create a regional food system allowing different areas of the country to produce much of the food consumed within the region (Cornucopia Project Newsletter: 1981).

Many "local food systems" are right in America's own backyard. In 1979, 33 million American households (42 percent) grew some of their own food. The total value of this produce reached $13 billion—an average yield of $386 for each garden (Gardens for All 1979).

Another strategy gaining popularity is the establishment of personal trading networks between farm and nonfarm families. In Japan, a common practice is for a small group of families to contract with a local farmer to produce their food. The prices they pay are usually less than retail, but more than wholesale, so both the farmer and the families benefit. Also "pick-your-own" farms are common in parts of the U.S., especially for fruit.

Foods co-ops and buying clubs

Food co-ops and buying clubs are nonprofit structures in which consumers buy directly from wholesale dealers or farmers, allowing them to save the money normally paid to middlemen. Buying clubs usually consist of several households that purchase bulk wholesale goods collectively. The clubs operate out of homes, churches, or community centers, with members contributing labor and transpor-

Focus 4-2

The story of beef

Today, Americans eat more meat per capita and pay less for it in terms of proportion of total income than any other people in the world. Although the U.S. has 1/15 of the world's population, it eats 1/3 of its meat. Beef has always been America's favorite meat. In the mid–1800s, steak was the most popular meal in the U.S., with Americans eating twice as much of it as their English counterparts.

As farming communities became established in early colonial America, the demand for beef was easily met. Each settlement was able to raise its own cattle. Even though cattle required three times as much land as grain, this posed little problem because at that time land seemed unlimited. But as the population of the East Coast grew, the pinch for space began to be felt and the large tracts of land needed to raise cattle were employed for other purposes.

If Americans were to continue to eat meat in large quantities, more grazing land was needed. The Western United States provided the vast lands required. When cattlemen arrived in Texas to set up their business, wild cattle were already there. Texas cattle were a tough breed whose ancestors had been imported by the Spaniards in the sixteenth century and abandoned in Texas. Within a generation of the cattlemen's arrival, these cattle had become domesticated as the notorious Texas Longhorns.

In the mid–1800s, the Western United States began supplying beef to the eastern part of the country. One drawback was the long distance separating producers from consumers. Cows had to walk many miles to reach the marketplace. A longhorn drive from west to east might consist of 2,500 animals with 1,500 miles to travel, advancing at a rate of 10 to 20 miles a day and requiring two to five months of steady plodding. Some drives ended in the Midwest, where cattle were sold and slaughtered. Others took a short break in a Chicago feeding pen to fatten up the animals, then went back on the road to New York. When the first herds of Texas Longhorn arrived in New York in 1854, citizens flocked to see them arrive (Root and de Rochemont 1976).

Cattle drives became more difficult in the late 1800s as land was enclosed. The open range was closed off as farms were fenced and cities grew up. Railroads offered a solution, revolutionizing the fashion in which beef was transported from the western plains to the eastern market. In 1867, the first shipment of cattle left by rail from Abilene, Texas. By the end of the nineteenth century, cattle drives came to a virtual halt and railroad transport took over.

The advent of the refrigerated rail car in 1882 also contributed to the availability of safer, fresher meat. Cattle could now be carried short distances to packing centers to be cut into carcasses and sent by refrigerated rail car to butcher shops in the East.

Beginning in the 1940s, a new system of feeding cattle was developed in the U.S. Instead of going from pasture to slaughter, with a possible short stop in a feedlot, most U.S. cattle now stay in feedlots for extended periods. Here they are each fed over 2,500 pounds of grain and soy products (about 22 pounds a day), hormones, and antibiotics (Lappe 1983). Prior to this time, relatively few cattle were fed grain, but by the early 1970s approximately three-fourths were raised on grain feed (United States Department of Agriculture 1961, Pimental 1980). Currently 90 percent of the soybeans, corn, oats, and barley grown in this country are fed to livestock.

Much controversy surrounds the current method of raising beef in the U.S. Since cattle convert grain into protein inefficiently, sixteen pounds of grain and soy are needed to produce a single pound of meat. In contrast, cattle are well-equipped to convert many fibrous plants (grass, wood pulp) that are inedible for humans into protein that we can eat. Therefore, many people object to the current practice of feeding cattle grain—which would be better used to feed the world's hungry people—and recommend instead that cattle be pastured on grasslands. Such ecologicol considerations have attracted considerable attention recently in light of Third World food shortages and have motivated many concerned citizens to adopt vegetarian diets.

Beef consumption patterns

Between 1910 and 1976, beef consumption increased 72 percent in the U.S. In 1976, the average citizen ate 180 pounds of meat; the vast majority of which (100 pounds) was beef. Americans passion for beef peaked in 1976 and then began dropping in 1977. According to USDA food consumption surveys, beef consumption dropped 6.1 percent from 1976 to 1981. This drop may be attributed in part to high prices, but an important factor was probably also health concerns.

Recent publicity has been directed at the health hazards associated with eating large amounts of beef. Beef is high in saturated fat and cholesterol, and thus is linked to the high incidence of heart disease in industrialized countries. Also, the current system of feeding large amounts of grain to cattle significantly increases the saturated fat content of beef. Choice grades of meat have 63 percent more fat than the standard grades (where less grain is fed to the cattle).

---

tation. Co-ops have more members, a greater variety of food, and permanent quarters. While some resemble large supermarkets, such as Berkeley (California) and Hyde Park (Chicago) Co-ops, more frequently co-ops are small enterprises that emphasize wholesome foods sold in bulk, rather than prepackaged products (Katz and Goodwin 1976). An estimated 250 and 350 storefront co-ops now exist in the U.S.

Personal dietary changes

A significant number of Americans are changing their eating habits. For example, in a USDA survey of 1,400 households made in 1976, in about half the homes, one or more persons said they were changing their diet due to health concerns. Food habits commonly adopted include avoidance of processed foods, use of more locally grown commodities, and decreased beef, milk, and egg consumption. The impact of consumers' dietary changes is evident in the host of new products boasting labels stating "no preservatives added", "contains all natural ingredients," "low sodium," "low cholesterol," or "nondairy substitute." Thus it appears that many consumer preferences can be registered at the checkout counter.

Diet and health of industrialized agriculturists

The abundance and variety of food supplies in industrialized societies enable most families to consume sufficient protein, calorie, and other essential nutrients to maintain good health. Widespread shortages are no longer a problem: only the poor cannot afford an adequate diet all year round (see Chapter 5 for a discussion of hunger and poverty in the U.S.). Although mild iron deficiency anemia is relatively common among children and women, especially in economically disadvantaged families, most forms of malnutrition are rarely found.

North Americans' dietary patterns are not without problems, however. High intakes of calories, fat, cholesterol, salt, sugar, additives, and preservatives have been linked in the U.S. to major health problems (NRS 1982, and Department of National Health and Welfare 1975). Obesity and its associated diseases (diabetes, heart disease, and high blood pressure) affect approximately 40 percent of the U.S. population. A sedentary lifestyle, combined with a food supply that offers literally thousands of calorically-dense products, contributes to North Americans' failure to balance food intakes with energy expenditures.

North Americans' high intake of marbled beef and fried foods, as well as the high fat content of many processed foods, contributes to diets rich in fat. Especially problematic are the high levels of cholesterol and saturated fats that have been linked to cardiovascular disease.

Nutritionists also are concerned about the high levels of sugar and salt consumed in developed countries. The average U.S. citizen ate over 100 pounds of sugar, including in that 240 candy bars and almost 300 12-ounce cans of soda, in 1979. (Some teenage boys consume as much as 400 pounds of sugar per year due to high-sugar snacks and beverages.) Sugar is known to promote dental caries and may contribute to obesity and related conditions such as cardiovascular disease. Sodium intakes also exceed what most experts consider advisable levels. The average U.S. citizen consumes 4,000 mg. to 8,000 mg. of sodium (two to four teaspoons of salt) each day. The ESA for sodium for adults is 1,100 mg. to 3,300 mg., but some people have lived well on as little as 220 mg. of sodium per day. Excessive intakes of sodium are linked to hypertension and its potentially fatal consequences, heart and kidney disease and stroke.

ESA
Estimated, safe, and adequate daily dietary intakes
(National Academy of Sciences, 1980)

Of equal concern are the additives and other chemical compounds found in many processed foods. In addition to colorings, flavors, and preservatives added by food technologists (see Highlight on Food Processing), many foods also contain pesticides, antibiotics, and residues of other chemicals used in the production phase.

This has raised many new questions about the safety of our food supply and how it should be maintained. If a substance causes cancer in rats, should we assume it is dangerous for us as well? What are the health risks associated with antibiotics? Should the need to control weight be considered in a decision to ban artificial sweeteners: How should we evaluate the relative value of production cost savings versus health hazards in legislating guidelines for food production? (Knutson et al. 1983).

Ultimately, the environmental, social, and health consequences of industrialized agriculture must be viewed as an issue of conflicting goals and values. For example, "the key to food selection for a large segment of the U.S. population is convenience and fun (for a growing number it is also maintenance of good health), while the food industry's major goal is production, diversification, and profit" (Jerome et al. 1980:37).

Agrarian values such as ownership of land and family farming must be reconciled with consumers' desires for a safe, nutritious food supply at reasonable prices. And conservationists' efforts to protect the soil and water must be considered in light of economic realities that make it more profitable to use environmentally destructive tools and techniques.

Resolution of these conflicts require the involvement of farmers and consumers as well as federal and state governments. Because the issues are complex and the need for resolution urgent, emotions tend to interfere with objective analysis and policy formation. As Knutson, et al. (1983:379) conclude:

> The basic volatility of agriculture and the importance of food to the survival of humankind complicate the problems of farmers, consumers and policymakers in arriving at mutually acceptable agricultural and food policy. This initially requires an understanding of the policy options, their consequences, and their interrelationships. Secondarily, it requires a willingness on the part of those affected by agricultural and food policy to recognize each other's interests and seek compromise solutions. This is not an easy task, but it is as important to agriculture as food is to life itself.

The importance and complexity of issues surrounding industrialized agriculture is reflected in the large number of publications on this topic. Unfortunately, it is also reflected in the degree of emotional involvement with which authors approach the subject. In reviewing the literature on industrialized agriculture and other topics discussed in this text—for example, the world food crisis (Chapter 7) and hunger in the U.S. (Highlight 5-1)—it is important to evaluate carefully the validity of data and the logic of the arguments presented. Publications that present only one side of the issue require particular scrutiny. Use of emotionally laden language is another sign that caution should be exercised. Although such discussions are often more readable, they can oversimplify, mislead, and polarize—making complex issues all the more difficult to understand. Consider, for example, the claims and arguments of two selections taken from the literature when preparing this chapter.

> A loaf of bread costs $7.66.
>
> Tomatoes, three large ones, $5.24.
>
> A ten-ounce jar of instant coffee comes to $45.06.
>
> Is this merely the shopping list of a paranoid housewife trapped in a frantic nightmare? Not at all.
>
> Based on recent reports to the White House, those are some of the food prices you may be paying at the end of the century (Rodale Press, 1982).

"Is There a Food Safety Crisis?"

Then came the consumer movement—which might better be called the anti-industry movement—of the 1960s, with a ready-made opportunity to attack the food industry . . . Coincident with their attacks on industry, the activists mounted a campaign to change people's food habits. They urged us to eat less processed food, avoid food additives, and cut down on animal products. They recommended that we eat a "natural" diet with more whole-grained cereals and other unrefined foods obtained from plants.

How successful have the activists been? I have no specific figures, but new reports and observations tell me that their efforts have not been in vain. In every group, one finds people who have changed their food habits. They are cutting down on salt, or they have quit eating bacon, or they have given up beer.

Well, what can we do about the controversy over food safety? . . . The first thing is to get our priorities straight. Let's put our efforts on the *real* hazards in life and quit dissipating our energies on hypothetical and imaginary dangers . . . Not a single fatality (has been) attributed to the much-criticized food constituents, pesticides, antibiotics and spray cans.

(Foster 1983:92)

Changing subsistence technologies

Throughout this chapter we have seen the relationship between a society's technology, its social organization, and its ideology. As technology changes in an effort to adjust to environmental conditions and to gain more efficient control over energy resources, social organization and ideological traits make concomitant realignments. Modernization of subsistence modes often has had disastrous effects on society's social, economic and political life, and not surprisingly, its nutritional status as well. Weiss's study of the Miskito Indians of Nicaragua offers a good example of the dangers so commonly associated with modernization and the need to proceed cautiously when altering subsistence technologies.

The Miskito live in villages along the coast of Nicaragua where they hunt sea turtles on the offshore islands. Trade with inland groups and land and sea resources enabled the Miskito to subsist with little trouble for many years. In the 1800's and early 1900s, the Miskitos relinquished much of their self-sufficiency in exchange for wage labor. They first worked in mahogany timbering, then banana plantations, and later pine lumber companies. When these resources were depleted, the companies left the area and the Indians were forced to return to their traditional subsistence activities, "mulling over memories of dollars and canned ham, and with no ready cash" (Weiss 1980:158). Fortunately, the ecosystem continued to provide sufficient food despite the degradation caused by outside companies.

Traditionally, everyone participated in subsistence activities. Women and young children helped maintain agricultural plots, while men cleared the land for crops and hunted sea turtles. The system produced sufficient food and an adequate diet for everyone.

Kinship ties were strong and people participated in large descent groups that offered traveling Miskitos support and hospitality from relatives living in other villages. Turtles brought into the village were traditionally distributed at the time of slaughter to an array of relatives. This smoothed irregularities in the food supply and maximized use of available resources, providing even the most unsuccessful households access to the primary protein source.

In 1968, another major shift occurred in the Miskito's technology. A commercial company built its first factory to procure and process sea turtles. "Again, the Miskito were invited into the economic marketplace, and again they entered. Once a subsistence resource, gathered for food, the turtle quickly become an economic commodity, sought for sale. Once the food needs of a local population determined when turtlemen went out and how many turtles they brought back. The demand was finite and within limits that the turtle population could sustain. Now, the virtually unlimited demand of a world market defines production, and turtle populations are being decimated" (Weiss 1980:163–4).

More than the turtle population has been affected by the shift to a cash economy. As the Miskitos devote more and more time to turtle hunting, they have less time to clear brush for garden plots. Since only men are considered capable of clearing land, fewer crops are grown and the potential labor of women and children is unused; they sit home while men pursue the green turtle.

Kinship ties are weakening also. Turtle meat, which was once distributed among kin groups as part of a system of reciprocity, now has a cash value. Turtle meat is now sold rather than distributed as a gift.

Another deleterious effect of the Miskito's changed subsistence technology is the peoples' decreased nutritional status and health. Weiss conducted a nutritional survey of the Miskito after they began turtle hunting on a commercial basis. The results were discouraging. Turtle meat still contributed 30 percent of the 45 grams of protein consumed by the average adult, while another 13 percent came from fish. Sixty percent of the fat came from coconuts. But the remaining protein, fat, and 73 percent of the carbohydrates came from foods purchased at the store. The Miskito were trading turtles, a high-quality source of protein and other nutrients, for white flour, white rice, and sugar. The flour was used to make plain or sweetened buns, sugar was now consumed at every meal (for a total of 42 pounds a year for each man, woman, and child) and many people used "their last few cents to purchase a small quantity of coffee and sugar, explaining that by drinking the mixture they won't feel as hungry" (Weiss 1980:164).

Thus, commercialization of turtle hunting produced an immediate and profound change in the Miskitos' use of local resources and destabilized their adaptation to the local environment. The turtle population is becoming depleted and the Miskito's nutritional well-being undermined to provide turtle meat at reasonable prices to distant markets. Thus, the turtle and the Miskito face a similar problem: the difficulty of surviving in a drastically changed technology.

Summary

- *Technology* is defined as the tools and techniques a group has developed for obtaining food, shelter, clothing, transportation, and protection from natural predators.

- Societies get their food in a variety of ways. The five major types of subsistence systems are *foraging, pastoralism, horticulture, intensive agriculture,* and *industrialized agriculture.*

- The subsistence technology followed by all human and pre-human groups until about 10,000 years ago involves hunting and gathering wild animals and plants; this subsistence mode is called *foraging.* Today there are only about 70 groups in the world that forage for the majority of their food. In these societies there is no class system or specialized occupations: everyone is involved in getting food. The wide variety in the wild diet allow foragers generally to enjoy an adequate diet, good nutritional status, and good health.

- *Horticulture* is a nonmechanized system of cultivating plants in small garden plots that relies on human labor and simple tools such as digging sticks. Horticulture is practiced by a large number of people throughout the world today. In southeast Asia, one-third of the total land used for agriculture is cultivated with this type of technology. While there are some inequities in the possession of wealth, the gap is not large enough to create major inequalities or lead to the formation of social classes. Many horticulturists' diets rely primarily on one or two high-carbohydrate, low-protein crops. Therefore, they are more susceptible to malnutrition than foragers when crops fail. Some horticulturists supplement their diet with foraged foods and so are able to maintain adequate health.

- *Pastoralists* get the majority of their food from herds of domesticated animals. Because they move from place to place to keep their grazing animals well-fed, some degree of nomadism results for all pastoralists. Often these groups trade with neighboring agriculturalists for grain and produce. Today many pastoralists are being driven from their lands by encroaching agricultural technologies. Their heavy reliance on blood and whole milk makes their diet high in saturated fat and cholesterol, increasing their risk of coronary heart disease. Pastoralists, however, have little or no cardiovascular disease. The saving factor seems to be that their blood vessels are quite large due to extensive exercise and so they can tolerate the high fat diet.

- *Intensive agriculture* is a form of plant cultivation that requires intensive labor, and land use, and tools such as hoes, plows pulled by draft horses, and irrigation systems. When agriculturalists grow food for their own use as well as for wealthier urban dwellers, they are called *peasants*. Significant differences exist in wealth and the society is stratified into social classes. Currently most peasant societies are experiencing a shift from food crops to cash crops and a cash economy. Rather than raising most of the food they eat, peasants now grow nonedible crops that are sold for cash. The cash is then used to buy food. Often the foods purchased are less nutritious than the crops the peasants traditionally grew for their own use.

- *Industrialized agriculture* is a highly complex food production system that uses machinery and fossil fuel to replace human and animal labor, as well as chemical pesticides and fertilizers and complex irrigation systems. While this technology is highly productive, many are concerned about some of the environmental, economic, social, and health costs associated with industrialized agriculture. The abundance and variety of industrialized societies' food supplies enables most people to consume a diet with adequate calories, protein, and other essential nutrients. Such groups, however, often have health problems associated with overnutrition—the overconsumption of calories, saturated fat, cholesterol, sodium, and sugar.

Highlight 4-1 Food processing: Nutrients lost and found

All raw foods are perishable. From the time of harvest or slaughter, raw plant and animal tissues undergo progressive deterioration by various biological actions. The rate of decay may be very fast, as in fish, to relatively slow, as in winter squash. One of the primary purposes of food processing is to slow these changes so that food will be edible at a later date (Harris and von Loesecke 1975).

Food is processed for a variety of other reasons too: to improve taste, to make foods safe to eat, to increase digestibility, and to allow for convenience. For example, olives that have not been fermented are extremely bitter and hard. Manioc, or cassava, a staple food for as many as 250 million people in the world, must undergo a complex leaching process to eliminate poisonous prussic acid (Farb and Armelagos 1980). Although humans cannot digest the cellulose and raw starch in some plant foods, cooking breaks down the cellulose and makes the starch more digestible. The convenience of frozen lasagne that can be popped in the oven after a harried day at the office is appreciated by many business people.

Nutritional changes due to processing are numerous, taking place before, during, and after treatment. Some processing techniques improve the nutritional value of foods, while others detract from it. An awareness of food processing's effects on nutrient content is important because processing techniques can often "make or break" the overall quality of a group's diet.

One way in which horticulturists have overcome the limitations created by a heavy reliance on one or two staple crops has been in the use of processing techniques that maximize the availability of scarce nutrients. Corn, or maize, offers a good illustration. As we have already seen in Chapter 2, maize is deficient in the B vitamin, niacin, and the amino acid, tryptophan, that can be converted into niacin in the body. In many parts of the world, people depending on maize as a staple crop have a high prevalence of pellagra, the niacin deficiency disease. In North and South America, however, this has not been the case. The reason lies in indigenous methods used to process maize. By soaking the maize in lime water, wood ash, or any other alkali solution before grinding it, tryptophan and niacin are made more available for absorption. Corn prepared in this way (e.g., corn masa treated with lime to make tortillas) provides enough niacin and tryptophan to prevent pellagra, thus compensating for the major nutritional deficiency in the staple crop (Katz 1983).

Another example comes from the American south during pre–Civil War days. Plantation slaves traditionally soaked their corn-bread in "pot likker," the liquid left from cooking greens, thus capturing precious nutrients. Because the custom became associated with the black culture, it was rejected by their poor white neighbors. In such a marginal subsistence economy, the preservation of these nutrients proved to make an important nutritional contribution; as a result, higher incidences of pellagra were recorded for poor southern whites than for poor southern blacks (Wood 1979).

Fermentation is another food preparation technique that offers substantial nutritional benefits. Fermentation lowers the pH of foods, enhancing their resistance to bacterial and fungal action. In addition to this preservation quality, fermentation improves the thiamine, riboflavin, niacin, and B-12 content of foods.

The nutritional benefits of food processing techniques used in other cultures have not always been well-understood. For example, before the beneficial effects of lime treatment on corn were identified, some nutrition educators attempted to persuade Mexican-American children to substitute white bread for more nutritious corn tortillas. Also, condiments, fermented beverages, and other seemingly insignificant foods only recently have been recognized for the important nutritional contribution they make to the diet. *Pulque,* a native Mexican drink produced from the fermented sap of the century plant, provides as much as 4 mg. of niacin (the Recommended Daily Allowance for adults is 18 mg.) per liter, as well as other vitamins and minerals.

Not all processing techniques enhance foods' nutritional quality. Modern rice and wheat milling techniques remove thiamine, B-6, niacin, riboflavin, vitamin E, fiber, and other nutrients. Populations in areas where polished rice and refined wheat are major dietary staples are at risk of developing beriberi and other deficiency diseases (see Chapter 2).

In the Mideast, where unleavened breads provide 50 to 70 percent of the energy intake, whole-grain flour is used. While whole-grain flours contain virtually all of the grain's original nutrients, they also contain a compound called phytic acid, or phytate. Phytate, a highly reactive substance, has the capacity to bind with minerals such as calcium, zinc, and iron in the intestine, forming insoluble compounds that cannot be absorbed. High intakes of phytate may contribute to the high incidence of

rickets, osteomalacia, zinc deficiency, and iron deficiency anemia found in the region (Haas and Harrison 1977).[2] In whole grain breads that are leavened, the action of yeast chemically alters the phytate so that it cannot bind with the minerals or inhibit their absorption. For this reason, the minerals in whole grain *yeast* breads are usable by the body.

The number of highly processed foods in the U.S. virtually exploded during the middle and latter part of this century. Prior to 1940, few foods were highly processed; manufacturers used relatively simple methods such as shelling peas and canning fruits and vegetables. In contrast, the food processing industry today uses over 3000 chemicals. These additives are used as preservatives, buffers, emulsifiers, neutralizing agents, stabilizers, flavors, colors, and serve many other functions.

Food additives are the subject of great controversy, and, as with most issues, there are at least two sides to the story. On one hand, food technologists point out that American, Canadian, and other industrialized nations' food supplies have never been more attractive, nutritious, and safe. They note the consistent quality of modern food products: The can of stewed tomatoes opened in Miami, Florida, contains the same quality of food as the one purchased in Montreal. More than ever before, consumers are free from the risk of acute food poisoning from spoiled food and food borne microorganisms because of refrigeration, advanced canning and processing techniques, federal inspection programs, and the use of preservatives and other additives. "The canning industry's record of safety is exemplary in that since 1940 it has produced more

---

[2]Osteomalacia is a condition marked by softening of the bones, leading to brittleness; osteomalacia occurs chiefly in adults and results from calcium-phosphorus deficiency.

than 800 billion containers of food with only five known deaths attributable to botulism from that food. During the same period, 700 deaths resulted from ingesting home canned foods" (Chou and Harmon 1979:20). The use of preservatives is also important for food systems that transport foods across long distances and store them for long periods of time.

On the other side of the controversy stand consumer advocates who claim that many of the additives and food processing techniques that provide consumers with color, variety, and protection from food poisoning are also dangerous to their health. The use of some additives has been linked to cancer, allergic reactions, and other health problems. Studies have shown that Red Dye No. 2, a once commonly used food coloring, causes cancer, increases fetal death rates, and impairs milk production in animals. In the face of these findings, Red Dye No. 2 has been banned. Many other additives are also suspected of causing health problems.

Highly processed foods also are criticized because of their typically high sugar, fat, salt, and calorie content.

In industrialized countries, the multi-billion-dollar food processing industry devotes much of its resources to creating a demand for new products that will compete with traditional ones for food dollars.

Because it is difficult to increase the amount of food consumed per person beyond 1500 pounds, food companies in a competitive market must create consumer demand for their products. So they develop and advertise new food items that promise more than the previous products. Consumers don't actually need anything new, therefore, the industry must search for something different and create a demand for change in order to increase sales and profit (Serrin 1980). Their success in this endeavor is easily seen in the modern supermarket, which now offers between 11,000 and 39,000 different food items, considerably more than

the 1500 items found in the average grocery store only 40 years ago.

Many of these new products attempt to imitate traditional foods: artificial chocolate, imitation vanilla cookies, sausages made with artificial meat flavor, and popcorn flavored with imitation butter. Some products such as breakfast cereals offer "improved nutrition" through vitamin and mineral fortification, while others offer convenience in the form of easy-to-prepare products with cooking times that are reduced or eliminated altogether. With more women in the work force, it is easy to understand the popularity of instant mashed potatoes, bottled spaghetti sauce, and frozen pizza. But consumers' tastes for new products have far exceeded the need for extended shelf life, fortification, or convenience. As Joan Gussow wryly observes in *The Feeding Web*, one might have predicted the popularity of novelty cereals for children or Hamburger Helper, but "one might *not* have predicted—as too absurd to imagine—a product like French Toast Batter Mix in which the customer, using *her* bowl, *her* milk, *her* bread, and *her* frying pan, replaces the "inconvenience" of beating a couple of eggs into milk with the convenience of beating in the contents of a $.25 packet of "sugar, whey solids, wheat flour, whole egg solids, tapioca, starch, dextrose, hydrogenated vegetable oil, salt, baking powder, lactose and artificial color!" (Gussow 1978:202).

Consumer advocates also criticize the food industry for its contribution to rising food costs. Most processed foods exceed the cost of their less-processed counterparts by a large margin. Of the hundreds of millions of dollars spent on food each year, almost half of it goes to purchase highly processed items (Serrin 1980).

Many North Americans, dissatisfied with highly processed foods, now seek more natural or less processed foods. Sales in health food stores have skyrocketed in the last ten years as people demand such items as peanut butter made only from ground peanuts and without the salt, sugar, fat, and preservatives added to commercial brands. The food industry has responded to these changing consumer tastes by marketing such products as low sodium canned soups, "natural" potato chips with no preservatives added, and caffeine-free soft drinks.

However, just because a product has the word "natural" printed on the labels, does not mean it's the real thing. The only natural ingredient in "Natural Orange Flavor" Tang is the orange oil that is artificially extracted from oranges. The remaining ingredients are refined sugar, citric acid, maltodextrin, calcium phosphates, vitamin C, artificial flavor and color, cellulose and xanthum gums, vitamin A palmitate, BHA, and alpha tocopherol.

5

Food in a
social context

Take a moment to consider how many people you come in contact
with each day. During the course of a single day, you might interact
with roommates, friends, family, coworkers, teachers, store clerks,
and waiters. Your ability to get adequate nutrition, shelter, and other
basic human needs requires interacting with other people.

> The amount of social interaction in a modern industrial society
> would stagger the imagination of the members of simpler socie-
> ties. Never before have people had so much contact with so
> many other people. To a large extent, this is the natural result
> of increasing urbanization: communities are larger, people live
> closer together, and increased contact is inevitable. Industriali-
> zation also has an effect; the home is no longer the workplace
> except for a small minority of men; children spend half their
> days in crowded schools; and women are increasingly drawn
> outside the home by a variety of responsibilities and opportuni-
> ties.
>
> *(Lenski 1970:251)*

Social interaction is guided by cultural norms that indicate how major tasks will be carried out and who will do them. Cultural traditions that define how people interact with one another and organize themselves in order to achieve common goals are referred to as *social organization*.

Groups set up guidelines for dividing food-getting tasks, distributing food, eating together, and what people occupying different positions in society should and should not consume. In some cases, these cultural guidelines can be unifying, as when people cooperate to produce food or share a meal together. In other cases the customs are divisive, as when people are denied adequate food because of their position in society.

Of course, not everyone follows the cultural guidelines for social organization exactly. People may reject some of the ideas shared by others or try new ways of doing things. Some groups experience greater amounts of nonconformity and change than others. But everywhere a certain degree of acceptance of the groups social organization is necessary to meet the basic needs of group life.

In this chapter we will examine the many ways in which food and eating habits are tied to social organization.

Food as a means of solidifying social ties

People often use food in building and maintaining human relationships. Food brings people together, promotes common interests, and stimulates the formation of bonds with other people and societies.

Almost everywhere, a food offering is a sign of love, affection, and friendship. Withholding it may be seen as an expression of anger or hostility, or as a form of punishment. Likewise, to accept food from someone signifies the acceptance of his or her offer and the reciprocity of the feelings expressed, while refusal may be viewed by some as a rejection of their kindness or an expression of hostility. Foster and Anderson (1978:268) note that "People feel most secure when eating with friends and loved ones and in most societies, public and private meals symbolically express these feelings. Normally we do not share a meal with our enemies; on the rare occasion when we do, the mere act of dining together signifies that at least for the moment antagonisms are laid aside."

Kinship and familial alliances

Around the world, the family unit is the basic building block of society and the context within which food preparation and consumption, procreation, and the fulfillment of other basic needs take place.

Meals eaten together strengthen family relationships and promote unity. It is sometimes the only time during the day when the family has a chance to sit down and talk. Food etiquette (e.g., table manners and appreciation of the cook) are taught to children along with ways to combine foods, colors, textures, and flavors into the cuisine of the family and larger society.

The importance of food and family meal sharing is evident in the strong sentiments attached to favorite family dishes and customs. Has the smell of one of your favorite dishes ever triggered a nostalgic flood of childhood memories? Perhaps after being away for several months, you have returned home to be served one of your favorite meals and became aware of the affectionate feelings associated with family dinners.

In all societies the family has important economic functions related to food production. Carrying out these activities and distributing food within the family strengthens kinship ties. In North America, as in most industrialized societies, the nuclear family comprised of a married couple living with their children is considered the typical family unit, although, as we shall see below, an increasing number of U.S. households now have different arrangements. Whether people actually live in nuclear, single-parent, or other types of households, family members share the major food getting and food preparation tasks. Money is used to buy food for the entire family, not just for the individual members who earn it.

nuclear family
A family group that consists only of a mother, father, and children

Food is stored in the house and made accessible to all. Grocery shopping, meal preparation, and food preservation is typically done with the entire family in mind. As children become old enough to carry out kitchen duties, they, too, contribute to food production by carrying out tasks such as shelling peas, husking corn, setting the table, washing the dishes, or taking out the garbage.

Most nonindustrialized societies define the family much differently than we do in North America. Typically, the extended family is one in which grandparents, aunts, uncles, cousins, nieces, and nephews—relatives you probably consider somewhat distant—are included in the primary family unit. Because the extended family plays such a limited role in industrialized societies, we are often surprised by the importance it plays in carrying out domestic activities in other societies. For example, the Ashanti of West Africa are organized into patrilineal units or extended families formed around men (the grandfather, father, sons, and grandsons) and the men's sisters. Traditionally, Ashanti men shared meals with their mothers, sisters, nephews, and nieces rather than their wives and offspring. Their wives did the cooking, however, so that at each meal there was a steady stream of traffic as children took food prepared by their mothers to their father's sister's house.

Focus 5-1

Changing U.S. families

During most of United States history, people lived in nuclear families. Until recently, only a small proportion of households lacked a parent or included a more distant relative such as a grandparent, aunt, uncle or other relative. Few people lived alone or with nonfamily members. Today the situation is quite different. In fact, the Bureau of the Census found that the number of families headed by a man or a woman without a spouse had climbed from 22 million in 1970 to 33 million in 1980. One out of every eight youngsters and nearly half of all black children now live in single-parent households (Sheils 1983). The number of people living alone or with unrelated people also has soared, so that nonfamily households now make up about 35 percent of all U.S. homes. When all types of living arrangements are considered, only about 60 percent live in nuclear family units.

Table 5.1   The shrinking family.   With divorce rates rising, families are increasingly headed by single parents, and more Americans are living alone. One in five U.S. households now consists of only one member.

Type of household	Number in millions	Percent of total
Male head of household, wife present	47.5	57.7
Male head of household, wife absent	1.4	1.7
Female head of household, husband present	1.8	2.2
Female head of household, husband absent	2.6	3.1
Single, never married	10.0	12.2
Divorced people	8.2	10.0
Widowed people	10.8	13.1

Source: Bureau of the Census

Other changes in family patterns include the increased number of married women who are working outside the home and the larger proportion of married households in which both partners work. In 1980, the number of households in which both partners worked reached 52 percent, up from 30 percent in 1960 and 41 percent in 1970 (Community Nutrition Institute 1983).

These changes have influenced U.S. dietary habits in several ways. First, employment outside the home has reduced the time available for menu planning, shopping, cooking, and other domestic activities. This is felt most strongly in single-parent households. Not surprisingly, the percentage of food dollars spent in restaurants has climbed substantially, to 26 percent of the total food expenditure by household, along with an increase in sales of convenience foods.

Second, fewer meals are shared with family members. One survey showed that 30 percent of all meals now eaten at home are eaten alone. For many this has been accompanied by the disappearance of the traditional three-meals-a-day eating pattern, with breakfast the most likely to be abandoned (Jerome 1979). For example, many of the 150 households studied by Jerome (1972, 1975) did not follow a consistent or routine dietary practice. Explanations about dietary patterns included comments such as these: "It depends on how we feel at the time," "sometimes we do and sometimes we don't," "it depends on what else is going on," or "most times . . . depending on the . . . children . . . mother . . . husband . . . friend," etc.

Meals are rare or almost nonexistent in some extremely poor urban families. Instead of sit-down meals, someone may go to the store and purchase food (usually something that is ready-to-serve), bring it home, and place it in the kitchen where it is consumed by all, at their convenience.

A third consequence of the changing American family structure is increased dietary individualism (Jerome 1979, Kahn 1976). With more people living and eating alone, family influence on eating habits has diminished. There is less opportunity to observe parents' food choices or discuss dietary practices. The nutritional consequences of these dietary habits depends upon each family's accommodation to the increased use of convenience foods, restaurants, and the "mini-meal" snack pattern so common today. Some families, especially those with an adequate income and accurate knowledge about nutrition and health, cope well. Others do not. Increased intakes of sugar, salt, fat, and additives from highly processed convenience foods and fast food restaurant menus place them at high risk of obesity, diabetes, hypertension, heart disease, and cancer.

It is unclear where these changes in family structure and diet will eventually lead. The changes are too rapid and too new to be fully comprehended. We are still unsure how we are adapting physiologically to the dietary practices associated with new family forms; genetic responses are even more obscure. What is clear, however, is the need for new information and new models of dietary patterns. Changing family lifestyles make many traditional views of dietary practices obsolete. No longer, for instance, can we assume that the mother has a major influence on what the rest of the family eats. Moreover, as family influences decline and individualism increases, it is more difficult to generalize about regional and ethnic dietary patterns. Today, more than ever before, it is necessary to recognize variation within as well as between groups.

Families in the Trobriand Islands are organized into extended family groups organized around the women. Referred to as matrilineal groups, these families consist of a woman, her offspring, sisters, brothers, mother, and grandmother. Often the women live near each other and share common property and economic obligations. The husbands live with their wives but belong to their mother's and sister's matrilineal group. When they marry they do not become a part of their wife's group, but always remain somewhat of an outsider. Activities traditionally done by males are carried out by the women's brothers, not their husbands.

Traditionally, a Trobriand household comprised of the husband, wife, and offspring grew yams primarily for use by the husband's sister's family. In return, a large proportion of the household's yams were supplied by the wife's brother. Because yams were distributed to members of the matrilineal group rather than the nuclear unit, a household might be working to produce food for families who were not even living in the same village. At harvest time, the biggest and best yams were transferred and displayed in front of the recipient's home, where the the producer received recognition for his gardening achievements and generosity. In this way, food built solidarity between brothers and sisters, thus strengthening the matrilineal family ties.

Building relationship with neighbors and friends

When you ask someone you've just met to come over for something to drink or go out for pizza, your offer carries social implications. Asking a neighbor over for a cup of coffee, for example, can be seen as an invitation into a relationship of recurring exchanges. Taylor (1976:144), who has analyzed the American coffee break as a gift exchange, notes that "the invitation to share a cup of coffee means 'come over and begin being my neighbor.' In other words, prepare to receive and reciprocate a whole series of possible exchanges of which coffee is only the first. Others will then follow, such as the classic requests to borrow the lawnmower or a cup of sugar."

The type of food and drink shared with friends often conveys meaning about the nature of the relationship desired or already achieved. Potluck dinners and cookouts suggest a closer degree of friendship than an invitation to morning coffee. Sit-down dinners preceded by drinks are served to close friends and honored guests, while cocktails alone are offered to acquaintances as well as friends (Farb and Armelagos 1980:103).

For North Americans working in non-Westernized societies, the use of food to strengthen friendship ties can sometimes be problematic. Imagine that you are designing nutrition programs for a rural community in the Peruvian Andes. You would like to build a friendship with the local teacher, who has impressed you with her understanding of the community and her pleasant personality. When she invites you to her house for dinner, you eagerly accept. Upon arrival at her home, your enthusiasm is heightened by the warm hospitality and interesting conversation. Then suddenly you are faced with the menu: an appetizer of ceviche (marinated, raw fish and octopus) pickled pigs feet, and a whole, baked guinea pig as well as several unfamiliar vegetables. What would you do?

When faced with such a situation it is important to recognize the strong association between food and social intimacy. If you choose not to eat the food, it would be helpful to know the local conventions by which invitations and food are properly declined. And if you choose to eat the foods you might strengthen social ties with your hostess. You might also find that you like them.

Strengthening economic and political alliances

Throughout history food has been used crossculturally to build economic and political alliances between groups. Recent uses of food for economic and political purposes include the wheat agreement signed between the U.S. and U.S.S.R. during the Carter administration and Richard Nixon's use of trade to improve Chinese/American relations.

Trade

Food trade has been used in all societies as an important means of economic distribution. Trade networks have always existed among foragers, horticulturalists, and agriculturalists. Today virtually all nations are involved in trade for some desired, if not needed, foods.

One of the classic examples in which food has functioned in a trade network with significant economic and political implications was observed in the Trobriand Islands. The "kula network" linked numerous island communities extending over a 200-mile area through the exchange of two ritual items: shell necklaces and shell armbands.

The kula armbands and necklaces were exchanged as traders traveled from island to island in canoes. They moved along a circular route, passing necklaces from one trading partner to another, in a clockwise direction. The armbands were passed in a counter-clockwise direction. As they moved along the route, armbands were exchanged for necklaces. Every aspect of trading was regulated by traditional rules. Only a limited number of men participated in the kula. Once they entered into a trade partnership, they were involved for a lifetime and the article was exchanged over and over. Great prestige was given to the man who possessed the kula armbands and necklaces and keen interest followed the cherished possessions' movement through the islands. The kula expedition served another nonritual function: a vast amount of food and other utilitarian products were exchanged between the islanders as they traveled the kula route. This trade of foodstuffs, while less ceremonial, strengthened political and economic alliances among the Trobianders.

Sometimes groups with very different lifestyles and technological adaptations become interdependent in ways that strengthen ties and enhance the nutritional adequacy of the diets of both groups. For example, the Pygmies of the Ituri forest in Zaire are foragers. They hunt a large number of animals and gather many kinds of wild foods. Their neighbors, the Bantu, are agriculturalists who produce most of their own food. The Pygmies and the Bantu have developed an arrangement by which the two groups exchange foods: meat hunted by the Pygmies is exchanged for agricultural products produced by the Bantu villagers. Both groups benefit nutritionally as well as economically from this exchange.

Today, all nations are economically interdependent because of their reliance on international trade. With few exceptions (e.g., China), most nations import much of their basic foods and rely upon exported foodstuffs and manufactured goods to pay for imports and internal development. In Chapters 7 and 8, which discuss the world food situation, we look at several developing nations that are now using grains to raise livestock to be exported to the United States (primarily for use in fast-food hamburger franchises) while they import basic grains for consumption by the poor. The resulting interdependence affects the nutritional as well as economic status of the trading nations.

Food as a gift

Another form of distributing wealth and building economic alliances is gift giving. Despite the giver's contention that it is a free presentation of goods that involves no obligation, gift giving is part of a network of distribution that is often intentional. Gifts serve to solidify social ties and build economic alliances. Friendship, kinship, and other relationships are reinforced and validated by the exchange of gifts.

Food is an appropriate gift for many occasions and, as such, serves to distribute wealth and strengthen social ties. Asking the boss over for dinner has economic as well as social implications. Soft drinks, beer, and snacks are offered to friends who help with residential moves or other labor-intensive projects. Grateful patients sometimes supplement their cash payments to physicians with food from their gardens or kitchens.

One of the most dramatic examples of gift giving as a means of distributing economic wealth and strengthening social alliances is the potlatch. Practiced by the Kuwakiutl and other Indian tribes of the Northwest Coast of North America during the early part of this century, the potlatch was an elaborate feast marked by lavish distribution of presents by the host and his relatives to guests from other families. Its distinctive feature was the ostentatious presentation of the gifts, sometimes accompanied by boastful speeches given by the host, extolling his generosity.

One of the potlatch's major functions was to redistribute wealth: Members of the tribe gave the chief who hosted the potlatch food and material possessions. Although some of the food was consumed at the potlatch, large quantities of leftovers were taken home. By distributing the extra food to other villages it offered a kind of neighborly protection against localized food production failures. When a village was threatened by food shortages, its members could attend potlatches and bring back supplies from hosts who were indebted to them from attending potlatches previously held by their own villages. Economic alliances were also enhanced because people often moved from villages that could not produce enough food and goods to hold their own potlatches to more productive villages. Thus potlatches served as a way of advertising the productivity of the village and recruiting labor from surrounding areas. As the Kuwakiutl have become involved in a cash economy the nature of potlatches has changed.

Political alliances

Closely associated with the economic function of food is its ability to enhance political alliances. Elaborate state dinners for visiting dignitaries are a common occurrence in North America as well as in many other societies. As Leininger (1970:163) points out, "food is a powerful force to solidify precarious or tenuous relationships with different political groups. Serving food before, during and after political meetings often dispels the 'heat' and interpersonal tension found in arriving at major political decisions." A similar use of food to build political support was Ronald Reagan's visit to a factory cafeteria, where he joined workers for their noonday meal—a symbolical gesture of unity.

The U.S. and Canadian governments also use food aid to build political ties. Unfortunately, as we shall see in Chapter 8, this type of "food diplomacy" often fails because recipient countries resent being asked to support U.S. views or activities in order to qualify for food shipments. The reverse situation, prohibition of food shipments, is also used for political purposes with equally erratic success. Consider, for example, the ineffectiveness of President Carter's embargo on wheat shipments to the U.S.S.R. as retaliation for its invasion of Afghanistan.

A final way in which food serves to cement political bonds is the association of alternative dietary styles with certain political ideologies. In the 1960s, the publication of Rachel Carson's *Silent Spring* brought new concern over environmental pollution caused by industrialized agriculture and food processing technologies. The civil rights movement and subsequent efforts to expand rights to other minorities (women, the elderly, gays, youth) led to widespread "self assertion with its accompanying activism, individualism, and expansion of consciousness" (Jerome 1979:196). New political ideologies emerged and the traditional American diet in general (and meat in particular) became a focus of protest, especially by the young. "The social environment and mood of the '60's and and early '70's likened the foods of the society to the polluted physical environment, to the American involvement in the conflict in Vietnam, and to most to the

Figure 5.1
Food and politics. These women's views on food and politics are worn for all to see.
(Lindenberger)

other societal problems" (Jerome 1981:41). Vegetarianism addressed many of these issues: the environmental threats of big business and big technology, capitalist greed, world food shortages, and a food supply contaminated with additives and pesticides.

Alternative dietary styles such as macrobiotics and the raw foods diet serve as an important expression of some groups' political and spiritual ideologies. Among members of the International Society for Krishna Consciousness, for example, food preparation and meals are important unifying activities, conducted with great care and devotion. All food is offered to God (Krishna) who gives it a sacred or transcendental quality. Once the food is blessed it becomes *prasadam* (a form of Lord Krishna) and must be handled in a proscribed way that protects its cleanliness and special spiritual status. When Krishna devotees distribute *prasadam* to passerbys in parks or invite nonmembers to share Sunday meal in their temple, they are offering far more than just tasty, nutritious food to their guests. They believe that *prasadam* brings a very special blessing to all creatures that consume it: the guarantee of a human body in the next life (reincarnation). *Prasadam,* then, is not only food, but a purifying substance as well as a vehicle for spreading Vedic ideology (International Society for Krishna Consciousness 1983).

macrobiotic diet
A diet that consists predominately of whole grains and vegetables, said by its practitioners to increase spiritual enlightment

Food and social status

Social status denotes the place an individual holds with reference to other members of society: child or parent, husband or wife, boss or employee. Status is one's position in the group's social organization. This definition of status as a position in society is somewhat different than the more common use of the term as a synonym for prestige. Social status does not necessarily imply superiority or rank, but is a set of rights and duties associated with the person occupying a certain position in a culture. Social status is based on gender and age in almost all societies.

Food and gender

In most cultures, food is linked to gender in several ways. Activities associated with food production are often divided by sex. As we have already seen in foraging societies, women gather vegetables and fruits while men hunt. Among horticulturalists, women plant, weed, and do most of the harvesting, while men clear the land and fence it in. Currently, in some societies, the women's movement is causing people to rethink job assignments based on gender, and as a result, some women are taking on such tasks as operating tractors while some men are taking responsibility as household cooks.

While women and men (particularly in the United States) are slowly beginning to cross over and take on some tasks formerly associated with the opposite sex, women in most societies still have the primary, if not sole, responsibility for cooking. Even women in industrialized societies who work outside the home rarely get much help in the kitchen from their husbands. A survey (Szalai 1973) encompassing the U.S., U.S.S.R., Yugoslavia, Belgium, Bulgaria, East and West Germany, Hungary, Peru, and Poland looked at data on the division of domestic activities in over 50,000 households. Nowhere were domestic activities divided equally between the sexes. "Husbands helped with household care and peripheral activities such as maintenance and repair to a degree that almost equaled wives' hours spent in cooking and primary housework. But the two sexes still rarely crossed over to help in each other's domain. . . . [Moreover] employed men after their contributions to the household still had 50 percent more leisure than the employed women" (Geile 1979:38).

Second, food is often distributed unequally between men and women. In many societies men eat first, children eat next, and women consume the leftovers. This practice is reflected in the low rates of malnutrition found in men in relation to women and children. (See Chapters 7 and 8 for a more detailed discussion of the malnutrition that affects women and children in developing countries.) Among some groups with limited food supplies, this practice may have developed because the men did strenuous physical labor in order to provide for the family and so they required extra calories.

Figure 5.2
Male/female differences in access to food. The Indian babies in this picture are two-year old twins, both raised at home; the one on the left, a girl, the one on the right a boy. The difference in their condition is due to the fact that the boy was nursed and fed first, his sister getting what was left over.
(UNICEF)

Sex discrimination in North America often takes a more subtle, but nevertheless widespread, form. For instance, in some families foods served at a meal are based predominately on the father's preferences. He may also be served first and given special privileges such as getting the best cut of meat or having the first chance at second helpings.

A third way food is tied to sex status concerns the types of foods considered appropriate for men and women. *Ms.* magazine recently printed an interesting letter about North American expectations in this regard. A woman wrote in reporting that whenever she went out to eat with a man and he ordered a salad and she ordered steak and potatoes, the waiter inevitably reversed their orders, giving him the steak and potatoes ("male food") and her the salad ("female food"). The book, *Real Men Don't Eat Quiche,* published in 1982, describes in detail which foods "real men" should and should not eat.

Finally, food restrictions are sometimes different for men and women, with most food taboos throughout history pertaining only to females. "In aboriginal Hawaii and other Pacific islands, women were forbidden the flesh of pigs and chickens as well as certain other foods; and the Tallensi of Ghana forbid the flesh of chickens and dogs to women though not to men." (Simoons 1961:110.) As women gain rights, such food restrictions have become less common.

Food and the life cycle

In every society, people pass through a life cycle marked by birth, puberty, marriage and/or reproduction, and death. Rituals typically mark a person's passage from one age status to another.

> Why are birth, puberty, marriage and death so frequently the occasions for rites of passage? Probably because of their public implications: the individual who is born, who reaches adulthood, who has a spouse or who dies is not the only person implicated in these events. Many other people must adjust to these momentous changes. Being born not only defines a new life but it also brings into existence or modifies the position of parent, grandparent, sibling, heir, age-mate, and many other domestic and political relationships. The function of rites of passage is to give communal recognition to the entire complex of new or altered relationships and not merely to the changes experienced by the individuals who ostensibly are the center of attention.
>
> *(Harris 1972:537)*

In the section below, we look at the special dietary practices associated with major phases in the life cycle: Infancy and childhood, adolescence, reproduction, old age, and death.

Infancy and childhood

North Americans view infancy and childhood as a period requiring special nutritional concern. Children's diets are selected to provide sufficient quantities of protein, calories, and other essential nutrients needed to support growth. Foods are also chosen based on their digestibility by the still-developing digestive tracts of infants and children. Because infants and children are considered too young to tolerate some items, they are not given the entire repertoire of adult foods. Parents are usually advised to withhold solid foods until four to six months of age, potentially allergenic egg white and orange juice after a year, and coffee and alcohol until adulthood or late adolescence. Childhood is also viewed as an important time for establishing future food habits that will sustain good health. Children are encouraged to "clean your plate," "take three bites of everything," and "eat your vegetables."

Some conceptions relating to children's dietary practices have significant health consequences. One example comes from peasant villagers in West Bengal, Bangladesh, studied by Derrick B. Jelliffe in 1957. There, infant food restrictions are ritually regulated. A special rice-feeding ceremony, the *mukhe bhat,* is held to make the child's transition from the critical first half year of life (when most infant mortality occurs) to late infancy. The ceremony is quite elaborate and requires the presence of all extended family members to give the child their blessings and presents. Up until the ceremony, foods that are considered unhealthful to infants (called *shokori* food), are restricted. The child may not be given rice, fish, eggs, meat, or a variety of other foods that are considered dangerous. In most families the *mukhe bhat* is carried out when the males are six months old and the females are seven months old. (This is similar to Western nutritionists' advice not to introduce solids until a baby is four to six months old.) However, if the family cannot afford the cost of the ceremony, the child is sick, or all relatives are not present, the ceremony is delayed. Unfortunately, this delay is accompanied by continued restriction of protein-rich foods and so increases the risk of protein/calorie malnutrition (Jelliffe 1957). (See Chapter 8 for a discussion of protein/calorie malnutrition.)

Other beliefs that interfere with adequate infant and child nutrition in peasant villages throughout much of the world is based on the classification of foods into "hot" and "cold" categories. (See Chapter 6 for a more detailed discussion of hot-cold classification systems.) Foods considered "hot" by West Bangladesh peasants include eggs, meat, milk, honey, sugar, and cod liver oil. Because these nutritious foods are considered hot, they are restricted when children have diseases also classified as hot (e.g., fever and diarrhea) as well as during hot weather (a good portion of the year). Similar practices are reported for Latin America and many other regions (Sanjur 1982). In poor children whose nutritional status is already marginal, these cultural practices can contribute to the onset of malnutrition, serious illness, and sometimes death.

Examples of beliefs that affect infant nutrition among North Americans involve the introduction of new foods. Though nutritionists advise against giving solid foods to children until after four to six months or substituting cow's milk for breast milk or infant formula until after a year, many parents reject these suggestions. Some view the consumption of solid foods and cow's milk as a sign that the baby is healthy and maturing faster than other children. As a result of eating solid foods and cow's milk when they are too young, some children may become overweight or develop food allergies.

The teen years

About the time of puberty, the rights and responsibilities of children begin to change. In much of the world adolescence is a brief period with a clearly defined and ceremonially observed end. Among the Shoshone Indians, as in many traditional societies, females' readiness for adulthood was announced by menarche. At the time of her first menstrual cycle, the Shoshone girl was isolated in a special hut where she was prohibited from eating meat. At the end of the isolation, her mother brought her new clothes—women's clothes—to mark her new status as an adult. Traditional male "initiation ceremonies sometimes involve circumcision and the revelation of hitherto secret knowledge; almost always they entail a change in diet and the relaxation of previous taboos . . ." (Farb and Armelagos 1980:83).

In contemporary North America the situation is quite different. Adolescence is a long, and, for some, difficult period, during which rights and responsibilities are ambiguously defined. The end of adolescence is not ceremonially defined. Depending upon state law, the eighteenth or twenty-first birthday marks the legal passage into adult status. Some bars recognize the transition and offer a free alcoholic drink to customers celebrating this occasion; however, in general, changes in age status and the accompanying role expectations are not socially marked. At what age, for example, did you become an adult? Thirteen? Eighteen? Twenty-one? Not yet?

Due to the rapid growth and sexual maturation that occurs during the teen years, nutrient needs may be greater than at any other time of life. A rapidly growing active boy of 15 may need 4000 calories or more just to maintain weight. Along with increased calorie needs, Recommended Dietary Allowances (RDA) for protein, the B vitamins, vitamin A, E, C, calcium, phosphorus, iodine, magnesium,

Recommended Dietary Allowance
The "levels of intake of essential nutrients considered . . . to be adequate to meet the nutritional needs of practically all healthy people." Derived by a group of nutritional scientists who advise the Food and Nutrition Board, a committee of the National Academy of Sciences—National Research Council.

and zinc also increase for teenagers. Teenagers of both sexes need more iron: teenage boys have an additional requirement for building up large quantities of red blood cells and teenage girls need more iron because of the onset of menstruation.

As teenagers become more independent, they assume greater control over what they eat. Parents and teachers no longer make dietary decisions for teens whose mobility allows them to eat when they want, where they want, and what they want. In some households, people in this age group are responsible for shopping and preparing foods for themselves and their families.

Research shows that of the 30.5 million American teenagers, 73 percent shop for food "quite a bit" or "occasionally" and in 1982 spent $44 billion on food. A survey of 1,000 teenage girls revealed that on the average, they made 4.1 meals for the family per week, *helped* prepare 4.8 family meals, and made 8.6 meals for themselves (Blakkan 1983).

In an attempt to express their individuality, teenagers sometimes deliberately try new things that are different from their parents' ways of life. In some cases, unconventional dietary habits such as vegetarianism offer adolescents a way to identify or distinguish themselves. Typically, however, behaviors that are different from the larger society are in strict conformance with the teen's own subculture. Teenagers are generally sensitive to peer pressure and often conform to norms shared by other members of their subgroup.

In North America, the fast-paced, independent lifestyle of teenagers affects their dietary habits significantly. Skipped breakfasts, increased snacking on empty calories, irregular meals, and frequent dining at fast-food restaurants are characteristic.

empty calories
A term used to denote calories from foods that contain no nutrients such as vitamins, minerals, or amino acids

An increased concern with physical attractiveness and body image are seen in the relatively high incidence of fad dieting, anorexia nervosa, bulimia, and the use of hormones to increase muscle mass.

Given the special nutritional and social circumstances of adolescence, it is not surprising that the diets of many North American teens fall below the RDA for some nutrients. Deficiencies in calcium, iron, vitamins A, C, and B complex are not uncommon. Due to the increased consumption of empty calorie snack foods and processed meals, the diet of some teens is also high in fat, cholesterol, sodium, and sugar, while it lacks fiber. The diets of some teenagers also contain large amounts of fast foods. As a result, they ingest too much fat, calories, and sodium, which can lead to health problems. Of course, not all teenagers eat poorly. Some people become particularly interested in nutrition during this time in their lives and eat quite well.

Table 5.2 Fat, calorie, and sodium content of some fast foods			
	Fat (gm)	**Calories**	**Sodium (mg)**
Burger King			
Whopper with cheese	45	740	1435
French fries, regular	11	210	230
Onion rings, regular	16	270	450
Wendy's			
Hamburger, double	40	670	980
Chili	8	230	1065
French fries	16	330	112
Dairy Queen			
Cheeseburger, double	37	650	980
Hot dog	16	280	830
Hot dog with chili	20	320	985
Fish sandwich without cheese	17	400	875
McDonald's			
Hamburger	10	255	520
Big Mac	33	563	1010
Filet-O-Fish	25	432	718
Arby's			
Regular roast beef	15	350	880
Chicken breast sandwich	28	584	1323
French fries	12	216	39
Potato cakes	9	190	476
Kentucky Fried Chicken			
2 piece original dinner	35	640	1480
2 piece crispy dinner	44	765	1480
Pizza Hut			
Serving Size: 2 slices of medium (13″) pizza			
Thin 'N Crispy			
Standard cheese	11	340	900
Pepperoni	15	370	1000
Supreme	17	400	1200
Supreme with extra cheese	26	520	1500

˙Source: Lynn Denney.

But because poor eating habits are so widespread among adolescents, they have been the target of many nutrition education programs. Unfortunately, many of these programs have failed. According to nutrition authors Eva May Hamilton and Eleanor Whitney (1982:481):

> If a teaching approach is to be effective it must not teach content alone. Students in a nutrition class can get A's on test after test, without undertaking any improvement in their own eating habits. Habit change occurs only when we choose to change it; we choose only when we want to change, and we want to change only when we feel the need. The way to begin to teach teenagers is to abandon all methods of pushing ideas at them, or forcing information into their heads and try to facilitate learning. Real learning takes place when the connection is made between what students feel is important—between what they want to know and the information being offered to them.

Reproduction

Reproduction is another phase in the life cycle that is associated with special dietary habits. Most societies recognize that eating habits of pregnant women affect the development of their babies; many prescribe special foods or avoidance of certain foods for the prenatal period. In the United States, women are advised by health care providers to increase their calories, protein, calcium, phosphorus, magnesium, folacin, and other vitamins and minerals to meet the increased nutrient needs of pregnancy and ensure a birth weight greater than five and one-half pounds. Milk is presented by many nutrition educators as a superfood necessary to obtain the Recommended Daily Allowances for calcium, while alcohol and coffee are to be avoided.

Of course, not all women comply with this advice. Conflicting beliefs, poverty, lack of prenatal care, or lack of exposure to nutrition advice, as well as a host of other circumstances, interfere with the observance of these dietary recommendations. In general, however, the pregnant woman is considered to be eating for two, weight gain is desired, and her cravings for pickles, ice cream, or other foods are accepted.

In contrast to North Americans who increase their food intake to produce large babies, women in some societies restrict weight gain and fetal size in hopes of minimizing the dangers of childbirth. This is especially important in populations that experience stunted growth and development due to nutritional inadequacy. The short stature and small pelvis of many poor women makes the birth of large babies extremely dangerous. This was recently pointed out by Wang (1983) at a conference on providing medical care to ethnic patients in the U.S. Wang, a pediatrician, treats many recent immigrants from Southwest Asia. The stresses of war, and escapes through forest trails or in small boats has compromised many refugees' nutritional status.

Figure 5.3
Food cravings during pregnancy. In most societies, pregnancy is a time women adopt special dietary habits.
(Lindenberger)

Once in this country pregnant women whose height is only 4'9" or 4'10" will enroll in the WIC supplemental food program (see Highlight 5–1 at the end of this chapter) and will be given a relatively abundant and nutritious diet. As a result many mothers are now giving birth to 8½ pound or 9 pound babies. Delivery of such a large baby is difficult for these women and often requires cesarean birth.

Many societies observe food taboos during pregnancy. "Even before becoming pregnant, the Mbum Kpan women of Chad in equatorial Africa are exhorted to eat no chicken or goat to escape pain in childbirth or the birth of abnormal children; after becoming pregnant, they avoid still other foods, such as the meat from antelopes with twisted horns, which might cause them to bear deformed offspring" (Farb and Armelagos 1980:73). Many food taboos are imposed to avoid "marking," or birthmarks. The Tanola woman must not touch black-eyed beans lest her child be born with black spots (Wood 197:132). Some North Americans still avoid looking too long at strawberries because they believe it can produce a similarly shaped birthmark on the fetus.

Cesarean birth
Also called cesarean section or c-section. Surgical incision of the abdomen and uterus for the delivery of a baby. So named because of the belief that Julius Caesar was born this way.

Focus 5-2

Pica

You've heard that some pregnant women crave pickles, ice cream and strawberries; but did you know that others crave and eat clay, laundry starch, and ice as well? The consumption of nonfood items is called *pica,* the Latin word for magpie—a bird known for carrying off and eating unusual things. Though clay, laundry starch, and ice are among the most frequently craved items, the desire for chalk, burned matches, and inner tube tires has also been reported.[1]

Geophagia, or clay eating, has been recorded throughout history, and, while found worldwide, it is most common in tropical areas.[2] In the U.S., geophagia is thought to be most prevalent among black pregnant women in the rural South. This may reflect a sampling bias, however, because many other groups have not been surveyed. Geophagia has been reported among whites, Mexican Americans, and Native Americans as well.

For most people who eat clay, not just any clay will do. In Ghana, for example, certain sites are held in high regard for the quality of their edible clay. The clay is formed into egg shapes and marketed throughout East Africa. In the U.S., clay from Georgia is considered to be especially good by some. The clay is sent to farmer's markets, where it is sold in shoe boxes (Farb and Armelagos 1980). Some eat clay plain while others add salt and vinegar and bake it to impart a smoked flavor. Others, unable to obtain good clay, have used laundry starch as a substitute. Despite its resemblance to clay (the texture is similar), laundry starch has none of the minerals found in clay.

Why do people practice pica? A review of the literature provides a wide variety of conflicting information on the subject. The five major hypotheses are:

1. *Pica is the body's response to the need to obtain certain nutrients.* Samples of clay eaten by people in West Africa have been analyzed for its mineral content. The calcium,

---

[1]Pica received media attention in the 1960s when some children living in poor urban areas were found to be eating peeling paint and plaster. When the paint is lead-based, this can produce lead poisoning. For this reason, the use of lead-based house paint has been outlawed.

[2]*Geo* · earth; *phagia* · eating

magnesium, potassium, iron, copper, and zinc levels have been shown to compare favorably with the mineral supplements given to pregnant women in modern societies (Farb and Armelagos 1980). Some speculate that the craving for clay is due to mineral deficiencies or increased mineral needs.

2. *Pica is a response to hunger.* Pica is prevalent among people with limited food available to them. Clay is free and filling. A one-pound box of laundry starch provides 1800 calories, making it an inexpensive source of energy, though it supplies no other vital nutrients (Bauwers 1978).

3. *Pica is a cultural phenomenon passed from generation to generation.* The stimulus for eating clay may be associated with women's early roles as gardeners and potters, which placed them in a position where consumption of clay was normal. Identity with the female community passed the tradition along (Lackey 1983).

4. *Pica is a response to physiological changes.* For example, dry substances such as clay and laundry starch absorb the excessive amounts of saliva produced during pregnancy. Some who practice pica say that eating clay or starch reduced nausea during pregnancy just as soda crackers do.

5. *Pica is a way of seeking attention.* Pregnant women who ask friends and family to help them secure hard-to-get items are expressing their need for support, love, and understanding. Along these lines, clay is taken as a gift to new mothers while they are recovering from childbirth.

Nutritional consequences of pica

Iron deficiency anemia is commonly associated with pica. Whether pica is the *cause* or the *result* of anemia is unclear, however. Some studies suggest that pica is stimulated by dietary deficiencies and can be corrected by iron replacement therapy. Others suggest that iron deficiency occurs as a result of eating nonfood items. Ingestion of clay may decrease iron levels by binding dietary iron, making it unavailable for absorption. Though laundry starch does not bind iron, if it is eaten in large quantities it replaces nutritious foods and leads to the development of nutrient deficiencies. Some people have reported eating up to two pounds of laundry starch per day (a total of 3600 calories), which leaves little room in the diet for nutrient-rich foods.

It seems that most who practice pica do so on a limited basis. For this reason, serious complications of pica are uncommon. However, in some unusual cases where pica has been practiced in its extreme form, it has led to bowel impaction, potassium depletion, and even death (Keys, et. al 1983).

Because of potential complications, it is helpful for health care providers to know if unusual items make up a large part of a woman's diet. But many women who practice pica are embarrassed about it and not likely to tell health workers. Interviewers have found that if they mention that they have talked to others who eat nonfood items, the respondents are more likely to share their practices. A question a nutritionist might ask is "I've talked to some pregnant women who say they crave things like clay, and laundry starch, and ice. Do you ever crave or eat them?"

Most likely, these taboos arise from a lack of information about physiological principles and a need to find causal explanations. Unfortunately, food observances often place an additional burden on an already anxious woman. And when the childbirth is unsuccessful, blame may be directed at her for violating these norms, adding an ill-deserved burden of guilt to the woman's sorrow and pain (Wood 1979).

Although some societies do not recognize the need for special dietary practices during pregnancy, with rare exception they observe postpartum food restrictions and proscriptions. For example, in Chinese culture, new mothers are sometimes given pig's stomach soup to improve the quality of their breast milk. One of the most common practices is to seclude the new mother and child together for a specified period of time, typically 20 to 40 days. Rest and confinement also includes the consumption of "strengthening" or "protecting foods" and the prohibition of foods believed to be harmful. Many traditional Latin American and Hispanic Carribean peoples observe a highly structured set of ritual obligations for 40 days after childbirth. The norms and rituals associated with this period, called *la cuarentena,* are described by Eric Wolf (1956:210) in an ethnographic study of a Puerto Rican coffee plantation.

> When labor sets in, the future mother retreats to the seclusion of a shuttered and unlit room, where ideally she must remain for a period of forty days *(la cuarentena)*. This custom has a double function. On the one hand, it exempts the woman from work and sexual intercourse for the period of her seclusion and puts her in to a role similar to that of an honored guest. She is fed chicken broth, prepared from the meat and fat of a bird usually reserved for festive occasions of hospitality. On the other

hand, her enforced idleness enables neighbors to extend their services to the family. A *compadre* or a relative will offer to help her prepare the precious broth, and a girl will come in to clean the house and help with the children. In turn, the secluded mother is expected to reciprocate these services on a similar occasion.

Many Cuban and Puerto Rican women in Miami, particularly those raised in the Caribbean, remember *la cuarentena*. And despite admonishments from grandmothers who claim they will "go crazy" if they wash their hair or go outside during the 40-day postpartum period, few abide by the proscriptions (Bryant 1978).

Currently the La Leche League (LLL) (see Chapter 3 margin glossary) uses a system somewhat similar to *la cuarentena*. In some chapters a project called "Meals for Mothers" is coordinated. LLL members take turns bringing nutritious meals to the new mother and her family, usually for a period of two to three weeks. In Chinese culture, new mothers are also sent gifts of food, including such items as wheat-flour noodles, chicken, and eggs.

Many postpartum dietary and other practices are helpful to the woman recovering from childbirth. Rest and seclusion allow her to establish a lactation schedule with the newborn. The assumption of cooking and other household tasks by family members and friends allows the new mother to eat well, focus on her child's needs, and adjust to new sleeping schedules.

Some postpartum food taboos, however, do not have a positive impact on the mother's health and nutritional status. The Mayla fishing village studied by Christine Wilson (1973) is representative of some communities. In that group rules prohibit many nutritious foods—fruits, vegetables, and fish—needed by postpartum and lactating women. Eggs, meat, and other high-protein foods are often restricted, lowering intakes of essential nutrients. Fortunately, however, balancing practices exist in many places to help offset the potentially negative nutritional implications. Some Mexicans, for example, restrict pork, beef, red beans, milk, cheese, and eggs, as well as all types of fruits and vegetables. However, families go to great lengths during the *cuarertena* to provide new mothers with chicken, black bean broth, soups, boiled milk, toasted torillas, and other nourishing foods (Sanjur et al. 1970, DeWalt 1983).

Old age

In some cultures, elders are highly esteemed for their wisdom and extensive life experience. Among foraging groups, band leaders are chosen from the oldest men in the group. Older women are also respected. In Chinese culture the best foods are often reserved for the elders.

Old age is not highly esteemed in all cultures, however. Access to food and other privileges vary considerably from place to place. Honigmann (1959) observes that elders tend to be held in highest esteem where they control inheritable wealth or where they are believed to exert control over the living after death (as ancestral spirits).

Elderly members of industrialized societies are often stereotyped as sickly, poor, and lonely, receiving little respect and assistance from younger people. As we shall see in the section below, although many elderly people face biological, economic, and social problems that affect their nutritional well-being, it is important to keep in mind that they are as diversified a group as any other age segment of our society. About one-third live at or below the poverty level, while others have enough money to support themselves moderately, and a few live quite luxuriously. Many senior citizens continue to work in part-time or full-time jobs. Some enjoy wealth and fame after retirement, while others have retired to a welcomed lifestyle free to pursue hobbies, travel, or other favorite pastimes. Only a small portion of the elderly fit the stereotype of the person forced to leave work and unable to find enjoyment (Whitney and Hamilton 1981).

Aging brings many biological changes that place the elderly at nutritional risk. The metabolism slows, decreasing calorie needs. Older people often produce less saliva, digestive acids, and enzymes than younger people. This may make some foods difficult to eat and digest. Dairy products may cause discomfort if eaten in large amounts because of the reduced activity of lactase, the intestinal enzyme that breaks down lactose. The gastrointestinal tract's motility (its involuntary folding and unfolding to move food along) is often decreased, allowing food to remain in one place much longer, producing harder stools and constipation (Rozovski 1983, Whitney and Hamilton 1981). Taste sensations also may diminish with age, so that some elderly people increase their use of salt, sugar, and other seasonings. This often causes problems for those with hypertension, diabetes, and/or obesity.

Older North Americans' dietary habits are influenced by a complex set of social, cultural, and economic factors that make it difficult for some to meet their nutritional needs. One factor is food acceptability. As some people become older, they may appear to become more rigid with respect to the foods they find acceptable. This is sometimes seen in nursing homes and other institutional food service settings. But, as with any age group, older people are often most comfortable eating familiar foods. And particularly when lifestyle changes dramatically, as when a person moves into a nursing home, eating familiar foods can make the transition easier.

As a result, the acceptance of institution meals (and the resulting nutritional status of residents) depends to a great degree on how closely menus correspond to residents' customary diets. In a study of nursing homes in Denver (Harrill et al. 1976), nutrient consumption was most adequate in a Jewish intermediate care facility that served Kosher foods similar to those that residents had eaten all of their lives. Studies of elderly persons living independently also show poorer nutrient intakes for those who recently have had to alter their diets (Learner and Kivett 1981, Clark and Wakefield 1975).

Again, however, it is important to stress that the elderly are a diverse group. While some may focus on an increasingly narrow array of valued foods, others may find that they now have the time to experiment and try new foods.

In addition to lifelong dietary patterns, many elderly people's diets are influenced by notions about what is considered appropriate for old people. Some foods are eliminated because they are perceived as "too strong" or "too hard" for the elderly, other foods are eaten in greater quantities because they have attributes considered desirable for older people. Prunes and foods high in roughage may be eaten to prevent constipation. Coffee and red meat are deemed by some as inappropriate in large quantities. As with other age groups, many food beliefs reflect an awareness of physiological changes and special nutritional needs.

Food availability comprises another set of factors that influences elderly people's ability to meet their nutritional needs. For the percentage who live below the poverty line, a major problem affecting food availability is economic in nature. When chronic illness requires special foods, many senior citizens living on fixed incomes find it hard to purchase products such as the often more expensive low-sodium foods they need. And because most are shopping for only one or two people, they usually purchase the smallest food package, giving them the highest unit cost.

Loss of mobility and lack of transportation also creates problems for some elderly people. With the flight of large chain stores from the central city to the suburbs, older people living in high-rise buildings or apartment complexes located in downtown areas are increasingly disadvantaged. Only small markets with a limited variety of generally quite expensive items are located in their immediate vicinity.

Finally, for the 5 percent of people over 65 who live in nursing homes or other institutions, food availability depends almost solely upon the institution's food service. Studies show a tremendous range in the dietary adequacy and variety of foods served in nursing homes. Even when menus are designed that offer residents 100 percent of the RDA for all essential nutrients, many residents do not consume them (Sempos, et al. 1982, Henricksen and Cate 1971, Clark and Wakefield 1975).

A third major influence on elderly nutritional status is the social environment in which the older person lives. For many, old age is a time of loneliness. Friends and loved ones may die and offspring may move away. Decreased mobility may limit their contacts with other people. Loneliness, of course, does not affect all older North Americans. For some, increased leisure time gives more opportunity to visit with family and friends. But for the six million people who live alone, and for many others, loneliness often contributes to malnutrition.

Because eating is as much a social activity as a biological activity, some people lose interest in eating when they are alone every day. Grocery shopping, storage, cooking, and clean-up may appear too demanding when cooking for just one. These tasks appear particularly meaningless to the older adult who is depressed or grieving for loved ones. Men who have relied on their wives for meal preparation as well as mealtime companionship may have more difficulty in dealing with widowhood. Some overcome these problems by sharing meals with friends and neighbors.

The impact of these biological, social, and cultural factors is seen in the relatively high incidence of dietary inadequacies and deficiency diseases found among the elderly. Nutrients found to be lacking most frequently are iron, calcium, vitamin D, vitamin C, folic acid and other B vitamins, vitamin A, zinc, and potassium. Nutrient deficiencies often are due to nutritional stresses of chronic illness as well as poor dietary practices. Iron deficiency anemia, for exam-

Figure 5.4
Nutrition for the elderly. This woman eats a nutritious lunch at a day care center for senior citizens.
(Lindenberger)

ple, is linked to blood losses associated with hernias, diverticular disease, and frequent aspirin use; potassium deficiency may result from renal disease or diarrhea; low folican levels may be due to the use of anticonvulsant and other drugs (Bryant, Johnson, and Van Willigen 1981; Kart et al. 1978; Thompson 1980).

Over the last century, the elderly population has grown dramatically in North America. Today, over 20 million people over the age of 65 live in the U.S. (Rozovski 1983). With its increasing size and longevity, this population has enjoyed heightened respect and attention from politicians and program designers. A variety of assistance programs such as Social Security, Supplemental Security Income, and the Nutrition Program for the Elderly (See Highlight 5-1) have been developed to benefit elderly Americans; funds for research institutes and special grants have been allocated to study the problems of aging in our society. With improved medical care and housing for older Americans, lifespan and population size is expected to continue to increase. Hopefully, the quality of those additional years will improve as well.

Death

The last transition of the life cycle is death. With rare exceptions, societies mark this event ceremonially.

> Death is an occasion when the routine of life is broken not simply for the deceased, but also for many other people. Kinship ties must now be reshaped, inheritances distributed, and new roles assumed by the survivors. Recognition by the community of this upheaval has its effect on the one activity common to everyone: the preparation and distribution of food. The disruption of community life is often symbolized by basic changes made in the customs of eating—fasting, temporarily extinguishing the hearths, placing new taboos upon foods, and special offerings of food to the gods.
>
> In many of the Polynesian and Melanesian islands, symbolic distinctions are made at a funeral between prepared and raw foods. The environment of these people provides many raw foods—such as coconuts, fruits, and edible roots—that can be easily obtained (except, of course, during times of drought or hurricane). Prepared foods, on the other hand, demand human intervention, and are symbolic of the social and domestic life that has been disrupted by death. On the island of Tikopia, the mourners are given prepared foods, such as puddings, which they associate with the continuity of life. At the burial itself, raw food from the dead man's garden is placed on the grave, symbolizing the product of his labors.
>
> *(Farb and Armelagos 1980:93)*

As in other phases of the life cycle, some dietary practices associated with death have important nutritional implications. The Tsembaga of New Guinea mark the passage of a warrior with a ritual pig slaughter. Several pigs are sacrificed and the pork is consumed only by close relatives. Though the Tsembaga perform these rites primarily for ideological reasons, (see Chapter 6) the consumption of a high-protien food such as pork during times of stress makes good nutritional sense as well in this essentially vegetarian population. Moving closer to home, in the U.S., friends and neighbors take food to families who are mourning the death of a relative. This custom provides relief from cooking and shopping when family members are preoccupied with making funeral arrangements and grieving.

Food and social class

All industrialized and most advanced agrarian societies are organized into classes. At the very least they are divided into two classes: the rulers and the ruled. More typically the society is made up of three or more distinctive strata. Definitions of the concept of class vary among social scientists. For many, a group may be considered a class only when its members have a consciousness of their identity as a class, exhibit a shared sense of solidarity, and act in an organized way to promote their collective interest. Other social scientists consider differential concentrations of power to be the essential feature of class structure. When major differences exist in access to basic resources—control over land, tools and techniques of production, energy, and supplies—classes are said to exist, whether the people agree or not (Harris 1980).

Because the class structure reflects different concentrations of wealth, social class has a powerful impact on diet and nutritional well-being. The chance for an adequate diet diminishes as the amount spent for food decreases. Below a certain point it is no longer possible to purchase the foods needed for an adequate diet. The use of poverty indexes or a poverty line to identify families at nutritional risk is based on government's recognition of the relationship between income levels and nutritional well-being.

Notions of a "poverty line" date back to the turn of the century. In the late 1800s, nutrition surveys revealed higher rates of malnutrition in working-class families than among those who were more affluent. One in-depth study conducted in Great Britan concluded that regardless of how wisely some poor families managed their budgets, they simply did not have enough income to purchase an adequate diet. The researchers calculated an income level, known as the poverty line, below which malnutrition eventually would result no matter how wisely or economically the family shopped. Supporting evidence came from studies that showed that the infant mortality rate for families below this line was 247 out of 1000 births, compared to only 173 per 1000 in families above the line. Further confirmation of the relationship between poverty and nutritional status came from two follow-up studies in the same country.

The U.S. government also uses a poverty line to evaluate the extent of poverty and identify people in need of federal assistance. In calculating the poverty index, the threshold income is adjusted for size and composition of family as well as current food costs.

The USDA developed "food plans" in the mid 1930s as a way of determining the cost of providing a family with adequate nutrition. These plans have been updated periodically and are now set at four cost levels: thrifty, low-cost, moderate-cost, and liberal. The USDA defines the cost of the thrifty food plan as the level at which a family can meet dietary requirements and uses it as the basis for coupon allotment in the Food Stamp Program.

Critics of the Thrifty Food Plan claim that it is unrealistic in today's economy. They argue that not even the most knowledgeable family with extensive resources could achieve adequate nutrition at that price and recommend a more liberal Food Stamp allowance.

The concept of a poverty line, when defined correctly, is helpful in dispelling the widespread myth that poor people "wouldn't be in such a bad fix if they'd just use good sense in how they spend their money." As Gifft, et al. explain:

> Such a simplistic charge fails to take into account the whole gamut of conditions of existence that characterize poor populations. The overriding influence on their lives is the lack of sufficient money to provide the barest necessities for decent living. To be poor means trying to keep expenditure down to an inadequate income, a situation that allows little or no flexibility. The poor consumer not only lacks money with which to make discretionary purchases, but his freedom of choice is also curtailed in matters relating to the time, place, amount, quality, and method of paying for his purchases. Because of all these limitations, the poor may frequently have to pay more than the affluent for the necessities of life. Though better management might alleviate some of the worst aspects of a poverty-ridden life, the best consumer practices cannot solve the problems of poverty; the hopelessness and resignation that tend to accompany the condition are detrimental to such efforts. It is difficult to disagree with those who declare that the principal need of the poor is money.
>
> *(Gifft et al. 1972:200–1)*

Poverty indexes are also useful in determining who should receive governmental assistance. Because poor nutrition contributes to numerous medical problems (low-birth-weight babies, anemia and failure to thrive in children, increased susceptibility to disease in all ages, and many other acute and chronic diseases), "investment of public funds for adequately feeding the nation's poor may in fact be less expensive in the long run than future high-cost medical care" (Presidential Commission on World Hunger 1980:156). (For a discussion of U.S. federal food and nutrition programs see Highlight 5-1.)

The nutritional status of poor Americans has improved dramatically over the last decade, largely because of federal feeding programs (Presidential Commission on World Hunger 1980:154). Yet, widespread unemployment and inflation have increased the number of people in need of assistance at the very time that federal and state budgetary cutbacks have limited the number that can be served. A 1 percent rise in unemployment, for example, adds 750,000 new recipients to the Food Stamp Program, a program that has been cut $6 billion since 1982.

This situation has been further complicated by the lack of nutrition information on the poor. How many Americans really need help? Where are they located? And what type(s) of assistance would be most effective? The government sponsored the first comprehensive nutrition survey, the Ten State Survey, focusing on the nation's poorest districts, in the late 1960s. Data on the poor also is available from the Health and Nutrition Examination Survey (HANES) and USDA's Nationwide Food Consumption Survey used to develop

Figure 5.5
Poverty in the U.S. became a public issue in the Sixties.
(USDA/1965)

the family food plans. The Canadian nutritional surveillance research, Nutrition Canada, also contains cross-sectional data. Analysts, believe, however, that this is not enough. They recommend that we have a truly comprehensive nutrition surveillance of the U.S. population on a continuing basis that would enable policymakers to identify the location, prevalence, and magnitude of marginal as well as acute nutritional inadequacies (Presidential Commission on World Hunger 1980:155).

Better nutrition surveillance and more effective feeding programs, while clearly important, represent only half the battle. Neither can provide jobs, reduce poverty, or otherwise eliminate the inequities in resource distribution—all required for a permanent solution (Presidential Commission on World Hunger 1980).

Food as a class marker

Because poor people have less access to expensive items and often must eat mostly low-cost foods, certain foods become associated with the rich and the poor. As abundance and prices change, so do the foods seen as "class markers." Today, lobsters are associated with affluence in the U.S., but in the seventeenth century, the situation was reversed. At that time, lobsters were in such abundance that they were considered "fit only for the poor, who could afford nothing better." When a group of new colonists arrived in Plymouth in 1633, Governor William Bradford was deeply humiliated because his colony was so short of food that the only dish they could present their friends was lobster ". . . without bread or anything else but a cup of fair water" (Root and de Rochemont 1976:51). Similarly, chicken was once reserved for guests on Sundays and special occasions. In the U.S. Calvin Coolidge's promise of a "chicken in every pot" represented affluence to his listeners. Today with highly efficient production methods, chicken prices have dropped and so has its status. Now, chicken is often featured in cookbooks and magazines as a money-saving meal.

Although the class differences affecting food practices may not be formalized as food taboos or actual restrictions, when class lines are crossed, people often take note. Imagine, for example, how a dignitary would react to being served beans and franks at a White House dinner or how some people would respond if they saw a person buying filet mignon with food stamps.

Castes When people are assigned to social strata based on characteristics acquired at birth (parents' social status or color) and there is little opportunity to achieve a different social ranking, we say that the society is organized into *castes.*

The most well-known caste system is that of the Hindus in India; a system that has become more flexible in recent years. In 1949, the government of independent India declared itself unequivocally opposed to the social barriers of caste and pronounced the system illegal. While this has weakened the system somewhat, many still recognize and adhere to it. Food is one area that is still strongly affected by the rules of the Hindu caste system. Despite laws prohibiting caste discrimination, many people from the upper castes still refuse to drink from glasses used by members of the lower castes. For this reason, railroads and other public places now use throw away styrofoam cups to serve their customers.

Maintenance of caste rankings is based in part on the use of food; conversely, a family's caste determines in part what foods are ritually available to it. In India, members of higher castes do not accept food prepared by members of lower castes. If a member of the Brahmans, one of the higher castes, visits the household of a lower-caste person, a Brahman woman is called in to cook for him. Only certain types of food may be given to a Brahman. Food cooked in water can only be given to a Brahman by another Brahman. Food cooked in ghee (clarified butter) may be accepted from members of other "clean castes." In many parts of India, the lower castes—"the untouchables"—such as leatherworkers and sweepers eat meat, including beef, when an animal dies. However, people in higher castes do not have access to meat, and many are completely vegetarian. Avoiding animal foods is thought to bring one closer to the ideal of nonviolence. Brahmans, in most places the highest caste, do not till the soil lest they inadvertently harm insects and other animals, thus breaking the rule of nonviolence.

Eating certain foods is a method of improving the status of one's caste. Although individuals are identified with the same caste for life (unless they commit an act that causes them to become "outcastes"), the status of the caste itself can rise or fall. Oscar Lewis (1958) studied the caste system of Rampur, a village 15 miles west of Delhi. There, most of the people are vegetarian. Until recently, the Camar caste, made up of leatherworkers and tanners, were an exception because they ate the cattle they skinned for leather. In midcentury, however, many Camars stopped eating meat in order to raise their caste's status.

The 12 castes in Rampur are intertwined with one another through a system of mutual obligations. The castes lower on the hierarchy owe labor and services to the Jats, one of the higher castes, who in turn provide them with goods, usually food. This system of mutual obligation is called the Jajmani system.

The following table, excerpted from the rules of service in Rampur, outlines the services that several castes are expected to render to the Jats and the rights earned through that service. Payment for services is frequently in the form of food.

Table 5.3 Rules of Service, Rampur		
Caste	Type of Service	Rights Earned Through Service
Khati (carpenter)	To repair agricultural tools.	One "mound" of grain per year along with "ori" right (2½ sirs of grain twice a year at each sowing season).
Lohar (blacksmith)	As above.	As above.
Kumhar (potter)	To supply earthenware vessels and to render services of light nature at weddings.	Grain to the value of the vessels. Additional grain at the son's or daughter's marriage, according to status and capacity.
Hajjam or Nai (barber)	To shave and cut hair; to attend to guests on their arrival and to render other services of light nature at weddings.	At each harvest as much grain as the man can lift by himself. Additional grain at the son's or daughter's marriage, according to status and capacity.
Khakrul or Bhangi (sweeper)	To prepare cow-dung cakes; to gather sweepings, to remove dead mules and donkeys; to collect cots for extraordinary needs, and to render services at weddings.	Meals and "radri" twice a day; at each harvest as much grain as the man can lift by himself and also at the son's or daughter's marriage, according to status and capacity.
Camar (leatherworker)	If a man assists in agriculture and gives all kinds of light services	he gets one-twentieth of the produce.
	If he does begar (compulsory labor), renders ordinary service, and removes dead cattle	he gets one-fourth of the produce and the skins of dead cattle.

Food as a symbol of prestige

Prestige refers to the social worth attributed to various social positions and their occupants. The use or display of expensive foods is used in many societies to communicate a person's social importance.

Among the Trobriand Islanders of the South Pacific, prestige is gained from displays of large yams in the family's yard. Yams are stacked in public view so the community can voice its praise of their quantity and quality. Among Latin American peasants, prestige is acquired from sponsoring a celebration of the village saint's birthday that includes the presentation of a ritual meal. Some peasants are known to use all their wealth—even go into debt—in order to benefit from the prestige associated with such sponsorship. North Americans are also concerned with prestige. Serving caviar and champagne at a party is a sign of high social class standing.

John Bennet, an anthropologist, has described how food functioned as a symbol of prestige in rural American society during the 1930s and 1940s. In the rural southern Illinois community he studied, many foods were classified and used according to their prestige value. Storebought foods, for example, were symbolic of the economic ability to purchase food; fresh fruit, candy, hamburgers, and oysters were prestigious because of their association with urban elites; foods used at picnics, church suppers, and holidays also held high prestige. In contrast, muskrats, yellow cornbread, wild game, and greens had low prestige value because of their use by poor blacks.

To some members of this rural community, food was more important as a prestige symbol than as a nutrient. Sharecroppers tried to pattern their diet to that of the more wealthy tenants and the riverside residents used food as a method of raising their social standing in the local rank order. But neither group had the resources to make the full diet modifications to move upward socially.

Unfortunately, the increased use of prestigious foods is often one of the first dietary changes to occur as a nation industrializes and/or becomes more affluent. In areas of Africa where sorghum and millet are traditionally grown, expensive wheat is now imported to meet the urban elite's demand for white bread. Red wine has replaced sour milk as the traditional offering at funerals in Senegal and in Chad, and sacrifices are now made to guardian spirits with red wine and lumps of sugar.

Often when people choose foods on the basis of prestige value, their nutritional health suffers. White flour, packaged bread, white rice, sugar, canned foods, baby formula, and soft drinks have high prestige value in many developing countries, yet are less nutritious than the natural, less-refined foods they replace. Such substitutions can have tragic effects. We have already seen how the replacement of brown rice with polished white rice led to an outbreak of the vitamin B_1 deficiency disease, beriberi, causing the debilitation and death of thousands of people in nineteenth-century Asia. (See Chapter 2 for more details.)

Food and ethnicity

An ethnic group is a group of people who share a similar cultural and regional origin, hold common norms and beliefs, and form part of a larger population, interacting with people from other segments of society. Frederick Barth, a well-known anthropologist, uses the following criteria to define an ethnic group:

- Its members share fundamental cultural values and norms that differ from other groups making up the larger population or nation.

- Its members communicate and interact together, reaffirming their ethnic identity.

- It is recognized by its members and others as a group distinguishable from other groups (Barth 1969).

Often many members of an ethnic group settle in the same section of a community, making the group highly visible. The _ction of the community they inhabit may be referred to in ethnic terms such as San Francisco's Chinatown or Miami's Little Havana. Ethnic members living in such places are likely to share many common cultural characteristics, including food habits, interact primarily with members of their ethnic group, and often marry someone from the same ethnic background. Members who do not live in ethnic enclaves are more likely to adopt cultural characteristics of the larger society—dress, language, etc.—marry outside the group, and eventually lose their ethnic distinctiveness.

To reaffirm ethnic identity, members frequently use traditional customs, including food habits, that set their group apart from others. These activities are referred to as *boundary maintenance* because they help to distinguish and clarify boundaries between cultural groups. Cubans living in Miami, for example, celebrate the Christmas holidays with a traditional family dinner on Christmas Eve and Three Kings parade at Epiphany. Besides the obvious emotional benefits that come with renewed ethnic pride, these boundary maintenance activities also build group solidarity. Use of traditional foods as a boundary marker is common in many groups: Italian pasta and spaghetti sauce, Polish sausage, Jewish matzah, German bratwurst and English tea and crumpets are easily recognized by ethnic members and outsiders alike.

All ethnic groups are exposed to the cultural traits and lifestyle of the larger society. Ethnic food habits, like other aspects of culture, change as a result of this contact. Unavailability of traditional foods, food processing techniques, work and leisure cycles, the entrance of women into the labor force, the effects of mass media, and meals shared with people outside the ethnic group all stimulate change.

To gain a clearer understanding of how ethnic food habits change, Judith Goode and her associates conducted an in-depth study of Italian-American food patterns in the Northeastern U.S. They found it valuable to categorize the traditional food practices in the following way.

- *the food item*—for example, pasta, tomatoes or sausage

- *the recipe*—which incorporates guidelines for combining food items and includes characteristics such as typical flavor combinations (garlic and oregano), modes of cooking (simmering, baking), and type of food (special cuts of meat)

Figure 5.6
A walk-up cafe in Miami's Little Havana.
(Lindenberger)

- *the meal format*—or the order in which courses are served to make a meal (for example, some foods are served together, others are served separately; antipasto is served before the main dish)

- *the meal cycle*—which refers to the patterning of different meal formats through time (for example, weekday meals, weekend meals, holiday meals)

Goode's findings revealed that changes in the traditional Italian-American diet had occurred at all levels: food items, recipes, meal formats, and meal cycles. One of the most significant changes was the addition of new meal formats such as "shortcut meals," which include hot sandwiches, and meals eaten at fast food restaurants and diners. Food items and recipes also had changed considerably. The meal cycle, however, proved more persistent. Even as food items and recipes changed, there continued to be great uniformity in the cycle of meals. Consistent with the traditional pattern, weekday meals were either a one-pot dish or platter. The week's end was marked by a fish or "fasting" meal on Friday evening, and a somewhat elaborate meal with several courses was served on Sunday evenings.

This study suggests that ethnic food habits cannot be simplistically categorized as resistant to change nor can they be said to be disappearing. Some aspects of the dietary pattern, such as specific food items, are replaced or elaborated, while other aspects such as meal cycle persist.

Another important finding was the lack of uniform Italian-American food pattern in the Northeast. As in all ethnic groups, a great deal of variation exists within the group. One cannot assume that the food preferences and meal patterns of one Italian-American is like that of his Italian-American neighbor. As in all communities, ethnic food practices are a mix of traditional and nontraditional influences. (See Highlight 5–2 "Hold the Grits: Regional and Ethnic Food Practices".)

Summary

- Social organization refers to the cultural traditions that people develop about how to interact with one another and organize themselves in order to achieve common goals. Food and eating habits are tied to social organization in many ways.

- People often use food in building and maintaining human relationships. Families, neighbors and friends often cooperate to produce, prepare, and share food. Throughout history, food has been used to build economic and political alliances between groups.

- American families have changed dramatically in the last 20 years. There are significantly more single-parent households, more women are working outside the home, and more people are living alone or with unrelated household members. These changes have influenced U.S. dietary habits in the following ways:

  - Increased sales of convenience foods and restaurant meals

  - Decreased the incidence of the typical three-meal-a-day eating pattern

  - Increased dietary individualism; people's eating habits are less likely to be like those of other household members.

- Societies link food to gender and age. Food production is often divided by sex and, in some groups, food restrictions differ for men and women. Food prescriptions are also associated with the major phases in the life cycle: infancy and childhood, adolescence, reproduction, old age, and death.

- Because the class structure reflects different concentrations of wealth, social class has a powerful impact on diet and nutritional well-being.

- People in the same ethnic groups are likely to share some common food habits based on the traditional cuisine of the group. It is important to remember, however, that a great deal of variation exists within ethnic groups and that food practices often are a blend of both traditional and nontraditional influences.

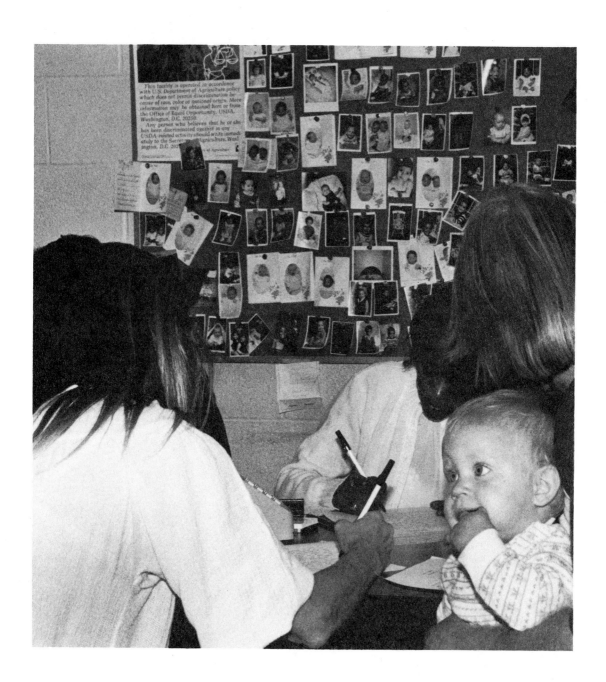

Highlight 5-1   U.S. federal food programs

Karen Miller is 28 years old and the mother of two. Her husband, Rob, also 28, has worked at a local tool and die factory for eight years. Recently the factory closed, and for the first time in 12 years, Rob Miller was without a job. After seven months of looking for work, he found a job at a local gas station. It pays one-third what his factory job paid. Karen and Rob were faced with another first: difficulties in being able to feed their children and themselves. After much discussion, they decided to apply for food stamps. Karen describes her experience:

My first visit to the food stamp office took three hours. There was a long wait and the interview took a long time. The whole thing was so new to me . . . I just didn't know the system. My worker asked me lots of questions about income and expenses. I didn't realize I needed verification—things like pay stubs and utility bills—so the interview could not be completed. I went home and gathered up receipts and took them back to the food stamp office the next day. We received a letter three weeks later saying we qualified for the program. Now every time I go grocery shopping, I just hope I don't run into anyone I know—there's such a stigma attached to food stamps. Maybe it's just my imagination, but it seems like people look into my basket at the checkout stand to see what I'm buying. Last week I bought some ice cream as a treat for the girls—it's been so long since they had anything special. You know, I almost felt guilty for buying it; like I didn't deserve it or something . . . Anyway, we're eating much better since we've gotten the stamps but I'll be glad when Rob or I can find a job that pays decent wages so we can get off the darned things.

The Millers are among the 22 million people in the U.S. who receive food stamps. The food stamps program and other federal food programs are the subject of much controversy. Some argue that federal food aid is a rip-off: draining hard-working, overtaxed citizens to support people who choose not to work. Others state that the programs are just a "band-aid" keeping us from addressing the basic causes of poverty and hunger. Still others claim that food assistance programs have significantly decreased hunger and malnutrition in the United States and should be expanded. To better understand this controversy let's take a closer look at U.S. federal food programs—their history, administration and impact.

The history of federal food programs

Before the Great Depression, there was little history of government aid for either farmers or hungry people. Herbert Hoover refused to distribute surplus wheat to the poor in 1931 but expressed the hope " . . . that the hungry and unemployed will be cared for by our sense of voluntary organization and community service" (Kotz 1970). But by 1934 the economic situation had become even more desperate and the government began distributing surplus flour, cornmeal, dried milk, rice, butter, and cheese to millions.

The first actual food stamp program began in 1939. It was a complicated system, difficult to understand and even more difficult to use. In addition, it offered only limited benefits for farmers (whose surplus products were guaranteed a market) and for the poor (whose diets were regulated more by availability of certain foods than by their needs and desires). The program was abandoned in 1943 when World War II created an increased demand for agricultural products. In 1961, the current food stamp program began under the Kennedy administration, initially as a pilot program. Recognition of the need for an ongoing program came in the late 1960s, as a response to several studies undertaken to assess the extent of hunger and malnutrition in America. The findings were sobering. A team of physicians sponsored by the Field Foundation reported widespread hunger and malnutrition in the rural south; the Citizen's Advisory Board cited case studies of people going hungry even though they received food stamps and the Ten State Nutrition Survey found nutrient deficiency among poor Americans. These studies received widespread media coverage, including the TV documentary, *Hunger, USA,* which showed clips of hungry American children with swollen bellies and apathetic stares. Americans were shocked to find such conditions right in their own well-fed, diet-conscious back yard. The mood in the country shifted dramatically from unawareness to urgency.

As a result of this nationwide consciousness-raising, Congress enacted a series of food program reforms. The Food Stamp and School Lunch Programs were expanded. The Supplemental Food Program for Women, Infants, and Children (WIC) was established along with the Title VII feeding program for the elderly. Between 1969 and 1979, the U.S. spent nearly $50 billion on these domestic food assistance programs.

Just how much has this expansion in government food aid contributed to improved nutrition among the poor? To answer this

question, in 1977 the Field Foundation sent the physicians who had visited the rural south a decade earlier back to retrace their steps. They reported to Congress:

Our first and overwhelming impression is that there are far fewer grossly malnourished people than there were ten years ago. Anemia was reduced; vitamin A levels were up. Growth patterns were better. This change does not appear to be due to an overall improvement in living standards . . . . In fact, life for Americans living in poverty remains as dark or darker than it was ten years ago. But in the area of food there is a difference. The Food Stamp Program, the nutritional component of Head Start, the School Lunch and Breakfast Programs . . . and WIC have made the difference.

Despite the results of this and many other studies showing that food programs have significantly decreased malnutrition in America, the conservative political climate of the late 1970s and early 1980s led to much concern over the high cost of the programs. And over a three-year period, $8 billion was cut from the food assistance programs.

The food stamp program

A common misconception about food stamp recipients is that they suffer such ignorance about buying and eating nutritious foods that no amount of food aid could improve their diets. Perhaps you have heard people make complaints such as this one: "I stood in the checkout line behind a woman who used food stamps and her basket was full of steaks and junk food." While this may be the case with some food stamp recipients, it is also true of some people who do not receive food stamps. Moreover, studies such as the one described below show that this is not the norm.

Donald West (1978), an agricultural economist, compared the food spending practices of middle-income food buyers with food stamp recipients. His studies have shown that both groups spent 36 percent of their food dollars on meat, poultry, and fish and 13 percent for dairy products. But the similarities ended there. The more affluent buyers spent their meat dollars on beef and veal, while the food stamp buyers spent more on pork and poultry. The middle-income buyers spend more on bakery goods, while the food stamp buyers spent more on flour. The middle-income shoppers purchased more ice cream and yogurt, while the food stamp users spent more on milk and eggs. More snacks and sweets were purchased by middle-income buyers, while the food stamp buyers spent slightly more on soft drinks.

In sum, the family on food stamps divides its food dollar in the same general way as the middle-income family, but economizes by buying less expensive foods. The families eligible for food stamps who elected not to receive them also were studied, and were found to allocate their food budget in much the same way as the food stamp shoppers, but out of necessity purchased less.

Another criticism made about the Food Stamp Program concerns the way in which it is administered. After talking with food stamp office staffers and recipients in Appalachia, Dr. Raymond Wheeler concluded that "there is an adversary relationship rather than service relationship with the poor. Encounters with food stamp officials are confusing, perplexing, demeaning and intimidating."

In an attempt to remedy some of the problems, the Food Stamp Act of 1977 was passed. It entitled recipients to new benefits and also required administrators to deliver those benefits in a manner that better met and respected the need of the recipients. Although this legislation certainly did not eliminate all problems, it greatly improved the program and allowed recourse if

recipients felt they were treated unfairly. Again, conservative policies of the early 1980s have weakened these gains by redefining eligibility criteria, removing many thousands of low-income people from the program, and reducing benefits for those continuing on it.

School breakfast and lunch program

Established in 1946, the National School Lunch Program enables private and public schools to provide nutritious lunches at a reasonable cost. All lunches are subsidized, but economically disadvantaged children are eligible for further price reductions or free lunches if the family income is low enough.

Most schools prepare lunches on-site in their own cafeteria, while others rely on centralized kitchens. In all cases, however, menu composition is based on federal guidelines. These nutritional standards are designed to ensure that the school lunch provides a child with at least one-third of his or her daily needs for certain nutrients as defined by the RDAs.

In 1966, the Child Nutrition Act established the National School Breakfast Program to complement the lunch program. It has not achieved the support nor exposure of the lunch program, but its aims are similar. When combined, the school breakfast and lunch are designed to provide the child with two-thirds of his or her daily nutritional requirements as defined by the RDA.

Recent research indicates that the school lunch and breakfast programs are effectively filling important nutritional needs. For example, data suggest that children with inadequate or no breakfast have more difficulty paying attention in class compared to their schoolmates and a marked improvement is reported in the nutritional status of children who participate in the breakfast program.

The benefits of an adequate free lunch program for poor children were demonstrated dramatically in a Baltimore program in which children were studied over a 14-year period. After introduction of the free lunch program the children scored impressive nutritional gains.

These programs are not without their critics, however. Many oppose the breakfast program on the grounds that providing breakfast is a parental responsibility. There is also much reluctance among school boards and administrators to take on another responsibility. Additionally, while few would claim that poor children are better off without the program than with it, some nutritionists have criticized the quality of school meals. Many programs serve lunches that do not provide the required one-third of the RDA for as many as 8 of the 13 essential nutrients, and most lunches and breakfasts are high in sugar, fat, and salt. Also, large amounts of food are often thrown away because the children don't like it. Food becomes nutrition only when it is consumed. A few schools have responded to these problems with creativity and imagination, setting up salad and fruit bars, featuring ethnic foods, and involving students and parents in menu planning.*

Despite the controversy, the school feeding programs remain the most widespread, best-funded child nutrition programs in the country. In 1977, 90,660 schools provided lunches to 26 million children, and 2.8 million of these also partici-

*When parents concerned about good nutrition band together, they can have an impact on the quality of the school food programs. The basic steps for organizing a parent group are outlined in *Eating Better at School,* a book published by the Children's Foundation and Center for Science in the Public Interest. This publication is available from CSPI, P.O. Box 3099, Washington, D.C. 20010.

pated in the breakfast program; a significant percentage in each program received reduced-price or free meals. Total program costs that year were $428 million.

Finally, many opponents of school feeding programs are critical of the way in which reduced-price and free meals are given to children. Although regulations are designed to guard against it, meal cards and other means of payment sometimes fail to conceal the difference between students paying full price and those getting discounts. The stigma associated with reduced-price and free meals acts as a strong deterrent to their acceptability. One woman whose husband left her with four children willingly accepted food stamps and financial aid for families with dependent children. But when told that her children qualified for free school breakfasts and lunches, she refused flatly: "I promised my children we would never come to *that;* you see all the kids at school can tell who gets free lunches, and even though we really can't afford it now, I made a deal with the kids that I'd never put them through that embarrassment."

The Women's, Infants and Children's supplemental food program (WIC)

The WIC program, started in 1970, represents a unique effort to combine preventative health care, nutrition supplementation, and education. In the WIC program pregnant women, infants, and children up to age five are provided nutritional assessments, vouchers for nutritious foods (such as milk, cheese, fruit juices, dried beans, eggs, cereal and iron-fortified formula), and nutrition education. Recipients must be both economically disadvantaged and at nutritional risk, based on measurements of height, weight, hemoglobin or hematocrit, dietary intake, and a history of nutrition-related disease.

The WIC program is directed at a critically important problem because of the link between a mother's diet and the birth weight of her infant, and the correlation between low birth weight, infant mortality, birth defects, and mental retardation. WIC's effectiveness in reducing infant mortality, low birth weight, and complications of pregnancy has been demonstrated by numerous studies. For example, a study conducted by the Harvard University School of Public Health, compared 627 WIC mothers with 329 non-WIC mothers and found that the predicted incidence of low birth weight was only 3.4 percent for WIC participants as contrasted with 14.6 percent for those not receiving WIC services.

The study also compared the total cost of providing WIC services and food with the cost of hospital treatment for low-birth-weight infants. In their sample, the Harvard researchers found a cost/benefit ratio of 3.1 to 1, indicating that for every taxpayer dollar spent on WIC services, $3.10 is saved in hospital costs for low birth weight infants that would have been born had WIC not been available. This does not include costs of maintaining physically and/or mentally impaired individuals on a long-term basis.

Title III nutrition program for the elderly

The Title III nutrition program, started in 1972 as the Title VII Program, is based on research suggesting that many people living alone are apt to have poor nutrition. If their nutritional status could be improved, they might avoid expensive medical problems and continue living independently in communities of their own choice rather than in institutions. Typically, the program is open to all people over 59 years old and

their spouses, regardless of income. Lunches are served at a central location such as a church or school; contributions are accepted from participants able to pay, and transportation is provided for those who need it.

Although every effort is made to encourage people to come to the group meal sites, volunteers deliver meals to elderly people who are homebound either permanently or temporarily. A study done in rural Kentucky (Bryant, fieldnotes, 1981) showed that the program made an important social as well as nutritional contribution to older people; bingo, card games, crafts, and a variety of other activities are featured before and after meals. One Title III participant said, "This gets me up and out of the house and gives me something to look forward to. Before I started coming to these meals I would go three and four days at a time sometimes without seeing another person."

Commodity food distribution

As mentioned earlier, surplus foods were distributed directly to hungry people in 1934. In 1982, the U.S. Department of Agriculture opened its warehouses again, this time to distribute surplus cheese and other products that had been stored as a part of the farm price support programs. While some recipients of commodity foods found the extra food to be helpful in feeding their families, others have criticized the program as offering little compensation to the thousands who have recently been cut from more helpful food programs.

The community's response to hunger

With the rise of unemployment, coupled with cuts in federal food programs in the early 1980s, thousands of U.S. citizens were forced into a new and rapidly growing segment of the population—the new poor.

Antihunger advocacy groups and others (e.g., the United States Conference of Mayors) documented a new wave of hunger in America, as increasingly large numbers of "street people" sought food at the Salvation Army and other soup kitchens.

Throughout much of the nation, local communities have responded by expanding existing food banks, soup kitchens, and other relief services, as well as forming new ones. One particularly effective program is *Second Harvest,* a national clearinghouse for surplus foods that serves over 60 regional food banks. (A food bank is a repository for surplus food that is distributed to charitable agencies or directly to the poor.)

Second Harvest solicits food from manufacturers and distributes it by truck to network food banks. By 1982 more than 100 companies had donated 30 million pounds of food to Second Harvest, an important step toward reclaiming the estimated 135 million tons of food that is wasted every year, at least 27 million tons of which is lost in the wholesale component of the food chain because it is outdated, imperfect or mismarked but still safe and nutritious food. From the regional food bank this surplus and salvage food is sent to local banks where volunteers further distribute food to on-site feeding programs and in food baskets to individuals and families in crisis.

Beyond federal food programs

Despite evidence that federal food programs improve nutritional status and health, these programs may not offer the best solution to the problem of hunger in America. Federal food programs were never intended to reduce poverty significantly nor to generate jobs. Rather, they attempt to improve the nutritional status of individual participants and serve as a support system for those unable to work: the elderly, the disabled, dependent children, and their mothers.

If we are to reverse the cycle of poverty and hunger that plagues millions of Americans today, we will have to implement a more equitable system for distributing resources and provide all citizens with an opportunity to earn sufficient income to purchase a nutritionally adequate diet.

Highlight 5-2* Hold the grits!: Regional and ethnic food practices

A woman from Atlanta was hospitalized in New York for minor surgery. Because she knew she was on a special, postoperative diet she tried her best to eat what was sent to her. Every day, sometimes twice a day, she got a bowl of what appeared to be Cream of Wheat. Though she disliked Cream of Wheat, she tried to choke it down. Not until days later, in conversation with the dietitian, did she realize that she had not been sent Cream of Wheat, but *grits,* and not because of any therapeutic benefit, but because she was from Georgia and therefore "naturally a grits-lover." She was somewhat amused but liked grits no better than she liked Cream of Wheat.

We tell the story to make a point. It is a common mistake to assume that because people are from a certain area or ethnic group they eat a particular way: "Blacks like corn bread, New Englanders love scrod, and Italians live on pasta." While we want to be aware of regional and ethnic food practices, we should avoid stereotyping and recognize the wide variation that exist within all groups. Food practices are the product of traditional and nontraditional influences: the families in which the mother and father were raised; contact with coworkers, schoolmates, and friends; restaurant menus; and mass media. Today fast and cheap transportation of foods has made regional and ethnic food differences less distinct. Items such as seafood are now available in the midwest, and warm-weather citrus crops are trucked north year around.

Because of the variation found within each ethnic group, health care providers need to be careful not to assume that all ethnic clients consume a traditional cuisine. While many Puerto Ricans still classify foods as "hot" and "cold", others consider this practice old-fashioned and would be offended if a health worker assumed that they held such "backward" beliefs.

For this reason, when working in a multiethnic setting, it is important to treat each person individually. Likewise, because each community varies, it is helpful to become knowledgeable about the specific group you serve. One way to familiarize yourself with the major features in ethnic or regional diets is to review the literature that has been published on members of that group, again remembering that much of what is practiced elsewhere may not pertain to your particular community. For those working with members of the major ethnic groups in the U.S. we have listed references that may help in preparing to work more effectively with them. Many of the references here are taken from Diva Sanjur's (1982) excellent bibliography on ethnic food practices.

---

*This highlight was written with the help of Karen Thompson.

Mexican Americans

Acosta, P. B. and R. Aranda
1972 Cultural Determinants of Food Habits in Children of Mexican Descent in California. *In* Practices of Low-Income Families in Feeding Infants and Small Children. HEW publication (HSA) 75–5605, Washington, D.C.: Government Printing Office, issued 1972; reprinted 1975.

Bowden, S.
1968 Nutritional Beliefs on Food Practices of Mexican-American Mothers. Thesis, Department of Economics, Fresno State College.

Bradfield, R. B. and T. Brun
1970 Nutritional Status of Califonia Mexican-Americans. American Journal of Clinical Nutrition 23:798.

Bruhn, C. M. and R. M. Pangborn
1971 Food Habits of Migrant Farm Workers in California. Journal of the American Dietetic Association 59:347.

Burma, John H., ed.
1970 Mexican-Americans in the United States. Cambridge, MA. Schenkman.

Burroughs, A. L. and R. L. Huenemann
1970 Iron Deficiency in Rural Infants and Children. Journal of the American Dietetic Association 57:122.

Cardenas, Jose, et al.
1976 Nutritional Beliefs and Practices in Primigravid Mexican-American Women. Journal of the American Dietetic Association 69:262

Clark, M.
1959 Health in the Mexican-American Culture: A Community Study. Berkeley, CA: University of California Press.

Czajkowski, J. M.
1964 Mexican Foods and Traditions. Storrs, CN: Connecticut Agricultural Extension Service.

Division de Nutricion del Instituto Nacional de la Nutricion
1969 Habitos de Alimentacion en una Region Fronteriza. Salud Publica de Mexico (No. 11)

Knight, Mary Ann, et al.
1969 Nutritional Influence of Mexican American Foods in Arizona. Journal of the American Dietetic Association 55:557–61

Lantz, E. M. and P. Wood
1958 Nutrition of New Mexican, Spanish-American, and Anglo Adolescents. I. Food Habits and Nutrient Intakes. Journal of the American Dietetic Association 34:138. II. Blood Findings, Height and Weight Data and Physical Condition. Journal of the American Dietetic Association 34:145.

Mann, V. R.
1966 Food Practices of the Mexican-American in Los Angeles County, Including a Method for Evaluating the Diet, revised. Los Angeles: Los Angeles County Health Department.

Sanjur, Diva, et al.
1970 Infant Feeding and Weaning Practices in a Rural Pre-Industrial Setting. Acta Pediatrica Scandinavica, Supplement 200.

Yanochik, A. V., et al.
1976 The Comprehensive Nutrition Action Program in Arizona. Journal of the American Dietetic Association 69:37.

Black Americans

Atwater, W. O. and Charles Wood
1897 1895–96 Food of the Negro in Alabama. Alabama Agricultural Experimental Station Bulletin, No. 3:15.

Bradfield, R. B. and D. Coltrin
1970 Some Characteristics of the Health and Nutritional Status of California Negroes. American Journal of Clinical Nutrition 23:420.

Brunson, R. T.

1962 Socialization Experiences and Socioeconomic Characteristics of Urban Negroes as Related to Use of Selected Southern Foods and Medical Remedies. Dissertation Abstracts 23:1824.

Coale, M. S.

1971 Factors Influencing the Food Habits of Negro Preschool Children in the Inner City. M.S. Thesis, Cornell University.

Cornely, P. B. and S. K. Bigman

1961 Cultural Considerations in Changing Health Attitudes. Medical Annuls of the District of Columbia 30:191.

Cussler, M. and M. de Give

1952 Twixt the Cup and the Lip. New York: Twayne.

Dickens, Dorothy

1928 A Nutrition Investigation of Negro Tenants in the Yazoo Mississippi Agricultural Experimental Station Bulletin, No. 254:5.

Fitzgearld, Thomas K.

1979 "Southern Folk's Eating Habits Ain't What They Used To Be . . . If They Ever Were." Nutrition Today. July/August: 16–34.

Hampton, M. C., R. L. Huenemann, L. R. Shapiro, and B. W. Mitchell

1967 Caloric and Nutrient Intakes and Teenagers. Journal of the American Dietetic Association 50:385.

Jerome, N. W.

1969 Northern Urbanization and Food Consumption Patterns of Southern Born Negroes. American Journal of Clinical Nutrition 22:12.

1980 Diet and Acculturation—The Case of Black-American In-Migrants. In Nutritional Anthropology, eds. N. W. Jerome, R. F. Kandel, and G. H. Pelto. Pleasantville, NY: Redgrave.

Jones, R. E. and H. Schendel

1966 Nutritional Status of Selected Negro Infants in Greenville County, South Carolina. American Journal of Clinical Nutrition 18:407.

Marquess, Carriemae

1977 Food Habits of Black Americans. Unpublished paper, Division of Nutritional Sciences, Cornell University, Spring 1977.

Mayer, J.

1965 The Nutritional Status of American Negroes. Nutrition Reviews (1965):161.

Moragne, Lenora

1969 Influence of Household Differentiation on Food Habits Among Low Income Urban Negro Families. PhD. dissertation, Cornell University.

Parker, S. L. and J. Bowering

1976 Folacin in Diets of Puerto Rican and Black Women in Relation to Food Practices. Journal of Nutrition Education 8(2).

Shapiro, L. R., R. L. Huenemann, and M. C. Hampton

1962 Dietary Survey for Planning a Local Nutrition Program. Public Health Reports. 77:257.

Walker, Burnese

1975 Selected Factors Influencing the Food Habits of Black American Females in Ithaca, New York. M.S. thesis, Cornell University.

Asian Americans

Brown, M. L. and S. F. Adelson

1969 Infant Feeding Practices Among Low and Middle-Income Families in Honolulu. Tropical and Geographic Medicine 21:63.

Brown, M. L. and C. H. Ho

1975 Low Income Groups in Hawaii. In Practices of Low Income Families in Feeding Infants and Small Children with Particular Attention to Cultural Subgroups. HEW publication 75-5605. Washington, D. C.

Casey, P. and I. Harrill
1977 Nutrient Intake of Vietnamese Women Relocated in Colorado. Nutrition Reports International 16:687–93.

Chan, Michelle
1977 A Preliminary Survey of the Food Habits of Chinese in Manhattan, New York. Senior honors thesis, Cornell University.

Chang, B.
1974 Some Dietary Beliefs in Chinese Folk Culture. Journal of the American Dietetics Association 65(4):436–8.

Chang, K. C., ed.
1978 Food in Chinese Culture: Anthropological and Historical Perspectives. New Haven, CN: Yale University Press.

Grivetti, Louis Evan and Marie B. Paquette
1978 Nontraditional Ethnic Food Choices Among First Generation Chinese in California. Journal of Nutrition Education 10:109.

Langlois, J.
1972 Moon Cake in Chinatown, New York City: Continuity and Change. New York Folklore Quarterly 28:83–117.

Lewis, Jane S. and Maria Fe Glaspy
1975 Food Habits and Nutrient Intakes of Filipino Women in Los Angeles. Journal of the American Dietetic Association 67:122.

Murai, Mary M.
1975 Discussion Section—Low Income groups in Hawaii. In Practices of Low-Income Families in Feeding Infants and Small Children with Particular Attention to Cultural Subgroups. HEW publication 75-5605. Washington, D.C.

Nong The Anh, Tran Kiem Thuc, and Jack D. Welsh
1977 Lactose Malabsorption in Adult Vietnamese. American Journal of Clinical Nutrition 30:468.

Pimental, Carmencita
1976 An Evaluation of Food Habits of a Selected Group of Filipinos of Preschool Age in the Washington, D.C. Metropolitan Area. M.S. thesis, Howard University, Washington, D.C.

Smith, D. S. and M. L. Brown
1970 Anthropology in Preschool Children in Hawaii. American Journal of Clinical Nutrition 23:932.

Tillotson, J. L., et al.
1973 Epidemiology of Coronary Heart Disease and Stroke in Japanese Men Living in Japan, Hawaii, and California: Methodology for Comparison of Dietetics. American Journal of Clinical Nutrition 26:177.

Wenkam Nao, S. and Robert J. Wolff
1970 A Half Century of Changing Food Habits Among Japanese in Hawaii, Journal of the American Dietetic Association 57:29.

Puerto Ricans

Bentz, L. and D. Sanjur
1981 The Effects of Environmental Changes on Nutrient Intake Among Puerto Rican Families, Federation Proceedings 40(3).

Colón, Mirta
1981 Home Food Production and Household Income as Predictors of Nutritional Status of Puerto Rican Preschool Children and Their Mothers. M.S. thesis, University of Puerto Rico Medical Campus.

Czakowski, J. M.
1971 Puerto Rican Foods and Traditions. Booklet, Cooperative Extension Service, University of Connecticut.

Duyff, R. L., D. Sanjur, and H. Y. Nelson
1975 Food Behavior and Related Factors of Puerto Rican-American Teenagers. Journal of Nutrition Education 7(3).

Fernandez, Nelson A.
1975 Nutrition in Puerto Rico. Cancer Research 35(3272).

Fernandez, N., et al.
1965 Nutritional Status of People in Isolated Areas of Puerto Rico. Survey of Barrio Mavilla, Vega Alta, Puerto Rico. American Journal of Clinical Nutrition. 17:305.

Fernandez, N., et al.
1968 A Nutrition Survey of Five Rural Puerto Rican Communities. Mimeo, School of Medicine, University of Puerto Rico.

Parker, S. L. and J. Bowering
1976 Folacin in Diets of Puerto Rican and Black Women in Relation to Food Practices. Journal of Nutrition Education 8(2).

Sanjur, Diva
1970 Puerto Rican Food Habits. Ithaca, NY: Cornell University.

Sanjur, D., E. Romero, and M. Kira
1971 Milk Consumption Patterns of Puerto Rican Preschool Children in Rural New York. American Journal of Clinical Nutrition 24:1320.

Sanjur, D., et al.
1972 A Community Study of Food Habits and Socio-Cultural Factors of Families Participating in the East Harlem Nutrition Education Program. New York State College of Human Ecology Research Report, Cornell University.

Tirado, Nilda
1978 The Changing Puerto Rican Diet: Implication for Nutrition Education. Paper presented at the Ethnic Foods Symposium, New York Medical College, March 8, 1978.

Roberts, L. J. and R. Stefani
1949 Patterns of Living in Puerto Rican Families. Rio Piedras, Puerto Rico. University of Puerto Rico Press.

Native Americans

Alford, B. B. and E. R. Nance
1976 Customary Foods in the Navajo Diet. Journal of the American Dietetic Association 69:5.

Bass, M. A. and L. M. Wakefield
1974 Nutrient Intake and Food Patterns of Indians on Standing Rock Reservation. Journal of the American Dietetic Association 64:36.

Carlile, W. K. et al.
1972 Contemporary Nutritional Status of North American Indian Children. *In* Nutrition, Growth and Development of North American Indian Children, eds. W. M. Moore, M. M. Silverberg, and M. S. Read, HEW publication (NIH)72–26. Washington, D.C.

Darby, W. J., C. G. Salsbury, W. J. McGanity, H. F. Johnson, E. B. Bridgforth and H. R. Sanstead
1960 Study of the Dietary Background and Nutriture of the Navajo Indian. Journal of Nutrition 60 (Supplement 2).

French, J. G.
1967 Relationship of Morbidity to the Feeding Patterns of Navajo Children from Birth Through Twenty-four Months. American Journal of Clinical Nutrition 20:375.

Gonzales, Nancie L.
1972 Changing Dietary Patterns of North American Indians. *In* Nutrition, Growth and Development of North American Indian Children, eds. W. M. Moore, et al., HEW publication (NIH) 72–26. Washington, D.C.

Harris, La Donna
1972 The Heritage of North American Indians. *In* Nutrition, Growth and Development of North American Indian Children, eds., W. M. Moore, et al., HEW publication (NIH) 72:26. Washington, D.C.

Kuhnlein, H. V. and D. H. Calloway
1977 Contemporary Hopi Food Intake Patterns. Ecology for Food and Nutrition 6:159.

McDonald, B.
1965 Nutrition of the Navajo, 2nd ed. U.S. Public Health Services, Division of Indian Health, Window Rock Field Office, Window Rock, AZ.

Martin, E. A. and A. A. Coolidge
  1978   Nutrition in Action. New York: Holt,
          Rinehart and Winston.

Moore, W. M., M. M. Silverberg, and M. S. Read, eds.
  1972   Nutrition, Growth and Development of
          North American Indian Children. HEW
          publication (NIH) 72–26. Washington,
          D.C.

Nance, E. B.
  1972   Food Consumption of 200 Navajo
          Adults Receiving USDA Donated Foods.
          M.S. thesis, Texas Women's University.

Owen, G.M., et al.
  1972   Nutrition Survey of White Mountain
          Apache Preschool Children. *In* Nutri-
          tion, Growth and Development of
          North American Indian Children, eds.
          W. M. Moore, M. Silverberg, and M. S.
          Read, HEW publication (NIH) 72—26.
          Washington, D.C.

Peterson, Mary A.
  1975   Indian and Alaska Native Low-Income
          Groups. *In* Practices of Low-Income
          Families in Feeding Infants and Small
          Children with Particular Attention to
          Cultural Subgroups. HEW publication
          (HSA) 75–5605 Rockville, MD.

Report of Subpanel on American Indians and
Alaska Natives: Eskimos, Indians and Aleuts.
  1970   White House Conference on Food, Nu-
          trition, and Health. Final Report. Wash-
          ington, D.C.

Scott, E. M.
  1956   Nutrition of Alaskan Eskimos. Nut. Rev.
          14:1–3.

Silverberg, M. M.
  1972   The Future of Native Americans. *In* Nu-
          trition, Growth and Development of
          North American Indian Children, eds.
          W. M. Moore, et al., HEW publication
          (NIH) 72–26. Washington, D.C.

Taylor, Theodore, W.
  1970   The States and Their Indian Citizens.
          Washington, D.C.

Van Duzen, J., J. P. Carter, J. Secondi, and C.
Federspiel
  1969   Protein and Calorie Malnutrition Among
          Preschool Navajo Indian Children.
          American Journal of Clinical Nutrition
          22:1362.

Wallace, H. M.
  1973   The Health of American Indian Chil-
          dren. Clinical Pediatrics 12–83.

General Works

American Dietetic Association
  1980   Cultural Food Patterns in the U.S.A. *In*
          Issues in Nutrition for the 1980's: an
          Ecological Perspective, eds. Alice L.
          Tobias and Patricia J. Thompson. Mon-
          terey, CA: Wadsworth Health Sciences
          Division. pp.244–260.

This chapter presents characteristics of the food
habits followed by ethnic groups in the U.S. It
also suggests ways to improve the nutritional
quality of these diets and recommends strategies
for making economical food choices, maximizing
the positive aspects of each dietary pattern.

Harwood, Alan, ed.
  1981   Ethnicity and Medical Care. Cambridge,
          Massachusetts: Harvard University Press.

The Editor provides an introduction that discusses the concept of ethnicity and how it relates
to issues of medical care in the U.S., and concludes with a chapter called "Guidelines for Culturally Appropriate Health Care." The book contains chapters on seven different ethnic groups.
Although the book focuses on health and medical
care, each chapter includes a section that defines
the group, provides a brief history of the group's
migration to the U.S., current population and
geographic distribution, and a demographic description of the group. It provides useful background information for readers interested in ethnicity. The intended audience includes health
care planners, medical educators, and behavioral
scientists.

Cassidy, Claire M.
1982   Subcultural Prenatal Diets of Americans. *In* Alternative Dietary Practices and Nutritional Abuses in Pregnancy, Proceedings of a Workshop. Washington, D.C: National Academy Press, p. 25–61.

Examines diets of several American subcultural groups, discussing food beliefs, cravings, and avoidances that may have negative effects on the health of the mother or fetus. Interestingly, Cassidy includes a description of "The Orthodox Middle-Class American Diet" as one of the alternative diets. She also looks at dietary patterns for "Health Foodists," Black Americans, Mexican Americans and Puerto Ricans, followers of Judaism and Islam, Asian Americans, and Asian Indians. Includes a section on "Common Lay Beliefs About Prenatal Diet" and an extensive bibliography.

Sanjur, Diva
1982   Ethnicity and Food Habits. *In* Social and Cultural Perspectives in Nutrition.

Englewood Cliffs, NJ: Prentice-Hall, Inc. pp. 241–284.

This chapter includes sections on six ethnic groups, providing a literature review, bibliography, and a discussion of dietary change for each group. For some groups, glossaries of ethnic food items are included.

Brown, Linda Keller and Kay Mussell
1984   Ethnic and Regional Foodways in the United States. Knoxville, TN: The University of Tennessee Press.

Essays of which examine the symbolic meaning of shared foodways in understanding inter- and intra-group behavior. The authors pay attention some of the theoretical problems, and the implications of foodways research for public policy. Topics addressed include: food festivals, food preparation techniques, meal cycles, seasonal celebrations, and nutrition education.

6

World view, religion, and health beliefs: The ideological basis of food practices

At a vegetarian restaurant in Washington, D.C. one of the authors took an informal survey asking diners if they were vegetarians and if so, why they did not eat meat. Responses included a wide variety of interesting reasons. A man from India cited the Hindu religious doctrine that prohibits meat consumption as one way to achieve the ideal of nonviolence. An American woman with a family history of heart disease chose the low-fat, low-cholesterol vegetarian diet as a disease prevention. Respect for animals combined with disapproval of the inhumane practices used in livestock production was another reply, and several people referred to todays' world food crisis, and stated they avoided meat as a way to protest the use of large quantities of grain to feed livestock while people in other parts of the world go hungry.

Each of these reasons reflects some aspect of the consumer's ideology. When we think of ideology, we usually think first of religion, folklore, art, dance, literature, and language—symbolic expressions of meaning and values. But ideology also embraces the entire realm

ideology
A systematic body of concepts, especially about human life and culture

of socially shared concepts about the universe and people's place in it. It includes goals for human existence and beliefs about the supernatural and its relationship to people. Ideology also consists of justifications for the social rules governing food production, division of labor, distribution of resources, marriage and child rearing, maintenance of law and order, and political relations with other groups. Finally, ideology consists of "thoughts about thoughts," as in formal philosophical or scientific systems (Harris 1975:158).

Several belief systems that make up ideology are particularly relevant to nutritionists. *World view, religion, health beliefs,* and their relationship to food practices are explored in this chapter.

World view

A major component of every society's ideology is its world view. World view refers to the way a group defines, categorizes, and explains physical objects and living things. It is a complex set of beliefs, values and norms describing "how the world works." Because of varying world views, people from two cultures looking at the same thing may describe it very differently. For instance, a simple description of the most basic observable components of this world—trees, land, and water—by a member of one society might prove to be completely unintelligible to a member of another. The Navajo Indian facing the East sees the world in the following way:

> The sage-covered earth is Changing Woman, one of the most benevolent of the gods, who grows old and young again with the cycle of each year's seasons. The rising sun is himself a god who with Changing Woman produced a warrior that rid the earth of most of its evil forces and who is still using his power to help people. The first brightness is another god, Dawn-Boy . . . The coneshaped mountains have lava on their sides, which is the caked blood of a wicked tyrant killed by the Sun's Warrior offspring. . . .
>
> *(Leighton and Leighton, cited in Honigman 1959:591)*
>
> A white man looking at the same landscape sees the yellow day coming up over miles of sage, copse of pinyon, three or four yellow pines in the soft light, distant blue swells of mountains, with here and there a volcanic cone. . . .
>
> *(Honigman 1959:591)*

Although everyone's view of the universe is greatly influenced by their society's particular world view, this aspect of ideology tends to be so implicit (taken for granted) that people are often unable to describe it. If interviewed by an anthropologist from another culture, for example, how would you describe the United States' world view? Take a minute and try to list some of the major assumptions North Americans make about how the universe operates.

Most likely you found this exercise difficult. Because this world view is so implicit, you are unlikely to discuss basic conceptions of the world and the overriding values that you believe should guide humankind. Moreover, you are even less likely to discuss these in cultural terms; that is, as one distinct way of looking at life that differs from the views held by others. Instead, you might assume that the values and beliefs that make up your world view are the "natural" or "correct" explanation of how things occur.

Because your world view, like that of others, is implicit, you also may not be well-prepared for how other societies' world views differ. When living and working in other countries, people are often perplexed by their hosts' behavior; when attempting to introduce changes, they are frustrated by the resistance and other confusing behavior they encounter.

In order to appreciate more fully how differing world views can affect Westerners' work in cross-cultural settings, we will look at several aspects of the world view held in the United States, and then compare it to how peasants (who comprise almost half the world's population) view the same phenomena.

World view in the United States

Despite a wide range of variety in ethnic background, religious affiliation, and secular interests, most people in North America share some basic attitudes and beliefs. Some observers from other societies, for instance, have been struck by our benevolence, humanitarianism, love of laughter, and use of humor as a sanction. On a more general level, the U.S. world view has been characterized as individualistic, rational, and pragmatic.

Individualism is a dominant theme permeating the U.S. lifestyle. The individual, rather than the family or society, is the center of consideration. Individual initiative is expressed in statements such as "pull yourself up by your boot straps" and "if at first you don't succeed, try, try again" (Hoebel and Frost 1976).

The poor and others who are unable to achieve financial success may be seen as lazy or somehow to blame for their failure. Self-reliance and autonomy are expressed through self-fullfillment, romantic love, personal achievement, and the use of time and money to meet individual desires.

Norge Jerome (1970) describes how individualism is expressed in Americans' food habits. She notes, for example, the autonomous

sanction
A mechanism of social control used to enforce conformity

pragmatic
Practical; having a problem-solving mentality

food selection and consumption of foods symbolizing reward, reassurance, nostalgia, warmth, comfort, and achievement—values that are central to the U.S. world view. Snacks are used as reward and comfort items; soups, milk, and ice cream are used to express nostalgia; steaks, caviar, and gourmet foods to symbolize success and power.

Rationalism is a second major theme in the U.S. world view. Faith in the rational springs from the proposition that the universe is a physical system governed by scientific laws. Mysticism and the supernatural are replaced by scientific explanations of cause-and-effect relationships.

The third theme is pragmatism. A "can-do" approach to problems is seen in the U.S., with an emphasis on biological sciences, agriculture, and technology as opposed to the humanities and social sciences. "Know-how" is valued more highly than ancient wisdom and tradition.

From rationalism, pragmatism, and an enthusiastic optimism comes the view that humans do not need to accept the world as it is; they can, and in fact they should, improve upon current conditions. Action rather than contemplation typifies many Americans as they fight social injustice, stamp out disease, declare war on poverty, and eliminate hunger (Hoebel and Frost 1976). The U.S. world view is also reflected in many Americans' attitudes toward natural resources. Concern over depletion of nonrenewable energy sources, for instance, is dismissed by the belief that we can always develop a new energy source to meet our needs.

With this rational, pragmatic approach to problems, nutritionists and other professionals take new ideas and improved techniques to poor, rural communities and expect peasants to accept their innovations with equal enthusiasm. More often than not, neither the ideas nor the professionals are well-received. As one technical agent reported:

> We carry manure and improved seeds in a trailer and offer to deliver them right at the door-step to induce these cultivators to use them. We offer them loans to buy the seeds and manure. We go to the fields and offer to let in water for them. We request them to try it out first in two acres only if they are not convinced. They could quadruple their yields if they would only take our advice and at least experiment. Still they are not coming forward.
>
> *(Kusum Nair, Blossoms in the Dust)*

What goes wrong? To answer this question, we will examine the peasant's world view and the conditions upon which that perspective is based.

World view in peasant societies

As you may recall from Chapter 4, peasants live in rural villages that comprise part of larger societies. Although they grow food primarily for their own farms, some items are grown to pay taxes and rent and to trade in nearby market towns. Since the first appearance of urban centers, the peasant's economic livelihood has been dominated largely by decisions made by wealthy elites outside the village. Often the peasant has no control over and little comprehension of taxes, legal restrictions, levys, or other orders imposed from the outside.

Peasant communities are also linked to the larger society by teachers, priests, and political leaders who visit and work in rural villages. Through them, ideas are borrowed from the larger society's world view and modified to fit traditional peasant values. Thus the peasant's world view is a product of centuries of contact with urban centers and long-standing political control and economic exploitation by urban elites.

Although specific religious beliefs, art forms, and other aspects of peasants' ideology vary from one region to another, several features of their world view are somewhat similar throughout the world. Of particular relevance in understanding their rejection of Westerners and many of their innovations is the peasants' suspicion of outsiders, their fatalism, and their notion of limited good.

Peasants are often suspicious of people from outside their close network of relatives and friends. To the well-intentioned North American health care provider, peasants' distrust and subsequent reluctance to try outsiders' innovations may be confusing. Certainly it creates frustrating barriers to change. This suspicion is quite understandable, however, when the history of their relations with outsiders is taken into consideration, for peasants have been exploited by outsiders for many generations (see Chapter 4).

An example of how this suspicious attitude affects change comes from Ecuadorian peasants living in the Andes mountains. Forest experts there tried for many years to give peasants eucalyptus seedlings to cover the denuded mountain slopes. Nothing seemed more logical than to reforest the land, protecting it while producing valuable timber that could make an entire village rich within 30 years. The only cost to the peasants would be a small fence around each tree and the time and energy to water it until it was firmly rooted. To the forest experts' amazement, the Indians refused the seedlings. Marvin Harris explains why:

> The Indians were keenly aware of the potential value of such trees. They had little confidence, however, that the men who were giving away the seedlings were simply going to forget

about them. Nothing could be certain until the fateful moment thirty years hence when the trees were full grown and ready to cut. Who could tell if the experts would not suddenly reappear and claim their timber? How could they be sure the whole thing was not merely a scheme to trick them into taking care of someone else's trees? Given the history of the Indian-Mestizo relations in Ecuador, it is difficult to dismiss these doubts as illogical or unrealistic.

(Harris 1975:464)

Another aspect of the peasants' world view that baffles most Westerners is their fatalism. Many peasants do not believe that success is necessarily derived from individual achievement. Individual initiative, hard work, and self-reliance are often insufficient, in the peasant's mind, to bring about desired ends. Success, like happiness, is seen as a function of the will of God, supernatural forces, or fate. When an infant dies, rather than blame the lack of medical care or other circumstances, parents may say that it was destiny; it was the child's fate not to live. In some societies, children are not given names until they have survived the dangerous initial months of infancy. In the face of the high infant mortality rates found in these communities, peasants anticipate the loss of children and protect themselves emotionally with the belief that some children are just not born for this world.

This fatalism may serve as a barrier to change. When the end results of an endeavor and ultimate happiness are thought to depend upon fate, why work harder or take greater risks than necessary? Regardless of the frustration it creates for outsiders, this view is understandable.

. . . in nonindustrial societies a very low degree of mastery over nature and social conditions has been achieved. Drought or flood is looked upon as a visitation from gods or evil spirits whom man can propitiate but not control. Feudal forms of land tenure and nonproductive technologies may condemn a farmer to a bare subsistence living. Medical and social services are lacking, and people die young. Under such circumstances it is not surprising that people have few illusions about the possibility of improving their lot. A fatalistic outlook, the assumption that whatever happens is the will of God or Allah, is the best adjustment the individual can make to an apparently hopeless situation.

(Foster 1962:66–7)

A third element in the peasant world view is the notion of "limited good." Many peasants see their world as one in which the good things in life are available in a limited and fixed quantity. If we remember that most peasants are poor and their land and other resources are limited, this concept of the universe is understandable. A correlation of this view is the belief that because the total amount of a good is set, personal gain is made at the expense of others. When one person gets ahead, the amount available for others diminishes. Thus, a peasant family who advances financially is the subject of envy, suspicion, and even accusations of witchcraft unless they share their wealth with others or hide all overt signs of economic advancement. This notion of limited good has mixed effects for peasant communities. On one hand, it may serve as a barrier to change: Why accept innovations that promise financial betterment if the fruits of additional work and risk-taking must be shared with others or create dissention and mistrust? On the other, this notion serves to maintain a narrow gap between rich and poor segments within the peasant community, promoting an equitable distribution of resources and, in some cases, preventing exploitation of environmental resources that would be gained at the expense of others.

An example of how the notion of limited good and other aspects of peasant culture can contribute to a successful change experience comes from Walderman Smith's case study of a Maya Indian community in Guatemala. Over 10,000 Maya Indians live in San Pedro, a modern and progressive textile town in the western highlands of Guatemala. Since its economy began to expand in the 1940s, conditions have improved dramatically for the Indians. Today, the presence of a physician, several lawyers, and hundreds of teachers as well as Indian-owned stores and locally-owned trucks sets this town apart from most other Indian villages. While numerous factors involving local and national conditions have contributed to the town's success, Smith explains how the Indians are aided by their notion of limited good. Because Indians want to avoid the envy of neighbors, they are careful not to display any new wealth but rather save and reinvest their profits. In this way, the notion of limited good encouraged these Indian entrepreneurs to maintain their current standard of living, deferring conspicuous forms of consumption in favor of reinvestment and giving them a competitive edge over businesses owned by non-Indians in neighboring communities.

Although the peasants' world view may perplex the Westerner especially when it impedes acceptance of his or her ideas, we do not want to imply that fatalism, suspicion of outsiders, and the notion of limited good are the major reasons development schemes fail, nor that peasants are inherently resistant to change. Empirical investigations of agricultural developmental projects, for example, show that innovations are most frequently rejected or misused because of risk aversion, lack of correct information, lack of access to essential resources, or inappropriateness of innovations to local conditions. Moreover, peasants are often quite willing to try new development schemes; particularly when the risks are minimal and the benefits clear.

Religion

> And you shall observe the feast of unleavened bread, for on this
> very day I brought your hosts out of Egypt: therefore you shall
> observe this day, throughout your generations, as an ordinance
> for ever.
>
> In the first month, on the fourteenth day of the month at eve-
> ning, you shall eat unleavened bread, and so until the twenty-
> first day of the month at evening. For seven days no leaven shall
> be found in your houses; for if anyone eats what is leavened,
> that person shall be cut off from the congregation of Israel . . . .
>
> *(Exodus 12:17–19)*

A second universal component of ideology is religion. Religion
is a system of beliefs that is expressed through rituals and symbols
and that is concerned with the supernatural. Religious behavior includes chants, prayers, myths, talks, ethical standards, and concepts
of supernatural beings and forces (Wallace 1966). Through its concepts of the supernatural and moral rightness, religion provides participants with an intellectual and emotional commitment to the ordered belief system on which social life is based (Hoebel and Frost
1976, Geertz 1965).

People everywhere relate to supernatural forces or entities, perform religious rituals, and incorporate the supernatural into their
daily lives. With the possible exception of China and the USSR, where
religion is still practiced in a secretive manner, all societies are characterized by religion of some type.

The specific ways in which humans define and relate to the supernatural vary widely, but despite this diversity all religions serve
many of the same functions. First, religion provides people with an
organized picture of the universe, various supernatural forces or entities, and their relationship to people. Religion offers explanations
for illness, death, and natural disasters and offers ritual practices for
controlling supernatural forces. Weather magic, fertility rituals, curing ceremonies, and rituals for attracting game offer the comforting
illusion of control where scientific and technological mastery are
lacking (Schwartz and Ewald 1968). Thus, by establishing an orderly
relationship between people and the supernatural, people use religion to make sense of the inexplicable and reduce anxieties associated with the unknown.

Religious rituals that involve prescribed foods or food avoidances are often used in this way. For example, in most societies pregnant and lactating women avoid certain foods believed to be harmful.
These food prescriptions give the woman a sense of security that she
is protecting her unborn child from harm. Some ritual practices are
nutritionally detrimental. Religious dietary restrictions placed upon

West Bengali children if the rice-feeding ceremony is delayed (the *mukhe bhat* described in Chapter 5) aggravate an already limited diet. Many of the foods considered ritually dangerous are high in protein and other nutrients needed by the growing child. These negative nutritional effects may, in part, be balanced, however, by emotional benefits (e.g., the sense of spiritual protection) gained by family adherence to this practice.

Religious ritual practices are also used to relieve anxiety about adequate food supplies. Communal hunting and agricultural rituals are practiced to ensure fertility of animals or soil, bring rain or make game more willing to be captured. The Christian farmer, for example, may pray for good weather and a bountiful harvest. Although all people recognize the need for hard, efficient work to obtain food, the level of technological know-how often leaves sufficient room for uncertainty. The hunter knows that the arrow kills and plants need rain, but he is also aware that the arrow may go astray and that the rain may come too late. In the face of such uncertainty, rituals are seen as a way to enlist cooperation of supernatural forces and ensure a successful outcome. Regardless of their technological efficiency, for most are probably worthless in affecting their stated purpose, these rituals serve an important function. They reduce the food producer's anxiety about his ability to secure adequate food. And by reducing this anxiety, efficiency may actually improve: the hand is steadied, movements become more skilled, behavior more flexible and members cooperate more willingly in team endeavors.

> Thus the improvement of confidence in the likelihood of success may very well be an important ingredient in achieving that very success. Ritual, by reducing anxiety and increasing confidence in hunting, agriculture, and other important activities, may very well be of material aid in direct proportion to the magnitude of the real risks involved.
>
> *(Wallace 1966:175)*

A second function served by religion is to enhance a feeling of unity and social solidarity. Religious ceremonies bring people together to participate in a common activity in an atmosphere heavily charged with emotion. Through this communal activity, people renew and reinforce their identification with the social unit and gain a heightened sense of social cohesion. Totemism, a feature of Australian aborigines' and some other societies' religions, exemplifies this function well. A totem is a certain plant or animal species considered sacred by a particular tribe or social group within a tribe. Members of the totem group identify in a special way with the totem, often through the belief that they are descended from an original totemic ancestor. Great respect is shown for the totem. It is neither killed nor eaten except in ceremonies where it has a ritual role in feasting. Social scientists view totems as symbols by which groups express their unity and identity. Among Australian aborigines, each sex, clan, and local group has its own totem. Totemic feasts bring people together to worship a symbol (the totem) of the group, and thereby, enhance their solidarity.

Among traditional Australian Arunta tribes, for example, each local group traces its descent from some mythological natural object—the kangaroo, wallaby, wittchetty grub, etc. Each group shares a complex set of myths describing the founding of the group by the totem ancestor. At initiation ceremonies, the entire tribe gathers for the boys' passage into adulthood. It is at this time, and not before, that they are taught the sacred lore about the tribe's totem. A ceremony is also preformed to promote reproduction of the totem species (Schwartz and Ewald 1968).

Today, while some aborigine tribes still worship a totem, many who have assimilated into Western culture have either abandoned the custom or combined it with new religious practices.

Religious ceremony and feasting is a familiar theme in Christian tradition as well. The Last Supper and its derivative Holy Communion are sacred meals in which participants share symbolically the flesh and blood of the Divinity. By partaking of Communion, religious followers reaffirm their faith and reinforce their sense of oneness with each other. Church picnics, potluck suppers, and sharing prayer before meals are other examples of activities practiced in the Christian religion that serve to solidify the group.

myth

A traditional story of presumably historical events that explains a belief, practice, or other component in a society's world view.

wallaby

One of the smaller kangaroos frequenting the forest and brush of Australia

grub

The thick, wormlike larva of certain insects

Figure 6.1
Family prayer. This Christian family says grace before each meal.
(Lindenberger)

A study of the relationship between religious participation and diet patterns of the aged (McIntosh and Shiffleet 1983) found that elderly people who participate frequently in religious activities have higher essential nutrient intakes and eat meals more regularly than those who do not. The nature of the resources exchanged and the ways in which these affect eating patterns, dieting, cooking, and shopping were not studied by these researchers. However, data collected in rural Kentucky (Bryant, et al. 1984) suggest that the elderly benefit significantly from church dinners and picnics and assistance with shopping, invitations to share meals, and gifts of foods from fellow church members.

A third function of religion is to reinforce cultural values and standards of behavior. Common goals and rules of conduct are embedded in religious codes such as the Ten Commandments. Rituals and symbols, many of which involve food practices, are used to evoke a sense of commitment to the moral order. Almost everywhere, religious codes restrict some foods; while several (e.g., Hinduism, Judaism, and Islam) include elaborate dietary laws. The Seventh Day Adventist religion restricts meat, tobacco, and alcohol and prescribes simple diets containing a balance of whole grains and other fresh foods.

Finally, many religious practices contribute significantly to a society's adaptation to the physical environment. These adaptive functions may not be obvious to members of a society; people follow these practices for *religious,* not *ecological,* reasons. They are, nevertheless, important to the professional who introduces changes that might inadvertently disrupt the ecological balance established by traditional religious customs. Food taboos offer a good example. Before the arrival of Christian missionaries, Bantu-speaking peoples throughout Southern Africa drank a fermented sorghum beer. In the late nineteenth century, the Bantu chief was converted to Christianity, and as a result forbade the people to prepare or drink beer. Unwittingly, the chief placed his subjects at nutritional risk. The sorghum beer had been one of their few sources of B complex and C vitamins, effective in preventing beriberi, pellagra, and scurvy. It also served as a sanitary source of drinking water because ingredients were boiled several times to make the beer. Thus, acceptance of a religious innovation—the prohibition of beer—had several unintended negative consequences for the group's adaptation to their environment.

The ecological functions of other religious practices involving food have also been explored. Food taboos among peoples living in tropical forests of South America have been shown to have important adaptative value. The religious restrictions placed on hunting and eating certain game animals protects otherwise endangered species and discourages hunters from expending energy on the animals that are most difficult (least "cost-effective") to hunt.

Focus 6-1

Jewish dietary laws

Perhaps the most elaborate set of dietary laws associated with religious beliefs are Jewish laws governing food and its preparation. Based on the Talmud, or the Old Testament as interpreted by scholars, these laws are still practiced by many orthodox Jews as a central part of their religion, but not all Jewish families practice these traditional dietary customs.

Jewish dietary laws can be divided into three elements. First, all animal and vegetable components of food must be derived from approved species. Approved species are defined by the laws of Kashrut, which deal primarily with animal foods. Approved animal species include four-footed animals that both ruminate (chew cud) and have cloven hoofs, birds that do not eat carrion, and fish with scales. All other animals, as well as their milk and eggs, are ruled unfit. These include the swine (which has a cloven hoof but does not chew cud), the rabbit and camel (which chew cud but do not have cloven hoofs) as well as carnivores, rodents, shellfish, birds of prey, eaters of carrion, and reptiles.

tithe
To pay or give a tenth part of income or possessions for support of a religious establishment

Most plant species are approved. Exceptions include untithed and crossbred (hybrid) grains and the fruit of trees that have born fruit for less than three years.

A second dictate requires that approved species must be prepared correctly. Warm-blooded animals for example, must be ritually slaughtered. The correct method of slaughtering animals is based on a principal of "pity for all living things" requiring that they must be killed with a minimum of pain. Hunting, which may inflict death in a cruel way, is forbidden. The *shokhet's* blade, used in ritual slaughter, must be so keen that there is no brutal tearing of the flesh or skin. A single, swift, almost painless stroke is used to sever both the trachea and jugular veins.

shokhet
Hebrew for "butcher"

Also, the blood of all slaughtered animals must be removed by ritual soaking. This involves an alternating sequence of soaking, rinsing, and draining that frees the meat of all blood, for consuming blood is strictly forbidden: "If any man . . . eat blood I will set my face against his soul and will cut him off from his people" (Leviticus 17:11).

Finally, milk and all dairy products may not be mixed with meat products. All approved, or "Kosher", foods are divided into three catagories: pareve, milkhk, and fleyshik.

Pareve foods include all *kosher* foods of plant or chemical origin, and of animal origin, honey, eggs, *kosher* insects, and *kosher* fish. These cold-blooded animals are not subject to the ban on blood, and rules for slaughter require only that the animal be spared unnecessary pain. *Pareve* foods cannot pollute other foods, and are ritually neutral. If *milkhk* or *fleyshik* ingredient is added to a *pareve* food, it ceases to be *pareve*.

Milkhk (dairy) foods include all dairy products produced from the milk of *kosher* animals: milk, butter, cream, cheese, whey, as well as their derivatives. Any food that contains a trace of these items is defined as *milkhk*.

Fleyshik (meat) foods are those produced from the meat of *kosher* mammals and birds, which must be slaughtered by a ritual expert and drained of blood. In the home, the housewife then ritually salts and bathes all exposed surfaces of the meat to remove remaining traces of blood. Only then does it cease to be *treyf* (impure), and is fit to be cooked and eaten.

(Regelson 1976:124)

The taboo placed on mixing kosher milkhk food with kosher fleyshik food is based on the Biblical command "Thou shalt not seethe the kid in the milk of its mother". This has been translated by Jewish scholars to mean the total separation of the two food categories. If they are brought together at any time they both become impure. Every effort is made, therefore, to keep them separate through the use of separate storage vessels and separate eating utensils, dishes, and cutlery. "These (foods and vessels) must be stored separately, and when washed separate bowls (or preferably sinks) and separate dishcloths (preferably of different colors to avoid confusion), must be used. If the meat and milk foods are cooked at the same time on a cooking range or even on an open fire in a closed oven, care should be taken that dishes do not splash each other and that the pans are covered" (Rabinowicz 1971:40). The kosher household, then, has two sets of dishes and cookware, one for meat and one for dairy food, used on regular occasions. They also have two additional sets of dishes reserved for Passover.

Meal planning is made less difficult by the inclusion of pareve, or neutral, foods that can be consumed with meat or milk. In many traditional communities, these foods (fish, flour, eggs, vegetables, fruits, salt, sugar, condiments, and beverages) made up the bulk of the diet. Meat, in fact, is an uncommon item reserved largely for the Sabbath, holidays, or when someone is sick.

In sum, Kosher dietary laws define which plant and animal species are fit for human consumption, how they should be prepared ritually, and what food categories may be consumed simultaneously.

Religious organizations such as the Seventh Day Adventists and the Church of Jesus Christ of Latter Day Saints (Mormons) have proven adaptive in modern North America. Their view of the human body as a temple not to be defiled by poor diets and unnecessary drugs has produced decreased incidences of cancer, heart disease, diabetes, and alcoholism among their followers.

The classic example of supposedly irrational dietary behavior which actually has adaptive value comes from India, where Hindu doctrine forbids the slaughter and consumption of beef. This taboo has long been cited as responsible for the creation of large numbers of aged, useless cattle that roam aimlessly across the countryside and throughout city streets, defecating, blocking traffic, and stealing food. Many Western economic planners have recommended improved animal husbandry techniques to improve the size and quality of India's cattle herds. Some have also claimed that the Indians are ignoring a valuable protein and energy food source and suggest that they replace this religious practice with a more nutritionally sound policy allowing beef consumption. Because the Indian population subsists on inadequate calorie and protein rations and suffer from frequent famines, it appears as if these recommendations are well founded and that the Hindu doctrine is foolishly endangering the society's chances for survival.

Quite the contrary, says Marvin Harris in his study of cattle within the context of the Indian ecosystem. Harris found that the way Indians treat their cattle "increases rather than decreases the capacity of the present Indian system of food production to support human life" (Harris 1975:568). In fact, the Hindu doctrine making cattle sacred has several important adaptative functions. Most Indian farmers, for example, rely upon cattle to pull plows and carts. By serving as cultivating machines, cattle play an essential role in traditional Indian agriculture.

Even though the cattle are scrawny because they live off the countryside, they can pull plows and carts well enough and do not require as much food as larger breeds. This is important for the peasant who has limited land and food and cannot afford to divert arable land for grazing space or take grain from his family to feed his animals. Cows, even the most scraggly and barren beasts, provide manure. Some of the dung is collected and used as cooking and heating fuel (a highly valuable product in a largely deforested country) and fertilizer for crops. The rest remains in the countryside and is swept by rains into fields where it, too, fertilizes the poor soil.

Indian cattle serve another adaptive function. By scavenging throughout the streets and countryside, they convert many items of little or no direct human value (such as grass) into products of immediate human utility: milk, dung, and draft labor. Moreover, they pro-

Figure 6.2
Sacred cattle of India.
(United Nations/1981)

vide a considerable amount of beef to those castes who eat cattle that have died from natural causes. Finally, the taboo placed on cows protects this valuable source of agricultural power, fuel, and fertilizer from being consumed during famines. If Indians were to eat their cows, they would have no way to produce crops when the next season began. Contrary to being useless, then, the sacred cow plays an important economic role in Indian society. In the words of Mahatma Gandhi: "Why the cow was selected for apotheosis [elevation to divine status] is obvious to me. The cow was in India the best companion. She was the giver of plenty. Not only did she give milk but she also made agriculture possible" (1954:3).

In sum, it is important to be sensitive to the wide-reaching functions that some religious-based food practices can have for a society. Attempts to change a client's diet or modify an entire community's diet patterns should include a careful assessment of the context in which religious food practices are found.

Health beliefs

biomedical health model
The health belief system
of industrialized coun-
tries based on modern scientific explanations

Three people with an increased body temperature and nasal conges-
tion may interpret the causes and treat the symptoms quite differently. A person who believes in a biomedical health model may describe it as a viral infection caused by contact with an infectious
person and treat it by staying in bed, drinking plenty of fluids, and
taking aspirin. A proponent of holistic health may chalk it up to stress
and use meditation and massage as the way to recovery. A person who
explains it in spiritual terms may search for a violation of supernatural norms and perform a ritual dance to relieve the symptoms.

Health belief systems include notions about how the body works
and explanations about what makes it healthy and ill. Health belief
systems can be understood by looking at the way in which symptoms
and illness are perceived and the preventative and curative practices
used, as well as the characteristics of the health care provider.

Perceptions of symptoms and disease

spirochete
Any of an order of slender
undulating bacteria in-
cluding those that cause
syphillis and relapsing
fever

goiter
An enlargement of the
thyroid gland, visible as a
swelling of the front of
the neck, caused by io-
dine deficiency

Cultures vary in what symptoms they see as indicative of poor health.
A set of symptoms considered serious in one society may be ignored
in another. Primary and secondary yaws (an infectious tropical skin
disease caused by a spirochete) were so common in parts of Africa
until recently that people did not regard it as a disease. Similarly,
in the 1930s, when goiter was widespread throughout parts of the
north central U.S. where the soil is iodine-deficient, its development
was considered by some to be a normal part of maturation.

The wide range of responses people may have to a set of symptoms is well illustrated in the case of spirochetosis. Known as pinta
(meaning "spotted"), this skin disease is caused by the bacteria *Trep-
onema karateum*. It begins as scaly plaques in childhood. These become blue, later turning pink, brown, blue, and black. Eventually the
affected areas become completely discolored, leaving the person
with a multicolored skin. Symptoms seem limited to the skin, although they also provide the person with resistance to syphilis and
yaws. Society's reactions to these symptoms have varied from scorn
to admiration. In some places the affected people have been
shunned, while in others they have enjoyed high status. In the early
sixteenth century, Montezuma, the Aztec emperor, selected pintados
(the spotted ones) to carry his carriage because of their attractive
skin coloration. Among some South American Indian tribes, the disease is so common that people who have it are considered healthy,
while those without it are regarded as ill (Wood 1979, Dubos 1980).

Another example spotlights malaria. Now regarded as serious,
this disease was not considered pathological during the nineteenth
century when it affected most of the settlers moving into the upper

Mississippi Valley. "As the frontier pushed westward, the cutting of forests, travel by riverboat, settlement in river bottoms, poor sanitation, and stagnant water increased the incidence of the *Anopheles* mosquito and peoples' exposure to it. In the beginning the 'chills' were regarded as a necessary element of the inevitable 'acclimatization' and after having 'shaken' for years people got so used to it that they hardly paid attention to a little 'ague'" (Foster and Anderson 1978:40–41).

Preventative and curative practices

Health belief systems everywhere offer people a variety of preventative and treatment measures to maintain health. The practices used in a given culture correspond closely with how illness is perceived. When illness is believed to result from magic, people avoid offending their neighbors who might direct evil forces against them. When people believe an illness such as kwashiorkor is caused by the breach of postpartum sexual taboos, they observe strict sexual abstinence. And when disease is believed to be caused by bacteria, sanitation is practiced carefully. Both these practices help prevent kwashiorkor.

Dietary practices are used by all peoples to treat illness, and by most to prevent it. In North America, nutrition has become exceedingly popular as a preventative measure, linked in the minds of some people to almost all diseases. At a public lecture given by one author, a member of the audience asked what she should eat to improve her hearing. Recent surveys show that a significant proportion of North Americans have decreased their intake of red meat and saturated fats in response to warnings that excessive consumption of these will lead to heart disease. Other changes that reflect a concern with preventive nutrition are increased sales of vitamin and mineral supplements, nutrition books such as *The Anti-Cancer Diet* and *Sugar Blues,* the popularity of hair analysis, and shoppers' heightened concern with product ingredients.

Perhaps one of the most widespread methods thought to prevent and cure diseases involves the proper balance of bodily humors (fluids), particularly hot and cold. These practices, and the underlying "hot-cold" classification of illness, are based upon the Greek humoral theory of disease. According to this theory, health is believed to result from a balance among humors. In ancient times, the body was considered to consist of four humors: blood, phlegm, black bile, and yellow bile. Each humor had two qualities—hot/cold or wet/dry. Blood was defined as hot and wet, phlegm as cold and wet, and so forth. Illness resulted from a humoral imbalance that caused the body to become too hot, cold, dry, or wet.

acclimate
To adapt to a new temperature, climate, environment, or situation

ague
Chills, fever, and sweating that recurs at regular intervals

When the system was introduced to the New World by Spanish and Portugese travelers in the late 1500s, Latin American populations dropped the wet/dry dichotomy and emphasized the hot/cold dimension. In parts of rural Latin America and much of the world, people still view the body in these terms and believe that illness results from allowing the body to become too hot or too cold, as when a person steps barefooted on a cold floor or stays in the sun too long. Another feature of this system is the classification of foods, beverages, and medications as having "hot" or "cold" capabilities, thus creating bodily imbalance.

Hotness and coldness are not determined by observable characteristics nor the physical temperature of the substance, although in some places cooking occasionally may make a cold food hotter. Normally, the quality of a food is determined by its effect upon the body, its medical use, or its association with natural elements. For example, "Chili is hot because it produces a burning sensation . . . . Ice is hot because it produces a burning sensation when applied to the skin. Certain medicines, like aspirin, are hot because they make a person sweat. Cabbage is cold because it produces gas or air (aire) in the stomach . . . ." (Cosminsky 1975:184).

These notions of hot and cold affect people's views of illness causation and are reflected in menu planning and the use of herbal medicines. A Mexican mother, for example, may put a bit of cinnamon (a "hot" spice) into her baby's formula (a cold food) to achieve a better balance. And when her child becomes ill with a cold, she may restrict foods classified as cold and substitute medicines and foods believed to be hot.

Although the hot/cold theory has been best described in Latin America, where it constitutes the major folk explanation for illness and treatment, traces of the hot/cold humoral model have been found in popular western health practices as well. "The rationale, or justification, for treatment that is clearly seen in Latin America has in most cases disappeared, but the practices themselves can be accounted for only as 'residual humoral pathology'" (Foster 1979:18).

Examples from industrialized societies include the belief that the body is particularly vulnerable to cold through the head, feet, and open pores (e.g., after bathing). Colds and chills may result from failure to maintain an even balance of warmth in the body. Going outside with wet hair, walking barefoot on a cold floor during winter, exposure to cool, night air, going into a cold room right after a bath (when the pores are still open), and exposure to drafts may cause illness. Traditionally, women were advised not to wash their hair, go swimming, or get caught in the rain when menstruating. Treatment practices based on the hot/cold theory include "feed a cold, starve a fever" (reflecting the need to balance the body's temperature in the face of excessive heat from a fever or chill from a cold) and special care to avoid cool temperatures, chills, or draughts when sick with a fever (Foster 1979:19).

Interestingly, many traditional folk remedies involving food and herbs have been shown to be effective from a scientific point of view. Work done by Bernard Ortiz de Montellano (1975) shows that many Aztec herbal remedies have physiological effects—usually the same effects claimed by native healers. For example, wormwood (Artemisia mexicana), used as a tonic and dewormer, contains an antihelminthic agent (santonin), as well as camphor (a mild stimulant and colic reliever). Wormwood is still used today to combat upset stomachs and intestinal worms in rural Mexico. The bark of willow trees (Salix lasidpelis) was used to stop rectal bleeding and treat fevers. It contains salicylic acid, an aspirin-like substance effective in lowering fevers and relieving pain. (It also enhances bleeding.)

Many agents found in herbal remedies are used in drugs today: digitalis (foxglove) for heart conditions, morphine (opium poppy) for pain, rauwolfia for hypertension, chaulmoogra oil for leprosy, and quinine for malaria.

Some foods used as medical remedies also contain pharmacologically active ingredients that correspond with their native use. Epazote, a spice used to fight intestinal worms, contains chenopodium graveolens, an effective antihelminthic. In Mexico it is classified as "hot" and used with beans ("cold") to provide a more balanced

wormwood
A European plant yielding a bitter dark green oil

antihelminthic agent
A compound that rids the body of intestinal worms

Figure 6.3
Medicinal herbs in China.
(World Health Organization)

meal and control intestinal worms. Onions, garlic, apples, and rad- ishes contain antibacterial properties. Grain stored in clay pots and mud bins, which allow for mold formation, often develops tetracy- cline. Etkin and Ross (1983) examined the antimalarial properties of plants used by the Hausa of Nigeria to treat malaria. The vast major- ity, 31 of the 35 plants studied, are used as food as well as medicine, and 23 of them are most abundant during the malaria season. Some of these were shown in their laboratory analyses to have therapeutic value. Moreover the plants' effectiveness may be enhanced when used as food as well as medicine. Thus, the Aztec, Hausa, and many other medical belief systems contain preventative and treatment practices that now are recognized as effective in biomedical terms.

Some of the folk advice common in the U.S. has been found to be true also. For example, the adage, "if you eat just before going to bed, you'll gain weight" has been borne out by research showing that fewer calories are stored as fat if you exercise immediately after eat- ing. The practice of eating homemade chicken soup when suffering from a cold or flu is useful because its steam can clear stuffed nasal passages and the broth contains fluid that is important in times of physical stress.

Health care providers: shamans, curers, and others

shaman

A priest who uses magic for the purpose of curing the sick

In aboriginal times an Eskimo man who continued to feel ill consulted a shaman . . . who 'walked about' the patient, examining him from all angles. Then he might touch the patient about the spot where the 'pain' lay. He licked his hands, then rubbed them over the painful area. Some shamans blew on the affected part, occasionally sucking it tentatively at first if the case was diagnosed as one of (object) intrusion. When these preparations were completed, the shaman began to sing.

(Spencer 1959:306 as cited in Foster and Anderson 1978:102)

In Aritama, a Spanish speaking mestizo village in Colombia, a curer, is called in when illness persists. After a few searching questions concerning the patient's enemies who might have caused the disease, the practitioner asks in detail about the food consumed during recent days or weeks, about any hallucinations, heavy physical efforts, or exposure to sun, rain, wind, or water. The pulse is taken. If it beats rapidly, a 'hot' disease is diagnosed, if it beats slowly, a 'cold' disease is suspected. Facial expression is studied carefully. . . . Some specialists examine the urine . . . . The pupils of the eyes are examined . . . . Fecal matter, sputum, and vomit are occasionally examined. Only then does the curer prescribe.

(Reichel-Dolmatoff 1961:289 as cited in Foster and Anderson 1978:102)

In the United States a . . . man asks for an appointment with his physician after several days of nagging abdominal pain that he suspects is something more than indigestion. The doctor 'fits him into' a busy schedule, examines him, presses his stomach, localizes the pain and orders a blood count. If the results are positive an appendectomy will follow.

(Foster and Anderson 1978:102).

Although the behavior of the Eskimo shaman, the Columbian curer, and the American physician may appear very different, there are actually many similarities between them. Throughout history curers have

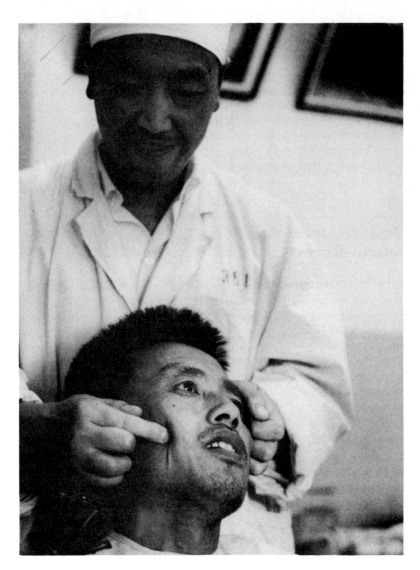

Figure 6.4
Acupressure. Acupressure is used in Chinese dentistry. Seconds after applying pressure, the dentist painlessly extracts a tooth.
(World Health Organization)

occupied a special role achieved through a selection process (inheritance, visions, dreams, instructions) and training (apprenticeship or medical school). Certification by previous practitioners, concern for professional image, receipt of payment for services rendered, and public belief in their special powers or skills are universal features of medical practitioners (Foster and Anderson 1978).

There is little doubt about the comparative effectiveness of Western medical practitioners and traditional healers in treating frank pathology. Antibiotics, immunizations, and modern surgery offer today's physician a degree of mastery that far exceeds the sand painting of the Navajos, object extraction by sucking, divination, and spiritual trance. However, as Wood (1979) points out, traditional healers offer many treatment forms with obvious value to the patient: massage, sweat baths, rest, social concern, and reassurance.

> . . . there remains much that modern medicine can absorb from traditional healers. The holistic approach to the troubled victim of some malfunction in his or her life, the involvement of family and friends, the sense of social solidarity and support, the expected and delivered explanations for the troubles at hand— all are vital adjuncts to any medical system. As members of the order Primates, we have a heritage millions of years old that renders us in constant need of the reassurance derived from physical as well as social "stroking."

> *(Wood 1979:333)*

Health belief system of mainland Puerto Ricans

To gain a better understanding of the complexity of health belief systems, let's examine the health belief system of a specific cultural group. An ethnic group whose medical system has received considerable attention in recent years is the Puerto Rican population living on the United States mainland. Our description of their belief system is derived largely from Alan Harwood's (1981) excellent summary in *Ethnicity and Medical Care.*

Population profile

Mainland Puerto Ricans, people either born on the island or to parents on the island, reached an estimated 1.8 million in the 1970s. The vast majority are located in New York, New Jersey, Florida, Connecticut, Illinois, California, Pennsylvania, Massachusetts, and Ohio. A significant segment of this population, approximately 30,000 to 40,000, work as migrant laborers. Because Puerto Ricans have been able to come to the mainland as U.S. citizens with no legal restrictions since 1917, a great deal of movement between the two places has occurred.

Today, considerable variation exists among families comprising the mainland population. In fact, Puerto Ricans are represented in all educational, occupational, and income catagories, and reside in rural and suburban as well as urban locations. Looking at the group as a whole, however, the Puerto Rican population on the continent is characterized as young and poor. Compared to a mean age of 28.6 for the total U.S. population in 1975, the mean age for mainland Puerto Ricans was only 19.4. Their median family income was $7,972 as compared to that of $16,000 for the nation as a whole in 1978; unemployment was high relative to other groups, and most workers were employed in jobs classified as unskilled. These factors, and the high incidence of families headed by females, have important consequences for health and medical care.

Perceptions of disease

Before examining Puerto Rican medical beliefs, it is important to point out the extent to which Puerto Ricans vary in their views. Some Puerto Ricans, especially those who have completed one or more years of high school education, adhere to popularized and orthodox biomedical theories (e.g., the germ theory), while those with less education tend to adhere more closely to folk theories of disease. The length of time spent on the mainland and the degree of exposure to the orthodox medical system also contribute to this intraethnic variation in medical belief systems. The nutritionist and other medical professionals are cautioned, therefore, to approach each Puerto Rican client individually in order to determine the extent to which folk, and/or orthodox beliefs are being used.

Typically, traditional peoples combine newly-adopted biomedical beliefs with their traditional system. Because most illnesses are believed to respond best to Western medicine, traditional treatment practices and healers are used less and less frequently. Often the tradtional healers are consulted primarily for culturally specific illnesses such as *susto,* for which biomedical practitioners offer little help, or after a disease has been designated as incurable by physicians.

susto
Spanish for "fright." A disease category known throughout Latin America and thought to be caused by a startling emotional or physical trauma that leaves the person immobilized or "soul-less"

The hot/cold theory

The Puerto Rican version of this widespread disease theory distinguishes between hot and cold diseases and between hot, cold, and cool foods and medications. Cold diseases such as arthritis are believed to result from excessive exposure to cold substances or states, as when hands are switched suddenly from hot to cold water. Influenza and colds result from exposure to drafts or going outside without sufficient clothing. Hot diseases are caused by an overindulgence in hot foods and medicine or by allowing the body to become overheated.

Because health is based on bodily balance, hot diseases are treated with cold or cool substances, while cold diseases are treated with medications and food classified as hot.

Spiritist theories

> Most Puerto Ricans of various Christian persuasions conceive of human beings as consisting of two aspects: a finite, physical body and an eternal, non-material spirit. Many Puerto Ricans also believe that the disembodied spirits of both deceased and divine beings play an active role in influencing the circumstances and behavior of the living. Only some Puerto Ricans, however, seek out spiritist mediums to diagnose and influence spiritual interventions in their own and others' lives.
>
> *(Harwood 1981:423)*

In line with this distinction between the material and spiritual aspects of the body, spiritist theories explain disease as resulting from material factors such as germs, or a hot/cold imbalance, disembodied spirits of divine or deceased humans, the activities of living people, or a combination of these. Most conditions are seen as materially caused and referred to medical professionals for care. Because a troubled spirit can complicate a material condition, spirit mediums are often used to supplement care regimens. Spiritists assist by diagnosing the spiritual problem, recommending ways to rid the body of noxious spiritual influences, improving relations with protective spirits, and counseling on interpersonal problems. Prayers, performance of special rites, use of herbal preparations, and participation in group sessions are common activities used by spiritists.

Viruses and other popularized biomedical concepts

As popularized in the mass media, the term *virus* is used to describe the symptoms of some colds or influenza. Virus colds are distinguished from chill-caused colds, although the criteria used to make this classification vary from person to person. Some Puerto Ricans also use the term to explain diarrhea or other intestinal disorders.

Other popularized biomedical concepts widely used by Puerto Ricans include the germ theory, parasitic infection, and allergy. Often these are incompletely understood, as when a behavioral restriction recommended by a physician is interpreted as the cause.

When a doctor recommends that a diabetic abstain from sugar, sugar is seen as the *cause* of diabetes. Of particular relevance to nutritionists is the Puerto Rican use of the term rickets (raquitis) and high and low blood pressure (alta y baja pression). Some, although certainly not all, Puerto Ricans use rickets to refer to tuberculosis in children, probably because both illness are commonly associated with malnutrition. High blood pressure is interpreted by some Puerto Ricans as too much blood and low blood pressure as too little, while weak blood (sangre debil) is the term used for iron-deficiency anemia.

Health care providers

Puerto Ricans rely most frequently on mainstream medical professionals for the illnesses they do not treat at home. In certain circumstances, however, depending on symptoms and cost, care is sought from alternative sources: pharmacists, herb shops (botanists), spiritists, curers (curanderos), or evangelical faith healers. These traditional healers may be consulted before going to orthodox medical professionals, such as when a woman asks her pharmacist for diagnostic and treatment assistance; they may be consulted secondarily when the medical facility fails to remedy the problem; or they may be used in conjunction with medical professionals. For example, spiritists often help chronically ill and terminal patients maintain spiritual peace while the physician provides biomedical treatment. Finally, some culturally-specific conditions require a special type of folk healer. *Empacho,* an indigestion believed to be caused by a bolus of food obstructing the intestines, is treated by a curandero. These healers administer massages, botanicals, and hot/cold remedies.

By and large these nonmainstream healers are not used in direct competition with medical services, and in some urban areas, medical and mental health clinics established successful referral networks with these healers, enabling patients to utilize both services simultaneously for maximum effectiveness (Bryant 1975).

Alternative health belief systems

Perhaps more common in this country than ethnic medical belief systems are the alternative health belief systems associated with the holistic health movement. Although a variety of differing beliefs and practices have gained popularity, several themes are characteristic of the movement as a whole: a value placed on natural foods and beverages and other practices such as natural birth control, natural sleeping cycles, and wearing clothing made of natural fibers; a belief in the body's ability to heal itself through proper diet, exercise, relaxation, massage, and other noninvasive procedures; and the use of proper diet as a major method of preventing as well as curing disease. Some of the more common foods that are to be avoided include meat, dairy products, and foods containing artificial substances.

With the rapid rise of the holistic health movement, most large towns and cities now feature a host of naturopathic doctors, chiropractors, holistic doctors, and nutrition advisors who offer help for a variety of ailments—arthritis, allergies, chronic back pain, fatigue, headache—as well as general medical care to promote longevity and enhance well-being.

Alternative health belief systems are not new in the United States. Their popularity, however, has surged over the last decade, at least in part because of dissatisfaction with the Western biomedical system. One source of dissatisfaction comes from modern biomedicine's inability to keep pace with consumers' expectations. Paradoxically, modern medicine's own dramatic successes also may be partly responsible.

nephritis
Inflammation of the kidney caused by infection, degenerative processes, or vascular disease

Because modern medicine has cured once-fatal diseases, reattached severed hands, transplanted organs, restored vision, and performed a host of other incredible feats, many people now expect cures for all their health problems. As a result many consumers are no longer willing to accept modern medicine's incomplete solutions to rheumatoid arthritis, chronic nephritis, cancer, and other diseases. They expect cures and when the biomedical system doesn't offer them, they look elsewhere for answers.

There are other reasons for dissatisfaction with modern medicine. Like all belief systems, the Western biomedical system is influenced by the cultural context in which it has emerged. The overprescription of drugs, frequency of unnecessary surgery, impersonality of the doctor/patient relationship, and restriction of hospital patients' visitors are just a few examples of practices the American health consumer is beginning to challenge.

Although physicians are typically the target of consumers' criticism, nutritionists also are being challenged by a host of alternative nutrition advisors practicing in health food stores and holistic health clinics. When consumers are told by a nutritionist that diet cannot cure arthritis, multiple sclerosis, or other maladies, many turn to alternative nutrition advisors who are willing to promise a dietary solution.

Because most people, like the mainland Puerto Ricans described above, combine biomedical remedies with other practices, the nutritionist needs to be aware of clients' dietary beliefs and practices. With this awareness, the nutritionist working with people who hold holistic or ethnic folk beliefs can more effectively combine biomedical nutrition beliefs and practices with the alternative system. (For a discussion of how this can be done effectively, turn to Highlight 6-1.)

Figure 6.5
Alternative health care providers. A variety of alternate health care providers practice at this office.
(Lindenberger)

Technology, social organization, and ideology

The last three chapters have discussed the ways in which a society's food and diet patterns can affect its technology, social organization, and ideology. The technological, social organizational and ideological sectors also have a synergistic influence on diet patterns. That is, because they are interrelated, all sectors have a combined effect in determining how the nutritional needs of a society will be met; this combined effect is greater than the effect of any single cultural trait.

A good example of how food habits are related to a society's technology, social organization, and religious beliefs in an interacting manner comes from Roy Rappaport's study of the Tsembaga in 1968. This slash-and-burn horticulturalist group lives in New Guinea. Their gardens produce sufficient taro (a starchy tuberous plant), potatoes, manioc (another starchy plant), greens, sugar cane, and other produce to provide a diet high in calories and adequate in protein.

synergy
Cooperative action of separate agents so that the sum is greater than the individual parts

nitrogen balance
A measure of protein status in the body. The amount of nitrogen consumed as compared with the amount of nitrogen excreted in a given period of time

Because the diet is comprised of 99 percent vegetable matter, however, the protein is of low quality. The diet is varied enough to provide the Tsembaga with just enough protein to achieve nitrogen balance, but added stress may bring a person into a state of negative nitrogen balance (protein deficiency).

The Tsembaga also raise pigs. However, the pork is only consumed at special rituals. These rituals are almost always associated with times of stress: illness, warfare, or death. Ritual norms specify when the pigs are to be slaughtered and who may consume the meat. During times of war, only warriors may eat pork; in case of illness, pork is consumed only by the patient and close relatives. It is to the Tsembaga's nutritional advantage to eat this high-quality protein at times of high stress. The person undergoing stress often requires a higher protein intake to protect against the breakdown of protein in the body and thus maintain nitrogen balance. One wonders if the custom was initiated after careful observation of the health pattern of people experiencing stressful situations.

Pigs serve purely technological functions as well. They act as garbage disposals by eating human feces and other wastes. Also they are used as cultivating machines. They are placed in garden plots at critical times when their rooting cleans out weeds and enhances the secondary growth of vegetation. Pig herds are usually kept small because in large numbers they require more food than is readily available, and they are likely to invade cultivated gardens where their presence is more damaging than useful.

The Tsembaga occupy a territory that is also inhabited by other groups. When hostilities break out with neighboring groups, a ritual cycle begins that has important consequences for the Tsembaga's adaptation to the physical environment, their social organization, and their nutritional status. Pigs and pig feasting play a central role in this ritual.

The ritual cycle begins when hostilities have been formalized and the opposing group is identified as the enemy. A number of taboos regulating food consumption are followed at this time. One important rule used as a means of regulating fighting is the ritual practice of eating heavily salted pig fat before going to battle. "The ingestion of salt, coupled with taboos on drinking (liquids of any kind), has the effect of shortening the fighting . . . . When everyone gets unbearably thirsty, fighting is broken off" (Rappaport, 1968:23).

The next stage of the cycle begins when one group surrenders. A ritual plant, the *rumbin,* is planted, ancestors are thanked for their assistance, and all the pigs except the juveniles are slaughtered. Some of the pork is consumed locally but most is given to allies from other villages who helped in the fight.

Although the fighting has terminated, obligations to the ancestors and allies have not been completely fulfilled until the *rumbin* is uprooted and a special pig feast, the *kaiko,* is held. Five to ten years are needed to increase the pig herds to the required size in order to hold the *kaiko.* During this time the group may not attack another group since the ancestors and allies have not been fully repaid for their assistance. A truce prevails until enough pigs can be raised to stage the feast. This, of course, gives the group a needed break from the destructive effects of fighting.

Once there are enough pigs to hold the *kaiko,* the feasting period continues for about a year. During this time, compatible groups are entertained at gatherings where guests are given the vegetable foods, women and men from neighboring villages court, and males dance. The dancing, which resembles fighting, is more than entertainment. It also advertises group members' strength as warriors and enhances their ability to recruit political allies for future wars. Economic products—salt and axes—are also traded during these feasts.

The ritual period concludes with major pig sacrifices. Rappaport observed between 7,000 and 8,500 pounds of pork distributed at one feast, the majority of which was given to 2,000 to 3,000 people from 17 local groups. On the last day of the feast, the *rumbin* is uprooted. At this time, the Tsembaga are free from their ritual obligation to ancestors and allies and are permitted to engage in warfare.

Rappaport's description of the Tsembaga illustrates the relationship between food habits and many other aspects of culture. The ritual has a number of functions. It mobilizes allies and at the same time results in the redistribution of pork among group members. The cycle is structured in such a way that pork, a high-protein food, is available during times of stress—illness, warfare, and death. The pig ritual also builds social, economic, and political alliances and limits the frequency of fighting. The size of the pig population is regulated by the ritual slaughter so as not to overtax the ecosystem. Obviously, the importance of the ritual slaughter of pigs by the Tsembaga can be fully appreciated only by viewing it within the social and ecological context in which it occurs.

Summary

- World view, religion, and health beliefs are among the ideological considerations that affect a person's health care practices and diet.

- The term *world view* refers to the way a group defines how the world works. People from two different cultures, looking at the same phenomenon, may describe it very differently. Knowing the history of a person's society and his past experiences is helpful in understanding his or her feelings and actions.

- Religion influences dietary practices in several ways. Religious beliefs sometimes prescribe or restrict certain foods. Through prayer and other ritual practices, people use religion to relieve anxiety about an inadequate food supply, and at formal and informal religious meals such as communion and church suppers people reaffirm their faith and sense of solidarity with each other. Many religious practices have adaptive value to the group.

- Health belief systems include notions about how the body works and explanations about what makes it healthy and ill. People vary in how they view symptoms and disease, what preventative and treatment measures they use to maintain health, and the kinds of curers they rely on.

- A society's technology, social organization, and ideology influence diet patterns in a synergistic manner: the combined effect is greater than the effect of any of the single cultural traits.

Highlight 6–1 Nutrition education: Bridging the communication gap

The surge of interest in nutrition that swept North America in the 1970s has been both a boon and a bane to the professional nutrition educator. One of the advantages today's educators enjoy is consumers' hunger (pun intended) for nutrition knowledge. In a survey taken in 1980, 55 percent of the people sampled rated their desire for more nutrition information as "strong." Probably never before have the U.S. and Canadian populations been so receptive to making dietary changes for the sake of good nutrition.

In the 1950s dietitians struggled to get people to listen to their advice. School children thought of the Basic Four as the "Basic Bore," and nutrition was equated with giving up the foods loved most for spinach, liver, and other unpopular items. Dietitians in the 1950s fought to get people's attention. Nutritionists of the 1980s have got the public's attention, but now must guide it in the right direction.

Unfortunately much of the public's excitement about nutrition has been stimulated by misinformation that often overplays the link between nutrition and health and promises easy answers to health problems. For instance, advertisers claim:

- "As a miracle cure from nature, bee pollen is being hailed by doctors around the world as the answer to eternal youth."
- "Vitamin E supplements will improve your sex life in just one week!"
- "Lose five pounds overnight. No pills, no exercise, eat your fill! Go to sleep, wake up and you've lost five pounds."

In contrast, nutritionists' messages seem quite pale. They will tell you candidly that they know of no food that provides eternal youth or guarantees sexual prowess. While they can recommend a diet that may reduce your risk of *developing* cancer, they promise no dietary *cure*. And the weight loss regime they recommend requires exercise and restriction of the many delicious, calorie-rich foods to obtain a mere one- to two-pound weight loss per week.

How can nutritionists be most effective in combating the nutrition misinformation that abounds in American culture today? For insight into the answer to this question, let's look at an exchange between a professionally trained nutritionist and a person who has become interested in nutrition through the popular media. Though the conversation is fictional, the authors have observed some others like it.

The scene is a health fair set up in a local shopping mall. A professionally trained nutritionist from the local university sits at a booth. She is ready to answer questions and hand out brochures to those who stop. Her goal is to give correct nutrition information and combat misinformation in a way that encourages people to improve their diets. Her first customers, a father and his daughter, arrive. The conversation goes like this:

Customer: I'm really interested in nutrition! I started buying whole wheat bread about a year ago. It's more natural than white bread. My body is in much better balance since I've gotten into nutrition. I take a teaspoon of brewer's yeast every day; it has really increased my energy level. I just recently started to give my daughter here, Lisa, 50,000 I.U.'s of vitamin A every day. It's also called retinol. She's doing better in school since she . . .

Nutritionist: I don't know where you heard that brewer's yeast increases your energy level, but that's incorrect. You're wasting your money on it. Just ask your doctor.

Customer: I know it works. Why, I read an article written by a naturopath that proves it. And not only that, I know from my own experience that I am more energetic now. Besides I don't trust any of those doctors anyway—they're all paid off by the American Medical Association. They don't want us to know anything about taking care of our bodies because then they'll lose money.

Nutritionist: That's not true. Also, its very dangerous to be giving your daughter large doses of vitamin A. It's fat-soluble and it can build up in her body and make her very sick.

Customer: It won't make her sick, it's natural. She's been feeling much better since she started taking it. Come on Lisa, let's go.

Obviously, something went wrong here. The customer did not change his beliefs and the nutritionist did not achieve her goal of correcting misinformation. What explains

this all-too-frequent impasse? First, the nutritionist and the customer were approaching the subject of nutrition from two different frames of reference. The nutritionist is trained in the biomedical belief system and believes that the scientific method is the correct way to determine nutritional information. The customer was challenging these basic beliefs. At the same time, the customer holds equally dear to him a set of beliefs that specific foods and large doses of vitamins are necessary for good health. The nutritionist was discounting his closely-held beliefs.

Even when a professional nutritionist counsels someone who shares her respect for science and biomedical nutrition knowledge, dietary changes may be difficult to achieve—(See Highlight 9 for a discussion of diet counseling strategies). However, the problem of changing food habits becomes even more complex when the values of the person to be influenced are different from the nutritionist's (Goldberger and Wheeler 1915). In our scenario, the customer did not value orthodox science nor its results and, in fact, actually distrusted it as a part of the "conservative establishment." In order to work effectively with a person who follows an alternate health system, we must first attempt to understand his food beliefs.

One of the most important steps that a nutritionist can take is to listen closely. Listening serves two functions. It provides useful information about what the person values and believes, some of which may be reinforced and used to promote good eating habits; and it demonstrates courtesy and respect to the person and his or her beliefs. The importance of listening should not be overlooked: it can go a long way toward establishing rapport and greatly increase counseling success.

Let's see how the nutritionist in our scenario could have improved her interaction with the customer if she had listened more closely and respected his values. As you re-call, the customer used the words "natural" and "balance" in describing his beliefs about health. Obviously he values these ideas. The nutritionist can use these same concepts in describing the dangers of taking megadoses of vitamin A. For example, she might warn him that megadoses aren't natural, and that they may "throw the system out of balance."

It is also useful for the nutritionist to establish a common ground with the person she is trying to influence. Find something you agree on, a belief you both share, and build on it. People are more likely to accept information from someone they can identify with in some way. Had the nutritionist in our story focused first on the food belief she and the customer held in common—eating whole wheat bread is good—she might have made more headway. Instead, she started out by bringing up a point they disagreed on—brewer's yeast's ability to increase vigor. Moreover, she denied a belief that he obviously held very dear; one that he had personally tested.

It is also helpful for the nutritionist to categorize the client's beliefs as advantageous to health, having no effect on health, or detrimental to health. Based on these classifications the nutritionist then can decide where to put her focus. Habits that are advantageous to health provide a good starting place for establishing common ground. Those practices that have no effect on health are probably best left undiscussed. Usually it is not worthwhile to disagree or undermine something that the person holds dear just for the sake of setting things straight. On the other hand, dangerous practices should receive serious attention.

Returning now to the nutrition booth at our hypothetical fair, let's categorize the customer's health beliefs. The practice of eating whole wheat bread is clearly beneficial to health, taking a teaspoon of brewer's yeast probably has little effect one way or

the other, while giving large doses of vitamin A to a young person is potentially quite dangerous. Thus, the nutritionist probably would have been more effective had she responded by applauding the customer's use of whole wheat bread, ignoring his beliefs about brewer's yeast, and attempted to persuade him to reduce or eliminate his daughter's vitamin A dosage. Using this approach, let's replay the conversation.

Customer: I'm really interested in nutrition!

Nutritionist: That's great! I am too!

Customer: I started buying whole wheat bread about a year ago. It's more natural than white bread.

Nutritionist: I agree. What kind do you buy?

Customer: "Earth Grains" and "Brownberry." I like them both a lot.

Nutritionist: I buy "Earth Grains," too. It's delicious.

Customer: My body is in much better balance since I've gotten into nutrition. I take a teaspoon of brewer's yeast every day; it really has increased my energy level, and I just recently started to give my daughter here, Lisa, 50,000 I.U.'s of vitamin A every day. It's also called retinol. She's doing much better in school since she started taking it.

Nutritionist: That's interesting. You know lots of people who used to take megavitamins have stopped since they've realized they aren't really "natural." In nature, vitamins come in small doses packaged in carbohydrate, protein, and fat—in other words, as food. When you take megadoses of vitamins you may upset the natural balance of your body.

Customer: I never thought of it that way, but what you're saying makes sense.

Nutritionist: Are you familiar with the term *fat-soluble vitamin?*

Customer: I've heard it.

Nutritionist: Vitamin A is a fat-soluble vitamin. If you get too much, it is stored in the body's fat rather than being passed out in the urine. Toxic levels can build up in the body. There are cases where people have gotten sick from taking too much vitamin A, and some have even died. Children are the most likely to be affected because they need less and they are smaller and more sensitive to overdoses.

Customer: I don't want to do anything to make my daughter sick. I think I'll quit giving them to her.

Nutritionist: I think that's a good decision.

Customer: Well, it's been nice talking to you. Goodbye.

In situations such as this, nutritionists often find it frustrating to listen to misinformation about nutrition. Because nutritionists have studied nutrition formally for many years, food is their field—their profession—making it difficult to yield to competing views. They may be particularly frustrated when someone who has never studied nutrition spreads misinformation and bad advice. As a student of nutrition you might have experienced similar frustration when you have

shared knowledge acquired in a nutrition class with a friend or relative and they disagreed with what you said, showing little or no respect for your credentials or training. But it is important to remember that everyone has some knowledge and beliefs about food. Almost everyone we come in contact with is going to have personal thoughts and views on the subject.

Despite their special training, nutritionists cannot afford to be dogmatic. Nutrition knowledge is always changing; we do not have the final word on many issues. In fact, nutritionists have had to "eat their words" on more than one occasion. Take, for example, changes in infant feeding practices. For years, nutritionists advised mothers to introduce solid foods during the first months of a child's life, citing data that showed infants had the capacity to digest it. More recently, research has suggested that while babies may be able to digest solid foods, it does not necessarily follow that such foods are always good for them. In fact, they may cause digestive problems and allergies if introduced too soon. At first, some nutritionists were reluctant to accept the delayed introduction of solid food, but now a widespread consensus exists that solids should not be started until the baby is four to six months of age. (Breast milk or infant formula are the only foods recommended before that time.) And some of the same health care providers, armed with the new truth, are now intolerant of mothers who introduce solids earlier than advised.

Similar reversals have occurred in therapeutic diets such as those used to treat diverticulosis and diabetes. Twenty years ago, high-fiber foods were believed to irritate the bowel and people with diverticulosis were advised to avoid bran, high-fiber vegetables, and fruits. Today's treatment plan is exactly the opposite: generous amounts of fiber are recommended as a way of "toning" the intestine. Similarly, diabetics, who were once taught to limit the amount of carbohydrates in their diets, are now encouraged to eat a diet high in complex carbohydrates. No wonder the public often is confused about nutrition and reluctant to embrace advice based on the newest scientific findings.

How do these often humbling changes happen? One reason is culture's influence on scientists. Take, for example, the impact of Louis Pasteur's discoveries on scientific thought. For years after he presented his findings on microbes, scientists tried to use this model of infectious diseases to explain other non-infectious maladies. We have already seen how Dutch researchers overlooked the nutritional cause of beriberi in a fervent search for a disease producing germ. A similar delay was encountered in the discovery of pellagra's cause. This disease was long known to be associated with diets in which corn was a staple. Yet, most researchers, still influenced by Pasteur's work, believed it was caused by an infectious agent or toxic substance in corn. In 1914, the U.S. Public Health Service sent Dr. Joseph Goldberger, a bacteriologist, to the southern U.S., where pellagra was endemic. He was assigned the task of finding a cause and possible treatment for the disease. In epidemiologic studies he noted that institution inmates who ate a diet of corn, fatback, and molasses contracted the disease while staff who worked and lived in the same environment, but who ate a diet with more animal food, did not get pellagra. Also, carefully conducted studies showed that healthy prisoner volunteers developed pellagra when given a diet similar to that eaten by people who had already gotten the disease. Because most scientists were convinced that this disease was infectious, Goldberger had to produce rather dramatic proof. To do this, he, his wife, and 14 volunteers ingested and were injected with secreta and excreta from pellagra victims. Finally, Goldberger and Wheeler produced black tongue (a symptom of pellagra) in dogs by giving them a pellagragenic diet. Although nicotinic acid had been known for some time, it was not until 1935, when it was shown to cure black tongue in dogs, did the B vitamin, niacin, become firmly established as the nutrient that prevented pellagra. Subsequent treatment of pellagrous humans and successful dietary prevention based on niacin added the final confirming evidence (Goldberger and Wheeler 1915, Goldberger and Wheeler 1928).

The lesson to be learned from these examples is that even with a reliable tool such as the scientific method, answers don't come easily. Research is often a lengthy process marked by many wrong turns and dead ends. Scientists often ask the wrong questions, use incorrect analytical models, fail to test their assumptions, draw inadequate samples, or apply the wrong statistical tests.

For this reason, we encourage you to carefully scrutinize all research, both old and new; avoid rigid, dogmatic views; and remain open to the many new ideas and changes that are forthcoming in the exciting field of nutrition.

7

The world food supply: Enough for all

It was the best of times, it was the worst of times, it was the age of wisdom, it was the age of foolishness, it was the epoch of belief, it was the epoch of incredulity, it was the season of light, it was the season of darkness, it was the spring of hope, it was the winter of despair, we had everything before us, we had nothing before us . . . .

Charles Dickens
A Tale of Two Cities

We are at a critical juncture in human history. Never before have we had a better opportunity to annihilate poverty and its common companion, malnutrition; yet never before have such a large number of people known desperate poverty and hunger. Today, we have the capacity to produce twice the food needed to feed the world's people; yet our technological interventions have disrupted many delicate ecological systems, challenging the earth's capacity to support its inhabitants. The future has never looked more promising; it has never looked more frightening.

ecology
the study of the interrelationship of organisms and their environments.

Predictions about population growth, food supplies, and environmental hazards offer many conflicting views of tomorrow's world. One thing, however, is crystal clear: The world food situation is changing, and it is changing at a mind-boggling pace. World food supplies are tied to numerous economic, political, and technological factors that are undergoing major modifications. Modest shortages that may raise the cost of bread in the United States or Canada by a few cents may have devastating effects in Bangladesh, Mali, or Guyana. Oil prices and malnutrition, international trade agreements, and rural poverty, political unrest, and hunger are all linked in ways that unite the world's diverse peoples into one. More than ever before, world peace and prosperity demand that we act together with determination, using imaginative new approaches to direct the changes ahead.

Background

Alarm about food shortages, malnutrition, and hunger has been a recurrent theme since 1798, when Malthus publicized his "Essay on the Principle of Population" warning that food production could not keep pace with population growth rates indefinitely. In this century, there have been three waves of fear about the world food situation: in the late 1940s, in the mid 1960s, and again in the mid 1970s. In all three cases, the crises resulted from temporary grain shortages created by drought or wars that affected major grain-producing regions (Sanderson 1975). Each shortage, however, brought with it concern that world food production was approaching its Malthusian limits and no longer could keep pace with population growth: one book predicted widespread famine by 1975 (Paddock and Paddock 1967).

A careful analysis of world food supplies fails to substantiate predictions of widespread famine in the near future. Although debate continues, it is generally concluded that Malthus and other forecasters were wrong. The most recent data show that the rate of population increase is slowing more rapidly than predicted, presumably due to increases in population density and improved economic, health, and nutritional status (Knutson et al. 1983). Technological achievements, especially the development of chemical fertilizers and high-yield varieties of wheat and rice, have increased food production more than enough to keep up with population growth, at least on a world wide basis. Technological advances in irrigation and other agricultural practices also have enabled people to cultivate new areas at a rate of 0.7 percent annually between 1950 and 1970 (Knutson et al. 1983). Together, increased productivity and expansion of cultivated land has brought the most dramatic increase in world food

irrigation
The process of supplying water by artificial means.

supplies that has been experienced since the original agricultural revolution 10,000 years ago. And recently, food production has outstripped population increases in most areas of the world, except Africa (Willet 1983).

> Globally, and throughout history, increases in output per acre were scarcely perceptible within any given generation. Only during the twentieth century have more and more countries succeeded in achieving rapid, continuing increases in output per acre, culminating a global turning point in the man-land food relationship.

(Brown and Finsterbusch 1972:109)

Accompanying this increased food production capacity is the ability to store grain surpluses and distribute them to areas experiencing food shortages. Improved storage and transportation facilities have made it possible for the first time to mobilize emergency relief to most parts of the world. Since World War II, the United States, Canada, and other nations have used their grain surpluses to assist many countries experiencing famine caused by climatic or political disruptions. In 1966 and 1967, one-fifth of the U.S. grain crop was used to relieve famine in India, preventing millions of deaths. Emergency assistance also relieved much of the suffering created by the 1972–74 drought that affected the Sahel region of Africa. In the world as a whole, only a tenth as many people died from famine in the last 25 years as in the same period of time just a century ago (Simon 1980).

Other recent developments contribute to an improved outlook. A network of financial institutions and technical assistance agencies (World Bank, Regional Development Banks, USAID) and international research centers is available to organize and finance worldwide assistance to promote agricultural development. The acknowledgement by national authorities in developing countries that agricultural promotion is a key component in the improvement of their people's living standards has been an important factor, as has been an improved understanding of the nature and limitations of agricultural technology, including a new recognition of the importance of developing simple, inexpensive technologies that are appropriate to the needs of small farms. (See Highlight 8–1.)

Because of these developments, many experts now believe that we have the capacity to eliminate widespread hunger and malnutrition by the turn of the century. While serving as the president of the Overseas Development Council, James Grant said, "that opportunity really didn't exist 25 years ago. It does now." He points to three poor countries, China, Taiwan, and Sri Lanka, and the State of Kerala in India, as examples of societies that already have overcome the worst aspects of poverty and malnutrition. Never before has the future held so much promise (The Hunger Project, *A Shift in the Wind,* 1978:4-5).

But despite the promises now appearing on the horizon, troublesome facts continue to cloud tomorrow's forecast. For even with all our technological achievements and their potential for improving humankind's nutritional well-being, chronic hunger and more subtle forms of malnutrition continue to afflict millions of people. Malnutrition is difficult to measure, and estimates vary widely. The United Nations Food and Agriculture Organization (FAO) estimates that in 1981, at least 420 million people had food intakes that fell below the critical minimum limit.

Some analysts put the number who are desperately hungry and suffer from clinical malnutrition at only 100 million, while others claim that the more subtle effects of hunger and malnutrition are underestimated in these reports; possibly as many as 1.3 billion do not get enough to eat. According to one report, " . . . the number of children under the age of five who die every year from starvation has been placed from 15 million to well over 30 million" (Crittendon 1981:13). Other estimates include:

Estimates of poverty and malnutrition vary widely (see Chapter 8). The number of poor people who are unable to get an adequate diet has increased as the population of the developing nations has expanded. This does not mean, however, that the proportion of the world's population that is poor or hungry has necessarily increased as well.

- The World Bank's calculation that 800 million people in noncommunist developing nations live in such absolute poverty that they do not have minimally adequate diets,

- The 1980 Presidential Commission on World Hunger estimates that "at least one out of every eight men, women, and children on earth suffers malnutrition severe enough to shorten life, stunt physical growth, and full mental ability" (Presidential Commission on World Hunger 1980:3).

- The Global 2000 report's projection that the number of malnourished people will increase from 400 to 600 million in 1970 to 1 to 3 billion in the year 2000 (The Global 2000 Report to the President 1980).

In contrast to these estimates, Thomas Poleman (1981) has dramatically reevaluated the number of truly hungry people in the world. He claims that some earlier estimates of world hunger exaggerated the extent of hunger to draw attention to this crucial problem. In doing so, however, they have made it seem that the possibility of feeding the world's people is hopeless. According to Poleman's estimates, the maximum number of people at nutritional risk is only about 309 million people, mostly women and children. This is less than half the number estimated by the World Bank.

Another problem even more widely publicized concerns the ecological pressures created by modern technology. Evidence of our

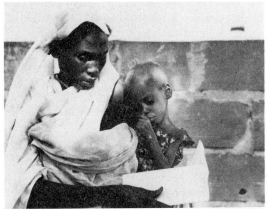

a. UNICEF/Maggie Murray-Lee

b. UNICEF/R. Farquharson

c. UNICEF/Arild Vollan

d. UNICEF/H. Dalrymple

e. UNICEF

Figure 7.1 a–e
Hunger

erosion
The wearing away or slow deterioration caused by the action of water, wind or glacial ice.

acid rain
Rain containing sulfuric and nitric acids; these acids form when oxides, injected into the atmosphere from the burning of fossil fuels, are converted into strong acids in the atmosphere. Acid rains fall over much of Europe, the northeastern United States, and Canada, and have a number of potentially harmful effects. Among their effects are their impact on soil chemistry, fish populations and microorganisms in the soil that are responsible for nitrogen fixation.

destructive impact on the ecology comes from many parts of our habitat: soil erosion, advancing deserts, air pollution and acid rain, deforestation and severe shortages of firewood, the accumulation of chemical pesticides, and pollution of ponds, lakes, and oceans. The economic and ecological costs of cultivating new lands, as well as the environmental damage associated with some of the newest agricultural practices, have made some scientists question whether we can sustain current production levels. Others fear for our very existence.

"Man has been a polluter for hundreds of thousands of years, but because his numbers were relatively few, he did little damage and was able to remain unconcerned about what damage he did do. He has only recently begun to accept some responsibility for his actions in this area, and one hopes he has accepted it in time" (Richards 1972:41).

In Chapters 7 and 8, we will look at both the exciting possibilities and problems that face humankind as it approaches the twenty-first century. First, however, a word of caution is in order. Current analyses and future projections of the world food situation must be studied carefully. Statistical analyses of agricultural productivity, food supply levels, poverty, and malnutrition often present very different—even conflicting—pictures of the world situation. There are several reasons for these often confusing discrepancies. First, data collection is extremely difficult. Imagine trying to determine the extent of malnutrition present in the earth's 4 billion human inhabitants. What nutrient levels would you consider inadequate? How would you measure dietary intake, nutritional status, or access to food supplies? Second, for many variables, a variety of measures can be made. Agriculture productivity, for example, can be calculated as the amount of food produced per unit of land, or per agricultural worker; as the kilocalorie of energy expended in production or in all phases of the food system; or, finally, as the ratio between inputs and outputs in monetary terms.

Future projections also must be viewed cautiously. Projections do not predict what will actually occur but rather depict conditions that are likely to develop if current trends continue unchecked. Of course, the accuracy of the data used to generate projections is also critical in terms of how well they can actually predict the future. Data stretching over a very short period of time, especially when that period is atypical, do not forecast future events nearly as well as data that represent changes caused by factors that will continue to influence events in similar ways both today and tomorrow. Unfortunately, statistics about food production, employment, and population growth in some developing nations are not highly accurate, and in a few cases are completely unavailable. Despite these limitations, projections of the world food supply, population growth, and other conditions abound; not surprisingly, considerable controversy and contradiction surrounds them.

A final problem is the tremendous complexity of the issue. The world food situation is a result of a multiplicity of interacting variables: agricultural and food policies, international trade agreements and economic market conditions, resource distribution, agricultural productivity, environmental conditions, and a host of dietary factors. In the following chapters, we present an overview of the world food situation, describing the major factors influencing food supplies and their distribution throughout the world. Our discussion is brief and thus we can explore only superficially many of the complex issues surrounding this topic. Keeping this in mind, let's attempt to answer two questions that lie at the heart of the world food problem: will we be able to produce enough food to meet the nutritional needs of the world's population as it approaches 5 to 7 billion in the year 2000? And, even if we have sufficient food, how will it get to the people in greatest need?

World food supplies

Most experts now conclude that sufficient supplies of food can be produced to meet the nutritional needs of the 5 to 7 billion people expected to be alive at the turn of the century (Willet 1983). This will be neither automatic nor easy, particularly if we are to avoid overstressing an already-vulnerable environment. An examination of the major factors influencing the adequacy of world food supplies—population growth, and availability of land and water, as well as agricultural, livestock, and fishing technologies—will enable us to better understand the obstacles ahead and the ways to overcome them.

Population growth

Although Neo-Malthusians' gloomy predictions about a population growing too rapidly to feed itself now appear inaccurate, we can foresee a point at which population growth, if unchecked, will overtax the globe's ability to produce sufficient food supplies. Therefore, the need to limit population growth is almost unanimously recognized as the most essential step in ensuring adequate food supplies for future population. Over two centuries ago, Reverend Thomas Malthus recognized that the population grows at geometric or exponential rates, while food production increases only arithmetically.

For this reason, he predicted that the population will eventually grow at a much more rapid pace than food production, ultimately leading to starvation.

As seen in Figure 7-2, population growth follows a J-curve; it grows by doubling—1, 2, 4, 8, 16, 32, 64, 128 and so on. If we plot the change in numbers, the line rises slowly at first, then after a series of doublings, it makes a sharp upward curve in the shape of the letter J. This is the exponential or geometric growth discussed by Malthus. Food production, which climbs in a more steady manner, is suddenly left far behind.

The effects of population growth on food supplies is clearest when we look at how the per-capita food availability—amount of food available per person—is calculated. An examination of the formula shows that if food production increases more rapidly than population size, per-capita food availability improves; if the population

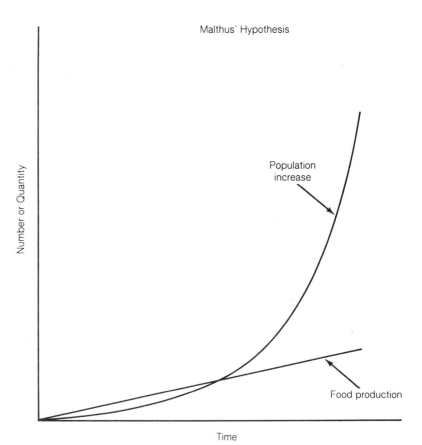

Figure 7.2
Arithmetic and exponential growth. In 1798, Thomas Malthus hypothesized that population would eventually exceed the food supply since population would increase exponentially and food production would increase only arithmetically.

PER CAPITA FOOD AVAILABILITY = $\dfrac{\text{TOTAL FOOD AVAILABILITY}}{\text{TOTAL POPULATION}}$

Figure 7.3
Per capita food availability equation.

grows more rapidly than food production, less food is available per person.

The history of the earth's population growth exemplifies what is meant by exponential growth and the J-curve. For the first million years, the human population remained relatively constant, growing at a rate of .001 percent each year. The domestication of plants and animals brought about a burst in the growth rate to .04 percent annually. At this rate the world's population grew from 5 million in 10,000 B.C. to 545 million in 1650. The next major change in the growth rate—to 0.29 percent—came about the time of the Industrial Revolution, bringing the total population to 728 million only one hundred years later. Death rates began to decline around the mid–1700s and the growth rate again jumped, this time to 0.45 percent a year. Since then the rate has risen more, and more rapidly: 0.53 percent in the early 1800s, 0.91 percent in the early 1900s and 2.10 percent in the 1970s. We now have come around the J-curve, reaching the 4 billion mark (Allaby 1977).

Another way to visualize population growth is through doubling times—the time required for population to double its size. From 2600 to 350 B.P., the population doubled on an average of every 1000 years. It doubled again in 1850, only 200 years later; then doubled once more 30 years later in 1930. The current doubling time varies considerably between nations, but averages 37 years (Caliendo 1979:177).

On the brighter side, population growth rates have been declining steadily in developing as well as developed nations. In fact, during the period from 1965 to 1970, population growth in the developing countries declined from 2.5 percent annually to an estimated 2.0 percent (Willet 1983). In developed countries, populations are growing about 0.7 percent a year (Knutson et al. 1983:98). As a result, some observers have changed their population projections to reflect slower growth rates and lower population levels for the future. Lester Brown at the World Watch Institute, for example, has readjusted his population projections downward from 6.3 billion to 5.4 billion for the year 2000. As the rate of population growth falls further after the end of this century, the needs for increases in food production will also decline, thus it may be that the period immediately ahead of us poses the greatest challenge (Willet 1983, Campbell 1975).

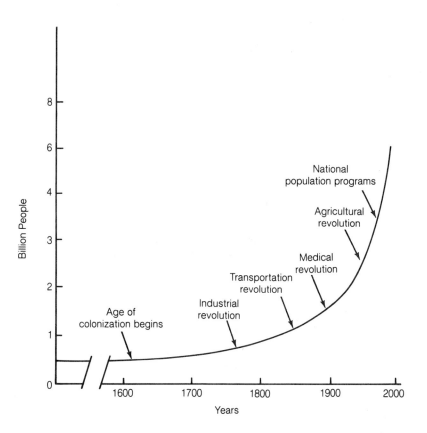

Figure 7.4
World population growth. The history of the earth's population growth can be character- ized as exponential, fol- lowing a J-curve.
(Adapted from Population Reference Bureau, Inc., World Population Growth and Response, 1965–1975: A Decade of Global Action. *Washington, D.C., 1976, p. 4.)*

Table 7.1   Past and present population increases

Year	Estimated population	Estimated annual percent increase in the intervening period
ca. 10,000 B.C.	5,000,000	—
A.D. 1	250,000,000	0.04
1650	545,000,000	0.04
1750	728,000,000	0.29
1800	906,000,000	0.45
1850	1,171,000,000	0.53
1900	1,608,000,000	0.65
1950	2,486,000,000	0.91
1970	3,632,000,000	2.09
1974	3,900,000,000	2.10

Reprinted with the permission of the Population Council from "World Population: Status Report 1974" by Bernard Berelson, Reports of Population/Family Planning, Number 15: p. 3.

Focus 7-1

On family planning

Why has population growth slowed, proving Malthus and his followers wrong? Knutson et al. (1983:92) point to "Malthus's failure to recognize that population growth slows with increases in per capita real income, with increases in population density, with improved health and nutrition, and with the realization that less food is available per capita."

One factor contributing to declining birthrates is the widespread promotion of family planning programs. Government policy makers in countries inhabited by 90 percent of the world's population promote some form of family planning. In China, women are encouraged to marry relatively late; it is not considered socially acceptable to marry before the mid to late 20s in towns, and early 20s in rural areas. Oral contraceptives are popular, but a variety of fertility measures, including abortion and sterilization, are employed (Allaby 1977:82).

Family planning programs, especially those in rural areas of developed countries, encounter many obstacles. First, each of the available contraceptives has significant disadvantages. Vasectomies and tubal ligations are not reversible; the diaphragm, condom, and oral contraceptives require discipline; intrauterine devices are associated with pain, bleeding, and increased mortality; and injectible contraceptives have been shown to cause serious side effects. Second, products must be distributed to areas with bad roads and poorly developed markets. Third, many programs are fraught with administrative, economic, and political problems. For example, the Indian government decided to offer free radios to men willing to have a vasectomy. Large numbers of radios were manufactured at low prices to supply the government program, but before the program could succeed, the radios appeared in the open market where men could buy them at reasonable prices and without having to have vasectomies (Allaby 1977:83).

Finally, family planning programs run into resistance in many rural communities because families want to have many children. As Robert McNamara (1977:37), President of the World Bank, has said, "It is a mistake to think that the poor have children mindlessly or without purpose—in light of their own personal value systems—

irresponsibly. Quite the contrary . . . poor people have large families for many reasons. But the point is, they do have reasons . . . ." Among their reasons are the following:

1. the need for children to take care of parents in old age and illness
2. extra hands to help with agricultural and household labor
3. religious beliefs that forbid birth control
4. a value on sons as a mark of success or good fortune or virility and the opportunity to pass on the family name and land.

Figure 7.5
Family planning
(AID)

Due to high mortality rates in developing countries, most families have many children hoping that several will survive to maturity. Allen Berg (1973:33) discusses the burden this places on poor families in *The Nutrition Factor.*

> Most families experience the loss of one or more infants or young children, and the uncertainty of their children's survival hangs over most couples. In many poor areas, where large percentages of children die before reaching a productive age, uncertainty and the overcompensation it induces are major factors in the common bearing of seven or eight offspring to assure two male survivors. A village study in India's western state Gujarat concluded 'families continued to have children until they were reasonably certain that at least one boy would survive. Once they had this number, they attempted to stop having more' . . . . A study using computer simulation indicates that with current estimated infant and adult death rates in India, a couple must bear 6.3 children to be 95 percent certain one son will be surviving at the father's sixty-fifth birthday. The average number of births in India per couple is 6.5.

Some scientists, like Julian Simon (1981), view large families in a positive light. He believes additional people contribute to increasing productivity through larger markets and economies, and more importantly, by contributions of increased knowledge and technical processes. While this may be true in areas where people are well-nourished and economically integrated into the market, it makes less sense where people's creativity and productivity are hindered by malnutrition. Government authorities in most poor regions, therefore, are attempting to limit population growth in an effort to enhance the per-capita food supply and the well-being of the general populace.

What these authorities have learned is that family planning programs do not work until families *want* to restrict the number of children they have. Health services, economic development, or other changes are needed to bring infant and child death rates down to acceptable levels before family planning can succeed. Because of this, students of population dynamics have come to see overpopulation as a *result* of underdevelopment, rather than a cause. As economic well-being increases, parents are motivated to limit the size of their families.

However, other analysts, such as Murdoch (1980), argue that a nation's overall economic development is insufficient to alter its growth rate; all segments of the country must benefit from the wealth and other improvements before economic development will slow population growth significantly. This explains the failure of economic development to slow growth in countries such as Mexico, in which wealth is distributed unequally between the rich and poor,

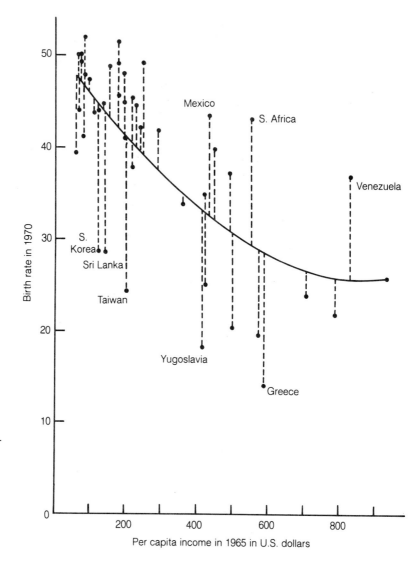

Figure 7.6
*Birthrate in 1970 com-
pared to per capital in-
come in 1965 (U.S. dol-
lars). The dashed lines
show the difference be-
tween the actual birth-
rate and the birthrate expected on the basis of
average income.*
(*William A. Murdoch,* The
Poverty of Nations, *Baltimore, MD: Johns Hopkins
University Press, 1980,
p. 61.*)

while other nations such as Sri Lanka that have concentrated on improving the economic situation of poorer segments have experienced lower birth rates. In Sri Lanka, the government has provided
assistance for the poor through food subsidies, free education, and
free health care. Also, its progressive tax structure works to ensure
that income is more equally distributed. Murdoch (1980:69–70)
notes, "this is not to suggest that Sri Lanka is a perfectly egalitarian
society. . . . But Sri Lanka has gone a long way toward equalizing the
availability of the basic requirements of a healthy and secure life for
the majority of its population."

The overall relationship in a number of countries is depicted Figure 7.6.

Even in the face of improved family planning programs, economic development, and declining birth rates, population size still continues to grow for a period of time due to the large number of women in the childbearing age range (15 to 45) resulting from high birthrates in previous years. Even if women in the reproductive period only have two children per family, their large numbers will cause the population to grow. It will take at least another generation before the number of childbearing women has declined and population growth can truly stabilize at a zero growth level. It is for this reason that Caliendo (1979:183) and others conclude that "although the declines in birthrates and natural increase levels that took place between 1965 and 1974 are encouraging in that they indicated that the world is heading toward a more slowly increasing population, they do not suggest that the population problem has been solved."

Food production

With population growth expected well into the twenty-first century, methods of increasing food production become critical. Thus far agriculture has more than kept pace with population growth in the world.

> In the developed countries agricultural production since 1955 increased at an average rate of 2.3 percent. On a per capita basis, the growth rate is 1.3 percent (reflecting annual increases in population). In the developing countries, the production growth rate is an even faster 2.9 percent. However, with more rapidly expanding populations, the per capita production grew at only 0.5 percent annually.
>
> *(Knutson et al. 1983:110)*

Growth of food production in developing countries is encouraging. As a group they have done well. When they are examined individually, wide variations in their agricultural performances are revealed: the lowest-income nations have done more poorly than the middle-income countries, and agricultural productivity in Africa has actually fallen behind its population growth (Willet 1983).

In sum, agricultural production is improving, although not as rapidly in some regions as others. In the developing countries, and for the world as a whole, it is keeping pace with population growth but not greatly exceeding it. Many studies suggest that agricultural productivity will have to grow at accelerated rates in order to eliminate hunger-imposed malnutrition. The FAO and International Food Pol-

Figure 7.7
Urbanization. Each year millions of acres of farm land are lost to urban expansions.
(USDA/Tim McCabe)

icy Research Institute conclude that annual food production will have to increase 3 to 4 percent in order to prevent massive food deficits in low-income countries (Knutson et al. 1983).

Food production can be increased in two ways: (1) cultivate larger areas of land, and/or (2) increase the amount of food harvested from the land now under cultivation (i.e., the area-to-yield ratio or agricultural intensity).

Land cultivation

The earth's surface has an estimated 32.9 billion acres of land. Only 30 percent of this area, approximately 9.8 billion acres, is potentially useful for agriculture. Lack of moisture, severe temperatures, and other environmental conditions currently prohibit cultivation of the remaining areas (Ehrlich et al. 1977:248).

The percentage of arable land actually farmed varies from region to region. For the world as a whole, only 3.5 billion acres are actually cultivated, leaving substantial room for growth. Asia and Europe are approaching their limit of arable land, but South America, Austrailia, New Zealand, and Africa currently farm only a small proportion of the available land.

During the past decade, the amount of land cultivated increased by 8 percent in developing countries, while their irrigated areas increased by 25 percent (Willet 1983:7). No doubt further increases will occur in the coming years, contributing to continued growth in production yields.

But, while opportunities to expand into new areas exist in all countries, these opportunities are not without substantial costs. Cultivation of virgin lands often requires expensive machinery to clear the land as well as to provide irrigation and drainage. China and India, for example, have found it difficult to expand their agriculture beyond current limits, and the USSR has had to abandon some of the lands it had attempted to cultivate in the late 1950s. In fact, Franke and Franke (1975:261) estimate that approximately $28 billion would be required to open enough new land to feed people added to the world's population annually.

Some of the new land, such as the plains in Argentina known as the Pampas, have the potential to be highly productive; other areas, especially in the tropical regions, are more marginal (Knutson et al. 1983:24). Soils are less fertile, more difficult to till, and/or more susceptible to erosion. Thus it is unlikely that expansion into new lands will contribute significantly to the increased production levels needed to feed the world's population in the future; increased productivity of land already under cultivation no doubt will be "the dominant method by which further increases will be achieved" (Willet 1983:7).

Agricultural productivity

As in the United States (see Chapter 4), "The distinguishing characteristic of agriculture in the developed nations is high productivity: high yield per acre, high yield per hour of labor, or both" (Nicholson and Nicholson 1979:49). The first country to experience a rapid and continuing increase in yields per acre was Japan around the turn of the century. Shortly afterwards, northwestern European countries such as Denmark and the Netherlands also experienced yield-per-acre takeoffs. In 1940, Australia, the United States, and the United Kingdom generated significant yield-per-acre increases. In all cases, the amount of grain produced per acre took a sharp steady upward

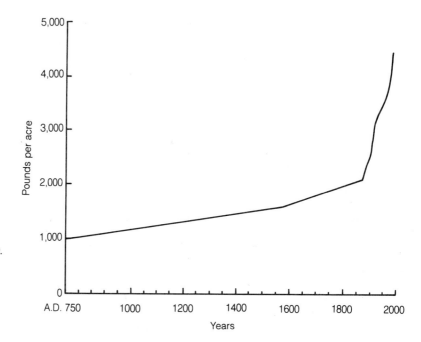

Figure 7.8
*Rice yields in Japan: A.D.
750–1960. Historical es-
timates from the Japa-
nese Ministry of
Agriculture.*
(USDA)

turn from previously static or barely noticeable increases (Brown
and Finsterbusch 1972:115–7).

The two most important breakthroughs responsible for increased yields were the development of chemical fertilizers and the
creation of high-yield varieties of wheat and rice. In the 1950s, plant
breeders developed new hybrid seeds capable of producing yields
that more than doubled the output of food harvested per acre when
used with fertilizer and proper amounts of water.

*See Highlight 7–1 for a
more thorough discus-
sion of the Green
Revolution.*

Commonly referred to as the Green Revolution, the new seeds
and other inputs, such as fertilizer, irrigation, and pesticides, have
spread rapidly since the 1960s through much of the developed and
developing world. In Asia alone, the acreage planted in high-yield
varieties of wheat and rice climbed dramatically from 1965 to 1975.

Despite the new agricultural revolution, outputs per acre and
per hour remain lower in most developing nations than in the developed world. Taiwan and Korea are noteworthy exceptions. With respect to rice, for instance, developing nations average, per acre, 3.75
tons annually in contrast to 13.75 tons in industrialized nations. Output per agricultural worker is 13 times lower in the poorer nations.

Because future food supplies depend largely on increased productivity, attempts have been made to introduce Western-style
mechanized agriculture into developing nations. While successful
on large plantations, mechanization and monoculture have proven

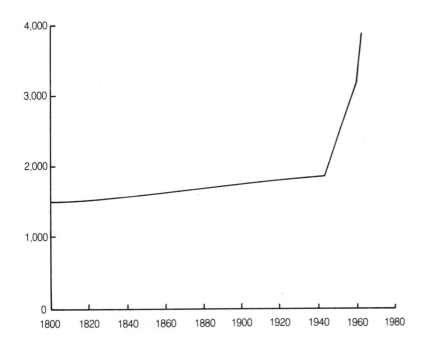

Figure 7.9
Corn yields in the United States: 1800–1963.
(USDA)

inappropriate for the millions of peasant farmers who make up much of the poor population in the developing world. On small landholdings, mechanization offers little improvement. Because land is limited, output per acre is the major concern and peasant agricultural practices (intercropping, multiple cropping, and close attention to individual plants) proves more productive than mechanized practices, where major gains are in output per worker, not per acre of land.

Moreover, geographical constraints on the use of machinery—steep hills, small plots—and lack of money to purchase machines and the associated inputs of fertilizers and pesticides make industrial agriculture inappropriate for most peasant farmers (see Highlights 7–1 and 8–1).

Comparisons of peasant or more traditional agriculture with industrialized agriculture differ greatly depending upon the productivity measure used. Industrialized agricultural practices are far more productive than traditional practices when hours of labor are compared. The industrialized agricultural laborer, using chemicals, pesticides, and machines, produces 120 times more food energy per hour than the average subsistence farmer, and over 650 times more than the !Kung Bushmen (Allaby 1977:234). The new methods also outproduce traditional methods in terms of land units. Monocropping with high-yield varieties of wheat and rice have more than quadrupled yields in many parts of the world.

monocropping
Planting a field with only one kind of plant. It is contrasted with "intercropping," in which several kinds of plants (e.g., corn, beans, and squash) are planted in the same field.

But these comparisons can be somewhat misleading. Often they are based solely on measurements of the major crop—wheat or rice—and do not take into account the other foods harvested in the small farmer's intercropped fields. The International Institute of Tropical Agriculture (Ward et al. 1980:574) cites data showing increases of 100 percent in total production when maize is intercropped with cowpeas, compared to cowpeas raised alone (regardless of the tillage method used).

Donald Innis (1980:4) gives an example of how assessment of productivity per unit of land can be misleading if the second, minor, crop is not considered along with the main crop.

> On a big rubber plantation, a corporate owner might well not be interested in growing cowpeas. But small farmers in Malaysia grow several secondary crops with rubber and are very much interested in the value of these crops. In addition they produce more rubber per acre than commercial plantations because they plant more trees. On commercial plantations, fewer trees per acre mean larger trees, less cost in tapping them, more rubber per tree and more profit per acre, even though less rubber per acre and no intercrops are produced. Some of the problems of measuring efficiency now become apparent.

Another problem in comparing yields per unit of land is failure to consider the long-term implications of various farming practices on soil structure, management requirements, and future yields.

> It is not always recognized that the effects of the soil on one year's cropping persist and influence the quality and yield of subsequent crops. It is therefore essential that the link between the past and present is recognized in methods of economic analysis. It would be wrong not to measure any major cropping change against its long-term implications for soil structure, management requirements, and yields. Comparisons of the profitability of "traditional" and "modern" agricultural technology will not be complete until the long-term implications of different technologies for future soil fertility and soil structure are taken into account.

(Sinha 1976:29)

Thus, the use of modern techniques that bring about short- or medium-range production benefits may create long-term damage to the soil structure or other natural resources if used indiscriminately. Higher yields today mean little if soil damage or pesticide accumulation reduce food supplies tomorrow.

Finally, a very different picture of productivity is created when the efficiency of entire food systems (agricultural production, transportation, food processing, and marketing) is measured in terms of energy inputs and outputs. Analyses of productivity in terms of energy ratios have become popular since OPEC raised its oil prices, causing fuel and fertilizer costs to skyrocket. As gas shortages developed and people came to realize the finiteness of fossil fuels, many people began examining agricultural systems in terms of energy inputs compared to energy outputs, or the amount of kilocalories of energy expended to produce a kilocalorie of food energy. As we saw earlier, in Chapter 4, industrialized systems make a rather poor showing. Because of their heavy reliance on chemical fertilizers and machines, agriculture (and the entire food system) in developed nations has become increasingly *inefficient* over the last 65 years with respect to the amount of energy from all sources needed to produce a kilocalorie of food energy.

In the section below, we look at some of the constraints on increasing productivity that affect industrialized and peasant farmers alike.

Water

Water poses the major limitation on the expansion of food production. Much of the land available for farming must be watered to produce food; most farmlands planted in high-yield varieties require careful water controls for optimal yields (Caliendo 1979:100). With proper irrigation and drainage, crop production can be increased in both traditional and modern farming systems. Currently, an estimated 500 million acres of farmland are irrigated. This is only one-seventh of the area under cultivation. Clearly the potential for increasing food productivity through proper water management is great. The major obstacles to realizing this potential are the availability of financial and technical resources for construction of irrigation projects, and careful maintenance. Construction costs alone place large-scale projects outside the reach of many developing countries.

Smaller-scale irrigation projects are becoming increasingly popular. Many Asian governments, for instance, are encouraging small farmers to finance their own tubewells or other small irrigation systems. Pakistani farmers installed 32,000 private tubewells during a five-year period in the mid-1960s; most farmers were able to recover the initial investment of $1,000 to $2,500 within two years. And for every 5,000 tubewells installed, an additional 1 million acre-feet were added to the annual supply of irrigation water. Because the tubewells are privately owned, water control is under the farmer's personal management, enabling each farmer to determine exactly how much and when water is delivered to his crop (Brown and Finsterbusch 1972:49–50).

tubewell
A small well for obtaining water from shallow strata; it consists of a pointed pipe driven into the ground.

acre-foot
The volume of water that would cover one acre of land to a depth of one foot.

Many technical factors also constrain the expansion of land through irrigation. If irrigation projects are not designed and maintained correctly, they create several problems. First, water brought in through irrigation channels percolates down through the soil to the ground water below. As it accumulates, the water table or the groundwater level rises. When the water table reaches the soil's surface, it brings with it salts such as magnesium, carbonates, sulfates, and sodium chloride from ancient subterranean deposits. Water evaporating from above also can leave salts that increase the soil's salinity. These salts can actually sterilize the soil. A second, but related, problem is waterlogging. As the water table rises to the surface, it reduces the amount of air and aerobic organisms held in the soil. Processes of decomposition are altered and plant roots die from lack of oxygen (Brown and Finsterbusch 1972:50–51). Many large-scale irrigation systems have created waterlogged, sterile soils. The ancient irrigation systems in the fertile crescents of Mesopotamia and the Indus Valley, as well as the recent Aswam Dam project, are among the more dramatic examples.

Obtaining groundwater through wells is relatively simple technologically but undesirable consequences can still result. Groundwater may be moving so slowly that the well cannot fill as rapidly as it is emptied. Obviously, much remains to be learned about intervening in the hydraulic cycle before these limitations can be fully overcome.

aerobic
The quality of living or occurring only in the presence of oxygen

hydraulic
Operated by means of water, especially through the pressure caused by the resistance of water forced through a tube

Soil nutrients

Plants need 13 nutrients for proper growth. All of these can be added to deficient soils. The most common nutrients manufactured as fertilizers are nitrogen, phosphorous, and potassium.

In fertilizers, nitrogen from the atmosphere is fixed chemically, usually using natural gas or a petroleum derivative to create ammonia compounds. Phosphorous is produced from rock phosphate. Potassium is mixed from minerals such as potassium chloride, and sometimes it is extracted from wood ash or seaweed.

Lack of any essential nutrient will decrease yields. Most often nitrogen is the limiting factor because it is taken from the soil in large quantities by plants, but is replaced slowly unless nitrogen-fixing crops are planted.

In traditional agricultural systems soil fertility is maintained through several means: application of animal manure, use of nitrogen-fixing plants such as legumes, and letting land lie fallow and then burning the ground cover. More recently, chemical fertilizers have also been adopted with great success.

When high-yield varieties are used, especially as part of a monoculture system, fertilizer is essential for optimal yields. As we have

fixation
Nitrogen fixation is the process whereby nitrogen from the atmosphere is assimilated by microorganisms in the soil and released for plant use on the death of the microorganisms.

already seen, fertilizer can more than quadruple the yields of some new varieties, making the use of chemical fertilizers the single most important factor in the increased agricultural productivity experienced in recent years.

The potential to further increase food yields with chemical fertilizers is especially great in developing countries. In 1972–3, the developing countries used relatively little fertilizer in comparison with the wealthier nations. In the United States, an average of 77.5 pounds of fertilizer was used per acre of arable land; in Japan, the average was 339 pounds per acre; while in India, it was only 14.2 pounds and in Laos it was less than 0.2 pounds per acre (Allaby 1977:159). Overall, the developed nations used 4.5 times more fertilizer than the developing countries (Sinha 1976:19).

The major constraints to increasing productivity with chemical fertilizers are availability and cost. As demand for fertilizers increased in the early 1970s, prices rose. Increased prices for natural gas and the petroleum derivatives used to make nitrogen fertilizer further boosted prices. Between 1971 and 1974, the average world price of one ton of fertilizer climbed from $40 to $360! This, of course, placed fertilizers financially out of reach for those farmers who needed it most (Marei 1978:29). Fortunately, fertilizer prices have begun to decline in the early 1980s due to manufacturing changes and more efficient distribution (Willet 1983:8).

Fertilizer shortages were another problem in the early 1970s. As shortages ended and prices dropped, fertilizer use rose in the late 1970s and early 1980s. However future shortages are still feared and research is currently being conducted to develop new crops with the ability to fix their own nitrogen.

Pests

Production and availability of food could also be increased significantly through better control of plant diseases and other pests. Losses of crops to pests have been studied in great detail by David and Marcia Pimentel (1979:13):

> On a world-wide basis, food losses to pests are high at present, world crop losses to pests are estimated to be about 35 percent . . . . These losses include destruction by insects, pathogens, weeds, mammals, and birds . . . . Post-harvest losses are estimated to range from 9 percent in the United States . . . to 20 percent in some of the developing nations especially in the tropics. The prime pests of harvested foods are microorganisms, insects and rodents.

> When post-harvest losses are added to pre-harvest losses, total food losses due to pests are estimated to be about 45 percent. *Thus, the pest populations are consuming* and/or destroying nearly one-half of the world's food supply. Surely this is a loss that we cannot afford . . . .

pathogen
A specific microorganism (such as a bacterium or virus) or substance capable of causing a disease.

Figure 7.10
*Pest control. AID has
trained Ethiopian techni-
cians, pilots, and me-
chanics to control in-
sects and plant diseases
by aerial spraying.
(AID)*

Pesticide use remains low in developing countries. Only 2 percent of the total cultivated area in India was treated with pesticides
in 1965. In contrast, 57 percent of U.S. acreage planted in corn was
treated with herbicides and 33 percent with insecticides (Sinha
1976:20).

Besides the cost, which can be substantial to the small farmer,
pesticides present another problem. Pesticides are highly toxic and
capable of affecting a broad range of plants and animals other than
the pests they are intended to kill; they circulate widely in air and
water currents, and in many cases accumulate much more rapidly
than they decompose. DDT, for example, accumulates in the tissues
of many species. It does not break down for approximately ten years,
thus as its use continues, DDT concentration in the environment
builds, threatening the extinction of many animals (especially predatory birds). "DDT is today found in the tissues of animals over a global range of life forms from penguins in Antartica to children in the
villages of Thailand, and it is even present in your tissues. [In fact,]
in the United States, concentrations of DDT in [some] mother's milk
now exceed the tolerance levels established for foodstuffs by the
Food and Drug Administration" (Brown and Finsterbusch
1972:174–175). Though use of DDT is now controlled in the U.S.,
effects on the current generation of breastfed babies are yet to be
seen. It is ironic that even breast milk—the best food for human
infants—has been contaminated by chemical attempts to improve
crop yields.

Because of the environmental hazards associated with pesticides, research is underway to develop alternate methods of controlling pests. Among these are:

1. Pesticides that are specific to particular species of insects, diseases or weeds and that do not affect other organisms

2. Pesticides that are relatively non-toxic and decompose rapidly

3. Biological controls, such as the release of sterile male members of a species so that population growth is stopped or greatly reduced

4. Breeding pest-resistant plants

5. Development and introduction of insect parasites and other organisms that prey on the pests

6. Integrated pest management that uses a variety of methods.

Given the potential that exists for decreasing the amounts of food lost to pests, a better understanding of control measures is of tremendous importance and offers great promise for future food supplies.

Climate

Climate usually refers to average weather conditions over several years. However, climates fluctuate, sometimes widely, and the day-to-day fluctuation in temperature, rainfall, and other conditions may have a tremendous impact on crop yields. Overall, the developed nations enjoy a climate that is more favorable to agricultural production than most of the developing nations, in which severe conditions (wet, dry, hot) are commonly found.

Unfortunately, we know amazingly little about climatic changes that influence food productivity, and we have even less control over their occasional catastrophic effects. Some scientists believe that the earth is experiencing a cooling trend; possibly a new period of glaciation is beginning. Others claim that temperatures have been rising. They show that as fossil fuels are burned, carbon dioxide rises into the atmosphere where it is trapped and creates a "greenhouse effect," holding in the sun's heat.

Research on these and other climatic processes is now underway. Meterologists are attempting to develop more sophisticated methods of predicting weather patterns and their effects on crops. In the meantime, the FAO, International Wheat Council, and other agencies recommend the establishment of grain stockpiles to be used in lean years. (The issue of grain surpluses will be discussed in greater detail in Chapter 8.)

Livestock production

Livestock production and meat consumption have become the center of controversy in many discussions of the world food crisis. On one hand, livestock are depicted as providing an unnecessary luxury foodstuff, animals are seen as direct competitors with humans for scarce grain supplies, and because of their inefficiency in converting grain protein to animal protein, they are considered an important factor contributing to future food shortages. As a result, reduced consumption of animal products is recommended so that more grain can be made available to the poor in developing countries. Data used to support this viewpoint can be quite convincing: Three billion head of livestock are maintained to supply the animal protein consumed in the U.S. alone. Although farm animals traditionally lived on forage, wastes, and surpluses (as when household pigs and chickens consumed spilled grain and kitchen scraps), today livestock consume 135 million tons of grain. This is 10 times more than the amount consumed by the entire U.S. population (Pimentel et al. 1980:843). Further, livestock in general, and sheep and cattle in particular, are inefficient converters of protein. Allaby (1977:20) compares the efficiency of various livestock forms and shows "quite clearly, that in terms of food energy and protein no livestock enterprise can compare in efficiency with vegetable crops . . . for every kilogramme of egg protein the hen must consume more than 4 kg. of grain protein; for each kilogramme of pork protein the pig must be fed 7.7 kg. of grain protein; for every kilogramme of poultry meat protein the hen must receive 5.9 kg. of grain protein; and, if we plan to produce beef in feedlots, fed on grain, then every kilogramme of beef protein represents an expenditure of 22 kg. of grain protein."

The effect of animal consumption on grain supplies is obvious when we compare the amount of grain consumed in the developed nations that use large quantities of meat with developing countries subsisting predominantly on grain. In India and Thailand, less than 200 pounds of grain is used by the average person each year. After setting aside 10 percent for the next year's seeds, the Indian family has less than 360 pounds, or under one pound per day for actual consumption. Nearly all of this is eaten directly as grain. At the other extreme, Canadians use almost a ton of grain per capita, with most of it used to feed livestock that they consume in the form of meat, milk, and eggs.

Perhaps the best evidence comes from the analysis of livestock production and its impact on grain supplies in specific developing countries. Billie DeWalt, for example, has examined the situation in Mexico and Honduras. In both cases he found that grain production failed to meet the population's nutritional needs largely because of increased livestock production. In Mexico, both productivity (yield per acre) and total grain production have climbed dramatically over the last four decades. More importantly, the production of basic grains has been rising at a faster rate than population rate so that the amount available per person is over 40 percent more than what it was in 1940. Yet Mexico has failed to eradicate its widespread malnutrition and must now import grain.

What has happened to the increased grain supplies? The picture becomes much clearer when consumption figures are considered. For as DeWalt (1983b:28) points out: "Mexico's food problem is not as much a production problem as it is a *consumption* problem. Mexican farmers are not only faced with supplying an adequate amount of food for the demands of the people but are also faced with providing for the appetites of that portion of the population that is able to afford an increasingly affluent diet." Large amounts of grain are diverted to support the meat consumption of affluent Mexicans who have increased per-capita pork consumption by 65 percent, poultry by 35 percent, and beef by 32 percent over a seven year period.

In Honduras, the situation is far worse. Much of the livestock raised there is intended for export to the United States and does not contribute significantly to increased protein intake in the country. In fact, per-capita meat consumption in Honduras actually declined by 20 percent from the early 1960s to 1979. Also, increased livestock production has brought about "a major change in the natural environment with pasture replacing forest land" (DeWalt 1983a:8). Small farmers cultivating land to produce food for their own households are becoming more scarce as larger landowners put their land into pasture for animals rather than renting or sharecropping to their landless neighbors.

Changes in resource use also are altering the social and economic life of local communities. (See Highlight 7–1.) Finally, diversion of grains to livestock is difficult to support in light of the shortfalls in basic grains projected for 1990 (DeWalt 1983b:2). Thus, in these countries as elsewhere, increased consumption of grainfed livestock can place enormous pressures on agricultural resources and tie up much of the increased grain produced through advanced techniques.

On the other side of the controversy are experts who argue that efficient use of grazing animals does not pose a threat for future food supplies. Indeed, livestock production may even increase the yield of high-grade protein and byproducts extracted from renewable sources, and one can think of cattle as living storage sites for surplus grain. Livestock, when used in these ways, can actually contribute to the resolution of malnutrition. Central to this view is the unique stomach of ruminants—cattle, sheep, goats, buffalo, deer, antelope, and other meat-producing animals. Ruminants' stomachs allow them to digest the cellulose in grasses and other plant material that humans cannot utilize as food. Horses, rabbits, and many other animals also digest cellulose, although less efficiently than ruminants. These animals convert vegetable matter into animal products, enabling humans to indirectly consume food that otherwise would be unavailable. Thus when fed grasses and other forage materials, animals become a complementary food source rather than a competitive element (Jacobson and Jacobson 1977:144–5).

Because many countries have large quantities of unused forages and large areas of marginal land suited only for grazing, important food gains could be realized by switching livestock from grain to forage feeds. In the United States cornbelt, cattlemen are mixing corncobs, cornstalks, straw, and even sawdust with molasses (to make it more palatable) and urea (to increase nitrogen content). Gains can also be made by switching pigs and other nonruminants from grain to feeds that do not compete with human needs.

Pigs in China are reared in large numbers on vegetable refuse, ground and fermented rice hulls, corn husks, sweet potatoes, soybean vines, water hyacinths, and other wastes (Jacobson and Jacobson 1977:145–6).

It is also worth noting that animals provide a full range of nonfood products and services needed in the developing world. Transportation, power to pull machinery, leather, wool, and manure for fertilizer and cooking fuel make animals a valuable part of the food production system.

Finally, livestock exports to developed countries generate funds that can be used to offset the costs of grain and other goods imported by developing nations.

Besides efforts to adjust the livestock production system so that it is more compatible with human needs for food, steps are being taken to utilize wild animal species for food and other products. The gazelle, impala, eland, kangaroo, and many other game animals are being considered for possible domestication. Perhaps most interesting is South America's capybara. The largest living rodent, it weighs over 100 pounds, reaches reproductive age in two years and bears 4 to 12 offspring each year. It forages for food along river banks and swamps where competition with other animals is minimal (Jacobson and Jacobson 1977:146). Insects and reptiles, now eaten as delicacies in many societies, are a less likely, but nevertheless potential, food source (Meyers-Rochow 1983).

Fishing

Many people believe that the sea offers a cornucopia of food; once we have exhausted the land's ability to produce enough food, we can turn to the oceans for an almost unlimited supply of high-grade protein. Indeed, for 25 years after World War II, the answer to future food shortages appeared to come from the sea. Catches tripled from 21 to

70 million tons of fish between 1950 and 1970. But this optimism was abruptly dampened in 1972 when fish catches dropped back to less than 55 million tons.

Many factors contributed to the declining yields and raised serious doubts about the ocean's ability to provide boundless food supplies in the future. The 1972 decline in world catches resulted primarily from the collapse of the Peruvian anchovy industry. Several theories have been proposed to explain the anchovy harvest's dramatic fall, with the best evidence supporting a combination of factors: overfishing, changing migratory patterns, and warming of the ocean current that sweeps by the Peruvian coastline. The anchovy industry is making a comeback, but still stands as a warning that limits exist on how much fish can be harvested at any one time (Allaby 1977:27–8). Other species that have declined are the Antarctic blue whales, California and East Asian sardines, Northwest Pacific salmon, Atlantic herring, Barents seacod and Antarctic fin whales (Brown and Finsterbusch 1972:89). Declining yields have not gone unrecognized, and original estimates of the amount of fish that could be harvested in a year have been readjusted downward.

While current estimates vary considerably, most experts now believe that we can increase ocean yields by almost 50 percent to about 100 million tons annually. Some increases are expected to result from advances in open sea fishing technology such as the use of helicopters, sonar, lights, and electrodes to locate and attract fish. Exploitation of underfished species, especially squid and lantern fish, and krill, a shrimp-like crustacean that lives in the Antarctic, also could expand world catches. Because of their small size, however, the new species are more likely to be used as fish meal than fillets. And critics are quick to point out that economically feasible catching, processing, and marketing arrangements have not yet been developed. Consumer acceptance of nonconventional species represents a very real barrier. Finally, large-scale fishing of krill may pose environmental hazards for whales and at least 30 other fish species that feed on them (Bondar and Bobey 1978:386).

To significantly exceed annual fish yields beyond the 100-million-ton mark, fish stocks not currently utilized would have to be used to create fish protein concentrate (FPC)—an odorless, tasteless, flour-like fish substance. The potential for producing FPC is great, but thus far it has failed to compete successfully in the marketplace. In a conference on the role of business in world food production, William Royce (1975:23) summarized the world prospects for the fishing industry this way:

1. An increase of about 50 percent in total production of conventional species over the next decade or two as production from the underfished stocks is developed.

Figure 7.11

Fish protein concentrate

a. Fish protein concentrate (FPC) processing plants convert fish into a powder which is nearly pure protein. (USDA/Warren)

b. Each month, 65,000 pounds of fish were processed into FPC at this Chilean factory. (AID)

c. Once fish has been produced into a meal or protein concentrate, it can be used to produce a variety of products such as these by the COPESA Company in Guayaquil, Equador. (AID)

2. Some increase in supply from the fully exploited stocks—
    which includes many of the familiar species of the North-
    ern Hemisphere. This increase is contingent on effective
    management, and without effective management a decrease
    in production is likely.

3. A large but uncertain potential for unconventional species
    if major catching, processing and marketing problems can
    be overcome.

4. Continuing modest increases in production from
    aquaculture.

It is clear that the aquatic food business must anticipate problems of a limited supply of the "name" species and a large supply of little known species that will require substantial business
resources to get to market. Further, it is clear that business must
seek help from governments, because governments are (or
should be) managing resources in public waters. Only governments are able to supply comprehensive data on the condition
of those resources, and only governments can sustain the
lengthy and sophisticated scientific work required to develop
aquaculture. Further, the risks involved in developing production from the unconventional resources are probably unacceptable to any business and governments must assist. But perhaps
the most important thing that business and government can do
is insist that government develop effective management of the
living aquatic resources. These requirements indicate that joint
venture between business and government will be the operating
mode in many countries.

Thus, it appears unlikely that the oceans offer a solution to future
food shortages. Even if conventional fishing could be developed to
overcome today's ecological barriers, increased yields would consist
largely of fish species with little or no value for human consumption.
Fish in general is not popular among most peoples of the world; it
is considered unfit to eat by many African and other peoples. Thus,
the acceptance of new species and new products such as fish protein
concentrate, which would significantly expand fish as a food resource, is doubtful at best.

Alternate foods

Science fiction has long suggested synthetic food and other exotic
solutions to humans' needs for nourishment. One concept that has
received serious attention recently is single-cell protein (SCP). Bacteria, yeasts, fungi, and algae are all being promoted as single-cell
protein sources that can be grown in large quantities. Petroleum
products, sewage, molasses, and other carbohydrates have been used
to support the growth of single-cell organisms with high protein concentrations. SCP has many advantages: growth rates are rapid (yeast

Focus 7-2

Aquaculture

One area of promise that has received much attention recently is aquaculture. Aquaculture is an ancient practice used by the Chinese, Japanese, and Egyptians. Oysters, mussels, and shrimp are still raised this way today. Unfortunately, many problems plague ocean ranchers. First and foremost is the lack of basic knowledge about marine science, fish diseases, and construction of safe aquatic environments. Second, marine fish and crustaceans are not easily protected from their pests and competitors; only small parts of the ocean are suitable for aquaculture structures, so that most successful schemes have focused on luxury items (shrimp and lobster) and have been produced by large corporations. Freshwater projects are less problematic but still limited to carp, rainbow trout, and a few other species. On the bright side, the Global 2000 Report to the President (1980:112) concludes that:

> There is cause for reasoned optimism when considering increased food production from aquaculture. Despite institutional, economic, environmental, and technological constraints, global yields are increasing. Intensive culture of high unit-value species—such as pen-rearing of salmon and raceway culture of shrimp—is approaching the point of economic feasibility, and extensive culture of animals that utilize very short food chains—such as oysters, mussels, and mullet—has the potential for enormous expansion with existing technology.

and bacteria need only 20 minutes to 2 hours to double their weight), labor needs are minimal, and production is not limited by land, water, climate, or waste-disposal facilities. Unfortunately, little is known about its safety when consumed in large quantities (Caliendo 1979:309–10). A more likely use for SCP is in the production of livestock feed. This places the consumer at least one step away from petro-protein organisms grown from sewage.

Another alternative protein source is leaf protein. Protein is extracted from otherwise inedible plant leaves, to produce a dark green, curd-like product. Although leaf protein is an excellent source of iron, calcium, magnesium, and vitamins E, A, and some B vitamins, it's taste and physical appearance detract from its success as a human food (Caliendo 1979:307–8). Most likely its uses will be limited to food fortification or supplementation, or livestock food. Despite these drawbacks, many companies are now experimenting with leaf protein. Batley James Enterprises, for example, has a California plant that produces ten tons of protein daily from alfalfa leaves. Some companies have achieved as much as 62.5 tons per acre! If large scale extraction methods are perfected, leaf protein offers an exciting new protein source especially suitable for food fortification and supplementation schemes.

Research on food production

In addition to research on climate conditions, pest control, and aquaculture, the National Research Council has identified other potential contributions possible through research. In the mid-1970s the National Academy of Sciences assembled 14 teams of experts to study the problem of future food production and make recommendations to "lessen the grim prospect that future generations . . . will be confronted with chronic shortages . . . and with the debilitating effects of malnutrition" (National Research Council 1977:iii).

In 1977, the teams published their report, *World Food and Nutrition Study: Potential Contributions of Research,* in which they state: "A strong research base is essential to all activities needed to increase the food supply, reduce poverty, and moderate the instability of supplies and prices. The role of research is to broaden the range of choices available to all those who affect world food supply and nutrition such as farmers, consumers, and government officials" (National Research Council 1977:4).

Food production is given high priority as a research topic. Particularly important are plant breeding and genetic manipulation, biological nitrogen fixation, pest management, weather and climate, management of tropical soils, irrigation and water management, fertilizer sources, and aquatic farm production systems. Perhaps the area of greatest potential, however, is the development of methods to increase the efficiency with which crops fix solar energy through photosynthesis. "Most plants capture no more than 1 to 3 percent of the solar energy they receive. Present knowledge suggests a theoretical maximum capture and conversion rate of 12 percent. The main research task is to learn how to increase significantly net photosynthesis per hectare of farmland and how to direct the increased material that would be created into edible food products (or perhaps into fuels)" (NRC 1977:76). If a plant's leaf structure and arrangement, growing period, and life span could be modified to enable it to capture more sunlight, crop yields would increase significantly. Basic research on biochemical and physiological processes by which green plants use energy in sunlight to convert carbon dioxide and water into food could open up new possibilities for genetic manipulation and chemical means of improving the plant's efficiency. The National Research Council study team estimates that between 50 to 100 percent gains in crop yields could be produced by increasing photosynthetic efficiency.

Other exciting research projects currently underway include the following: (1.) Development of salt-tolerant crops that can grow in the saline soils created by poorly managed irrigation projects (Epstein et al. 1980:399), (2.) Genetic manipulation of the protein content of crops to enable staples such as wheat and rice to producer higher quality protein, (3.) The use of wild plants such as quinoa (a cereal used by pre-Columbian Indians) to produce hybrids that are nutritionally superior and more resistant to environmental stresses such as pests and drought (Martin 1980:1), (4.) The use of fertilizers, lime treatments, and other soil management systems that reduce soil degradation (Brady 1982:849), (5.) Development of plants with higher percentages of usable material; hybrids already have increased the edible percentage of corn plants from 24 to 43 percent and farming practices have increased wheat's edible percentage from 23 to 46, (6.) Development of small-scale, inexpensive technologies that small farmers can utilize to increase their yields (e.g., windmills for low-lift irrigation, animal-drawn weeding machines, rainwater collection tanks, and low-cost tools).

See Highlight 8–1 for a more thorough examination of the exciting possibilities offered by these appropriate technologies.

Figure 7.12
Enough for all: Southeast Asian peasants in their rice fields.
(AID)

Summary

- Careful analyses of world food supplies fail to substantiate predictions of widespread famine in the near future. Although debate continues, it is generally concluded that food production has outstripped population growth (except for Africa) and the world will have sufficient food to sustain itself through the remainder of this century.

- Population growth rates have been declining steadily in developing and developed nations as a result of family planning programs and economic development. However, because of the large number of women in the childbearing age range, the population will continue to grow for at least another generation. Therefore, the population problem cannot yet be considered resolved.

- Thus far, agricultural production has more than kept pace with population growth in the world. Cultivation of larger areas of land and increased yields from the land already under cultivation can be used to increase food production further.

- Increased agricultural productivity depends on several factors: water supplies, availability of nutrients needed to support plant growth, pest control, and climate.

- With increasing meat consumption in much of the world, livestock production has received considerable attention. Besides efforts to adjust livestock production techniques (use of marginal grazing land and types of feed that do not compete with human needs), steps are being taken to utilize wild animal species for food and other products.

- Although fish is being used in many new ways to feed people and their livestock, earlier hopes that the oceans would provide boundless supplies of high-grade protein and offer a solution to future food shortages now seem unrealistic.

- Synthetic and other alternate foods (single-cell protein, leaf protein), development of salt-tolerant crops, use of wild plants, and research into other methods of increasing food supplies also promise to contribute to future food production.

Highlight 7-1 The Green Revolution: Production benefits and social costs

The term "Green Revolution" is one that we have heard frequently over the last several decades. It is used to refer to several aspects of agricultural change since World War II. Strictly speaking, "Green Revolution" describes the development and use of new agricultural technology, including high-yield varieties of seeds (HYV) and the cultivation techniques developed to go with them. The new technology includes chemical fertilizers and pesticides, mechanical preparation and cultivation of the soil, and irrigation. In its broader sense, the term has been used to refer to a hoped-for transformation or modernization of agriculture in underdeveloped countries resulting in an increase in the availability of food, reduction of food shortages, and elimination of hunger and poverty.

It is important to keep both of these uses of the term in mind because they do not necessarily go together. As we shall see in Chapter 8 much of the problem of hunger in poor countries is the result of national and international economic and political policy that results in widespread poverty. Nonetheless, the scientific advances that have produced better seeds and technology for food production have had a tremendous impact on the ability of the world to feed itself, both now and in the future. These advances have not been without costs, however, including damage to the environment and difficult social problems. Again, as we have seen, the social costs are closely tied up with the political and economic structure within various countries and the world.

The history of plant breeding for desirable food characteristics and higher yields is as old as agriculture itself. The history of

domestication has been a process of selecting plants that yield more food than their wild cousins. In the beginning, the selection of better crops was in the hands of the individual farmer. The scientific basis of plant improvement came with the work of Darwin in the mid-nineteenth century and the discovery of the laws of inheritance by Gregor Mendel in 1865. Mendel's work was overlooked for nearly 40 years and not rediscovered until 1900. Since then, the breeding of food crops using scientific principles has gained increasing momentum. The most important work, however, has taken place in the last 40 years.

The first significant increase in potential grain yields due to the development of plants with greater genetic potential came in 1961 when the first semi-dwarf winter wheat developed in the United States was released. Even more important was the development of two semidwarf spring wheats developed in Mexico by the International Maize and Wheat Improvement Center (CIMMYT). The CIMMYT wheats were adapted to a wide variety of climates and could be grown from Canada to Australia. At about the same time, dwarf varieties of rice were being developed at the International Rice Research Institute (IRRI) in the Phillipines.

Semidwarf wheat and rice are more productive for several reasons. The plants respond better to the presence of nitrogen: that is, they have narrower leaves, which reduces the amount of shade that lower and inner leaves get and allow for more photosynthesis. When fertilized, they produce more grain-filled heads. Traditional grain plants, which are taller and have weaker stems, will fall over when the heads are very heavy. This is called "lodging." The lodged grain may be lost or eaten by animals. The shorter semidwarf varieties are less likely to fall over and lodge, so the heavy heads of grain are protected. Also, the shorter plants are more efficient producers of grain. That is, they spend less of their energy producing leaves and stems and more to produce grain.

It must be kept in mind, however, that the improved yield of grain from the new "miracle" seeds produced in the 1960s is dependant on the use of fertilizer, and in most cases the careful use of water, usually through irrigation. The high-yield varieties do not yield any better than traditional varieties when fertilizer is not applied or sufficient water is not provided. In fact, under these conditions traditional varieties frequently do better. After all, they are the result of many generations of selection by farmers under the very conditions of poor soil and unpredictable rainfall in which they are grown. The HYVs are most useful when they are cultivated using the entire technological package that includes chemical fertilizer and, frequently, chemical pesticides and herbicides, mechanical plowing, and irrigation. The extra inputs necessary in order to perform the "miracle" can be very expensive in relation to the resources available to small farmers in rural areas of poor countries.

Nevertheless, the adoption of HYVs and the technology they require has been rapid in many areas and has had dramatic effects on the production of grains in many parts of the world. Norman Borlaug, one of the scientists that developed the semidwarf wheat at CIMMYT, writes:

When high-yielding semidwarf varieties of Mexican wheat were introduced into India during 1966 to 1968, national production stood at roughly 11 million metric tons and average yields were less than 1 ton per hectare. The high-yielding wheat varieties quickly took over, and by 1981 wheat production had increased to 36.5 million metric tons, largely as a result of a 100 percent improvement in national wheat yields. The 1981 harvest represents sufficient additional grains to provide 186 million people with 65 percent of the carbohydrate portion of a diet containing 2350 kilocalories per day (1983:692).

Plucknett and Smith (1982) note that the wheat varieties released by CIMMYT in the 1960s now account for virtually all of the wheat grown by Mexico. In Sonora, the state with the greatest wheat production, yields an average of 4 tons per hectare (2.46 acres), as compared with 0.7 tons per hectare with the traditional varieties. The area planted with HYV rice has also increased dramatically in Asia. IRRI rice accounts for one-fourth of the rice grown in the world today (Plucknett and Smith 1982).

The success of HYVs of maize has been much less. The costs of producing maize using these seeds is high and the land can often more profitably be used for other crops. Almost one-fifth of the land in Mexico planted in maize is in HYVs. In Kenya, HYVs account for 800,000 hectares of land.

The spread of HYVs of rice, wheat, and maize has reduced or even eliminated the need for food imports in some poor countries. India has been self-sufficient in grains in most years since the introduction of HYVs of wheat and rice; Bangladesh has come closer to feeding itself. The Philippines has only occasionally had to buy rice since 1970, and in 1980 exported 250,000 tons of rice.

Because of the early successes with IRRI rice and CIMMYT wheat (and, to some extent, maize), these three crops have received a great deal of emphasis, often to the exclusion of other crops. In fact, monocropping of these cereals has been emphasized even in areas in which legume crops were important dietary staples and were traditionally intercropped with grain. Other crops, such as cassava, sorghum, millet, yams, beans, sweet potatoes, and potatoes, considered minor in much of the developed world but of great importance in many developing countries, have been ignored.

Fortunately, the dramatic results of work at the IRRI and CIMMYT have fostered the establishment of new international centers to focus on the improvement of legumes and other crops traditionally produced in the developing world. Individual countries are also beginning to sponsor agricultural research in areas important to the Third World. The United States Agency for International Development (AID), for instance, recently set aside funds to conduct research on millet, sorghum, beans, cowpeas, and peanuts.

Seeds developed by the Green Revolution have had an important role in increasing the availability of food in the world. However, they also bring with them several ecological problems. One is the loss of crop diversity as the new seeds replace a wide variety of older plants. As a result, a great deal of diversity in genetic material is lost. This can be dangerous if, for instance, an entire area is planted in the same hybrid seed and a new or old disease or pest emerges that severely damages the crop. Because of their lack of diversity, all of the crops planted are susceptible. Also, because the number of different varieties of plants grown throughout the world is smaller than before the introduction of HYVs, many experts fear we may be heading for massive crop failures. For this reason, germ plasm banks for storage of seeds of many diverse kinds of crop plants are very important. They provide genetic material used by many different countries for development of new and better varieties of seeds.

A second problem is the environmental effects of the chemical fertilizers and pesticides required to grow HYVs. Large scale use of pesticides on rice in India appears to be associated with a rise in malaria as the mosquitos become resistant to the insecticides used. Contamination of food with

pesticides is a problem of unknown dimension.

Perhaps the most profound and difficult effects to assess are the broader social consequences of the Green Revolution. As we saw in Chapter 4, the vast majority of peasant farmers are poor, and unable to afford the more expensive HYV seeds and technology (fertilizers, pesticides, machines) that accompany them. Thus, the wealthier farmers are able to benefit from the HYVs while the poor farmers, who need it most, cannot. This, in turn, leads to increasing disparity between the larger, richer landholder and the poorer small farmers in most areas in which Green Revolution technology has been adopted (Griffin 1974). In fact, in many places, the new technology has allowed larger landholders to more profitably cultivate their own fields, pushing tenant farmers and sharecroppers off the land. Moreover, in many instances the adoption of machines to carry agricultural labor has further reduced the need for laborers, and increases unemployment for laborers.

In this way, then, the Green Revolution has been a major factor in causing the poor and landless to leave the countryside to join the growing ranks of the urban poor. Such migration of people from agriculture need not be a problem if a well-developed industrial sector exists to provide them with jobs. But this is exactly what developing nations lack.

Finally, the Green Revolution has revitalized agriculture enough in the Third World to allow larger landholders to move to even more profitable cash crops. It is ironic that Mexico, which became self-sufficient in food grains as a result of the green revolution technology, has now lost self-sufficiency as farmers have moved away from the production of food to the production of cash crops for export. A further aspect of the Mexican food situation is that sorghum, originally developed in the United States for use as animal feed, is so productive that Mexican farmers find it more profitable to produce sorghum for animal feed than maize for human food. The sorghum goes to produce meat. Unfortunately, the poor of Mexico cannot afford to eat the now more abundant meat (DeWalt 1984).

In response to a recognition of the negative effects of the Green Revolution and a failure of the new seeds and technology to produce the social transformation that many expected, many researchers have turned to a new model of agricultural research and development to produce seed and techniques that are more geared to the needs of the small and poor farmer. Several very similar approaches are subsumed under the general term "Farming Systems Research and Extension" (FSR/E). FSR/E is an approach to the problems of the small farmer that begins with an assessment of the social and economic constraints confronting the farmer, as well as the technical problems of crop production. The new technologies are then designed to fit into the already-existing farming system. In fact, the farmer often is made part of the research team by conducting on-farm research; that is, testing new seeds and methods of cultivation on the farmers' own fields to see whether they really are better than traditional techniques and can be profitably adopted. The technology is geared to be appropriate (see Highlight 8–1 on Appropriate Technology).

The FSR/E approach is being adopted by the international centers and many research programs in Third World countries. FSR/E is not a panacea for the agricultural, social, and economic problems for the poor farmer in developing countries. It does not address many of the structural problems between the elites and the poor, nor does it address the problems of the urban and nonfarm poor in these countries. It does, however, offer a new way of supporting the small farmer, and, as a consequence, continued improvement in the availability of food. Therefore, FSR/E may provide a firmer base from which small farmers can exert influence and pressure on the wealthy toward the achievement of social justice.

8

The world food crisis
and resource
distribution

Are we to say that a world which can send a man to the moon,
which can cure the majority of diseases, and can produce machines to solve the most complex mathematical problems
within seconds can still deny to millions of its inhabitants sufficient basic food to keep them alive? It sounds incredible. In
fact, it seems probable.

(Marei 1978:iiii)

The world currently produces almost twice the amount of food
that it needs to feed its 4 billion inhabitants, yet ". . . . for hundreds
of millions of [poor people], life is neither satisfying nor decent. Hunger and malnutrition menace their families. Illiteracy forecloses
their future. Disease and death visit their villages too often, stay too
long, and return too soon" (McNamara 1973:106–107). The poor
have little or no land, no jobs and no money to buy food. To eliminate
the malnutrition associated with poverty, the poor will either have
to be supported through aid and charity from the rich, or produc-
tively integrated into the world economy so that they can earn their

own way (Presidental Commission on World Hunger 1980:49). In this chapter, we examine factors affecting distribution of food and other resources as well as strategies that can be employed to bring about a more equitable economic order and alleviate hunger.

Economic development and underdevelopment

At the heart of poverty and malnutrition lie deep social and economic inequities between developed and developing nations, as well as between the wealthy elites and the poor within these nations.

Development can be defined in economic terms by Gross National Product (GNP)—the annual gross national product of goods and services produced per person. Or it can be viewed as the amount of food and energy consumed per person, which, like GNP, is significantly higher in developed than in developing nations. It also is reflected in infant and child mortality rates, life expectancy, and other measures of health and nutritional well-being.

Put more poignantly by Tanzania's president, Julius Nyere:

> Under the economic, political, and social systems at present operating, the world's people are divided into two groups; those with access to its resources, and those without access. Those with access to existing resources—the rich—can afford to invest heavily in the production of greater wealth, so they get richer. The poor have very little to invest; their productivity consequently remains low, and they remain poor. Worse still, the market laws of supply and demand mean that the wealth of the few diverts the world's resources—including the labor of others—from meeting the real but ineffective demand of the poor into satisfying the luxury desires of the rich. Land and labour are used to cultivate grapes instead of grain; palaces are built instead of houses for the workers and peasants.

> *(Presidential Commission on World Hunger 1980:19)*

Today, the world can be divided into two broad catagories: the 25 *developed* countries in North America, Europe, Japan, Australia, and the USSR—that account for one-third of the world's population, and the more than 100 developing nations of Asia, Africa and Latin America inhabited by the other two-thirds of the world's people. Although diversity exists within both groups, important generalizations can be made when contrasting developed and developing nations. Some of these are summarized in Table 8.1.

One of the most outstanding characteristics of developing countries is the high rate of malnutrition, especially among women and

Table 8.1   Developed countries versus developing countries

Developed countries	Developing countries
•High GNP: $6200 per capita	Low GNP: $150 per capital in low income nations; $750 per capita in middle income nations
••Low percent of income spent on food (15 to 35%)	High percent of income spent on food (70% in Latin America, 90% in India)
•Positive export/import ratio	Negative export/import ratio
Abundant diet with high meat consumption; malnutrition rare	High rates of clinical malnutrition in children and women
Slow population growth (0.7%)	More rapid population growth (2.0%)
Highly industrialized and urbanized	Little industrialization; primarily rural
•Intensive energy use (approximately 5016 kilowatts per capita, per year)	Little use of energy (52 kilowatts in low income nations; 524 kilowats in middle income nations)
Many health care facilities and professionals	Few health care facilities and professionals
High literacy rates (99%)	Low literacy rates (23% in low income nations; 63% in middle income nations)
Low infant and child mortality rates and long life expectancy	High infant and child mortality rates and short life expectancy

•Source: World Bank, *World Development Report:* 1978.
••Source: Community Nutrition Institute: 1980; Monckeberg
1983:13. Some studies suggest that as the percent of family
income on food exceeds 30%, and as it becomes more difficult
to select the quality and quantity of foods needed, the diet
becomes distorted.
(Caliendo 1979:130–145; 351–355)

children. Regardless of the figures used to estimate the number of
people affected, 100 million or 450 million, hunger and malnutrition are intolerable in a world that has mastered the ability to prevent
it. In the words of James P. Grant, Director of UNICEF (1983:1):

> No statistic can express what it is to see even one child die in
> such a way; to see a mother sitting hour after anxious hour lean-
> ing her child's body against her own; to see the the child's head

turn on limbs which are unnaturally still, stiller than in sleep; to want to stop even that small movement because it is so obvious that there is so little energy left inside the child's life; to see the living pink at the roof of the child's mouth in shocking contrast to the already dead-looking greyness of the skin, the colours of its life and death; to see the uncomprehending panic in eyes which are still the clear and lucid eyes of a child; and then to know, in one endless moment, that life has gone.

Among the world's poor, women and children are at highest risk of malnutrition. Not only do most developing societies place greater value on men than women, but because they are larger, men require diets containing larger amounts of calories and essential nutrients. Also, most poor people recognize the logic in feeding their male producers first, for they are considered major wage-winners. Because women are more important earners than children, frequently it is the youngest family members who are the first victims of food scarcity. "It is not that their parents don't love them. 'An inactive child is not as damaging to a family's survival as an inactive adult' . . . . if there is not enough food for the whole family, the working adults tend to take for themselves the largest share" (Minear 1975:18).

Figure 8.1
Starvation
(UNICEF)

Hunger is defined as "the physiological as well as psychological discomfort caused by the lack of food" and *malnutrition* describes "bad nutrition, or more scientifically, 'a condition in which there is an impairment of health, growth, or physiologic functioning resulting from the failure of a person to obtain all the essential nutrients in proper quantity or balance'" (Caliendo 1979:6–7). Put in more descriptive terms:

> No fear can stand up to hunger, no patience can wear it out, disgust simply does not exist where hunger is; and as to superstition, beliefs and what you may call principles, they are no more than chaff in a breeze.

> *Joseph Conrad*
> Heart of Darkness

Malnutrition comes in many forms: vitamin and mineral deficiencies, caloric deficits, and protein/calorie malnutrition. In its initial stages, a deficiency may be so mild that physical signs are absent and biochemical methods generally cannot detect the slight changes. As tissue depletion continues, the biochemical changes can be measured in body fluids and tissues. With further depletion the physical signs become apparent, until finally the full-blown deficiency can be easily recognized.

Protein/calorie malnutrition, commonly called PCM, is the most widespread nutritional problem in developing nations. Its most easily identified forms are kwashiorkor and marasmus, both of which are found predominantly in children under six years of age.

Initially recognized by Dr. Cicely Williams in West Africa, kwashiorkor is the indigenous name used to describe the disease that occurs when a child is displaced from the breast by another baby. And indeed, the condition clinically recognized as kwashiorkor most frequently develops several months after switching a child from breast milk to a starchy diet providing adequate caloric intakes but insufficient protein.

indigenous
Born or developed naturally in a country or region

Unfortunately, mothers in developing countries have begun to wean their children earlier or substitute bottle feeding for the superior practice of breastfeeding. Economic pressures that encourage mothers to work away from the homestead; advertising by formula companies that presents bottle feeding as the modern, sophisticated way to feed a baby; changing norms for male-female relations and modesty; and the lack of social support and assistance in the postpartum period are among the many factors contributing to the decline of breastfeeding and the subsequent rise of protein malnutrition (see Highlight 10–2: "Breastfeeding").

In its more extreme forms kwashiorkor has the following characteristics: moderate to severe growth failure and muscles that are

infiltration
Entrance into the tissue of
some abnormal substance,
or a normal substance in
excess

poorly developed and lack tone. Edema is usually severe, resulting in a large pot belly and swollen legs and face and masking the muscle loss that has occurred. The child has profound apathy and general misery; he or she whimpers, but does not generally cry or scream.

Marasmus results from a diet lacking in calories, although protein and other nutrients may be well-balanced. Severe growth failure and emaciation are the most striking characteristics of the marasmic infant. The wasting of the muscles and lack of subcutaneous fat are extreme. Marasmus differs from kwashiorkor in several ways: the onset is earlier, usually in the first year of life; growth failure is more extreme; there is no edema; and the liver is not infiltrated with fat. The period of recovery is much longer. In both marasmus and kwashiorkor, height and weight for height are markedly retarded.

In addition to these extreme types of PCM there are many combinations of intermediate forms. In fact, for every child with frank kwashiorkor or marasmus, there are 99 children with more subtle or milder cases that go unnoticed.

Vitamin and mineral deficiencies also are relatively common in poor peoples' diets. Iron deficiency anemia affects millions of women and children throughout the developing world. In a 1982 document, FAO estimates that "about one half of non-pregnant women, two-thirds of pregnant women and 30 percent of preschool children" have hemoglobin levels established by the World Health Organization as indicative of anemia. Goiter, vitamin A and iron deficiencies are found in many regions of the developing world. Vitamin A deficiency, for example, is prevalent in India and Southeast Asia. Approximately twelve million people suffer from night blindness because this vitamin is lacking in the diet. The FAO estimates that one quarter of a million children go blind each year as a result of vitamin A deficiency. Goiter caused by iodine deficiency affects another 200 million (Food and Agricultural Organization 1982:5).

There is little doubt that malnutrition is the major cause of infant and child mortality in developing nations. One study found that nutritional deficiency was a factor in more than 60 percent of all childhood deaths from infection, and in the first and second years of life, a major contributor to deaths from all causes (Willet 1983:12).

Malnutrition has other long-lasting effects that are not revealed in infant and child mortality rates. First, it reduces the body's ability to resist infection and disease. PCM supresses certain immune responses, leaving the child vulnerable to many childhood illnesses, pneumonia, diphtheria, and other diseases. A deficiency of certain vitamins, such as A- and B-complex, also affects immunity; ascorbic acid deficiency impairs resistance to bacterial infections; and when malnutrition causes the skin and mucous membranes to bruise and break open, the body is more easily invaded by organisms (Caliendo 1979:26). Once a malnourished person succumbs to illness, his or her nutritional status is further jeopardized by loss of appetite, diarrhea, and vomiting. Sweat, fever, and intestinal parasites increase nutrient needs and aggravate nutritional deficiencies. This is visible in the comparison of death rates in developed and developing nations. Deaths due to measles are 100 times higher in Chile and Bolivia than the United States; in Mexico, they are 180 times higher.

Second, severe malnutrition is believed by many to impair brain growth and reduce learning abilities. In an excellent review of existing studies on animals and humans, Caliendo (1979:46) concludes that more research is needed to sort out the complex relationship between the effects of malnutrition and poor housing, poor sanitation, poor health, low levels of education, ignorance, and a climate of apathy and despair. Clearly malnutrition's strong association with mental development and learning are cause enough for concern.

Third, malnutrition affects productivity and decreases the span of working years. In *The Nutrition Factor,* Allan Berg (1973:9–17) argues that the poorly-nourished fail to achieve their genetic potential in physical size or prowess; their capacity for work is reduced, as is their life span. Increased medical costs, lost work days, and reductions in work capacity affect economic growth and serve as obstacles to development in poor countries. The elimination of malnutrition, then, makes good economic sense for developing nations.

The many imbalances between rich and poor nations have their legacy in the colonization of much of Africa, Asia, and Latin America, and in the Industrial Revolution. After the Industrial Revolution, European countries were forced to search for new sources of raw materials, cheap labor, and new markets for their industrial products. Beginning in the sixteenth century, many tropical colonies were used to grow sugar, cotton, tea, tobacco, sisal, hemp, and copra. To maintain their new markets and keep plantations profitable, the colonial powers retarded the development of industrialization in their colonies. Few industrial projects were established in their overseas possessions and, in some cases, colonial subjects were prevented from learning the skills on which industry depends (Tannahill 1973:321). Moreover, to keep labor costs down and profits high, slavery, taxes, forced labor, and schemes making the production of certain crops mandatory were established in many colonies (Harris 1980:353).

This century has brought independence to most colonies, and yet underdevelopment persists. Why? One of the major problems facing former colonies is their late start. The Presidential Commission on World Hunger, for example, reported that although developing nations must be responsible for attaining their internal economic growth and nutritional security, "the success of their efforts will be

Focus 8-1

The myth of the Protestant ethic

Some analysts have tried to explain the discrepancies between the developed and developing nations in terms of Europeans' Protestant work ethic or their entrepreneurial spirit. People in underdeveloped nations, they argue, are less resourceful, unwilling to work hard, or unwilling to make the financial sacrifices required by economic progress. But as Marvin Harris (1980:352–353) points out:

> Anthropology provides little support to the notion that the root cause of underdevelopment is the absence of an ethic of hard work, frugality, and reinvestment. Indeed, this ethic is actually present in many of the non-Protestant regions where underdevelopment is most conspicuous. The problem is that hard work, frugality, and reinvestment are by themselves no guarantee of entrepreneurial growth. If these attitudes are expressed in a political economy that systematically prevents the formation of capital and that fails to reward even the most energetic efforts, they will have little effect upon raising per capita income. . . .

Instead, he believes, as we do, that the unequal development of the industrial and nonindustrial countries is a heritage of economic and political imperialism in the colonial and postcolonial eras.

strongly conditioned by an international economic order which they did not create, but which affects them in important ways." This international economic order is shaped primarily by industrialized nations' needs. For instance, developed nations, to a large extent, establish trade relationships and set the prices of many basic commodities. Thus, "the decision-making power on international economic issues still remains heavily weighted against the developing countries, which are penalized for having begun the development process late in the game, well after their predecessors had established ground rules that do not favor newcomers" (The Presidential Commission on World Hunger 1980:21).

Other factors affecting development in the postcolonial period identified by Marvin Harris (1980:358) include: access to natural resources, population size and density, the nature of exploitation used during the colonial period, the extent to which the new country remains tied in politically and economically subordinate ways to its previous ruler, and the conditions under which it gained its independence. Did the former administration withdraw hastily because the colony became nonviable economically, failing to prepare the indigenous population to take over power, or did the colonies benefit from unifying liberation efforts?

Today, as in the colonial era, developing countries are not a homogeneous group. Some developing nations have large amounts of exploited resources while others do not. Some export food while others import much of what they eat. In some areas, especially poor African countries, slow food production growth is only one sign of the complex economic and social problems so often associated with traditional societies.

Taiwan has successfully joined the industrialized capitalist world; China and Cuba have built successful socialist economies; while Haiti, Bangladesh, and many African nations appear to be losing ground. In general, economic growth has been slow in the poorest nations while middle-income countries have experienced expanding trade and more rapid economic development. In many instances, political and agricultural reform, as well as widespread education, have been part of these countries' successes (International Bank for Reconstruction and Development 1980:20–23).

Because of the diversity within the developing world many schemes have been used to categorize these nations. Table 8.2 lists major classifications of less-developed nations, with a description of the criteria for classification.

Perhaps most commonly, nations are referred to as *developed* (those already industrialized and wealthy), or *developing* (those still struggling to develop the agricultural and manufacturing sectors of their economies). They also are often divided into the "First World" (highly industrialized, Western-style democracies), "Second World" (the Soviet bloc), and the "Third World" (the less-developed, under-developed, or developing nations). Regardless of how they are classified, the differences between rich and poor nations are significant. One hundred and fifty years ago the per-capita income in developed nations was *2 times* that of developing nations. In 1979, it was more than *20 times* greater (Caliendo 1979:130). Today, the gap between many developing nations, particularly those in the middle income group, and industrialized nations is beginning to close (International Bank for Reconstruction and Development 1982:20–23). For example, differences in infant and child mortality rates and life expectancy between low-, middle-, and high-income nations were smaller in 1980 than in 1960. Also, as per-capita income climbs in the more rapidly developing nations, many economic, social, and nutritional differences between middle-income and industrialized nations can also be expected to grow smaller.

Table 8.2	Classifications of less developed nations
Source of classification	**Description**
United Nations List of Least Developed Countries (LDCs)	Created in 1971; updated in 1975. Includes 29 nations with low GNP per capita, minimal industrial sectors, and widespread illiteracy.
Most Seriously Affected Countries (MSAs)	Composed in 1974. Purpose is to identify nations most in need of international assistance. Revised 1975 list includes 45 nations.
World Food Council Food priority countries list	Adopted in 1976 as a policy tool to indicate hunger and malnutrition. Characteristics of nations listed include annual per capita income of $500 or less; annual cereal deficits of 500,000 tons, and/or 20 percent of estimated consumption by 1985; significant PCM; potential for rapid increases in food production and distribution; serious balance of payments constraints.
World Bank Grouping according to per capita GNP	Countries whose per-capita GNP is: less than $200 (38 countries) $200–499 (42 countries) $500–1999 (64 countries) $2000–4999 (29 countries) More than $5000 (15 countries).
International Development Association (IDS) list	Low-income developing nations (33 nations with annual per capita GNP of $200 or less). Middle-income developing nations (56 nations with average GNP of $375 or less). Higher-income nations (with average GNP of more than $375).
Consultative Group on Food Production and Investment	List of 18 countries with chronic and widespread malnutrition, and where assistance may increase food production and nutritional levels.
International Food Policy Research Institute	Four categories of food-deficit nations: the two most critical categories are "very severe food-deficit" and "serious food problems" countries.

Unfortunately, these gains are not shared equally by all citizens living in the developing nations. Although rapid growth is almost always associated with a reduced incidence of poverty (Croswell 1981:2–4) the amount of wealth that trickles down to the poor is

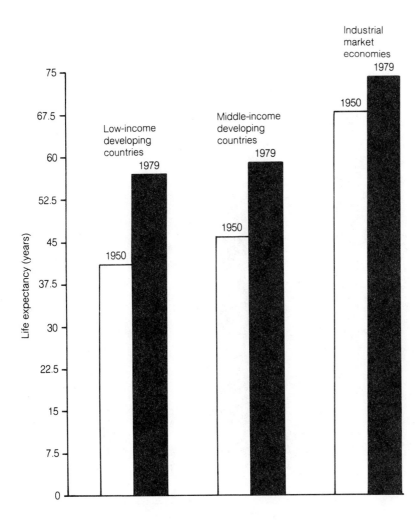

Figure 8.2
Life expectancy in coun-
tries with low-income,
middle-income, indus-
trial market economies:
1950 and 1979.
(International Bank for Re-
construction and Develop-
ment, World Report: 1982,
Washington, D.C., p. 24.)

quite small compared to that enjoyed by the elite. India's poor, for
example, were only marginally helped by increased food production
in the 1960s. In most countries, a sizeable portion—in some cases
as much as 40 or 50 percent—remain desperately poor (Molina
1983:47).

Resource distribution

Countries vary in the degree to which their national incomes are distributed among their citizenry.

> Brazil and Taiwan, for example, have roughly the same national
> per capita incomes, yet, in proportion to their populations, Bra-
> zil has three times as many people living in absolute poverty as

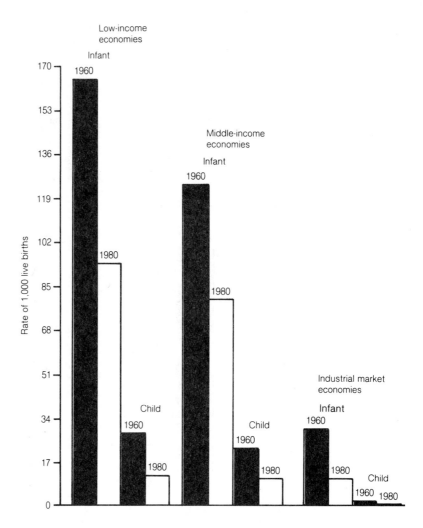

Figure 8.3
Infant and child mortality in countries with low-income, middle-income, and industrial market economies: 1960 and 1980.
(International Bank for Reconstruction and Development, World Report: 1982, *Washington, D.C., pp. 150–151.)*

asset
Anything owned that has exchange value (usable to pay debts)

Taiwan. The difference is that the national income of Taiwan is distributed more evenly than Brazil's. In most developing nations, income is highly concentrated. In Senegal, Peru and Turkey, for example, the poorest 40 percent of the population receives less than 10 percent of the national income. Such wide gaps between rich and poor are rooted in the inequitable distribution of income-producing assets, such as farmland, cattle, education and jobs.

(Presidential Commission on World Hunger 1980:21)

Land distribution and agrarian reform

Land is the major form of wealth in agrarian communities, and, as with other resources, agricultural land in most developing countries

Figure 8.4
Unequal distribution of
wealth: Bombay, India.
(United Nations/JP
Laffonte)

is concentrated in the hands of a relatively few wealthy families. Typically, a few wealthy farmers own large tracts of land that they farm
using the modern techniques associated with the developed nations,
while the great majority of peasants own tiny plots cultivated with
traditional tools and techniques. In many poor nations, as much as
80 percent of the farms are 12 acres or less, and over 50 percent are
under 2.5 acres. Land distribution in individual countries exemplify
this inequity: in Latin America one-tenth of the farmers own 90 percent of the farmland, while more than 60 percent of the rural poor
are landless; in the Philippines, Pakistan, and India, 20 percent of the
farmers own about half the land (Presidential Commission on World

Hunger 1980:22; Minear 1975:16). Worldwide, the number of landless agricultural workers currently exceeds 100 million and is growing.

Although many peasants own their small garden plots, others must rent from landlords. Landlords typically have been depicted as harsh, cruel rulers who have little incentive to improve farm production. "It is undeniably true that peasants in many parts of the world have suffered various deprivations, even indignities at the hands of landlords, and that landlords in general, and absentee landlords in particular, have not been very interested in agricultural development" (Sinha 1976:49). Not all landlords, however, fit this description. Some landlords have made important contributions to agricultural development and have treated their tenants with respect. In India, for instance, landlords have financed major irrigation projects, advanced low-interest loans for construction of wells, contributed to environmental improvement projects, and cooperated with government agricultural experiments (Sinha 1976:50).

In many regions, income disparities between landlords and tenants have been small and partially offset by complex duties and responsibilities of the rich to help the poor. In other areas, income disparities have been accepted as part of tradition. But more recently, especially with the introduction of advanced farming techniques and machines, the traditional status quo has been disrupted. Increased yields have been associated with increased disparities in incomes, farm machinery has caused unemployment to grow among farm laborers, and the poor have become more aware of their poverty. Occasionally, these changes have resulted in outbreaks of violence and heightened interest in land reform (Allaby 1977:338).

land tenure policies
Policies governing the right to own land and the length of time it is owned

Land tenure policies in many developing countries retard food and agricultural production. Poor tenants and small farmers are unable to maximize use of their land. They do not have the money or credit needed to purchase fertilizer or pesticides needed to increase yields with the new seed varieties. Land tenure, then, is seen by many as a serious obstacle to technological change and increased agricultural productivity (Presidential Commission on World Hunger 1980).

Agrarian reform

"Sometimes argued with ballots, sometimes argued with bullets, and mostly argued with words, the debate about land reform has surfaced time and time again in the 20th century" (Eckholm 1978:13). Land reform is used here to refer to the redistribution of property or land rights for the benefit of small farmers and agricultural workers.

Land reform schemes have varied considerably: some have occurred gradually (Peru) and peacefully (Japan); others through violent revolutionary changes (China, USSR). Not all land reforms have

been successful. Some governments have failed to back up reforms
with credit, farm supplies, or other economic assistance, thus causing small farmers to lose their newly gained possessions. In other
countries opponents of reform have prevented reallocation from actually occurring. But where reforms have been successful, important
gains have been achieved in agricultural production as well as social
justice. In Mexico, for example, over 2 million families have been
placed on the land. Employment has risen from 50 to 100 percent
over previous levels, and agricultural output has increased from 3.5
to 8 percent annually over the last 30 years. Taiwan offers another
example. The number of families owning land increased from 33 to
59 percent during the reform period, 1949–1953. As a result, the
World Bank reports that "the productivity of agriculture has increased, income distribution has become more even, and rural and
social stability have been enhanced" (Eckholm 1978:13).

Because traditional land tenure systems act as obstacles to technological change, some experts have argued that land reform is essential to increase agricultural productivity and alleviate hunger.
Pierre Crosson questions this notion. He recognizes that a number
of countries have made significant progress in agriculture after redistribution of land. Many of these countries, such as Taiwan and
Mexico, also have enjoyed other types of technical assistance and
progress (e.g., irrigation, foreign aid, and credit) that may have contributed equally to their successes. Crosson also points to countries
(India, Pakistan, the Philippines, and Thailand) where substantial
technological progress has occurred in the absence of significant
land reform. Crosson concludes, therefore, that:

> We have too little understanding of the relationship between
> systems of land tenure and technological innovation to predict
> how important present tenure systems may be as obstacles to fu-
> ture technical progress in LDCs (less developed countries).
> That they may impede progress seems certain, but it is equally
> certain that land tenure reform is not a generally necessary con-
> dition for innovation. This discussion of land tenure systems
> thus ends on a note of uncertainty.
>
> *(Crosson 1975:522)*

Aside from the impact of land reform on agricultural productivity, the issues of economic equity and nutritional well-being must be
dealt with. In agrarian societies, access to wealth is almost exclusively tied to land use and/or ownership. The landless must work as
farm laborers or find nonagricultural employment, both of which are
exceedingly scarce in rural communities. Unless industrialization is
proceeding rapidly enough in urban areas to absorb the rural poor,
land reform represents one of the few means of redistributing wealth
and giving the poor a chance to get ahead.

Nutritional well-being of the poor also is tied to land tenure systems. For instance, Costa Rican families who farm small plots of land (under 3 hectares) are 2.3 times more likely to have undernourished children than those with larger farms (over 6.5 hectares) (Valverde et al. 1977).

Larger landowners typically produce cash products that reap better profits on the international market than crops sold locally. Thus, even though their farms tend to be highly productive, the yields do little to improve the diet in surrounding communities. Also as DeWalt (1983a) has shown for Central America, larger landholders are changing cropland to pastureland, leaving less land available for small farmers who rent from larger landowners. A similar situation has accompanied the Green Revolution in several developing countries (See Highlight 7–1, "The Green Revolution"). Land reform is associated with the production of basic grains and other food consumed locally, enabling farmers to better feed their families.

Even though the benefits can be great, land reform schemes are difficult to implement. "The successful change of long-standing rights and rental practices is not something that can be accomplished with the mere passage of a law by some sympathetic politicians . . . . The unspoken dilemma facing many Third World governments is that by promoting the emergence of new peasant groups, they could be endangering their traditional sources of political support—and in some cases the economic interests of their own leaders as well" (Eckholm 1978:16).

Historically, the most successful efforts to eliminate poverty have been rapid governmental changes in distribution of land and all other forms of wealth, combined with the creation of new jobs and expansion of education and health services. These changes in long-standing political and economic systems require an extraordinary degree of political commitment as efforts to meet the basic needs of the poor clash with the individual political freedoms valued in western democracies.

Such measures are, of course, the most politically sensitive that most political leaders can take. In many instances they threaten the government's very survival. In other cases, however—as in Nicaragua most recently—it is the reluctance to undertake these same reforms that causes governments to fall. At the least, redistributive measures are sure to alienate powerful segments of the society. Therefore, the long-term success of efforts to achieve structural change is largely dependent upon firm unyielding commitment by local political (as well as social, economic and religious) leaders. Political, financial, and technical support from the outside, as well as supportive trade and investment policy, can often strengthen local resolve and help the process of implementation.

(Presidential Commission on World Hunger 1980:33)

Credit, marketing, and price systems

Access to land often is not sufficient to ensure an adequate income. Many small farmers cannot survive without support in the form of credit for small loans and markets to sell produce and buy supplies at fair prices. In many developing nations, the lack of these institutions inhibit productivity and foster rural poverty. It is not uncommon for small landholdings to be mortgaged, sold, or turned over to money lenders because farmers do not have sufficiently large incomes to purchase supplies or pay high interest rates.

Credit The small farmer, as any other businessperson, requires money for investments. Long-term investments include land improvements, housing, irrigation, and agricultural tools and machinery. Short-term investments commonly are made for seed, fertilizer, livestock feed, veterinary services, and wages to pay extra help. Without credit to make these investments, many farmers cannot make small land holdings productive.

Credit may come from a variety of sources. Developed nations have an elaborate system of government and private banks, cooperatives, credit unions, and other lending institutions.

In some developing countries these formal credit sources are relatively unavailable to farmers, who turn instead to friends, relatives, neighbors, landlords, shopkeepers, and other informal money lenders. Some governments offer a limited number of subsidized loans at low interest rates. But if these sources cannot provide him with the money needed, bankruptcy may result; at the very least, the farmer may be forced to sell goods, livestock, or other products at low prices.

Increasing amounts of credit are essential for rural development and agricultural productivity. Individual governments and regional development banks can greatly enhance the formation of a self-reliant small farm population by expanding sound credit to the rural population.

Markets As farming moves away from the subsistence level, markets become increasingly important as a source of farm supplies and a place to sell produce. In addition to a place for exchanging foods, successful markets require transportation systems, food processing, and storage facilities. Without these services, it is difficult to assemble large quantities of food or make goods available year round. In most parts of the world, postharvest crop losses are great due to difficulties and delays in getting food to the market place and inadequate preservation techniques. Losses due to rodents, molds, spillage, and spoilage are particularly high in tropical countries where postharvest losses generally approach 20 percent. Wastage also is high in areas where high-yield varieties are planted uniformly over large areas. This genetic uniformity provides an ideal ecological

genetic uniformity
Single genetic strain of a crop, planted uniformly over large areas

Focus 8-2

The Mexican food system

To exemplify how a government can use price supports and consumer subsidies to improve the nutritional status of its citizenry, we turn to Mexico and its program, the Sistema Alimentario Mexico, commonly known as the SAM.

The SAM was introduced against a depressing background. Despite widespread land reform since the 1920s and increased agricultural productivity brought by the Green Revolution (see Highlight 7–1), Mexico was importing increasingly large amounts of basic crops, the gap between rich and poor was widening, and millions of Mexicans were malnourished. Also agricultural production was concentrated among large landowners who qualified for credit and used much of their land to grow cash crops exported to other countries.

The SAM was proposed by President Lopez Portillo on March 18, 1980, and included several important programs. Subsidies were provided to promote production and consumption of basic food crops—principally maize, wheat, and beans—in which the government subsidized both the price the farmer received as well as the amount the consumer paid. In some cases, the guaranteed prices proposed were 30 percent higher than what farmers had received in previous years and proposed consumer prices of a range of basic foods were subsidized by 70 percent, thus assisting the poor to buy a minimum basket of foods worth 13 pesos for only 9 pesos (Redclift 1981:12). Agricultural credit and crop insurance, cheaper fertilizers, and improved seed varieties were made available to farmers who produced basic food crops. The objective behind these proposals was to encourage farmers to grow more of these basic food crops, decreasing the need to import them from other countries. The government hoped for self-sufficiency in maize and beans by 1982 and in wheat, sunflower seeds, and rice by 1985 (Redclift 1981). In addition to the political implications of self-sufficiency, increased productivity would lower costs of these basic foods and help improve the nutritional status of consumers. Finally, an education campaign was launched to teach the public about good nutrition. This measure was proposed in response to national nutrition surveys that showed that daily calorie and protein intakes were below accepted levels for approximately 19 million Mexicans, and as many as 25 percent of Mexican children were malnourished (Redclift 1981).

Although the cost was enormous—27 million pesos or $1 billion—Mexico's newly-discovered oil was expected to generate the necessary funds. Initially, the SAM appeared successful, increasing production of basic food crops as intended. However, in the final analysis, the SAM failed to achieve its goals. Internal opposition grew from a variety of sources, including local strong-men who complained that the extension of credit and open marketing threatened their traditional hold on small farmers. More critical, however, was the drop in oil prices that undermined SAM's financial support. When a new president, Miguel de la Madrid, took office in 1982, one of his first acts was to dismantle the SAM, bringing an end to an innovative governmental program designed to encourage self-sufficiency and improve nutritional status for the poor.

---

environment for pests and leads to increased losses (Pimentel and Pimentel 1979).

Many improvements can be made in roads and waterways that will speed handling and thus decrease postharvest losses. Insect- and rodent-proof storage facilities and more efficient drying and preservation methods could contribute significantly to increasing the amount of food that reaches the consumer (see Highlight 8–1). Recognizing the importance of marketing systems, the Food and Agriculture Organization has organized regional conferences in Asia, Latin America, and Africa to assess current needs and begin steps to improve marketing institutions.

Price polices   Food prices are another essential feature of agricultural systems. Prices influence production and consumption levels, both of which have direct nutritional significance for the poor. When prices fall, consumption of most items climbs. However, if prices fall too low, farmers do not make enough profit to pay for production costs, and may stop growing that crop. When prices rise, consumption of most items falls, especially among the poor. If consumption drops low enough, and farmers cannot sell their products, incentives to increase productivity are damaged.

It is not surprising, then, that many governments establish policies to manipulate prices in order to protect the farmer, the consumer, or both. Commonly, price supports (guaranteed minimum price levels) or subsidies are used as incentives to producers when the government wants to increase food supplies. Price ceilings (maximum price levels) are used to protect consumers from rising prices when supplies are scarce. Special commodity subsidies or other discriminatory prices are used to assist consumers, while at the same time providing incentives to producers. The Food Stamp Program is one example of a discriminatory policy that redistributes wealth;

subsidy
A grant of money paid by a government to a private producer of goods to assist an enterprise considered to be for the public good

commodity
Any article that is bought and sold; especially in this case, a product of agriculture

India's fair price stores that provide wheat and rice at reduced prices to the poor is another.

In all cases, government price intervention must be conducted cautiously. Price policies are complex to operate and often have unintended consequences. These include policies that artificially hold down prices paid to farmers for their produce and consumer prices for food, export taxes, and other export controls on food.

Employment and industrialization

With population growth expected through at least the beginning of the twenty-first century, the agricultural sector will have difficulty providing employment to all who need it. Already, many developing countries suffer from an overabundance of unemployed laborers, stiff competition for available jobs, and low wages for those who are employed. Development planners are keenly aware of the need to expand jobs outside the agricultural sector to accommodate those pushed off the land by rapid population growth.

The world labor force is expected to grow by 1.6 to 1.9 percent annually, reaching 2.6 billion by the year 2000. Over three-quarters of this growth will occur in the developing nations (Sinha 1976:36).

Recent growth in nonagricultural employment in developing countries offers some optimism. However, future growth may not be able to keep pace with current rates in all countries. Already, some developing nations are finding that manufacturing growth, especially in light industries, is slowing (Sinha 1976:46). Also, many of the cities in these nations are administrative and trading centers created to facilitate exchange with other countries. They offer relatively few jobs to the millions in search of them (Poleman 1975:517).

The problem of large-scale unemployment and underemployment is now recognized by the World Bank and U.S. Agency for International Development (USAID) as well as the developing nations' governments, who are now funding numerous schemes for enhancing labor-intensive rather than mechanized, capital-intensive forms of development. However, it seems clear to most economic analysts that a radical reexamination of urban and rural development is required (Sinha 1976:46). This may imply massive welfare schemes, and other completely new alternatives. "It almost certainly also implies substantial social and political change" if we are to avoid civil strife and the "misery and vice" about which Malthus warned us (Poleman 1975:518).

Developmental assistance

Economic development of poor nations is essential for a long run solution to the hunger problem. However, as we have just seen, in many nations, economic growth and redistribution may take many years before they impact on the lower 40 percent who are poverty stricken (Willet 1983:22). Until then many nations rely upon development assistance from richer nations. Development assistance, also known as foreign aid, comes in many forms: money, goods, food, credit, technical assistance, and research. The United States provides two basic types: bilateral and multilateral. Bilateral assistance is given directly to the recipient country. Multilateral assistance is distributed to developing countries in combination with assistance from other nations through international organizations, the World Bank, the United Nations and Regional Inter-American Development Banks (Knutson 1983:147–148).

About two-thirds of bilateral agricultural assistance (as opposed to that designated for industrialization or other nonagricultural purposes) goes to middle-income countries, while almost all multilateral assistance goes to the poorest nations (International Bank for Reconstruction and Development 1982:50–51). For the low-income nations, foreign aid makes up a large part of the resources flowing into them from outside; it is less significant in the middle-income countries.

In the United States, bilateral assistance was initiated with the Marshall plan, immediately following World War II. At that time the United States was the single largest donor nation, known for the high quality of its technical assistance. Unfortunately, both the United States' generosity and quality of performance have declined in recent years. Although it is still the largest donor in terms of dollar amounts, the United States now runs behind Canada and ten other Western countries when assistance is determined as a percentage of the gross national product (Presidential Commission on World Hunger 1980:110).

There are four major tools of development used in bilateral and multilateral assistance: commodity assistance or food aid, institution development, technical assistance, and research (Knutson 1983:148).

Commodity assistance

A major component of Canadian and U.S. bilateral assistance is food aid. In fact, Canada's first major venture into foreign aid was a $10 million wheat shipment to the newly independent India. At the 1974 World Food Conference in Rome, Canada committed 1 million tons of cereal grain and $45 million in nongrain foodstuffs annually for the 1975–76 and 1977–78 seasons (Cohn 1979).

Over the past 25 years, the U.S. has given about $1 billion in food aid, making its contribution approximately one-third of the official development assistance budget (Presidential Commission on World Hunger 1980:95, 140). U.S. food aid policy is derived from Public

Law 480, the Food for Peace Act. This legislation has four basic goals: "To provide humanitarian assistance, to spur economic development within recipient countries, to develop markets for U.S. agriculture commodities, and to promote U.S. foreign policy objectives" (Presidential Commission on World Hunger 1980:140). Throughout its history, emphasis has shifted from one objective to another. Originally it favored the American farmer by disposing of grain surpluses outside the U.S. economy (where surpluses would not lower American farm prices) and developing markets for American commodities. In the late 1960s, the legislation's humanitarian objectives came to the foreground as food aid averted starvation in India and elsewhere; during the Vietnam War, food was used as military aid and a component in U.S. foreign policy.

Figure 8.5
U.S. commodity assistance. In many nations, food aid is highly valued. After the salad oil is gone, the can becomes a water jug.
(AID)

The impact of food aid has been the subject of much debate. Those arguing food aid's benefits point to its many effective uses. For refugees of natural disasters and political conflicts, food aid offers temporary relief from famine. In relocation projects, food aid is used to sustain people after they are located in new housing until they can set up agricultural activities and produce their own food. Food aid can help a poor nation reduce its balance of trade deficits by offsetting the costs of food imports, thus easing the way for other development activities. Finally, food aid is used as an incentive to attract mothers to maternal and child health centers where food is distributed along with medical care.

Critics of food aid believe that commodity assistance is generally used inappropriately with damaging results on recipient nations. According to Joseph Willet (1983:17), for example:

> Even when there are no surpluses, the actual transfer of huge amounts of grain as gifts into developing countries would have catastrophic impacts on the local farm economies of the receiving areas. Many authorities consider that the effective use of food aid is severely limited by price-depressing effects, which hinder the incentives of both officials and farmers to develop efficient farm systems in the aid-receiving countries. Depressed prices, caused by over-large imports of subsidized grain or other commodities, can have direct effects on the incomes of many poor farmers.

In addition to diminishing small farmers' incentives to produce when prices are low, governments may rely on food aid instead of increasing agricultural development to insure food supplies, and focus on developing the nonagricultural sector. This, in turn, hinders the development of self-reliant agricultural systems and proper integration of the industrial and agricultural economies. Also, the availability of food aid allows governments to ignore the full implications of their population growth rates and delay the introduction of family planning policies and programs (Allaby 1977:8).

Food aid also is criticized because it often fails to help those who need it the most: the poor. In countries that use food aid to offset expensive food imports, the total amount of food available does not increase. The poor cannot gain better access to food unless it is distributed to them directly, and this is often difficult in developing nations where roads are poor and transportation limited.

Another problem arises when donated commodities such as wheat or corn replace more nutritious items in the local diet. A demand is established for these new foods. Because they are not grown locally, when commodity assistance allotments are reduced or stopped, the newly-demanded foods cost significantly more than the traditional foods they replace, putting financial pressure on already limited food budgets. Families in Asia and Latin America, for instance, were introduced to wheat through the Food for Peace program. Many of them are now paying dollars for American wheat and other products to replace local produce.

The U.S. food policy also has been criticized for its failure to focus on humanitarian as opposed to political or economic objectives. The Presidential Commission on World Hunger (1980:108, 141) criticized the U.S. food aid policy in particular, and development assistance policy in general, because it did not give highest priority to the neediest countries.

> Foreign policy interests play a major role in determining the allocation of development assistance funds among and within developing countries. Despite rhetorical bows to "the poorest of the poor," more than half the budget for bilateral development assistance goes for "economic support" to political allies of the United States.

When development assistance or agricultural exports are used "as tools to achieve specific foreign policy goals," we speak of food diplomacy (Knutson et al. 1983:162). Food aid may be used as a tool of diplomacy in a positive way, as when assistance is given with no strings attached to countries the United States views as politically strategic. Israel and Turkey were major recipients of food aid in the 1950s, and South Vietnam in the 1960s and 1970s. Today, the United States provides most of its foreign aid to strategically important countries such as Egypt, Israel, and the Caribbean (Hanley 1981). When food diplomacy is punitive, aid or exports are contingent upon specific action by the recipient government. The United States has used commodity assistance in this fashion on several occasions, such as when food aid contributed to military disengagement in the Middle East in 1974. Punitive food diplomacy often has proven ineffective and created resentments; e.g., when the U.S. government failed to persuade Indian officials with promises of food shipments if they supported policies in Southeast Asia during the 1960s. Similarly, resentments intensified when food aid to India was made contingent upon the adoption of family planning programs (Knutson et al. 1983:162–3).

Finally, the original justification for food aid—widespread food shortages in the Third World—has been challenged. As we have already seen, food production has more that outstripped population growth in all areas except Africa.

> It has been assumed up to now that food aid is needed because there is a shortage of food in the Third World. The Third World is thus seen as a vast refugee camp with hungry people lining up for food from the global food aid soup kitchen. This view is

false. Some disasters aside (and these are important areas for food aid), the basic problem is not one of food, but poverty. Free handouts of food do not address this problem, they aggravate it.

(Jackson and Eade 1982:93)

Institution development

Institution development involves the expansion of industries, public services (education and health facilities), and agencies to enhance research and development. Most commonly, this is in the form of grants or loans made for building irrigation systems, credit agencies, universities, data collection systems, and fertilizer plants, and improving marketing. The major sources of institutional development from the United States come through its agency for International Development (USAID) and its donations to development banks, particularly the Inter-America Development Bank and the World Bank (Knutson 1983:148–9).

"The World Bank, established in 1945, is owned by governments of 135 countries. The Bank, whose capital is subscribed by its member countries, finances its lending operations primarily from its own borrowings in the world capital markets . . . . Bank loans generally have a grace period of five years and are repayable over 20 years or less. They are directed toward developing countries at more advanced stages of economic and social growth" (World Bank 1980:3). Institutional development projects funded by the bank include roads, railways, telecommunications, electrification of rural communities, ports and power facilities, irrigation projects, water and sewage plants, low-cost housing, and small industry. Their major strategy is emphasis on investments that directly improve the well-being of the poor in developing nations by making them more productive and by integrating them into the development process. Although the Bank sponsors development projects that commercial banks find too risky, it does demand repayment of its loans. And with the exception of the poorest countries, borrowing nations are charged a small interest rate extended over 15 or more years. Money for financing these loans is derived primarily from member nation contributions (Simons 1981:63).

Technical assistance

Technical assistance, the provision of expert advice and assistance in specific areas, is often a necessary step in both institution and agricultural development (Knutson et al. 1983:149). The World Bank, USAID, FAO, and many other agencies offer developing nations this form of aid. In 1980, the World Bank alone allocated $807 million

Figure 8.6
Irrigation. With help from the Food and Agriculture Organization, the Yemen government has undertaken several irrigation projects, supplying water to cotton, sorghum, and other crops.
(United Nations/Kay Muldoon)

to expert supervision, implementation, and engineering. Often technical assistance is a substantial component included in the Bank's loans for large-scale projects; e.g., $49 million of the $210 million loaned to India for irrigation, and $7.2 of the $38 million loaned to the Philippines for fisheries training (World Bank 1980:76).

FAO offers technical assistance in soil conservation, water management, land reform strategies, nutrition intervention programs, and plant and animal breeding (Knutson et al. 1983:149).

Research

We have already discussed the exciting potential that research offers for increased food production (See Chapter 7). Until recently the United States was the center of agricultural research, but now multilateral organizations and developing nations have joined in the endeavor. Currently 13 major research centers are funded by an association of countries called the Consultative Group on International Agricultural Research (CGIAR). These include the International Maize and Wheat Improvement Center, the International Rice Research Center, and others. The World Bank also funds a variety of research projects in agricultural and institution development. Developing countries also have picked up a substantial portion of research costs, so that as a group, their expenditures now exceed those of the U.S. (Oram 1983:3–8).

By 1975, only 18 percent of global agricultural research expenditures came from the U.S.—an encouraging sign reflecting widespread recognition of the long-term benefits gained from research (Knutson et al. 1983:150).

Focus 8-3

Women and food

An issue that crosscuts many of the development problems we have discussed is women's role in producing as well as preparing food. For example, in many subsistence or food production systems, women are active farmers. In fact, women account for an estimated 60 to 80 percent of agricultural labor in Asia and Africa. In Latin America the percentage is somewhat lower, although an estimated 40 percent of agricultural labor is provided by women (Blumberg 1981).

Even these figures, however, may significantly underestimate women's food production. There are several reasons for this underreporting. First, many nations do not include women when compiling labor statistics. Second, most nations focus their agricultural reports on cash crops, typically grown by men, rather than crops produced for family consumption. Third, most reports fail to include all aspects of the food production and preparation system, omitting activities such as storage, processing, and local marketing which are conducted primarily by women. Finally, many countries report their statistics in terms of land use, noting how much of the land cultivated is devoted to certain crops. Because women traditionally are involved in production on uncultivated land (in gathering foods, small animal production, and milk production) or small garden plots, their activities are greatly underreported. Cloud, for example, points out that:

> It is one of the characteristics of gardening [horticulture] that a great deal of food can be produced in a small space, but this very characteristic tends to work against women. For example, consider this quote, "Cereals are the major crop; many varieties are grown on about 65 percent of the cultivated land . . . . Peanuts and cotton occupied about 25 percent of the cultivated area. Small amounts of manioc, yams, sugar cane and tobacco were produced on the remaining 10 percent of the cultivated land" (Matlock and Cockrum 1976). *Women's crops are invisible in this account of land use.* This invisibility may also contribute to the lack of development resources available for some kinds of food production.
>
> *(Cloud 1978:15; cited in Blumberg, 1981)*

Figure 8.7
*Korean peasant and
child.*
(AID)

Because of these reporting problems, Blumberg (1981:33) has
prepared an analysis of African women's participation in the food
production system, including production and distribution, and
household/community work. For each activity, he reports women's
work in terms of "units of participation"—or the percentage of labor
which is performed by women—0.70, for instance, means that
women carry out 70 percent of the work of that responsibility. We
can see from Table 8.3 that African women are responsible for all
labor associated with food processing, cooking, child care, and washing. They also are responsible for the greatest share of food production, marketing, fuel-gathering, water collection, and community
self-help projects. Women and men carry out roughly equal proportions of animal husbandry and food storage (important in minimizing
postharvest food losses).

While women always have been important food producers, their
role has increased since colonial times. As colonial rulers forced or
encouraged men to work on plantations or in mines, women were left
in their villages with increased responsibility for food production.

Table 8.3   African women's participation in:
(a) Production/supply distribution;
(b) Household/community

Responsibility	Unit of participation*
Production/supply/distribution	
Food production	0.70
Domestic food storage	0.50
Food processing	1.00
Animal husbandry	0.50
Marketing	0.60
Brewing	0.90
Water supply	0.90
Fuel supply	0.80
Household/community	
Bearing, rearing, initial education of children	1.00
Cooking for husband, children and elders	1.00
Cleaning, washing, etc.	1.00
House-building	0.30
House repair	0.50
Community self-help projects	0.70

*Units of participation are calculated on the basis of estimates of women's time as a percentage of all the time expended in a particular task. Units of participation were proposed in: Data Base for Discussion on the Interrelations between Women in Development, their Situation, and Population Factors, UN Economic Commission for Africa, 1974. Units of participation were determined first for areas within countries, then for countries, then for Africa.

(Blumberg 1981:33)

Also, more recently, some development schemes have encouraged men to plant cash crops (see Chapter 2), which often have resulted in increased production of the family's food by women.

One result of the male bias in reporting agricultural production has been to overlook and devalue women's contribution to food production. At a conference sponsored by the Association for Women in International Development (AWID) held October 1983, many expressed the opinion that agriculture's failure to meet Africa's food needs is in large part due to the fact that the technology to improve production was made available to the wrong people. That is, it was given to men and not to women.

World food security

Since widespread food shortages in the early 1970s, much attention has been focused on the establishment of international regional and national reserves. Grain reserves are used to prevent severe shortages, offset high consumer prices produced by poor yields, and provide stable farm prices. When natural disasters or political conflicts disrupt agricultural production in one region, the effects are often felt around the globe. World production shortfalls of less than 10 percent have raised prices for wheat and rice by 200 percent or more. As prices climb, wealthy consumers easily can absorb the higher prices and unknowingly draw supplies from the poor. "Modest shortages, which may raise the cost of bread in the United States by a cent or two a loaf, can result in severe shortages in Bangladesh, or Mali, or Guyana" (Presidential Commission on World Hunger 1980:89–90). To avert these shortages and protect farmers and consumers by stabilizing prices, grain is reserved when yields are plentiful and released into the marketplace when yields are low. This prevents farmers from bankruptcy when prices fall during abundant years, and poor consumers from being priced out of the market in lean years.

Optimum size of grain reserves depends upon their planned purpose. Famine relief would require much less than that needed to stabilize prices or improve nutritional status among the poor.

At the 1974 World Food Conference, the Food and Agriculture Organization (FAO) agreed to coordinate the formation of international and regional grain reserves. Many nations committed themselves to reserve targets and policies. Thus far, however, India is the only developing nation to establish significant grain surpluses.

embargo
A trade restriction on a particular commodity

In 1980, as a result of the embargo in grain sales to the USSR, the United States built up a reserve of 4 million tons. This government-held reserve was isolated from the wheat market by a Food Security Wheat Reserve Act designating it for emergency humanitarian needs in developing countries (Willet 1983:16). The United States also committed 4.47 million tons of food aid under the Food Aid Convention of 1980. The FAO, World Food Council, and other international food groups do not believe that this is enough. They proposed that an international reserve of 9 to 18 million tons be established to assure that developing countries can purchase grain in times of shortage.

Negotiations between nations as well as international agencies have included control over purchase and release, responsibility for costs of acquisition and maintenance, and financial assistance in buying from reserves, as well as establishment of an optimal size for reserves.

Recognizing the need for World Food Security, the Presidential Commission on World Hunger (1980:100) recommended that the

United States increase its reserves substantially and press for a resolution of issues impeding the establishment of global reserves.

The next year, in 1981, negotiations broke down. "The U.S., supported by other leading grain exporters, opposed international control on coordination of national actions concerning grain stocks, and in December 1981, The International Wheat Council announced that efforts to develop an alternative approach" had failed (Willet 1983:16). That same year the FAO announced that world cereal reserves were expected to drop far below the level considered a minimum for world security.

The international economic order

> Contrary to widespread views, hunger and poverty are not just problems to be overcome through more vigorous local initiatives by poor nations. The pace of economic development in general and the alleviation of hunger in particular will depend importantly on far-reaching changes in many aspects of international realities as well. International economic relationships involving trade, debt, finance, and investment constitute the basic framework within which poor nations will be able to improve their own standards or living . . . . Trade, after all, is the single most important determinant of a country's economic activity that can be influenced by outside forces.
>
> *(Presidential Commission on World Hunger 1980:49–50)*

Trade

No country is completely self-sufficient. All nations are dependent on trade with other countries to provide food, goods, and services that are in short supply at home. International trade is increasing among developed and developing nations alike. Trade in grains, for example, almost doubled from 1970 to 1980, and total agricultural export in the U.S. increased from less than $10 billion in 1972 to over $42 billion in 1981. The rate of growth of exports in developing countries (5.4 percent) was slower than developed nations (6.7 percent), but nevertheless substantial. Developing nations also expanded the amount of trade among themselves (World Bank 1980:17). The terms under which international trade is conducted has a major impact on the developing nations' ability to fight poverty and hunger.

Theoretically, the international market economy is based on open and expanding trade agreements, free exchange of money and technology between nations, readily available supplies of raw material, and international institutions working together cooperatively.

International trade is regulated by several international agreements such as the Bretton Woods Agreement and the General Agreement on Tariffs and Trade (GATT), which define trade rules and establish procedures for negotiating tariffs and other economic arrangements between nations. GATT is a treaty which contains a code of principles and means of resolving disputes between the 90 participating nations. The major purpose of GATT is to prevent nations from erecting a series of retaliatory trade barriers (Knutson et al. 1983:138). In actual practice, international trade has been increasingly controlled by taxes and tariffs, embargoes, and other trade barriers. Restrictions on the foods and goods imported into a country are the most common form of trade barrier. Tariffs, for example, do this by placing a tax or fixed charge to the value of the shipment. Beef might cost $1 per pound when it arrives, but $1.10 after the tariff. Tariffs are used to make foreign goods less attractive to consumers, and thus protects producers within the importing country. Other important restrictions commonly used are quotas, which set limits on how much of a product may be imported, and levies, which set a minimum price for imported goods (Knutson et al. 1983:122).

Exports are also encouraged by governments who want to expand exports by lowering their prices. This often is done through subsidies, in which the government pays the producer a fixed price on each shipment exported. This has the effect of lowering the price on the international market below what is being paid at home, and therefore encouraging producers to sell their goods abroad. Subsidies give the producers a competitive edge over other exporters (unless they, too, offer a subsidy). Export taxes have the opposite effect. By raising the price of goods exported, they reduce international demand and promote domestic consumption. Quotas and embargoes (suspension of trade) are also used to control exports (Knutson et al. 1983).

Governments erect trade barriers to protect certain producer or consumer groups, usually those with enough power to secure governmental support. U.S. efforts to control consumer prices through embargoes on the export of agricultural products and domestic price control discourage increased production. This has the overall effect of decreasing agricultural production and increasing the average price of food throughout the world (Knutson et al. 1983:25). For this reason, the effort to lower agricultural trade barriers is seen as an important means of improving the world food problem. Unfortunately, there has been little progress in this direction (Willet 1983:2).

Balance of trade

When the value of a country's exports exceeds the value of its imports, the country enjoys a positive balance of trade. When its imports

tariff
A system of government taxes, usually placed on imports

export taxes
Charges levied on a percentage of the value of goods sent to another country (or region) by local producers

cost more than its exports, the balance is negative. Dramatic increases in crude oil prices during the 1970s created tremendous pressure on oil-importing nations. Most developing countries also had to cope with increased prices for the manufactured products they imported, a growing dependence on food imports, and slow-downs in their export growth. As might be expected, many developing nations were pushed into negative trade balances and large deficits.

A fundamental problem in developing nations' trade relations concerns the type of materials they export. Most have a heavy reliance on only one or two raw materials (as opposed to manufactured or processed goods). Raw materials generally bring low prices and suffer from wide price fluctuations. This is particularly serious now that many developing nations are using money gained from exports to pay for basic grains and other imported foods (Willet 1983:18).

Because prices for raw materials have declined relative to manufactured goods, some developing countries have increased their industrial production. In Taiwan a shift toward an export-oriented economy was partially responsible for its recent economic success; per-capita income rose from less than $1,000 in the 1950s to $1,300 in 1978. For the underdeveloped world as a whole, sales of manufactured products grew from $8 billion in 1960 to over $64 billion in 1978. But again the developing nations encountered difficulties in international trading. Tariffs on finished and semifinished manufactured products are high, but in recent years, highly discriminatory import restrictions have been established in developed nations to limit competition from poorer countries where lower labor costs give them an advantage (Presidential Commission on World Hunger 1980:60). These trade barriers have proven effective in preventing poor nations from building international markets to support expanding industries at home. They also have contributed to the developing nations' sky-rocketing debts.

By 1975, the developing nations that imported oil had amassed a debt of $39,600 million, a significant rise from the $8,300 million owed in 1970 (World Bank 1980:19). By the end of 1979, trading debts exceeded $300 billion. Loan repayments and interests alone reached $40 billion, so that one out of every five dollars of their trade earnings was turned over to creditors in industrialized nations (Presidential Commission on World Hunger 1980:68). For many, trading debts brought slowed economic development as loan repayments and interest used up money originally set aside for agricultural programs, institution building, education, and research. Furthermore, much of the pressure to produce crops for export has come from a need to pay off these debts. In some cases, this has further exacerbated food shortages and, ironically, the need to import food (Caliendo 1979:136).

The politics of world hunger:
Synopsis and proposed solutions

Our analysis of world food production and distribution has shown that poverty is the underlying cause of world hunger. Most developing countries are characterized by an inequitable distribution of wealth between a small group of elites and the much larger proportion of the population that is poor. The poor are malnourished because they cannot afford to purchase the foods needed for an adequate diet; if they are farmers, they cannot afford the seeds, fertilizers, and land needed to grow more.

In addition to the inequitable relations between rich and poor within nations, poverty and malnutrition also result from inequities between industrialized societies and the Third World countries. As we have seen, these inequities have existed since colonial times, when Third World nations were used to produce raw materials and food for the colonial powers. The dependency created by colonial policies has been replaced by international trade policies and practices that favor the industrialized nations, preventing developing countries from breaking out of their dependence on developed nations for loans, aid, direct investments by commercial firms, and markets for their exports (Murdoch 1982:309). Moreover, it is the need to sell cash-producing crops and goods on the international market that has stimulated many countries to shift from producing basic foods to cash crops such as cotton, sugar and coffee. This, in turn, has contributed to the widening gap between the rich who can afford the technology and land needed for cash crop production and the poor who cannot (DeWalt 1984).

Because international and national politics are intertwined, both must be addressed in any attempt to end world hunger. First, wealth must be distributed more equally within Third World countries, and second, the relationship between rich and poor nations must become more equitable. The remainder of this chapter examines solutions proposed to redistribute resources within developing nations and between the industrial and Third World countries. Our discussion draws heavily upon William Murdoch's clearly outlined analysis in *The Poverty of Nations: The Political Economy of Hunger and Population* (1982).

Redistribution of wealth within developing nations

Solutions proposed for the redistribution of wealth and power within developing nations can be classified into two categories: reformist approaches that advocate gradual change, and more revolutionary approaches relying upon the rapid rise of radically socialist governments (Murdoch 1982:313).

Reformist approaches focus on gradual change brought about by negotiations between elites and the poor, forming a reformist coalition. According to this view, elites in developing nations will recognize the need to give up some of their privilege and power in the short run in order to survive in the future. Once the coalition is formed, governments would gradually redistribute the wealth. While this approach may be appealing, it is unlikely to take place on a wide scale. Elites have not demonstrated an interest in sharing their wealth; on the contrary, they have proven quite adept at eliminating reformists and others who challenge their power. In Central America, for example, many reformists have been killed, jailed, or exiled, creating even greater polarization and civil strife within these countries. Also, although the Mexican government has advocated a number of reformist ideologies throughout this century, this country continues to have one of the largest gaps between rich and poor. For this reason, Fagen (1978:199), like many others, concludes that:

> Although some among [the LDC elites] may genuinely wish to assault class privilege and maldistribution, they are relentlessly pulled back toward policies that favor the few rather than the many . . . sustained progress [toward equitable distribution] is structurally out of the question. Only profound changes in the developmental strategies currently in use (and most probably in the elites currently in power) will significantly alter this situation.

Those who look to socialism, brought by either revolution or election, as a cure for the inequities in developing nations are also likely to be disappointed (DeWalt 1984:11). First, the building of a socialist economy and socialist society is a difficult and ongoing process that prevents many socialist revolutions from creating the reforms that they promise. Burma offers a good example. After the 1962 revolution, the Burmese military government committed itself to construction of a socialist society. But as Fenichel and Khan (1981) show in their analysis, these objectives were in many ways unsuccessful. When faced with economic problems, Burma has permitted foreign investments and reactivated the private sector, allowing much of the nation's industry and agriculture to be privately owned. Burma is not unique. Gerand Chaliand, a participant-observer in several recent revolutions, and William Murdoch (1982:315) conclude that:

> Very few of the revolutions that have occurred have resulted in radical restructuring of the economy. The revolutions of the past thirty years have been undertaken mainly by the small middle class (often led by intellectuals) when that class has been prevented from promoting and benefiting from economic growth. As a consequence, most revolutions have occurred only at the top of society and have not resulted in thoroughgoing social change.

Second, there is little reason to expect widespread successful revolutions by either urban poor or peasant farmers in the Third World countries. The elite ruling class has had several decades to consolidate their economic and political power. Only when assisted by a major world power can peasants in developing nations be expected to successfully achieve a socialist revolution. And then there is always the question of whether the opposing world powers will allow the revolutionary socialist government to persist.

International redistribution of wealth

At the international level, two major strategies have been proposed for redistribution of power and wealth: a new international economic order, and increased self-sufficiency among developing nations.

A new international economic order

Recognizing the limitations current international trading relationships place on developing nations' ability to develop economically, many Third World nations have called for a new international economic order.

> The basic concepts of establishing such a new order include policy and program proposals such as:
>
> - Revamping the present international credit system by phasing out national currencies and replacing them with a new international currency
>
> - Dismantling affluent-nation restrictions on movements of goods, services, and people
>
> - Control by developing countries of primary production, processing, and distribution of their national resources
>
> - Renegotiation of all past leases and contracts given by developing countries to multinational corporations
>
> - Restructuring the United Nations to give it greater operational powers and to increase poor-nation voting strength in the World Bank and International Monetary Fund.
>
> *(Knutson et al. 1983)*

In 1974, the United Nations passed a resolution expressing the determination of its member states, including the industrialized countries, to revamp the international trade situation with "higher and steadier prices for raw materials and broader markets for (developing countries) manufactured exports . . ." (Murdoch 1982:317).

Also, the debt burden of developing countries would be eased, aid and investments increased, and other improvements made.

In 1980, the Presidential Commission on World Hunger also endorsed the need to create a new international economic environment which supports the goal of balanced, self-reliant development. The Commission's report recommends that price support schemes be established to give poor nations a more dependable deal on raw material exports; tariffs and other trade barriers be reduced to allow developing nations to sell more labor-intensive clothing, textiles, footwear, and electronics to developed nations; and developing nations be allowed to convert their current debts to the United States into local currencies specially earmarked for development projects and activities (Presidential Commission on World Hunger 1980).

While most analysts agree that more equitable international trade relations must be established as part of the fight against world poverty and hunger, many doubt that substantial change will occur. Discussions and resolutions promoting a new international economic order have taken place for over a decade, and yet there has been no noticeable improvement in the developing nations' standing in the international economic order. Despite the U.S. and other industrialized nations' initial enthusiasm, little change has been implemented and "even talk on the New Order [has] run out of steam" (Murdoch 1982:319). According to Mahmond Mesteri, a U.N. spokesman for the developing countries economic situation, "the basic problem is the refusal of most of the developed countries, and particularly the principal industrialized countries, to commit themselves seriously to economic reform" (Mesteri 1979:17). Other experts point out that even if developing nations were to gain an advantage at the international bargaining table, economic growth would be slow and not necessarily distributed equitably within developed nations. Thus, the call for a new international economic order is unlikely to be answered in a way that would offer substantial relief in the near future.

Self-sufficiency as a route to equity and growth

An alternate and more radical view of international trade holds that the economic interests of rich and poor nations are far too different to be resolved through negotiations; overall, international trade will always be unfavorable to the developing countries. Therefore, they are encouraged to emphasize internal development and self-sufficiency.

The path to self-reliance is not simple and no doubt would require different strategies for different countries. The essence of this approach, however, is outlined by Murdoch (1982:320):

This is hardly the place to attempt to lay out development plans for an enormous array of LDCs; however, some features are probably generally applicable. The preferred strategy would seek to minimize dependence on foreign capital, at least during the early stages of development; where possible, it would use locally abundant resources rather than imports; it would greatly reduce foreign investment, especially by transnational corporations; it would minimize foreign loans that required western-oriented economic policies, foreign aid that the LDCs could not control, or foreign aid that accentuated internal biases or external dependence. Trade with other LDCs, especially regional trade, would be emphasized, where appropriate, since this would help to avoid dominance by foreign capital-rich nations. Where western technology had to be imported it would be analyzed, modified, and adapted (as the Japanese did so brilliantly) so that local technical skills would be developed, paving the way for the creation of indigenous technology in the future.

All of this would depend for its success, of course, on a radical redistribution of internal political power. However, once such a transformation were achieved, dependence would be reduced and the LDCs would come to the international bargaining table in a much stronger position.

China offers one of the most successful examples of a nation's ability to develop self-reliance and minimize foreign intervention. After the revolution ended in 1949, the People's Republic of China (PRC) turned inward, attempting to meet its citizens' basic needs for food and health care—efforts now recognized as highly successful. The PRC also limited trade with Western nations and even refused international disaster relief during its initial period of isolation. In recent years, the PRC has reestablished world trade on a limited basis, but presumably from a much stronger bargaining position.

Other nations have tried to pursue the path to self-reliance. Mexico, as we've already seen, established the SAM in an unsuccessful attempt to achieve self-sufficiency in basic food crops. Some countries have also attempted to improve their international trade situation by banding together. OPEC, for example, has been highly successful in controlling oil prices. However, no other attempt at building self-reliance or creating price cartels have proven effective. Some analysts believe that strictly authoritarian rule such as that found in China may be necessary to bring about the internal direction needed to achieve self-reliance. They also point out that internal policies must be developed to distribute the economic benefits of self-reliance to the poor, or this strategy, like many others, will fail to resolve the poverty that underlies world hunger.

Conclusion

In our exploration of the world food situation, we have found that there are no easy answers; no quick solutions. The problem of widespread malnutrition cannot be eliminated through any one technological discovery or any single developmental scheme. Increasing the amount of cultivated land, producing more food per acre, improving yields from fishing and agriculture, and developing new alternative food sources each can contribute to a solution. But there is no "technological fix" for world hunger.

Because malnutrition throughout the world is the result of deep social and economic inequities, any attempt to resolve world hunger needs to address the issues of redistribution of wealth and power between industrialized and developing nations as well as between the rich and poor living within these developing nations.

Thus far, no single reformist nor revolutionary proposal for distributing wealth equitably has proven successful on a large scale. The rich continue to maintain a firm grip on their power and wealth. It is difficult to foresee how the earth's poor will claim their share of the planet's resources. But as improved communication brings the world closer together, transmitting news of the industrial nations' abundant wealth to remote villages everywhere, we can be certain that discontent will grow among the poor, pressing all peoples to find a solution to the inequities.

Fortunately, population growth rates are slowing and crop yields are increasing in many poor as well as rich nations, giving us more time to join the poor in the pursuit of an end to world poverty and hunger.

> Social justice is not simply an abstract ideal. It is a sensible way of making life more livable for everyone. Thus, for the developed nations to do more to assist the developing countries is not merely the right thing to do, it is also increasingly the economically advantageous thing to do.
>
> *(Robert McNamara, President, World Bank, from the Presidential Commission on World Hunger 1980:11)*

Summary

- At the heart of poverty and malnutrition lie deep social and economic inequities between developed and developing nations, as well as between the rich and poor within these countries.

- Land is the major form of wealth in agrarian communities, and as with most resources, it is concentrated in the hands of a relatively few wealthy families.

- Access to land often is insufficient to ensure an adequate income, and therefore, many small farmers cannot survive without support in the form of credit for small loans and markets to sell produce and buy supplies at fair prices. Governments vary in their abilities to meet these needs.

- Many developing countries suffer from an abundance of unemployed laborers, and therefore must expand jobs outside the agricultural sector to accommodate those pushed off the land by rapid population growth.

- Many developing nations rely upon richer nations for developmental assistance in the form of money, credit, technical assistance, research, and food aid.

- All nations are dependent on trade with other countries to provide goods that they do not produce and markets for their exports. The international market economy is controlled by taxes and tariffs, embargoes, and other trade barriers that place developing nations at a disadvantage.

- Because international and national politics are intertwined, both must be addressed in any attempt to end world hunger. Wealth and power must be distributed more equitably between industrialized and Third World nations as well as within these countries. Thus far, no single proposal— reformist or revolutionary—has proven successful in combating the underlying cause of world hunger: poverty.

Highlight 8–1 "As if people mattered": Appropriate technology

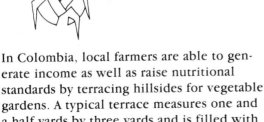

In Colombia, local farmers are able to generate income as well as raise nutritional standards by terracing hillsides for vegetable gardens. A typical terrace measures one and a half yards by three yards and is filled with organic compost; the only cash outlay is for seed. The average family makes seven terraces, each of which can produce three vegetable crops a year (McRobie 1981).

Pedal-operated mills that can grind hard grains to any degree of fineness are in use in parts of Africa. These mills, made from materials available locally, save village women hours of tiring pounding (McRobie 1981).

Health care workers in India who don't have access to elaborate laboratory equipment are taught to test for iron-deficiency anemia through simple physical exams such as checking for paleness of the lips, gums, tongue, and inner surface of the eyelids (Werner and Bower 1982).

What do these three accounts have in common? They are all examples of *appropriate technology*. Also known as intermediate technology, this type of technology falls midway between using very simple tools and techniques (such as cultivating land by using digging sticks) and highly technological modern machines and methods (such as $20,000 tractors designed for use on 3,000-acre farms).

Appropriate technologies are distinguished by their *smallness, simplicity, inexpensiveness, and compatibility with the physical and social environment* (Schumacher, 1981). Any one of these criteria, or a combination of them, increases the technology's value in underdeveloped re-

gions. Though the concept of appropriateness is well-accepted now, 20 years ago more complex, sophisticated technologies prevailed. At that time many agricultural scientists and engineers thought that farmers and others in developing areas would fare best by adopting Western methods and machines. But the developing world is overwhelmingly a world of smallness. Four-fifths of the farms are 12 acres or less. Large-scale technology does not fit in small communities, but unfortunately, often the only available technologies are designed for big markets in highly populous areas. For example, in 1969 a community in Zambia wanted to make egg trays from waste paper; they needed about one million trays per year. The smallest machine produced at that time made one million a month! Because the machine would not be utilized fully, its cost was impractical. Today smallness is coming to be valued in rich as well as poor countries. "Experience shows that whenever efficient, small-scale equipment is made available the demand for it comes not merely from the Third World, but even more insistently from affluent societies as well" (McRobie 1981). A catalogue of small-scale farm equipment, originally intended for use in developing countries, was so successful in the U.S. that an American publisher has added U.S.-manufactured small farm equipment and reissued the guide for sale to small American farmers.

In developing technologies that are appropriate for developing societies, techniques and tools must be relatively simple so that skills and resources already existing in the society can be used and demands for highly specialized skills and locally unavailable resources are minimized. It has sometimes happened that the newest, most complex hardware is sold to people who do not have the resources to maintain it. George Foster describes such an incident:

> In 1957 in the Helmand Valley of Afghanistan I was shown irrigation works designed and built by American engineers and technicians to standards as high as could be devised on drafting tables. For all the technical excellence, however, serious problems were encountered in the local distribution of water to farmer's fields. American agricultural agents told me the degree of sophistication and responsibility needed to operate and maintain the superbly designed gates, valves and ditches was higher than could be reasonably expected of American irrigation farmers. Yet many of the Helmand Valley farmers had only recently been resettled from traditional nomadic life.
>
> *(Foster, 1962:181)*

Today, many engineers are interested in designing technologies that are better suited to developing areas. The aim of one program in Tanzania was to develop a range of tools that could be made and repaired by the villagers themselves. Workshops were set up in villages to show people how to make the tools. Within a year, villagers were producing oxcarts, handcarts, cultivators, wheelbarrows, and maize shelters (McRobie 1981).

Modern technology typically is *capital-intensive* as opposed to *labor-intensive*. A capital-intensive technology is one in which techniques and tools are expensive, requiring large amounts of capital or money, but usually not requiring much labor. A labor-intensive technology is one in which the techniques and tools are inexpensive but require large outputs of human labor. Using capital-intensive technologies in poor areas where there is abundant labor, high unemployment, and scarce capital makes little sense. In many instances, the introduction of modern machines to Third World countries has contributed to unemployment and widened the gap between rich and poor.

Figure HL8.1
Appropriate technology for planting. (Billie DeWalt)

One center in south India has focused on increasing job opportunities among the rural poor. For example, a small dairy processing plant employs local villagers who make butter from locally produced milk. The plant pays the villagers 6 percent more for their milk than they could get get by selling milk to urban milk depots. The center also returns the buttermilk residue to the villagers free (McRobie 1981).

The final criteria for appropriate technology is that it should be compatible with the physical and social environment. We have already seen the harmful effects highly mechanized agriculture can have on the environment. E. F. Schumacher (1977), pioneer of appropriate technology, states that technology should be carried out "as if people mattered." Therefore, technologies that cause unemployment or create mindless, demeaning work do not qualify as "appropriate."

Appropriate technology in developed countries

Even though the concept of intermediate technology was developed with the Third World in mind, many industrialized countries are finding that they, too, need a new kind of technology, one more appropriate to the new conditions they face: fuel shortages, environment destruction, increasing unemployment, and the human revolt against dehumanizing work.

This interest in appropriate technology is evident in the growing number of people practicing organic gardening in the U.S., Britian, and Canada. The U.S. magazine *Organic Gardening* now has a circulation of over 1 million. Job enrichment programs, profit-sharing, employee gyms, and day care centers for employees' children are other examples of industrialized countries interested in practicing technology "as if people mattered."

Appropriate technology in health care systems

The concept of appropriate technology also can be applied to health care systems. The same criteria—small, simple, inexpensive, and compatible with the physical and social environment—are necessary for health care systems to be effective in developing areas.

In most developing countries health care systems have been copied from the West, where health care is in the hands of doctors and is centralized, hospital-based, marked by advanced technology, and very expensive. Poor countries, with a health budget of perhaps as little as $1.00 per person, are looking for ways to spread health care to as many people as possible.

One means of doing this effectively is to train local people as auxiliary health care workers. Training varies from three weeks for some Kenyan village workers who learn about hygiene, child care, and nutrition, to three years for medical assistants in Tanzania. Many appropriate health care programs are quite effective. An evaluation team visiting the Bonashasthaya Kendra community health project in 1977 found decreased rates of skin problems, diarrhea, smallpox, and maternal deaths. Birth and death rates had both dropped (Cooley 1978).

People in Africa, India, and Mexico have designed appropriate methods for measuring nutritional status. Measuring arm or leg thickness has long been recognized as one of the easiest and best methods for checking to see whether children are healthy. A well-nourished child has thicker arms and legs than a poorly-nourished one. From age one to five, the circumference of a child's upper arm does not normally change much. In modern medical facilities, skin fold calipers are used to measure nutritional status. Calipers which cost as much as $500 are out of the reach of many poor communities. But ingenuous substitutions can be made. In parts of Asia and Africa, one traditional method used to measure the thickness of a child's arm is with a bracelet made of wire that has an inside diameter of 4 centimeters. If the bracelet will not slide past the elbow, the child is well nourished; if the bracelet slides easily onto the upper arm, the child is poorly nourished (Werner 1982).

People in industrialized countries also are becoming interested in appropriate health care, as evidenced by the strong movement toward holistic medicine. Some people are replacing elaborate medical treatment and expensive medications with simpler remedies such as nutrition, exercise, and stress reduction. The widespread popularity of books such as *How To Be* *Your Own Doctor . . . Sometimes* and *Family Guide to Health* illustrates the increased interest in this appropriate health care.

Summary

Recognition that part of the solution to the world food crisis lies in the developing world's ability to feed itself makes the use of appropriate technology highly significant. It also poses an important challenge: it is relatively easy to make modern, sophisticated technology more complicated; but far more creativity is needed to make it more simple!

One way to measure the thickness of a child's arm is with a bracelet like this:

If the bracelet will not slide past the elbow or calf, the child is **well nourished.**

If the bracelet slides easily onto the upper arm or slips down to the ankle, the child is **poorly nourished.**

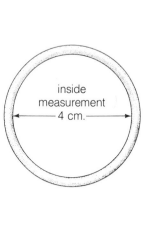

inside measurement 4 cm.

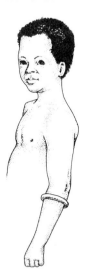

Figure HL8.2
Bracelets used to measure upper arm and leg thicknesses.
David Werner and Bill Bower, The Hesperian Foundation. P.O. Box 1692, Palo Alto, California, 94302.

9

Understanding
dietary change

I have the audacity to believe that people everywhere can have
three meals a day . . . . I believe that what self-centered men
have torn down other-centered men can build up. I still believe
that one day mankind will bow before the altars of God and be
crowned triumphant . . . . I still believe that we shall overcome.

Martin Luther King, Jr.
Nobel Peace Prize Acceptance Speech, 1964

Perhaps never before has the challenge been more critical or
more difficult: Many developing nations are threatened by widespread hunger and social upheaval because of the inequitable distribution of food and other resources. It will not be easy to implement
the changes needed to avert food shortages and long-standing poverty in the Third World. Industrialized nations appear more secure
with their abundant supplies of grain, meat, fruits, and vegetables.
Yet they, too, are caught in a dilemma of meeting consumer demands for an ever-abundant supply of attractive, convenient, and diversified food products while minimizing the environmental degradation and health problems that can result from an industrialized
food system.

Consumers in North America have more extensive nutrition knowledge than ever before, but because many are unable to apply it to their daily lives, obesity, diabetes, heart disease, hypertension, and other diet-related diseases continue to afflict a significant proportion of the population. These dilemmas will not be resolved easily.

For those of you determined to take on today's challenges, an understanding of culture change processes and intervention strategies is valuable. In this chapter we look in depth at the *directed change* process: "That situation in which someone, or some group, interferes actively and purposefully in the social behavior of others" (Gallaher 1973:476). More specifically, we examine changes that are advocated and directed by nutritionists, nutritional anthropologists, and policy makers.

To better understand change processes and how to manage their direction, we draw on social science research. Of major concern to the nutrition interventionist are factors affecting how people accept the ideas they promote. We focus, therefore, on three components in the directed change process, noting certain characteristics of each which influence peoples' receptivity to change. These are potential adopters, advocates of change, and the innovations themselves.

Potential adopters are key figures in our discussion of the change process. They are the targets or recipients of directed change efforts. Nutrition intervention is directed at convincing them to accept new ideas and adopt new practices. In studying the nutrition change process, our primary objective is to determine why some adopters accept change and others reject it. Part of our discussion will revolve around certain attitudes and values held by adopters that make them more open to new nutrition ideas.

The *advocates of change* are the people promoting new ideas, practices, and products. Sometimes called change agents, these people usually are nutritionists, educators, or other professionals

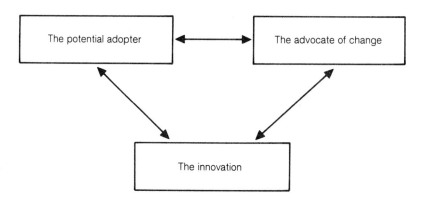

Figure 9.1
The three components of directed change.

whose work is devoted to improving the health and nutritional well-being of potential adopters. We will examine certain attributes of advocates that determine how well they can influence others to change.

An *innovation* is any idea, practice, or material object perceived as new by an individual. Innovations may arise through discovery and invention or they may emerge from social interaction as cultural traits diffuse between and within social groups. Here we are not concerned with whether or not something is objectively new as measured by the lapse of time since its first appearance, but rather with the individual's perception of newness and reaction to innovations. Thus, if a dietary practice, belief, or product is new to the individual, it is an innovation.

Every innovation is an idea or set of ideas. Some innovations have only an *idea* component, while others have a *physical* component; the idea is given overt expression through material or behavioral form. Acceptance of a new dietary trait that has both an idea and a physical component invokes an action that can be observed; the acceptor buys a new food product, practices a new agricultural method, or adopts a new cooking technique. Innovations that only have an idea component cannot be adopted in a way that is directly observable. Some food guides, for example, now include beans in the "meat group". This innovation—a new way of categorizing foods—demands that people change how they perceive beans. Acceptance of the innovation is not directly visible, but expressed indirectly through behavior; for instance, as beans are served instead of meat for a main course.

Characteristics of the adopter

Certain attitudes and values affect people's perceptions of innovations. One of the most obvious examples is the value some people place on change itself. Although an attraction to novelty is typically associated with industrialized nations, many people in developing countries also value newness as a sign of modernity. Throughout the world, advertisers capitalize on this value by promoting "new," "improved," and "modern" products. Clearly, the individual who places a value on change is more receptive, overall, to innovations than the person who does not.

Other attitudes and values also influence peoples' receptivity to innovations and their general readiness to change. Three sets of attitudes and values that play an especially important role in the adoption and rejection of dietary innovations are discussed below. These are dependence on authority, the expectation of change, and conceptions of pride and dignity.

Dependence on authority

In all societies except small tribal bands, people rely on specialists for information and advice about religion, government, technology, and other aspects of life. We have seen that the number and variety of specialists increases as society becomes more complex, and that society's dependence on these authorities for solutions to its problems also grows. When a body of knowledge like nutrition grows and becomes specialized, most people do not master its complexities, but turn instead to experts for guidance. As Homer Barnett explains:

> The more intricate the knowledge, the greater must be the dependence, if there is any appeal to the specialists at all. People everywhere take the word of their prophets and their medicine men. American culture, with its multiplication of specialties and the extreme complication of many of them, offers a good example . . . . Indeed, because of specialization, Americans are constantly listening to the voice of authority from some quarter. This dependence has become a habit with us. As a people we have an almost slavish regard for "experts" in any field.
>
> *(Barnett, 1953:67)*

The rate and nature of change in a social group is influenced by how the authorities that people depend upon view change. In the United States and Canada, for instance, representatives of science and technology are highly innovative, devoting time and energy specifically to the search for new solutions to their problems. In contrast, our religious authorities typically take a conservative stance and discourage major changes in belief or ritual, while our politicians are divided between those that defend the status quo and others who push for radical changes in our economic and political system.

Some people place a great deal of faith in the advice of these authorities. They are easily influenced by professionals or other "experts" and reluctant to accept innovations promoted by lay persons. For example, a woman convalescing after abdominal surgery spoke to a dietitian about her slow recovery. The dietitian found that the patient was eating a very limited diet and recommended eating more protein foods and taking a multivitamin and mineral supplement as a way of hastening the healing process. The client responded to the dietitian's advice eagerly and stated emphatically that she would start right away. The patient's mother, who was also in the room, remarked to the dietitian, "I'm so glad she heard that from *you*. I've told her that several times but she just ignored my advice."

Many lay people perceive formal education in health science as essential, even though they may not consider training specifically in nutrition as important. In fact, two national surveys conducted in 1979 (Community Nutrition Institute 1979:4) found that the majority of Americans have high confidence in physicians as a source of nutrition advice while nutritional education from other sources was ranked much lower in its impact.

Unfortunately, many physicians are unable to meet these expectations because of limited nutrition training. This situation is improving, however. Medical schools are adding nutrition courses to their curricula and many physicians are obtaining nutrition information through continuing education classes.

Other degrees and titles also are respected as signs of authority by smaller segments of the North American population. Naturopaths, homeopaths, and chiropractors are gaining popularity as nutrition advisors. Many of the people who look to these alternative health care providers for advice are somewhat distrustful of professionally trained clinicians, often viewing M.D.'s, R.N.'s, and R.D.'s as overly conservative members of the medical establishment. On the other hand, many Americans are suspicious of alternative forms of health care and totally dismiss these perspectives as quackery. Clearly, North Americans have a diversity of attitudes toward nutrition experts.

In sum, people often rely on specialists to create new solutions to their problems and guide them in evaluating new ideas and practices. The degree of dependence on authority for directing dietary change is greater in some societies than others, but in all instances, it is valuable to know who is respected as an authority and in what ways people depend upon their chosen authorities for advice and direction in nutrition matters. By understanding people's attitudes toward authority, the nutrition change agent will be better able to evaluate his or her own status as an expert and enlist the support of those who are most respected, and hence most influential, in directing change.

Expectation of change

An attitude closely associated with dependence on authority is the expectation of change. In some societies, governmental and industrial authorities provide the people with new, effective solutions to their problems. The public then begins to expect—even demand—that authorities produce more changes to further improve their lives. With this expectation, the people grow increasingly receptive to change and more willing to adopt innovations. Thus, the expectation of change in itself serves as a stimulus to the acceptance of change. Innovation thrives in an atmosphere that anticipates it.

The expectation of change "is a cultivated attitude with variable limits and areas of relevance, depending upon the society. Most often it is limited to select aspects of the culture" (Barnett 1953:56). For instance, the Samoans traditionally

> expect each individual among them to be unique in everything that he does. Imitation is deplored. Every woman has her own design on tapa cloth, even different designs for each piece and the opposite ends of the same piece. Every person is expected to improvise song and dance steps for himself. Likewise for house builders, tattooers, and other specialists. The expectation of deviation even extends to religion and political organization, both for individuals and villages. Innovation is the rule . . . .
> (Barnett 1953:57)

In contrast, Gallaher's (1961) study of a midwestern American town showed that while Plainvillers expect rapid technological change and readily accept new agricultural practices, cooking appliances, and time-saving devices, they do not anticipate equally rapid change in other areas such as religion. Finally, some societies such as traditional Zuñis, do not anticipate change in any area of their culture.

Not all change that is expected is also welcomed. People may anticipate innovation in technology, religion, or political organization, but at the same time prefer the status quo. Changes in childrearing practices, dating, and sexual relations are unwelcome to many older North Americans, and yet they are seen as inevitable. Likewise, emigrants often view the rapid changes encountered in a new country as destructive to their traditional values and family structure and yet these changes are fully expected (Barnett 1953:59). Even if change is not desired, it is more likely to be accepted when it is anticipated than when it is not.

With respect to dietary change, interventionists face two challenges. First, in societies that do not expect dietary changes to occur, nutrition educators usually encounter resistance to new ideas or programs. Because nutrition change is not seen as natural or good, it proceeds more slowly than in situations where it is expected. Typically, nutrition educators find that people are suspicious of their motives and skeptical of the benefits of the products or programs they are promoting. Clearly, a great deal more preliminary work is needed to create an atmosphere conducive for innovation in these societies before a successful change program can be launched.

A second challenge to nutritional interventionists is found in societies where rapid dietary change *is* expected. In these situations, the nutrition specialists upon which people have come to depend for change often are unable to generate innovations at a rate acceptable to the people. The result is a growing sense of frustration with the status quo and the authorities responsible for producing and guiding the change process. In the United States, for instance, people are accustomed to a rapid and steady development of new and improved food products, cooking appliances, and ideas about dietary methods to prevent and cure disease. The attitude that change *should* and *will* occur in this area is a stimulus to the production and acceptance of dietary innovations. But it also contributes to frustration with government authorities when they either oppose popular innovations or fail to generate new and better solutions. High-dosage vitamin and mineral supplements provide a good example. The use of nutrient supplements as cure-alls is both expected and valued so highly by some that attempts to place them out of reach of the general population have been unpopular and unavailing. In the early 1970s, when the FDA attempted to limit the over-the-counter sales of potentially toxic vitamin and mineral supplements, consumers and vitamin manufacturers staged an extensive protest campaign that effectively persuaded Congress to nip the FDA's proposal in the bud.

In addition to public pressure on authorities to make the expected changes, people's frustration with the status quo also motivates them to turn to others who promise the desired solutions. Today the anticipation that a quick and painless weight reduction plan will be rapidly forthcoming tempts many people to try an endless variety of fad diets. A glance at the covers of women's magazines and weekly newspapers stacked in the aisles of grocery store checkout counters reveals people's insistence on fast and easy weight control. In Great Britain alone, annual retail sales of slimming aids were estimated at $30 million during 1970 (Lynch 1970:48). And in the United States, products such as *Dexatrim* compete with other diet pills, diet foods, and a multitude of gadgets using promises like "I *guarantee* you can lose up to 13 pounds in the first 10 days . . . . up to 25 pounds in 30 days . . . . up to 37 pounds in 60 days . . . . the *safe* way." (*The Globe* 1980:8). No wonder, then, that people pay dearly for these products and pass quickly over the ADA's 1200-calorie plan or other diet regimes that require great discipline and delayed gratification in order to shed a mere pound or two weekly. The expectation of rapid dietary change also is a major force behind the public's acceptance of some inaccurate health food claims. Public health nutritionists must deal with misinformation and exaggerated claims that undermine the less sensational, albeit empirical, information they offer clients about diet and health.

In sum, the expectation of change is an important attitude, with many implications for the dietary change process. Its absence usually points to widespread resistance and skepticism of directed change efforts, while its presence can create unrealistic demands for innovation and accompanying frustrations that can undermine policymakers' carefully formulated plans for progress. In either case, nutrition interventionists stand to gain a great deal by recognizing recipients' attitudes towards change as well as the types of dietary innovations that they may expect.

Pride and dignity

> Anthropologists have noted that an innate dignity in personal bearing and a pride in their way of life characterize the peoples among whom they work. This correlates with the ethnocentric position of most people vis-a-vis their cultures, and it is reflected in a strong—not to say rigid—belief about the behavior appropriate to recognized roles.
>
> *(Foster 1962:69–70)*

While all people are proud of their culture, specific definitions of pride and dignity vary crossculturally. Formal table manners in one society may appear odd to those from another cultural background.

Cultural definitions of pride and dignity are likely to pose conflict for the nutrition interventionist in several ways. These conflicts arise from the appropriateness of formal student roles in educational programs, acceptability of certain foods for human consumption, pride associated with performance of certain roles (e.g., cooking), and attitudes toward gifts, welfare, and other forms of public assistance.

Nutrition educators frequently rely upon lecture-discussion groups, seminars, and workshops to transmit information to people

Figure 9.2
The innovation. A traveller in an arid region of the Uzbek, USSR uses a portable solar heater to boil water.

[United Nations/
S. Meteeitsa (TASS)]

of all ages. In North America, adult education is widespread; parents as well as children attend classes and lectures without losing face. This is not true everywhere, however; in many societies, formal education is appropriate for children only. Adults may appear undignified if they occupy student roles. The following quote from Dube's study of change in India pertains to many other communities as well:

> The idea of an adult education class sounds excellent, but few adults want to adopt the role of a school child and enroll in these classes. The few who do join these classes also eventually give up because of the general amusement their position arouses. It must be remembered that we are dealing here with a population which is very sensitive concerning matters of honour and is unwilling to risk any ridicule.

> *(Dube 1958:136)*

Even in cultures where adult education is widespread, many people find classroom programs unacceptable because such activities remind them of bad experiences they had in school when they were young.

When working with adults who find student roles humiliating or undignified, nutrition educators have little chance of gaining acceptance for programs that resemble activities used to educate youth. Even among peoples that readily participate in adult education, the age, sex, and ethnic differences between the teacher and the students, as well as other aspects of the educational process, must be designed to conform with local definitions of appropriate behavior for maximum acceptance.

Another conflict commonly encountered by nutrition interventionists arises from beliefs about the appropriateness of certain foodstuffs for human consumption. (See Chapter 3 for a more thorough discussion of foods considered appropriate by different groups.) These food beliefs and taboos make it undignified to eat certain foods. Indians in the Bolivian Andes, for instance, perceive milk as a type of animal excrement similar to urine. As we saw in Highlight 1–1, many other people have similar beliefs or avoid milk because it causes gastrointestinal distress.

When powdered milk has been sent in vast quantities from Canada and the United States to malnourished peoples in India, Africa, and Latin America, it has been rejected. "A.I.D. powdered milk has been thrown away by the ton, fed to animals, used as fertilizer, paint, even pavement for airplane runways" (Heyneman 1971:305). North Americans are often astonished to find that their gifts are not put to the use for which they were intended.

People are, of course, proud of how they perform certain roles, particularly how they care for their children. A public health nurse encountered a conflict in Mexico when she condemned the local feeding practices for babies, telling mothers that they should give their babies milk instead of the traditional diet. When she made little progress, she suggested that they feed their babies with water in which beans were boiled. The babies' health improved dramatically, and when the nurse pointed this out, one mother replied: "Oh, but we are feeding them milk now, too. We have followed your advice about the milk ever since you stopped calling our own food bad."

Ward Goodenough (1966:462–63) speaks to the same issue in this advice given to program administrators:

> It is difficult, indeed, to avoid the implication that the project administrator disapproves of the local foods when he tries to introduce new ones in order to improve the diet. The very existence of the project may be an implied insult, and taken as such. In promoting his program, therefore, the administrator may find it politic to emphasize that he is concerned with ways of increasing the quantity rather than the quality of available food, or again that he is interested in helping people obtain a greater variety of foods rather than substituting a better food for the present inferior one.

A final area of conflict frequently noted arises from people's attitudes towards gifts, welfare, and public assistance. Many innovative programs have failed to gain acceptance by people holding negative attitudes towards outsiders' help. For example, a government-sponsored Child Development Service in Florida planned to establish a day care center and lunch program for economically disadvantaged Latins in a section of Dade County. Several months prior to the Center's opening, a survey conducted among the community residents revealed resistance to the program. While the vast majority of respondents said that day care center services were needed and welcomed in the area, few people interviewed were willing to use the center for their children. Further questioning revealed the reason for the discrepancy: the program was associated with other government-sponsored programs like food stamps. Potential participants feared that they would be stigmatized as "poor" or "welfare cases" if they sent their children to the program (Bryant 1974).

Unfortunately, programs formed with the best intentions also can prove insulting to the people they hope to help. In one of the Middle Eastern countries, a North American oil company decided to offer its Arab workers one nutritious meal each day. While the plan was designed to increase efficiency of the poorly nourished workers, the company also wanted to improve its employees' welfare. At the very least, it was hoped, the plan would gain the workers' good will. A well-equipped cafeteria was built and workers were offered nutritious food at a nominal charge. The workers not only rejected the program in its entirety, but claimed that the Americans had insulted them by treating them as inferiors. Dismayed, the company investigated to find out what had caused this reaction. The answer proved to be the cafeteria pattern of providing the food. Only beggars in this country stood in line to be fed. By having workers pass through a cafeteria line, the company had implied that they were beggars, without self-respect, dependent on the company for a handout (Fathauer 1960:335).

In contrast, a program in Yap, a group of Micronesian islands in the U.S. Trust Territory of the Western Pacific, proved to be successful because it appealed to Yapese pride and traditional ways. This nutrition education program was initiated through the Yap District Health Department with the objective of promoting increased consumption of nutritious, locally produced foods and decreased use of expensive, nonessential imported foods that contributed to dental caries, obesity, and diabetes.

A project promoting locally produced coconut juice in place of soft drinks started in 1975. Local grocery stores agreed to stock drinking coconuts and display promotional materials. Educational materials included comic books and posters that described the nutritional superiority of coconut juice over soft drinks and emphasized that increased sales of locally grown coconuts would improve the Yapese economy. Shortly after the campaign began, a political cartoon, not originated by the program, appeared in the newspaper. It depicted a canned soft drink as a character representing unpopular foreign political influence being kicked by a coconut representing Yapese sentiments.

As a result of the campaign, coconut sales increased dramatically. Cold drinking coconuts are now sold at public events, movie theatres, restaurants, and most grocery stores. Moreover, tax receipts show that soft drink sales decreased significantly after the program started. Though many factors contributed to the success of this program, in the word of Nancy Rody, the program coordinator, "my observation is that change originating from older values was accepted by the community and was not seen as something imposed from the outside" (Rody 1978).

Characteristics of the advocate for change

The directed change process is like many situations involving persuasion: success depends in large part on the advocate, the person promoting the innovation. Common examples of advocates or change agents include salespersons, VISTA volunteers, teachers, and nutrition educators. In advertising, advocate-acceptor relations are indirect and impersonal, relying on the printed word, television, or radio messages as the means of contact and persuasion. Most nutritional interventionists, however, work directly with their clients to discuss and influence their ideas and behavior.

Typically, advocates are professionals who influence innovative decisions in a direction they deem desirable. Although nutrition interventionists most often promote new ideas and practices, occasionally they are advocates of the status quo, attempting to slow or stop innovations believed to be harmful. Efforts to combat dangerous fad diets are a common example.

Much advice has been written for the person occupying the advocate role. This includes community development textbooks, village level worker manuals and guides for the overseas administrator (see Goodenough 1966, King 1965, and Brownee 1978). These texts contain valuable information on communication techniques, coping with culture shock, and other stresses commonly experienced by change agents. But all too often, these guides and those who read them fail to recognize the important role that certain attributes of the advocate play in the intervention process. For, as we shall see below, success as an interventionist may depend to a great extent on personality, prestige, personal relations with potential acceptors, degree of similarity with potential acceptors, and personal credibility.

Personality

Personality is one of the most inescapable advocate attributes. The shy, reticent person has a far more difficult time persuading others to adopt new ideas than the out-going, sociable individual. Nutrition interventionists, like encyclopedia salesmen and public relations specialists, find their personalities important assets or liabilities when trying to convince others to "buy" new ideas or goods.

We all are familiar with how an offensive personality affects our receptivity to persuasion. A suggestion—any suggestion—offered by someone whose manner creates antagonism is likely to be rejected regardless of the essential merits of the advice. Although the advocate and not the innovation is the offender, both are subject to rejection.

A good example of this comes from the history of science. Louis Pasteur's personality was a powerful liability, affecting the acceptance of his many brilliant ideas. Barnett (1953:322) tells us that even when Pasteur's "most sympathetic biographers seem to be agreed that he struck the majority of his contemporaries as an insufferable egotist with not a little of the paranoiac about his behavior. He was dogmatic, cocksure, conceited, contentious and extremely sensitive to criticism." Despite his many outstanding contributions to science, Pasteur's personality almost prevented him from gaining a seat in the Free Association of the Academy of Medicine. (He won by a single vote.) More importantly, Pasteur's unpopularity created violent antagonisms to his medical discoveries, delaying their acceptance.

An appealing personality is an equally powerful asset. Engaging people with likeable mannerisms will attract attentive consideration to both themselves and the ideas they advocate. People are more likely to listen, consider their opinions, and emulate advocates by adopting their ideas or practices.

Thus, personality can be a powerful asset to liability to the architects of change. Within limits, personality is flexible and can be manipulated to fit the persuasion situation, making it even more valuable as an attribute.

Prestige

Many commercial advertisements use people with widely recognized prestige to advocate their products: it is hoped that the advocate's prestige will motivate people to adopt a product in order to be more like the advocate or indirectly win his or her approval. Athletes, movie stars, and other celebrities who attribute their success, at least partially, to dietary factors are proving to be effective advocates for many nutrition products. Mary Lou Retton, the Olympic gymnast and gold medalist, tells American television viewers that she eats Wheaties—the "breakfast of champions"—for strength and good health. Two former Miss Americas, Bess Myerson and Phyllis George, have written popular diet books. In these cases, personal success and notoriety rather than formal education, qualify the advocates as authorities.

The health educator in Yap, who successfully promoted coconuts also found that local celebrities can be quite effective in eliciting dietary change. She used film strips featuring two well-known Yapese women to promote breastfeeding and homemade baby food at meetings with village mothers and in hospital clinics. The increased incidence of breastfeeding and homemade infant food that occurs on the islands was attributed, in part, to the use of respected local persons (Rody 1978).

Prestige is a difficult concept to dissect because it encompasses so many interlocking components: competence, past accomplishments, reputation, wealth, and in many cases, ascribed characteristics such as sex, age, or nationality. Furthermore, a person's prestige varies according to the audience, the situation, and the subject at hand. A person may be highly respected and admired among literary circles but virtually unknown to blue-collar workers. Or as with the punk rock image of the 1980s, elements of prestige recognized by some youth invoke completely different responses in their parents.

The prestige of an advocate, even when widely recognized by her audience, may not be sufficient to influence others to alter their ideas or behavior. For instance, the wife of a recent Mexican president was unable to influence the women in her country to breastfeed rather than bottle feed despite her prestige as an advocate.

Personal relations

Advocate relationships with potential acceptors range from stranger or professional acquaintance to neighbor, friend, and even close relative. The relationship often will affect the advocate's ability to persuade others to adopt his or her novel idea. As we have seen, in many communities people look primarily to professionals for leadership and direction in change, while others are more skeptical of innovation and unwilling to adopt something new unless it has been tried first by neighbors, friends, or relatives. People who are open to advice from professionals or advocates outside their communities typically accept innovations first, and therefore, are called "early adopters" (Rogers 1971:184). Those who are more resistant to change and follow community members rather than professionals are called "late adopters."

Because professional change agents who come from outside a community are largely ineffective in persuading late adopters, it is often beneficial to recruit early adopters from within the local community to support the innovation. The effectiveness of using these in-group advocates is illustrated in Bryant's (1978) research on infant feeding practices among Cubans, Puerto Ricans, and Anglos in Dade County, Florida. In this study, mothers did not adopt advice from nutritionists or physicians about controlling infant weight gain unless it was also advocated by a friend, relative, or neighbor. In other words, someone the mother knows personally had to support the professional advocate or the innovation was rejected. For this reason, diet counseling is often more effective if a friend, neighbor, or relative attends the session and reinforces the advice given by the nutritionist. (See Highlight 9–1 for more information on social supports.)

The importance of personal relations between advocates and acceptors makes a strong case for living in or near the recipient's community. Homer Barnett (1953:323) tells us how "After I had lived in a Palauan Village for several months, I was often asked for an interpretation of some new American regulations, such as the request that polygamy be abandoned or the order that fallen coconut logs be burned to destroy beetle larvae. The natives were uncomprehend-

Palaua
A group of 20 small coral islands extending between the Philippines and the Caroline Islands

ing and sometimes distrustful of the motives behind such requirements. They felt more assured that they should cooperate with the
officials if I could find nothing inimical to their interests in the law."
Because he was a member of the Palauan community and hence incorporated into their personal relationships, Barnett was accepted
as an advocate. Those Americans outside the community were not.

Homophily

Homophily is the degree of similarity in age, sex, ethnicity, and
other attributes between advocates and their clients. Heterophily is
the degree to which they are different. Communications research
has shown that homophily is an important advocate asset (Rogers
and Shoemaker 1971:240–3).

Unfortunately, interventionists usually differ significantly from
their clients in educational background, social status, and wealth. In
heterophilious relationships such as these, values and interests are
not always shared, making communication difficult indeed (Rogers
and Shoemaker 1971:241). Thus many interventionists work
closely and effectively with clients who are the most like themselves: those with the most education, wealth, and a cosmopolitan
orientation. They may fail to convince or avoid working with the clients least like themselves: sometimes the people who need assistance most.

Recognizing the ineffectiveness of advocates who are dissimilar
to their clients, many programs recruit interventionists from the
population being served. Village-level workers in India (Dube
1958), neighborhood workers in the United States (Bryant 1974),
and other advocates selected from the target community have
proven highly successful for this reason.

When it is impossible or impractical to recruit change agents in
this way, people still can be selected that are similar in some attributes with their clients. Canadian programs sending nutritionists to
Mexico, for example, could assign educators to special groups by
matching them according to age and sex. In this way women could
work with women and men with men. The educators then could
focus activities around issues important to the specific groups they
are serving, building upon the attributes and experiences shared
with program participants.

This is done in a program called Community Advisors for
Breastfeeding Mothers (CAB), designed to promote breastfeeding
among economically disadvantaged and minority women in Lexington, Kentucky. In CAB, advisors are recruited, and to some extent assigned to clients, so as to maximize their similarities with the population served. Unlike other breastfeeding support groups (e.g., La
Leche League), most CAB advisors are members of minorities, work-

ing mothers, and personally experienced with economic hardships. Because of this homophily, the needs, interests, and problems of clients are shared to a large extent with advisors. This enables counselors to share first hand experience as well as technical advice with the mothers seeking help. (For more details see Highlight 10-2.)

Credibility

A final advocate asset is credibility. Credibility refers to the expertness and trustworthiness of the change agent. Clients' beliefs about an advocate's knowledge, intelligence, training, and competence form their assessment of her expertness. Trustworthiness is based on clients' evaluation of the agent's sincerity and personal motives for promoting change.

An advocate's credibility may be affected by other attributes as well. Educational background and titles, sex, age, social status, personal relations, homophily, and other characteristics or accomplishments contribute to the determination of an individual's credibility. Men, for example, are less credible sources of information on breastfeeding than women. Obese dietitians are less credible than thin ones. And, as we have noted above, physicians are more credible sources than nutritionists to many Americans.

A person's credibility also is affected by perceptions of the advocate's intentions. When a person is recognized as having a definite *intention* to persuade others, there is an increased likelihood that she will be viewed as having something to gain, and hence, as less worthy of trust. Casual and nonpurposive conversations are effective means of persuasion because the recipients do not have the critical, defensive attitude that they may have in situations where they know others are trying to influence them.

Credibility, then, is an important asset to the interventionist. Based on perceptions of competence and trustworthiness, a person's credibility is limited to certain areas of expertise; it is not a fixed attribute and can be damaged by the promotion of highly objectionable ideas or a negative evaluation of the advocate's intentions.

It should be noted that no single advocate attribute is more powerful than the others. For some people, some of the time, prestige will outweigh personal relations or even personality. In some instances, heterophily may prove almost inconsequential in the persuasive process, while in others it is a major deterrent to change. Nutrition interventionists, therefore, must be aware of each asset and liability they carry into the nutrition change setting, adjusting their own activities and the work of colleagues to maximize their effectiveness as advocates.

Characteristics of the innovation

Eating less sugar and more high-fiber foods, exercising regularly, rotating crops, boiling water—all are examples of changes that health care providers might encourage people to make. Eating at a new type of restaurant, adopting a macrobiotic diet, using a new cooking appliance, or trying a new hybrid seed exemplify innovations that people may choose to make.

Each of these ideas have certain attributes that enhance or detract from their appeal to potential adopters. Certain innovation characteristics have been shown to have especially powerful influences on people's receptivity to change. They include complexity, compatibility with existing beliefs and values, relative advantages (efficiency, health, pleasure, economics, prestige), and penalties (illness, legal sanctions, public ridicule, religious concerns).

By understanding these characteristics, interventionists are better able to predict an innovation's chances of being accepted. Interventionists also can manipulate the change (for example, make it less complicated or more pleasurable to carry out) thereby making it more attractive to potential adopters.

Complexity of the change

Complexity is "the degree to which an innovation is perceived as relatively difficult to understand and use" (Rogers and Shoemaker 1971:154). Many researchers have found that the complexity of a novelty impedes its rate of adoption. Thus, a cooking technique that

Figure 9.3
Comparing the old and the new.
(AID)

appears easy to master will be adopted more readily than one one that appears difficult.

Any dietary change makes certain performance demands upon the person who adopts it. Many innovations require that users read in order to follow instructions; some require the individual to calculate and tabulate the amount of nutrients daily; some force the adopter to remember lists of foods that can and cannot be eaten; others require that the person acquire new planning, shopping, and cooking skills. All require some relearning or reconditioning.

Therapeutic diets can be especially demanding in their complexity. The often-used diabetic exchange list diet, endorsed by the American Dietetics Association is a good illustration. To follow this diet correctly, the diabetic must remember how items are grouped, measure foods according to predetermined portion sizes, and exert willpower to consume only those items and the quantities prescribed by the diet. Most importantly, the patient must understand the exchange system.

Just how easy is the exchange system to understand? Foods are grouped according to nutrient composition and designated as food exchange groups. There are six exchange groups: milk, vegetables, fruit, bread, meat, and fats. Food items within any given group can be exchanged freely as long as the designated portion sizes are followed. Thus, one small apple can be exchanged for a cup of watermelon or 7 inches of honeydew melon because they all contain approximately equivalent amounts of protein, carbohydrate and fat.

There are several ways in which the exchange system can be misunderstood. Interviews with clients referred to a mid-western diabetes clinic, for example, show that some people believe that exchanges are made *between* food groups rather than *within* each group. Moreover, many people think that they cannot eat fruits, vegetables, or other items that are not specifically named on the food exchange lists. This creates unnecessary and unintended restrictions for members of many ethnic groups and individuals who like foods such as chitlings or malanga that are not included in the lists given to patients. Also some of the groupings are difficult to remember. For example, bacon is placed in the fat group, not the meat group; cheese is in the meat, not the milk group; and potatoes are grouped as breads, not vegetables.

Other problems encountered with the exchange system concern serving sizes. All items in the exchange system are listed with designated serving sizes. These portion sizes are important because they are what determine carbohydrate, protein, fat, and calorie content of the diet; but some patients are not accustomed to cooking with these measures (cups, inches, ounces) and thus do not calculate portion sizes correctly. Moreover, many people do not have the

chitlings
The small intestine of calves or hogs prepared as a food

malanga
A tuberous vegetable popular among Cubans and other Caribbean groups.

Table 9.1a–g   The American Dietetics Association's Diabetic Exchange List

'The U.S. exchange system presented here is based on material in *Exchange Lists for Meal Planning,* prepared by committees of the American Diabetes Association and the American Dietetic Association in cooperation with the National Institute of Arthritis, Metabolism, and Digestive Diseases and the National Heart and Lung Institute, National Institutes of Health, Public Health Service, U.S. Department of Health and Human Services (formerly U.S. Department of Health, Education, and Welfare).

Table 9.1a   Milk list (12 g carbohydrate, 8 g protein, 80 cal)[a]

Amount	Food
Nonfat fortified milk	
1 c	Skim or nonfat milk
1 c	Buttermilk made from skim milk
1 c	Yogurt made from skim milk (plain, unflavored)
⅓ c	Powdered, nonfat dry milk, before adding liquid
½ c	Canned evaporated skim milk, before adding liquid
Low-fat fortified milk	
1 c	1% fat fortified milk (count as 1 milk and ½ fat exchange)
1 c	2% fat fortified milk (count as 1 milk and 1 fat exchange)
1 c	Yogurt made from 2% fortified milk (plain, unflavored) (count as 1 milk and 1 fat exchange)

[a]A milk exchange is a serving of food equivalent to 1 c of skim milk in its energy nutrient content. One milk exchange contains substantial amounts of carbohydrate and protein and about 80 cal.

Table 9.1a   (continued)

Amount	Food
Whole milk (count as 1 milk and 2 fat exchanges)	
1 c	Whole milk
1 c	Buttermilk made from whole milk
1 c	Yogurt made from whole milk (plain, unflavored)
½ c	Canned evaporated whole milk, before adding liquid

Table 9.1b   Vegetable List (5 g carbohydrate, 2 g protein, 25 cal)[a]

Amount	Food
½ c	Asparagus
1 c	Bean sprouts (alfalfa, mung or soy)
½ c	Beets
½ c	Brussels sprouts
½ c	Cabbage
½ c	Carrots
	Carrot juice: See Fruit List
½ c	Cauliflower
½ c	Celery
½ c	Cucumbers
½ c	Dark green vegetables
½ c	Beet greens
½ c	Broccoli
½ c	Chards
½ c	Collard greens
½ c	Dandelion greens
½ c	Kale

[a]A vegetable exchange is a serving of any vegetable that contains a moderate amount of carbohydrate, a small but significant amount of protein, and about 25 cal.

Table 9.1b *(continued)*

Amount	Food
½ c	Mustard greens
½ c	Spinach
½ c	Swiss chard
½ c	Turnip greens
½ c	Eggplant
½ c	Green pepper
½ c	Mushrooms
½ c	Okra
½ c	Onions
½ c	Rhubarb
½ c	Rutabaga
½ c	Sauerkraut
½ c	String beans, green or yellow
½ c	Summer squash
½ c	Tomatoes
½ c	Tomato juice
½ c	Turnips
½ c	Vegetable juice cocktail
½ c	Zucchini

Table 9.1c Fruit list (10 g carbohydrate, 40 cal)[a]

Amount	Food
1 small	Apple
⅓ c	Apple juice
½ c	Applesauce (unsweetened)
2 medium	Apricots, fresh
4 halves	Apricots, dried
½ small	Banana

[a]A fruit exchange is a serving of fruit that contains about 10 g of carbohydrate and 40 cal. The protein and fat content of fruit is negligible.

Table 9.1c *(continued)*

Amount	Food
½ c	Blackberries
½ c	Blueberries
¼ small	Cantaloupe melon
½ c	Carrot juice
10 large	Cherries
⅓ c	Cider
2	Dates
1	Fig, fresh
1	Fig, dried
1 half	Grapefruit
½ c	Grapefruit juice
12	Grapes
¼ c	Grape juice
⅛ medium	Honeydew melon
½ small	Mango
1 small	Nectarine
1 small	Orange
½ c	Orange juice
¾ c	Papaya
1 medium	Peach
1 small	Pear
1 medium	Persimmon (native)
½ c	Pineapple
⅓ c	Pineapple juice
2 medium	Plums
2 medium	Prunes
¼ c	Prune juice
½ c	Raspberries
2 tbsp	Raisins
¾ c	Strawberries
1 medium	Tangerine
1 c	Watermelon

Table 9.1d   Bread-starchy vegetable list (15 g carbohydrate, 2 g protein, 70 cal)[a]

Amount	Food
Bread	
1 slice	White (including French and Italian)
1 slice	Whole-wheat
1 slice	Rye or pumpernickel
1 slice	Raisin
1 half	Small bagel
1 half	Small English muffin
1	Plain roll, bread
1 half	Frankfurter roll
1 half	Hamburger bun
3 tbsp	Dried bread crumbs
1 6-in.	Tortilla
1¼ oz loaf	Pita (Syrian) bread
Cereal	
½ c	Bran flakes
¾ c	Other ready-to-eat cereal, unsweetened
1 c	Puffed cereal, unfrosted
½ c	Cereal, cooked
½ c	Grits, cooked
½ c	White rice, millet, wild rice, or barley, cooked
⅓ c	Brown rice, cooked
½ c	Pasta, cooked (spaghetti, noodles, or macaroni)
3 c	Popcorn, popped, no fat added
2 tbsp	Cornmeal, dry
2½ tbsp	Wheat flour
3 tbsp	Buckwheat flour, dark or rye flour
2 tbsp	Cornmeal, dry
3 tbsp	Miso

Table 9.1d   *(continued)*

Amount	Food
¼ c	Wheat germ
¼ c	Oats, dry
⅓ c	Wheat berries, cooked
Crackers	
3	Arrowroot
2	Graham, 2½-in square
1 half	Matzoth, 4 x 6 in
20	Oyster
25	Pretzels, 3⅛ in long x ⅛ in diameter
3	Rye wafers, 2 x 3½ in
6	Saltines
4	Soda, 2½-in sq
Dried beans, peas, and lentils	
½ c	Beans, peas, lentils, dried and cooked
¼ c	Baked beans, no pork, canned
Starchy vegetables	
⅓ c	Corn
1 small	Corn on cob
½ c	Lima beans
⅔ c	Parsnips
½ c	Peas, green, canned, or frozen
1 small	Potato, white
½ c	Potato, mashed
¾ c	Pumpkin
½ c	Squash (winter, acorn, or butternut)
¼ c	Yam or sweet potato
Prepared foods	
1	Biscuit, 2-in. diameter (count as 1 bread and 1 fat exchange)
1	Corn bread, 2 x 2 x 1 in (count as 1 bread and 1 fat exchange)

Table 9.1d   *(continued)*

Amount	Food
1	Corn muffin, 2-in diameter (count as 1 bread and 1 fat exchange)
5	Crackers, round butter type (count as 1 bread and 1 fat exchange)
1	Muffin, plain (count as 1 bread and 1 fat exchange)
8	Potatoes, french fried, 2 to 3½ in long (count as 1 bread and 1 fat exchange)
15	Potato chips or corn chips (count as 1 bread and 2 fat exchanges)
1	Pancake, 5 x ½ in (count as 1 bread and 1 fat exchange)
1	Waffle, 5 x ½ in (count as 1 bread and 1 fat exchange)

Table 9.1e   Meat and meat-alternate list (7 g protein, 3 g fat + variable added fat; 55 cal + calories for added fat)[a]

Amount	Food
Lean meat	
1 oz.	Beef—baby beef (very lean), chipped beef, chuck, flank steak, tenderloin, plate ribs, plate skirt steak, round (bottom, top), all cuts rump spareribs, tripe

[a]A meat exchange is a serving of protein-rich food that contains negligible carbohydrate but a significant amount of protein (7 g) and fat (3 g), roughly equivalent to the amounts in 1 oz. of lean meat; contains about 55 cal.
[b]Blue, brick, camembert, cheddar, edam, farmer's, gorgonzola, gouda, gruyere, liederkranz, limburger, mozzarella, muenster, neufchatel, parmesan (3 tbsp), ricotta, swiss.

Table 9.1e   *(continued)*

Amount	Food
1 oz	Lamb—leg, rib, sirloin, loin (roast and chops) shank, shoulder
1 oz	Pork—leg (whole rump, center shank), ham, smoked (center slices)
1 oz	Veal—leg, loin, rib, shank, shoulder, cutlets
1 oz	Poultry—meat-without-skin of chicken, turkey, cornish hen, guinea hen, pheasant
1 oz	Fish—any fresh or frozen
¼ c	Canned salmon, tuna, mackerel, crab, lobster
5 (or 1 oz)	Clams, oysters, scallops, shrimp
3	Sardines, drained
1 oz	Cheese, containing less than 5% butterfat; all varieties made from skim milk
¼ c	Cottage cheese, dry and 2% butterfat
½ c	Dried beans and peas, cooked (count as 1 lean meat and 1 bread exchange)
¼ c	Baked beans, canned
¼ c	Soy flour (count as 1 lean meat and ½ bread exchange)
2 tbsp	Brewer's yeast, powder (count as 1 lean meat and ½ bread exchange)
Medium-fat meat (count as 1 lean meat and ½ fat exchange)	
1 oz	Beef—ground (15% fat), corned beef (canned), rib eye, round (ground commercial)
1 oz	Pork—loin (all cuts tenderloin), shoulder arm (picnic), shoulder blade, Boston butt, Canadian bacon, boiled ham
1 oz	Liver, heart, kidney, sweetbreads (high in cholesterol)

Table 9.1e   *(continued)*

Amount	Food
¼ c	Cottage cheese, creamed
1 oz	Cheese—mozzarella, ricotta, farmer's cheese, Neufchatel
3 tbsp	Parmesan cheese
1	Egg (high in cholesterol)
⅓ c	Soybeans, cooked
4 oz	Soybean curd (tofu), 2½ x 2¾ x 1 in

High-fat meat (count as 1 lean meat and 1 fat exchange)

1 oz	Beef—brisket, corned beef (brisket), ground beef (more than 20% fat), hamburger (commercial), chuck (ground commercial), roasts (rib), steaks (club and rib)
1 oz	Lamb—breast
1 oz	Pork—spare ribs, loin (back ribs), pork (ground), country-style ham, deviled ham
1 oz	Veal—breast
1 oz	Poultry—capon, duck (domestic), goose
1 oz	Cheddar-type cheeses[b]
1 slice	Cold cuts, 4½ x ⅛ in
1 small	Frankfurter

Meat alternates

2 tbsp	Peanut butter (count as 1 lean meat and 2½ fat exchanges)
4 tbsp	Peanuts (count as 1 lean meat, ½ bread, and 2 fat exchanges)
4 tbsp	Pumpkin or squash seeds (count as 1½ lean meat and 2 fat exchanges)
4 tbsp	Sesame or sunflower seeds (count as 1 lean meat and 2½ fat exchanges)

Table 9.1f   Fat list (5 g fat, 45 cal)[a]

Amount	Food
Polyunsaturated fat	
1 tsp	Margarine (soft, tub, or stick)[b]
⅛	Avocado (4-in diameter)[c]
1 tsp	Oil—corn, cottonseed, safflower, soy, sunflower
1 tsp	Oil, olive[c]
1 tsp	Oil, peanut[c]
5 small	Olives[c]
10 whole	Almonds[c]
2 large whole	Pecans[c]
20 whole	Peanuts, Spanish[c]
10 whole	Peanuts, Virginia[c]
6 small	Walnuts
6 small	Nuts, other[c]
1 tsp	Tahini
1 tbsp	Hommous
1 tbsp	Pignolia nuts
Saturated fat	
1 tsp	Margarine, regular stick
1 tsp	Butter
1 tsp	Bacon fat
1 strip	Bacon, crisp
2 tbsp	Cream, light
2 tbsp	Cream, sour

[a]A fat exchange is a serving of any food that contains negligible carbohydrate and protein but appreciable fat (5 g), totaling about 45 cal.
[b]Made with corn, cottonseed, safflower, soy, or sunflower oil only.
[c]Fat content is primarily monounsaturated.
[d]If made with corn, cottonseed, safflower, soy, or sunflower oil, can be assumed to contain polyunsaturated fat.

Table 9.1f *(continued)*

Amount	Food
1 tbsp	Cream, heavy
1 tbsp	Cream cheese
1 tbsp	French dressing[d]
1 tbsp	Italian dressing[d]
1 tsp	Lard
1 tsp	Mayonnaise[d]
2 tsp	Salad dressing, mayonnaise type[d]
¾-in cube	Salt pork

Table 9.1g   Unlimited foods (negligible cal)[a]

Amount	Food
	Diet calorie-free beverage
	Coffee
	Tea
	Bouillon without fat

[a]These are "free foods" that contain negligible carbohydrate, protein, and fat and therefore negligible calories.

Table 9.1g *(continued)*

Amount	Food
	Unsweetened gelatin
	Unsweetened pickles
	Salt and pepper
	Red pepper
	Paprika
	Garlic
	Celery salt
	Parsley
	Nutmeg
	Lemon
	Mustard
	Chili powder
	Onion salt or powder
	Horseradish
	Vinegar
	Mint
	Cinnamon
	Lime
	Raw vegetables—chicory, Chinese cabbage, endive, escarole, lettuce, parsley, radishes, watercress

utensils (measuring cups, spoons, scales) required to measure the portions accurately, creating another barrier to compliance with the system.

Unfortunately, these problems with the food exchange system usually result in an inability or unwillingness to meet the dietary requirements of the diabetic diet. In some cases, the person attempts to follow the plan but because of misunderstandings surrounding the exchange system he consumes an unbalanced diet. The patient also may abandon the plan and turn to friends, the media, or food faddists for advice that is easier to comprehend and thus adopt. Some people give up entirely.

Many dietitians help the patient overcome these barriers by making diet instructions less complex and easier to understand. Non-insulin-dependent diabetics, for example, are given a list of simple instructions in place of the food exchange. They are advised to decrease simple carbohydrates (e.g., sugar, honey, candy, syrups), decrease saturated fats and cholesterol (e.g., animal fat, lard, hydrogenated vegetable oils, eggs), increase complex carbohydrates (e.g., potatoes, rice, whole grain breads and cereals), and use polyunsaturated fats (e.g., vegetable oils).

Not all diabetics respond well to a simplified, relatively unstructured plan. Some people want a very detailed plan in which menus for each meal are specified and nutrients or exchanges can be counted. Also, some diabetics and most renal patients cannot afford as much flexibility in daily intake as others and still meet the nutritional requirements for their particular health needs. The physician and patient provide the information needed to decide which type of plan will be most effective.

Another means employed for making therapeutic diets easier to adopt is giving detailed instructions and demonstrations of cooking methods that patients are not accustomed to using. Under ideal circumstances, this is done in the patient's home or a demonstration kitchen at the counseling site so that the dietitian or nutrition aide can work with the patient until the new techniques are mastered. When kitchen facilities are not available, measuring utensils, photographs, and other props are used to demonstrate preparation methods. This type of education is most effective when it occurs in a familiar setting, using real foods and utensils, and giving the person time to learn and practice new skills.

Compatibility with current beliefs

Compatibility is the "degree to which an innovation is perceived as consistent with the existing norms, beliefs, and practices of the receivers" (Rogers and Shoemaker 1971:145). In general, innovations that do not conflict with existing traits are more readily accepted than those that do. Therapeutic diets, for instance, may be incompatible with some societies' schemes of classifying food. As discussed in Chapter 6, many societies in India, Latin America, the near East, and elsewhere classify foods, illness, and medicines as hot or cold. The exchange list diet would not be compatible with this belief system, but modification might be possible.

Many Americans believe that potatoes, bread, and other complex carbohydrates are fattening. When attempting to lose weight, dieters often avoid these foods. Nutritionists' advice to include these carbohydrates instead of more calorically dense fats may be rejected as incompatible with these beliefs.

Dietary innovations also may be incompatible with existing norms such as those pertaining to the proper preparation, storage, or appearance of foodstuffs. A classic case of incompatibility between norms and nutritional intervention is reported by Apodaca (1952:35–9). In the Mexican-American community that he studied, a county extension agent introduced hybrid seed corn to local farmers. One half of the farmers planted the seed and doubled their yield over the traditional seed. But soon the farmers abandoned the use of the new superior-yielding seed. The seed was discontinued because the farmers' wives complained that the hybrid corn made meal that did not have the proper texture, color, or taste for making tortillas. In this way the new corn violated local norms for acceptable tortillas.

Although the incompatibility of novelties with existing traits may present barriers to acceptance, it does not automatically preclude acceptance. Traditional beliefs, values, and practices are not unchangeable. Beliefs can be changed in some instances to fit new customs that are highly valued, and even when they cannot there often is a way around them. Health care professionals encounter this situation frequently in patients who believe that grapefruit burns fat. If the patients do not change their belief, the health professional may include grapefruit into a diet plan along with other foods in such a way that the diet's nutrient composition is not altered.

Relative advantage of change

Rogers and Shoemaker (1971:138) define relative advantage as "the degree to which an innovation is perceived as being better than the idea it supersedes." A new belief, product, or practice is judged with reference to something that is believed, done, or known by the potential acceptor. There is always some basis for comparison; some existing trait (material or nonmaterial) is associated with the novelty. An innovation, then, is perceived as more or less beneficial than previous forms in terms of its efficiency, health benefits, pleasure, financial gains or losses, and the prestige that it bestows on its adopter.

Let's see how relative advantages work by examining how they influence our receptivity to a new automobile. As we shop, salespeople tell us about each model's many advantages. We learn of the car's efficiency (engine size, performance records, EPA mileage rating), cost, certain pleasure features (color, reclining seats), and the prestige it bestows on its owner. Although people may consider all these advantages, the relative weight assigned to any one varies considerably from person to person. Some buyers are concerned primarily with efficiency, while others select automobiles primarily for their prestige. Because of this, the salesperson is careful not to emphasize one advantage when the customer is more interested in another. This is true with dietary innovations as well. The nutrition interventionist may stress a diet's efficiency in promoting health, while the client is more concerned with taste. In the pages ahead, we shall explore how each of these advantages can influence a person's receptivity to dietary change, and how an understanding of their impact can be used by nutrition educators to enhance the directed change process.

Efficiency of the change

Efficiency refers to the effectiveness of a new idea, item, or practice: its ability to function well. Efficiency encompasses the speed and ease with which the task is accomplished as well as the degree to which it functions. To assess an innovation's efficiency, first, we must know its function(s). Food, as we have seen, has many: It alleviates hunger, promotes health and well-being, relieves boredom, and contributes to a host of social and religious activities. Although a single food may contribute to all of these ends, a product typically is selected on the basis of just one or two of its functions. The large number of Americans selecting processed foods because of their convenience rather than their nutritional value, economy, or taste is an obvious example.

Because some consumers are primarily interested in food to meet one function while others are motivated by different concerns, advertisers may promote a product in several ways to appeal to the needs of different audiences. This is illustrated in a Canadian study that showed that marketing style and communications have the ability to cause substantial differences in how a single commodity is perceived. In this instance, advertisements for a new convenience food called "Complete-With-Meat-Meals" were designed to reach three unique marketing groups. The groups, labeled Speciality, Simplicity, and Basic, were comprised of subjects who had in common the following factors identified through a 67-item lifestyle questionnaire.

1.   Specialty: enjoyment of outside activities,
         enjoyment of cooking and entertaining,
         enjoyment of dining

2.   Simplicity: making cooking easier,
         liking prepared foods,
         lacking in organization

3.   Basic: economy consciousness,
         enjoyment of family life,
         enjoyment of traditional meals

Three advertisements were created to feature the same product, each using distinctive styles. The first advertisement appealed to the "specialty" group by capitalizing on the consumer's image of herself as an active, sophisticated individual. A second ad emphasized the ease of preparation in order to attract consumers in the "simplicity" group. And a third ad included details of particular interest to consumers in the "basic" group: price per serving, assurance that the product was a "real meal," and a picture of the smiling family anticipating the meal.

For a wide variety of dietary innovations, ranging from high-yield hybrid seeds to improved cooking appliances, efficiency weighs heavily in people's decisions to accept or reject them. But how is efficiency evaluated, and how easily is the efficiency of old and new traits compared? If a therapeutic diet makes the patient look or feel better, the results are readily observable; the old and new diets can be compared easily. But if the diet does not have an immediately observable impact, its efficiency is not easily assessed. For this reason, an innovation is more readily accepted when its efficiency is highly visible than when it is not. The recent popularity of the protein-sparing diet, for instance, is in part because of the very rapid weight loss (due predominantly to water, not fat loss) experienced on this regimen. Reduction in body size is easily noticed. Food allergies are another example of diet restrictions that sometimes bring about a rapid relief of symptoms, and therefore are more easily accepted as effective. These innovations demonstrate three important components of the visibility which enhance acceptance of an innovation: The changes are measurable, relatively rapid, and perceived as positive.

For those diets that do not have an immediate observable impact, there are several methods of demonstrating the diet's efficiency. Perhaps the most common and most effective method is to use the patient's weight, hematocrit, serum cholesterol, or other biochemical and physiological indicators as a way of measuring the diet's impact on health. By watching serum cholesterol levels decrease, hematocrit rise, or blood glucose normalize, the patient becomes aware of the diet's efficiency. These laboratory tests, if incorporated into the ongoing treatment plan, provide systematic feedback of the diet's success or failure.

The efficiency of other dietary novelties such as food products and cooking appliances is made visible through home demonstrations, free trial periods, and samplers. Coupons and sales that offer an introductory discount tempt the consumer to adopt the product on a trial basis, thus enabling a comparison to be made between the old and new. Superior attributes of the new product, it is hoped, will be sufficient to ensure continued acceptance even at its regular price.

protein-sparing diet
A diet that involves a caloric intake of 200 to 700 calories in the form of a liquid protein preparation; the diet results in quick but potentially dangerous weight loss

A common problem associated with efforts to make visible the efficiency of a new item should be noted. Unreal promises, overstatements, and unrealistic expectations may gain initial adoption of an innovation, but when the benefits fail to materialize disappointment and rejection result. In diet counseling, patients that expect to lose five to ten pounds a week quickly abandon a diet plan that yields a modest two-pound loss per week. Unfortunately, many patients have obtained unrealistic expectations and misinformation about a given diet's efficiency and the amount of time required for results to be achieved. Misinformation about an innovation's efficiency can be as damaging to adoption and continued compliance as no information at all.

How the change will affect health

Concerns about the relationship between diet and health are increasing throughout many western nations and play a major role in selection of food for many people. In fact, the 20 percent decrease in red meat consumption per person noted in the 1970s largely reflects North Americans' concern about the relation of saturated fat and cholesterol to heart disease (*Nutrition Week*, 1983).

The extent to which people are willing to alter their diet for health reasons varies. While some people may be willing to forego dessert two meals per week, others may make great efforts to avoid even a single grain of sugar in their food.

In some individuals, certain foods cause gastrointestinal distress, allergic reactions, or acute physical responses that limit the range of foods eaten. The rapid onset of illness after trying a new dish can be a dramatically convincing reason to avoid it in the future. Feeling poorly when blood glucose levels rise after eating sugar serves as a strong incentive for some people with diabetes to avoid sweets.

The *fear* of becoming sick, weak, or debilitated from eating something new is an equally powerful deterrent to dietary innovation. In Yugoslavia, North Brazil, and Mexico, attempts to introduce enriched corn and manioc meal were resisted because people feared it would make men impotent (Read 1966:59). And in parts of Europe, the belief that potatoes caused leprosy delayed this vegetable's adoption for nearly two centuries (Young 1970:14). There are ways to overcome these kind of fears (assuming, of course, they are unfounded) when introducing dietary change. For example, educational materials concerned with enriched corn or manioc meal could depict a well-respected male from the local community endorsing the product. Or members of a prestigious group (such as well-known athletes) could be shown using the dietary innovation.

How enjoyable is the change?

Pleasure derived from acquiring and using innovations is another important consideration in people's receptivity to something new. If a person enjoys cooking with a new utensil, he is more likely to buy it and use it regularly. The taste and appearance of food produced by a new hybrid crop is often the deciding factor in whether or not farmers grow it. The lack of satisfaction arising from a diet such as the Rice Weight Loss Diet makes it difficult for people to follow the regime for any appreciable length of time. In this way, pleasure or absence of it affects the rate of acceptance of a new object or practice. Conceptions of pleasure, of course, vary greatly among individuals and ethnic groups so that what is satisfying to one may be displeasing to another. Taste is a good example of this. The taste of mangoes is so pleasurable to some people that they are willing to pay three or four times more for them than other types of fruits, and yet others refuse to eat them no matter how little they cost. Likewise, people's perceptions of texture and color of food differ significantly.

The technological change literature abounds with examples of people rejecting agricultural or dietary innovations because of dissatisfaction with the taste, texture, or other pleasure-giving qualities of the new product. New hybrid strains of corn in Mexico, wheat in India, and potatoes in Peru have been rejected despite superior yields, resistance to pests, and superior nutritional qualities because they weren't as pleasing to eat as the traditional strains.

Today the use of careful planning and implementation can make use of people's beliefs, values, tastes, and dislikes. For instance, ethnographic interviews with female household heads can be used to provide data about preferred tastes and textures of commonly eaten grains. Such information can help agronomists develop more acceptable hybrid strains. Also, when distributing or promoting the seeds, extension agencies can provide culturally-appropriate food preparation ideas and recipes along with the seeds. Or demonstrations can be conducted, describing the productive advantages of the seeds and encouraging people to taste the products. Women's organizations in many rural areas provide an ideal setting for communicating with women about dietary innovations.

While pleasure is a powerful motive to acceptance of a new food or diet pattern, the long-term consequences of the novelty may offset the immediate satisfaction. For example, many avoid foods they like but suspect of containing carcinogens. Although a delicious meal is preferred over a poor-tasting one, many people restrict some of their favorite foods in order to protect their health.

Cost of the change

Financial considerations loom large in many decisions to accept or reject an innovation. The cost of something new may make it unobtainable no matter how desirable the novelty is in other regards. Let's look first at how this affects diet counseling. As the price of food rises, the cost of the therapeutic diet becomes an increasingly important determinant of acceptance or rejection. If expensive food and food supplements are part of a diet plan, adoption may be limited to those people who can or will spend extra money for nutritional purposes.

Often it is possible to replace expensive foodstuffs such as meat with less expensive items like beans and rice, eggs, or peanut butter. This becomes difficult, however, if several types of food are restricted. One client seen at a large urban medical center was placed on a low salt diet to treat toxemia of pregnancy (a practice no longer recommended because a low-sodium diet actually may aggravate toxemia). Later a public health nurse making a routine maternity visit took the client's diet history and discovered that she had an extremely low protein intake. Further discussion showed that the woman was adhering religiously to the low-salt diet sheet she had been given at the medical center. The sheet advised her to avoid peanut butter, tuna fish, canned beans and cheese—her usual inexpensive protein sources. This was particularly unfortunate because a low protein intake is now thought to contribute to toxemia. A call to the physician changed the diet order, counseling convinced the patient to try these foods again, and enrollment in the Women, Infants, and Children Program (WIC) provided food supplements to ensure adequate protein intake.

Because cost is the major constraint for many patients, it is important that each dietary restriction recommended is truly necessary. Frequently allowances are made in standard diet plans to enable a patient to purchase a balanced diet without undue economic strain. By helping a patient plan a week's menu and marketing list, the dietitian determines if a diet plan is economically feasible. When costs are not considered in formulating diet recommendations, adherence often declines.

Cost also influences farmers' receptivity to many agricultural improvements. The Green Revolution in Mexico provides an example. The adoption of the agricultural innovations needed to obtain increased yields—hybrid seeds, fertilizers, and pesticides—benefit Mexico's large farmers who can afford to purchase the fertilizer and other inputs. These farmers have experienced higher yields and greater profits. Similar benefits have not been shared by smaller farmers because they do not have the funds to purchase fertilizer,

toxemia of pregnancy
A cluster of symptoms seen in pregnancy, including edema (swelling) and often hypertension and kidney complications

pesticides, and other items needed for this type of agriculture (Wellhausen 1976:134). In this case, as in many others, the innovation's cost deters adoption by those who need it the most. Because cost is an overriding concern for so many, promoters often use incentives to make an innovation more attractive. Discounts in the form of introductory offers are a typical example. In the WIC program, part of the rationale behind giving out nutritious supplemental foods is the hope that mothers will continue to purchase those foods even after they have left the program. While this strategy has proven successful in some cases, people often abandon the item once the incentive is removed so that change is short-lived and neither beliefs or values are modified.

The other side of the economic coin is profit. Desire for increased economic gains from agricultural endeavors is a strong factor in the farmer's receptivity to many innovations. We have just seen several instances in which the taste or texture of produce overrides economic considerations derived from a crop's yield or pest resistance, but in all of these cases, the crop is used primarily for home consumption. The reaction is quite different when a crop is grown primarily for cash purposes. In India, this difference was illustrated in one community's reaction to two new hybrid seeds. The first, a new wheat strain, promised greater yields and improved resistance to drought. Wheat was a staple in the local diet and when the new seed produced flour with a different taste, it was rejected. Sugar cane, on the other hand, was a cash crop. The new sugar cane seeds brought higher profits and were more acceptable to the local farmers. Even though it was considered inferior in taste and food value, it was adopted (Dube 1958:63–4).

As with other advantages, both economic gain and cost are relative. A man will pay more dearly for water in a desert environment than when he is near freshwater springs. One person may think a microwave oven is overpriced; yet the blind man may consider the price worth the relief from fear of being burned by a conventional oven. In sum, financial considerations play an important but complex role in the selection of innovations.

Social advantages of the change

Often the prestige associated with an innovation gives the acceptor a social advantage. A twenty-room mansion or Rolls-Royce is coveted as much or more for the prestige it bestows upon its owner as for its efficiency or pleasure-giving attributes. Prestige is a major social attraction of many new practices and goods for some people. Industrial firms capitalize on the desire for prestige in many of their promotional campaigns.

Even without the aid of Madison Avenue or multinational corporations, prestige attracts people to many commodities and practices. Some are desirable in other ways; many are not:

> A problem agents may encounter is that less nutritious foods have the highest prestige as the things rich men eat. We heard a story recently about university students in an oriental country where rice formed the staple food. According to this story some of the students would have to drop out of class periodically for medical treatment against beriberi. They knew the cause of beriberi and far from considering the illness a disgrace looked upon it as something of which to boast. Only the wealthy could afford to live on polished white rice. To suffer from beriberi, like having a Cadillac in front of one's door, was valued as a form of conspicuous ostentation. Under these conditions where prestige foods are less nutritious, a rise in the affluence of the community can lead to a reduction in the standard of health.

> *(Goodenough 1966:465–6)*

Another common occurrence is the relatively high prestige associated with foods purchased in stores as opposed to that prepared at home. In many peasant communities, canned meat, white bread, and soft drinks are served to honored guests and used at special occasions because they function as symbols of affluence and modernity. Unfortunately, these high-prestige foods usually are less nutritious than the traditional, wholesome, home-prepared items that they replace. It is not uncommon to see nutritional status decline in populations that adopt more processed food products on a wide scale. In the early eighteenth century, for example, tea and white rice were regarded an an occasional luxury and used primarily by urban, affluent families. Some of the less affluent desired what the more wealthy consumed, and by 1850, tea and white bread had entered the diets of the entire nation. Fortunately, in some places, North America for example, homemade foods are regaining prestige and highly processed less nutritious foods are losing status.

Like other advantages of an innovation, prestige can frustrate or enhance the interventionists' efforts to direct change. An understanding of the potential adopter's perceptions of advantages enables the change agent to utilize, perhaps even manipulate, an innovation's perceived benefits in order to improve the nutritional status of the recipients.

Disadvantages of the change

Just as an innovation gives its adopters many advantages, certain disadvantages may result from its acceptance. Penalties commonly associated with dietary innovations include legal sanctions, public ridicule, and religious concerns. The fear of being penalized in these ways greatly detracts from an innovation that otherwise may be appealing.

Do laws impede the adoption of the change?

Legal sanctions also deter the acceptance of some innovations. Actually many laws are designed purposefully to prohibit the adoption of new ideas and practices believed to be dangerous or fraudulent (Barnett 1953:371). Authoritan leaders and regimes often prohibit or tightly regulate the introduction of foreign ideas. For instance, in the Soviet Union it is illegal to import magazines and newspapers from other countries. With respect to dietary innovations, many nations have established food laws to protect consumers against adulterated foods and fraudulent promotional claims. The establishment and enforcement of these laws is carried out by governmental agencies such as the Food and Drug Administration (FDA) in the United States and the Institute of Nutrition in the USSR.

Many products never reach the consumer because they fail to meet government requirements or standards. Some products are marketed with warnings designed to deter acceptance.

And other products are prohibited from using questionable claims in advertising or packaging. One humorous example comes from the beginning of this century: "Soon after the first Federal Pure Food and Drugs Act was enacted in the United States in 1906, the father of that law, Harvey Washington Wiley, then charged with its enforcement, confronted a phrase on the label for processed food called Theobroma. "I do not think," Dr. Wiley wrote (1910) for his fellow enforcers, "that we should officially validate such a phrase as 'A food fit for the Gods.' We presumably are not acquainted with the character of nourishment used by the immortals" (Young 1970:10).

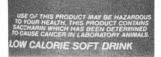

Figure 9.4
Legal sanctions and dietary innovations. As this diet soft drink label illustrates, some products are marketed with warnings to deter acceptance.
(Lindenberger)

For more on Dr. Wiley, see Chapter 2.

Reaction to the change

Adverse public opinion is still another type of penalty which can impede dietary change; this may take the form of censure or ridicule. For example, a school survey conducted in a midwestern town revealed that some children who are diabetic do not notify the teacher or cafeteria manager of their special dietary needs. Moreover they frequently fail to comply with their dietary guidelines. Why? Because they fear public ridicule and stigmatization for being different than their classmates.

Religious concerns

Finally, fear of supernatural punishment prevents some people from accepting new foods and practices. On Manam Island, off the North Coast of New Guinea, the natives traditionally believed that a person who ate the food that he himself had helped to grow was liable to supernatural punishment. They believed that he would become seriously ill and might die. Therefore, housewives after cooking the evening meal, make exchanges with one another before serving their families (Hogbin 1958:70).

As noted in the beginning of this section, each attribute's overall influence on receptivity to adaption is relative. Cost may play a major role in some decisions, efficiency in others, and penalties in still others. The relative weight of any one attribute depends upon the type of innovation being assessed as well as the needs and interests of the potential adopter. Some people value efficiency over prestige in selecting appliances, but choose clothing on an entirely different basis. For this reason, it is common to find an innovation accepted for completely different reasons than those intended by its promoter. The nutritionist who encourages a woman to lose weight for health reasons may not realize that her patient's losses result more from a desire to be thin than her fear of developing diabetes. Similarly, groups of people within a population may adopt a novelty for very different reasons. For example, sanitary wells in India, proposed as a source of clean, hygienic water, were widely accepted.

> In accepting this programme the motives of the people were different. The well-to-do people contributed towards it because they wanted to oblige the village level worker and other project officials by cooperating in a project which could be shown to visiting outsiders to impress them. (Others) were enthusiastic about it because they wanted to enhance the prestige of their group by having something bright, new and impressive.

> *(Dube 1958:129–30)*

But none of the adopters, it should be noted, said they built the wells for health reasons.

Summary

- Directed change is "that situation in which someone, or some group, interferes actively and purposefully in the social behavior of others" (Gallaher 1973:476).

- Peoples' willingness to accept new dietary ideas or practices is influenced by certain characteristics of the innovation, the person advocating change, and the potential adopter or consumer.

- Attributes of the adopter or consumer that are most influential in the directed change process are dependence on authority, the expectation of change, and conceptions of pride and dignity.

- A critical element in nutrition intervention, like many situations involving persuasion, is the advocate. Successful nutritional intervention may depend to a great extent on personality, prestige, personal relations with potential acceptors, degree of similarity with potential acceptors, and credibility.

- Certain innovation characteristics shown to have especially powerful influences on peoples' receptivity to change are complexity, compatibility with existing beliefs and values, relative advantages (efficiency, health, pleasure, economics, prestige) and penalties (illness, legal sanctions, public ridicule and religious concerns).

- By understanding these characteristics, nutrition interventionists are better able to predict an innovation's chances of being accepted. They also can modify the change, making it less complicated or more pleasurable, for example, thereby enhancing its attractiveness to the potential adopter.

Highlight 9–1 Diet counseling: Helping people stick with it

Peoples' inability to follow therapeutic health care practices is recognized as one of the most serious problems facing the health care field today. Failure to follow recommendations leads to unnecessary illness, hospitalizations, and repeat outpatient visits, all of which undermine preventative and curative efforts and increase health care costs.

Adherence rates to diet therapy are particularly discouraging. On average, only about 50 percent of patients on long-term diets will follow them with any regularity, and rates as low as 20 percent have been reported for weight loss (Stunkard 1981).

In a recent survey of elderly residents in a rural Kentucky community, for example, only 42 percent of those given therapeutic diet instructions by a nutritionist, nurse, or physician said that they try to follow the diet, and diet histories reveal that even these people often have difficulty carrying out therapeutic diet recommendations correctly (Bryant, Johnson and VanWilligen 1982). Even when special diets are a central part of treatment for life-threatening diseases such as diabetes and hypertension, adherence rates are disturbingly low. For example, a review of adherence studies among diabetics conducted by West (1973) cited failure rates of 22 percent to 89 percent for children and 45 percent to 66 percent for adults.

Because no diet or other treatment plan is effective unless it is applied, patient adherence has become the subject of much research. This highlight reviews some of the strategies that appear promising for helping people to "stick with it."

In addition to findings of other researchers, we draw upon our own experience at the Lexington-Fayette County Health Department where nutritionists prescribe therapeutic diets to over 700 clients a year.

Before we begin our review, let's take a more personalized look at factors that influence dietary change. For this exercise you will need two sheets of paper, each divided into three columns. On the first sheet of paper, write "Successful Dietary Changes" over the left hand column and then list the diet changes you have made to improve your health. Leave several lines between each item. Next, in the middle column, note all the obstacles or barriers you encountered that made it difficult to change. Then, in the right hand column write down all the things that helped you achieve your goal. Include knowledge (e.g., research shows high-fat diets are linked to breast cancer) and feelings (fear of cancer, determination to change) as well as behaviors (reminder on refrigerator, switch from steak houses to Chinese restaurants). Now consider how relatives, friends, or health care providers helped you achieve your dietary goals. What did they say or do that was particularly helpful? Once you have finished this analysis of the obstacles and factors motivating your successful changes, repeat the exercise on the next page for your future dietary goals—changes that you would like to make but thus far have not carried out satisfactorily. List each change you have tried to make, the obstacles in your way, and the factors that have helped so far.

Keep these lists available as you read this highlight so you can add to your analysis when you recognize other factors that might help or hinder adherence to your dietary goals.

Patient education

Education is an important component in diet counseling. Obviously adherence is not logically possible unless the client first understands and remembers the diet instructions. Therefore, many educational techniques have been developed for improving clients' comprehension and recall. These are described below.

1. *Limit the number of messages and amount of information conveyed in a single session.* Large numbers of statements have been found to greatly reduce patient recall (Ley 1976, 1977). Our experience suggests that diet counseling is most effective when only two or three key points are covered in a single session. When prescribing therapeutic diets (e.g., for Type I diabetics) that involve numerous diet changes, we find it best to schedule a series of visits, presenting the most crucial information for the initial session, and other recommendations at later meetings. Thus, the first session with a newly diagnosed diabetic client may focus on avoidance of concentrated sweets and timing meals with insulin injections. Other topics such as the importance of fiber, decreased fat intake, and appropriate calorie level and shopping and cooking tips could be covered during follow-up visits. It also is helpful in each visit to emphasize the most

crucial information first, emphasizing its importance throughout this and other sessions.

2. *Keep diet instructions simple.* This can be accomplished by presenting recommendations in simple sentences and selecting written materials that are easy to read. When working with clients who have little formal education or who cannot read well, achieving the proper level of simplicity is especially important.

3. *Make recommendations as specific as possible.* Most clients find it helpful to be given brand names, recipes, addresses of stores that carry certain products, or even menu plans. This information allows the client to translate therapeutic diet recommendations into dietary behavior.

4. *Use repetition to enhance recall.* In addition to repeating recommendations at the end of a session, many nutritionists find it useful to summarize the major points in writing or give the client printed material to read at home. Followup visits provide another opportunity to review the major recommendations presented during previous visits.

5. *Ask the patient to review key recommendations or dietary changes covered in the session.* Being careful not to pose these questions as a test or examination, the nutritionist can ask the client to review the major points he or she remembers as well as changes she plans to make. This not only aids the clients' recall but provides a check for congruence between the counselor's and patient's understanding of diet instructions. Sometimes health care providers incorrectly assume that they have explained a treatment plan clearly and learn only after the therapy fails that the patient has misunderstood the instructions. One rather dramatic illustration comes from a university teaching hospital where newly diagnosed diabetics are trained in the proper methods to inject insulin and then practice by injecting water into an orange. When one patient returned to the

hospital several days after discharge with dangerously high ketone levels, he was asked about his diet and insulin injections. The reason for his poor metabolic control soon became apparent: the man was carefully injecting the insulin into the orange and then eating it.

Although the recommendations listed above can greatly enhance patients' understanding and recall—both of which are necessary prerequisites for adherence—information alone is not always sufficient to enable a client to change. In fact, in a review of education strategies for improving adherence to medical regimes, Haynes (1976) estimated that education alone achieved success in only half the cases.

Looking at your own list of dietary changes, consider how effective information or dietary advice has been in helping you modify food practices. Would additional knowledge be sufficient to overcome obstacles preventing you from achieving your goals? Or do you find that you already know far more about what you should eat than you can put into practice?

Because information is a necessary but often insufficient motive to dietary change, patient education is usually combined with other strategies for improving compliance. The approaches that appear most promising for diet therapy are:

1. Tailoring the diet to the client's lifestyle,
2. Eliciting the client's participation in development of the treatment plan,
3. Providing support and encouragement, and
4. Eliciting social support from friends, relatives and others.

Tailoring the diet to the client's lifestyle

When tailoring a diet, instructions are designed to fit the client's daily routine, estab- lished dietary habits (meal patterns, cooking styles), and food preferences. Efforts are made to minimize the amount of change introduced into the client's lifestyle, making the diet easier to follow (Dunbar and Stunkard 1979).

Tailoring treats patients as unique individuals. The health care provider and the client explore the client's food preferences, daily routine, social patterns, religious beliefs, and budgeting constraints that may affect diet habits in search of areas requiring special modifications in the diet plan. The businessman, for example, who eats most lunches and meals in restaurants may need instructions on how to select appropriate items from menus; the Seventh Day Adventist is given a meatless diet, and the Italian American whose family practices many traditional food customs is prescribed a diet that utilizes many traditional food items and recipes.

Eliciting client participation

This strategy attempts to heighten the patient's sense of responsibility for his own health care. The patient is encouraged to collaborate with the health care provider in monitoring and caring for his own health. This theme is a break with the traditional notion of the patient as one who is largely a passive recipient of care who follows orders from the professional. In contrast, the active patient acts in mutual participation with the counselor, selecting dietary goals and determining ways to achieve them. Nutritionists at the Lexington-Fayette County Health Department, for example, explain the importance and methods of decreasing saturated fats and cholesterol to clients with arteriosclerosis, and then ask the client to select the specific changes they would like to make to limit their intake. By encouraging a client to start with a goal that is relatively easy to achieve, they enhance the client's chances of success and likelihood of making other dietary modifications. This one-step-at-a-time approach has proven effective in working with some clients who previously were unsuccessful in following therapeutic diets. This and other ways of encouraging the client's active participation is especially important in treating chronic diseases such as diabetes or hypertension, in which long-term adherence is critical to health maintenence (Garrity 1981:218).

Although there are many ways to heighten a client's participation and sense of responsibility, the approaches that are used most commonly in diet therapy are written contracts and self-monitoring exercises.

Patient contracts In contracting, patients negotiate a written agreement with a health care provider to perform certain behaviors (e.g., count calories, avoid high-fat dairy products, exercise daily). The goals are stated as positive, specific, behavioral objectives (e.g., I will do ten minutes of aerobic exercises three times a week). In most cases, a reward is designated for successful completion of the contract. The written contract is then signed by both parties and often one or more witnesses.

Contracts have been shown to be highly successful in several studies of patient adherence to medical regimes (Garrity 1981). However, their success seems best with short-term goals (Dunbar et al. 1979).

Contracts offer several benefits. First, the process fosters a reciprocal relationship between the client and counselor that encourages the patient to actively plan her treatment and assume responsibility for its success. Second, the contract is a formal, public commitment to change. Compared to promises and plans made in private, public commitments are far more likely to be carried out (Lewin 1958). Third, the negotiating process offers patients to express their

beliefs and expectations about diet therapy and allows the counselor to clarify any misinformation and resolve differences in what is expected from therapy.

Self-monitoring Another technique commonly used to enhance adherence is self-monitoring. With self-monitoring, the client records dietary intake, a food history, weight, or some other measure of dietary progress. "Self-monitoring is an active measure for the individual, especially early in treatment, when the mere monitoring of the variables may alter food consumption" (Adams et al. 1981:1066). Research has shown that weight loss is enhanced by self-monitoring of food intake and body weight.

Self-monitoring is most effective if the recording materials are simple to use, the client is trained in the technique, recording is done immediately before or after the behavior, the client is given feedback on her progress, and the number of behaviors recorded is limited (Barlow 1976; Dunbar and Stunkard 1979).

Providing support and encouragement

Counselors also can assist their clients in learning how to adopt new dietary practices by providing encouragement and understanding. In fact, in several studies, health care professionals' support has proven effective in improving people's ability to follow a variety of health recommendations (Garrity 1981).

One of the most effective means of providing support and encouragement involves listening to clients express their emotions and concerns about their condition and the therapeutic diet plan. For instance, imagine that you've just learned that your blood pressure is high and you will have to take medication and follow a special diet to control it. Or imagine that you've had diabetes for the last ten years and have always had

3 Day Food Diary For _____

Day I

	Food	Amount	Brand	Where Eaten	Why/Time
Meal					
Snack					
Meal					
Snack					
Meal					
Snack					
Meal					
Snack					

Day II

	Food	Amount	Brand	Where Eaten	Why/Time
Meal					
Snack					
Meal					
Snack					
Meal					
Snack					
Meal					
Snack					

Day III

	Food	Amount	Brand	Where Eaten	Why/Time
Meal					
Snack					
Meal					
Snack					
Meal					
Snack					

Activity Record   Use Total Times

Day	1	2	3
Sleeping hours			
Sitting: — includes, riding in car, TV, school, eating, homework			
Walking/housework			
Active playing			
Exercising			
Any Other Name Them _____			

Figure HL9.1 *Self monitoring in dietary changes: The dietary record. Research has shown that weight loss is enhanced by self-monitoring of food intake and body weight.*

difficulty following the diet. In either case you would probably have many feelings about the disease and the diet. If the disease is newly diagnosed you may have feelings of fear and anger to deal with; if it's been uncontrolled for years you may feel frustration and hopelessness at the mere mention of the word "diet." When you talk to a nutritionist you may find yourself so preoccupied with feelings about the subject that you tell her all about them rather than discussing your diet.

In situations such as these the most helpful thing a nutritionist can do is provide support through listening. Listening effectively is an art and health care providers who do it well have been shown to be successful in helping clients make positive changes (Svarstad 1974). Effective listening is characterized by looking interested, not interrupting, and encouraging the client to tell you more by asking questions that demonstrate your interest.

While it may be difficult at first to give up valuable education time to allow the patient to talk about things not directly related to nutrition, it is usually time well spent. In fact, many people can be so distracted by their fears and other concerns that they are unable to listen and/or learn effectively. After they have had an opportunity to express their concerns, they usually are better able to concentrate on the dietary information and how to put it into practice.

Eliciting social supports   In almost all diet counseling situations, the health care professional has very limited contact with clients. Even when followup sessions are attended regularly, time spent with a client rarely exceeds an hour per week and typically occurs within a clinic setting.

It is no wonder, then, that relatives, friends, and neighbors who may see the client throughout the week and participate in food selection, preparations, and consumption often exert more influence on the client's diet habits than the counselor.

Many studies have shown that social support can enhance people's ability to follow a variety of therapeutic diets. Family cooperation, for example, has proven effective in helping people lower their cholesterol level (Witschi et al. 1978), lose weight (Stunkard 1981, Brownell et al. 1978, Rosenthal et al. 1980, Fremouw 1980) and control obesity in children (Brownwell et al. 1983) and infants (Bryant 1982). Advice or encouragement from relatives and others also has been shown to have a significant impact on mothers' willingness to follow health care professionals' advice about infant feeding and their ability to breastfeed for the length of time desired (Bryant 1978).

How can health care professionals use social supports to increase adherence to the diets they prescribe? First, family and friends can be asked to participate in counseling sessions, group classes, or other educational activities. Many clients believe it is helpful if their spouse agrees to change menus and cooking styles, or their children agree not to eat tempting foods in their presence until the client loses weight. In some instances, family members even may be willing to follow the diet plan along with the patient.

Second, the client can be asked to identify the way that friends and relatives help and hinder adherence to the diet plan. Many obese women, for instance, report that their husband's criticism of their weight or eating habits actively stimulates them to overeat. With an understanding of what clients find helpful, the counselor and client can then advise relatives and friends how to be more supportive.

Third, support networks can be established in the form of special groups and support programs. The power of social supports is perhaps best illustrated by the widespread success of Weight Watchers, TOPS (Take Off Pounds Sensibly), and Overeaters Anonymous, which use encouragement and understanding of fellow members to foster weight loss. La Leche League, a group of experienced breastfeeders, has also demonstrated the impact social support groups can have on behavior—in this case lactation (see Highlight 10-2).

To conclude this exploration of dietary adherence, let's reexamine your list of successful changes and future dietary goals. As you review these, consider these questions: Has social support, self-monitoring, other types of activity, or a sense of responsibility in health matters helped you improve your diet? In what ways has education been important in helping you meet your dietary goals? Have you found it difficult to tailor nutrition advice to your daily life and, if so, how could your goals be better adapted to your lifestyle? How can these strategies help you achieve your personal nutritional goals and more effectively counsel others?

10

Nutrition programs and strategies

Imagine that you are employed by the public health department in a major North American city. You are approached by an influential Puerto Rican leader and asked to develop a program to combat iron-deficiency anemia and obesity among children in her community.

Or suppose that you are a nutritionist working for the Ministry of Health in a Southeast Asian country. You are appointed to the National Nutrition Planning Commission responsible for developing a five-year plan for the country.

Finally, imagine that you have been asked by a corporate business to provide nutrition education with the goal of decreasing heart disease among employees. In each of these situations, how would you proceed?

Each day nutritionists search for solutions to problems much like these. The quality of their answers determines in large part the degree of success they achieve in helping others. In this chapter, we describe five major types of nutrition intervention strategies and programs: nutrition education, supplementary feeding, formulated foods, fortified foods, and consumer advocacy.

Nutrition education

> An important part of the nutrition gap is the information gap. Although lack of purchasing power is a major constraint, many nutritional deficiencies would be moderated if people knew how better to use the resources already at hand.
>
> *(Berg 1973:74)*

We have seen that beliefs in some societies restrict the use of high-protein foods like fish and eggs among pregnant and lactating women; that many traditional weaning foods are low in protein, while more nutritious foods are withheld for fear that they will cause illness; and that many dietary practices, like the withdrawal of solid foods in treating sick children, provoke rather than cure nutrition problems. Malnutrition, then, also may prevail in industrialized societies; although adequate food is available to the majority, some consume too much of the wrong kinds of foods. When this is the case, acquainting people with the value of available resources and persuading them to change traditional practices can be a successful intervention strategy (Berg 1973:75).

A variety of education methods are used to combat poor nutrition resulting from inadequate information. These are often referred to as *person-to-person, educational media,* and *combined approaches.* The person-to-person approaches are:

Lecture-Discussion, involving the presentation of information and encouragement of questions and other responses from the participants.

Panel Discussion, where a group of people (three to five) are brought together to talk about a chosen topic. Questions are then asked by the audience.

Demonstration, in which verbal information may be supplemented by a demonstration. Participation by the group members make this particularly effective. An example is a demonstration of cooking techniques with audience participation.

Problem Solving, in which the nutrition problem is presented and discussed in terms of an individual (real or fictional) situation, the underlying causes, and what can be done. What is known about the problem and the participants' values may be incorporated into the discussion. This helps develop people's ability to make informed decisions about their health.

Nutrition educators have long recognized that audience participation is a key component in the success of person-to-person methodologies. In fact, many nutrition education programs reported in the *Journal of Nutrition Education* during recent years attribute their success to the use of learner- as opposed to teacher-oriented methods. Activities involving self-discovery, learner choice, and decision making are more successful than lectures, written materials, or other methods which confine the audience to a relatively passive role.

One of the most successful applications of comprehensive nutrition education in underdeveloped countries has been through Mothercraft Centers. These rehabilitation centers teach mothers to feed and care for their malnourished children through demonstrations. Originally formulated by J. M. Bengoa in 1955, Mothercraft Centers are still in existence and are designed to meet the special constraints imposed by severe poverty, illiteracy, and maldistribution of food within the family. Bengoa's basic idea is to identify malnourished preschool children, encourage their mothers to bring them to a center, and involve mothers in the nutritional rehabilitation of their own children. A major feature of the program is the use of foods and equipment available to mothers in their own homes (King 1971:10).

Typical operation of a center includes nutritional screening of village children, selection of 30 to 35 severely malnourished preschoolers, and education of their mothers during a three- to four-month rehabilitation process. Children are brought to the center six days a week and each mother remains one day a week. During their stay, mothers learn why certain foods are good buys, how to select and prepare nutritious meals, and how to improve sanitary conditions within the limitations of local resources.

Mothercraft Centers, overall, are considered a successful method of reducing—even eliminating—malnutrition in preschoolers. In some villages, centers have been closed because malnutrition is no longer a problem.

The centers are not without problems, however. Failure to involve fathers in the educational processes and a focus on curative rather that preventative nutrition have been cited (Bengoa 1964). Also, person-to-person methods are severely limited in terms of outreach. Moreover, the small audience served often makes these methods quite costly. Cost, of course, is relative; it must be considered in light of how much it can buy, and how much is available to spend. Person-to-person methods often are an effective means of improving health status, and in that sense, they are a bargain. But for reaching a large population, the costs of person-to-person methods remain out of reach for most countries.

See Highlight 9–1 for more discussion of person-to-person approaches.

Focus 10-1

Costs involved in person-to-person outreach

To give you an idea of the costs involved in person-to-person approaches, Berg estimates several components in a comprehensive nutrition education program in rural India. To be effective, a person-to-person program would have to reach 65 million farm families in 567,000 mostly isolated villages.

- "To provide a single visit by a mobile audiovisual unit to each village would take eight years if each district had its own van (twenty times the seventeen vans the Indian government had in 1970)."

- "The education portion of the applied nutrition program carried on through the *balwadi,* the community facility for preschool children, reached a small fraction of the target group— less than 2 percent in Tamil Nadu, one of the most nutritionally conscious states. At the rate of increase planned by the government—200 new *balwadis* a year—it would take more than 150 years to cover the target population, assuming population size did not increase."

- "Based on the cost figures of the Haitian Mothercraft Center program, a nutrition education and rehabilitation program undertaken in India on a comprehensive scale would cost $1.5 billion" (Berg 1973:79–80).

Educational media

Because of the problems associated with person-to-person approaches, educational media are becoming increasingly popular as a nutrition education method in both developing and developed nations. The most common media forms are television and radio broadcasts, billboards, posters, audio cassettes, brochures, comic books, puppet shows, and folk theater. In nonindustrialized countries techniques also include messages printed on school workbook covers and slates, signs on bicycle rickshaws, calendar art, pictorals, and pictures on large boulders or village walls.

A relatively new nutritional use of media is the advertising campaign. For example, media attention given to the link between diet and heart disease in North America has raised the public's consciousness about the subject. Campaigns coordinated by health associations, newspaper columns, and magazine articles have been given significant credit for encouraging North Americans to change their dietary habits, resulting in a decreased rate of heart disease in the 1970s (Public Health Service 1982).

Advertising or mass media campaigns typically transmit messages that are short, easily understood, specific, and focused on a single set of behavior changes. Successful media campaigns have several important characteristics. First, they are realistic and doable. Second, good messages offer consistent, sound advice; one message reinforces or builds on previous ones. Campaigns have a common theme and appearance. Comic books, for example, contain the same messages and logos as wall paintings, posters, and television spots. Third, good messages are culturally relevant.

Media campaigns generally are more effective in changing attitudes or increasing awareness than in modifying dietary behavior. This may seem strange in light of the tremendous impact of media on soft drink sales, infant formula and the like, for it is true that media has excelled in promoting thousands of commercial products. But convincing people to change beliefs, abandon traditional dietary practices, and accept new nutrition concepts is quite different:

> The role of mass media in selling social change is unlike its conventional function—selling nutrition is not like selling soap, but like the much more difficult and abstract job of selling the concept of cleanliness. It is not merely a matter of curing a headache by selling an aspirin; people must first be convinced that they have a headache.
>
> *(Berg 1973:81)*

The Manoff International Project in the Philippines provides a good example of mass media's impact on dietary attitudes and behavior. Manoff International designed a series of short radio messages to improve infant feeding practices. A needs assessment had revealed that infants between six and twelve months of age failed to grow normally because their mothers did not provide sufficient nutritious food to supplement breastfeeding after the sixth month. Interviews with nutrition and medical authorities in Manila showed that nearly all Filipino families had foods available that could be added to the traditional weaning foods, making the diet more nutritious.

Radio messages were designed to:

1. increase the number of mothers who begin supplemental feeding by the child's sixth month,

2. decrease the number of mothers who believe babies cannot digest small amounts of oil, fish, and green vegetables, and

3. increase the number of mothers who add chopped fish, green vegetables, and cooking oil to the supplemental food.

Before designing the radio messages, a survey of over 100 families was conducted to learn how Filipinos perceive infant health and feeding, their knowledge of nutrition, family structure, sources of nu-

Figure 10.1
The use of radio in nutrition education. In many developing countries, radio is the most accessible medium available for providing health education.
(AID)

Focus 10-2

Media relations

Establishing relationships with newspaper, television, and radio professionals is an effective way to spread nutrition messages at a low cost. The relationship can be mutually supportive as nutritionists provide media personnel with interviews, story ideas, information, and consultation, and in return are given an opportunity to disseminate nutrition messages. Television and radio news programs and talk shows, newspaper articles, and public service announcements provide an effective means of reaching large numbers of people.

Becoming acquainted with news professionals through phone calls or personal visits is an important first step. Because the media business is fast-paced and deadline-oriented, it is important to keep contacts brief. For the same reason, it is essential to follow through on agreements in a timely fashion.

Even though nutrition is currently quite popular, media coverage can be difficult to obtain for topics that are considered unexciting. For this reason, one author and a coworker found that they could attract the desired coverage by organizing a newsworthy event. To bring their message, 'Eat Whole Grains,' to the public, they produced "Day of Bread," a whole wheat bread baking contest using several local radio and newspaper personalities as judges. As you might expect, they got excellent media exposure for their message (Greist and Markesbery 1979).

Establishing contact with food and health writers of local newspapers can increase the number of nutrition articles printed. Nutritionists can provide information and interviews for such columns; in some cases, local papers will contract with nutritionists to write a regular column. Two of the authors write a monthly column, *Food Rap,* for a local food co-op newsletter that reaches over 4,000 people. Not only do the articles disseminate information, but also heighten the writers' visibility, resulting in increased requests for nutrition education programs (Courtney and Markesbery 1983).

Another option open to nutritionists is the use of public service announcements (PSAs): short messages sent to the media that are printed or aired at no cost as a public service to nonprofit groups. PSAs can be used to promote a nutrition message or advertise programs and services.

Guidelines for writing PSAs include the following:

1. Briefly describe your message, noting the what, when, who, where and how of your message.

2. Put the most important information first.

3. Address the PSA to a specific individual rather than to the station or an unidentified person, such as the Public Service Director.

4. Use agency letterhead stationary whenever possible.

5. Type the PSA in capital letters and double-space it.

---

trition information, radio listening habits and other aspects of rural life. Based on survey findings and interviews with nutritionists, six radio messages were prepared. These were translated into the local language, recorded by popular radio personalities, and tested on a pilot population. Messages were then modified to overcome problems noted in the pilot tests. Finally, they were broadcast on each of the 15 commercial stations in one province, with an average of three to four spots played daily for one year.

An evaluation of the project revealed mixed success: 75 percent of the target group households had heard the message and substantially larger percentages of families agreed with the messages transmitted (i.e., add cooking oil, fish, or vegetables to infant porridge) than before the project began. However, less than one third were actually carrying out any of the recommended practices. The project was highly successful in changing attitudes but only mildly effective in altering behavior.

Educational media: pros and cons

One of the greatest advantages of educational media is their ability to transmit information to large numbers of people quickly. In Western societies, television, radio, and newspapers reach the vast majority of the population. In developing societies, media are more limited: television reaches only the affluent, and newspapers and radio are unavailable to many economically disadvantaged and geographically isolated segments of the population. Cultural and linguistic differences within countries and high illiteracy rates create additional problems for mass communication programs. Nevertheless, educational media remain the most efficient method of reaching large numbers of people with relatively few resources (Berg 1973:81).

Another advantage is the relatively uncomplicated and inexpensive administrative demands of media campaigns. Neither extension agents nor neighborhood workers, for example, have to be trained and supervised. Also, television and radio stations often offer free broadcast time for public service or educational announcements. Mexico, for instance, reserves 12.5 percent of all commercial radio and television time for governmental use (Manoff 1973:128). In the U.S., the Federal Communications Commission (FCC) suggests that stations commit a certain percentage of TV and radio air time to public service announcements.

Mass media is limited, however, in several important ways. The kinds of nutrition problems that it can deal with are limited; not all nutrition issues can be communicated with easily understood, emotionally appealing messages that prompt a concrete behavioral change. Messages cannot always be made culturally relevant. This is especially true if they are broadcast to an ethnically mixed audience. A considerable degree of similarity in cultural background and nutrition problems must exist for mass-produced messages to work at the local level. Some have solved this problem by targeting messages to one specific group. Because of the lack of local control and quick feedback, major problems may not be discovered until too late. In one Latin American country, a campaign was conducted to persuade mothers to give a homemade lemonade preparation to children suffering from diarrhea. Later it was discovered that many women used the lemonade as a magical medical cure because of the "over-sell" approach, and assumed that no other medical treatment was necessary (Perrett 1977:26–7).

Combined approaches

To maximize the benefits of both person-to-person and media methodologies while overcoming some of their limitations, many educators use a combined approach. Media forms often are used to reinforce and supplement the more personalized methods of instruction.

The Nutrition Change of the Month Project is one U.S. program using a combination of methods. Developed to improve diet habits of elementary school students, the Nutrition Change of the Month Program focuses on one dietary innovation at a time; e.g., replacing white bread with whole wheat or changing from sweetened to unsweetened cereal. Students in each grade select the change for a particular month. Teachers, school food service personnel, and parents join them in promoting the change by using a combination of educational techniques. Students plan school menus, select recipes, form taste testing panels, make posters, and help develop handouts for parents. The principal announces the Change of the Month over the

Focus 10-3

Food advertising

The U.S. food industry spends $3 billion each year to promote its wares to the public. Most food advertisements encourage an already overfed America to consume even more calorically dense, nonnutritious foods. Unfortunately, such advertisements are quite effective and have contributed to many nutritional problems.

The nutrition advocacy group, Center for Science in the Public Interest (CSPI), petitions the Federal Trade Commission (FTC) to remove deceptive advertising from the airwaves. In 1981, for example, Wonder Bread was forced to pull an ad that erroneously claimed that white bread was as nutritious as whole wheat bread. Action for Children's Television (ACT), a Boston based consumer group, claims that advertising aimed at young children is a moral issue: it constitutes electronic exploitation of young people. As a result of ACT's work, the number of commercial minutes on children's Saturday and Sunday morning programming has declined from 16 minutes per hour to 9.5 minutes and commercials for candied vitamins have been forced off the air.

intercom each week during the month. Teachers show films and discuss benefits of the change and how it can be implemented. (Bryant 1981).

An especially successful combined approach in many developing nations is the radio forum in which programs providing nutrition, agricultural, and health innovations are broadcast to organized listening groups. The forum or local group typically meets weekly in a public building or other designated place and listens to a radio broadcast 15 to 30 minutes in length. The program may include rural news, answers to questions submitted by local listening groups, reports on group activities and successes, and a talk or dramatization about a topic of common interest. The group leader then directs a discussion of the message, using flannel boards, posters, or other audio visual aids to reinforce the radio message. She also assists the group in deciding what individual or collective action should be taken. Because decisions are group-based, proposed actions are more likely to be carried out and maintained. Countries

KIDSFOOD

| BETTER EATING |
| THROUGH |
| EDUCATION |

"FOOD ADS"

SELLING FOOD

"Be a Pepper!"

"You Deserve A Break Today."

"Coke Is It!"

Though the slogans are different, the message is the same: buy our food!

Food advertising has come a long way since it first started in the late 1800's. At that time, the founders of A&P used 8 horses to pull a red wagon with the store's name painted on it through the streets of New York. This was their way of getting people to remember A&P.

Today food ads are much fancier. In fact, $ 3 billion is spent each year on food ads in the U.S. alone. And as you've probably noticed, the least nutritious foods are the ones advertised most. When was the last time you saw an ad for a carrot?

Many ads make it seem that if you buy their product you will be like the person in the ad. Some examples are listed below:

THE AD	THE MESSAGE
"I'm a pepper. He's a pepper. Wouldn't you like to be a pepper, too?"	You will be popular if you buy *Dr. Pepper*.
"Tab, for the beautiful people."	You will be good looking if you drink *Tab*.
"Stimoral, at last, chewing gum for the rich."	People will think you're rich if you chew *Stimoral*. (This is called snob appeal.)

MAKE YOUR OWN

Many of the foods that are advertised can be made at home.

• A better soft drink—Mix 1/2 cup juice with 1/2 cup club soda.

• A crunchy snack—Mix together popcorn, peanuts and raisins.

• Homemade cereal—Mix 1 cup oats, 2 tablespoons brown sugar, 2 tablespoons oil, 1 teaspoon cinnamon and 1/4 cup nuts together. Place on a cookie sheet and bake at 200° F. for 30 minutes or until oats are toasty. Stir in 1/4 cup of raisins.

On the average, people between the ages of 9 and 14 see 8,500 to 13,000 T.V. commercials for food and drink each year.

SOME DETECTIVE WORK

Many people think some food ads are unfair because they are not easily understood. Learning how to spot the tricks that advertisers use can make watching T.V. fun, as you "catch" advertisers in their tricks.

Here are some examples that will help you spot advertising tricks:

Scare tactics —	"60% of American children don't get enough vitamin A."
Bent truth —	"Our bread has as much calcium as an apple." (But an apple doesn't have much calcium.)
Sales pitch —	"You need our protein powder." (We do need protein but we can get it from real food.)
Incomplete truth —	"Need energy?" "You need our candy bar." (We do need energy, but we can get energy from good food.)
False claims —	"Our cereal will give you more get-up and go!"

Citizen groups have worked to make advertising more fair. One group, *CSPI*, works to get ads that are tricky taken off the air. Another group, *Action for Children's Television (ACT)*, works to change or get rid of ads aimed at young children. They think that the ads for toys, candy, sugary cereals, and other "junk foods" shown with Saturday morning cartoons take advantage of young children. Many children like the cute bears and dolls, prizes and games that are used to sell the products. They do not know enough about nutrition and advertisement to see it for what it is.

WHAT YOU CAN DO

✓ Don't fall for the tricky ones. Watch food ads closely. What are they *really* saying? What kind of food is being sold?

✓ Let the food companies know that you don't like bad ads. Write them a letter. Don't buy their products.

✓ Write ads for good foods. Hang them on the walls at school or read them over the school's loudspeaker system. Most ads are 30 seconds long.

ADVERTISING IS EXPENSIVE

American food advertising costs went from $2 billion a year in 1950 to $ 3 billion in 1978! For some new, hot-selling brands, we pay up to 35¢ on every dollar for the ads that sell them to us. Here are some comparisons to show how the cost of advertising affects the sales price:

House Brand	Cost	Name Brand	Cost	% Higher
Flour, all purpose	$1.35	Gold Metal	$2.75	104%
Salt, iodized, 26 oz.	.22	Morton	.33	50%
Rice, enriched, 2 lb.	1.05	Uncle Ben's	1.69	61%
Peanut Butter, 12 oz.	.83	Jif	1.15	38%

Sponsored By
Suburban Woman's Club

Figure 10.2
KIDSFOODS, a nutrition newsletter distributed to sixth grade students each month, devotes this issue to food advertising (Courtney and Markesbery 1983; art by Chris Ware.)

Tips for a Low Sodium Diet

USE THESE FOODS:

- Fresh or frozen meats –
  chicken, turkey, fish,
  veal, and <u>lean</u> beef, pork
  and lamb (<u>limit</u> to three
  ounce servings), eggs

- Dried beans (pinto,
  navy...)

- Peanut
  butter

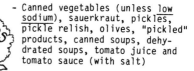

AVOID THESE FOODS

- Bacon, sausage, luncheon meats
  (bologna and salami...), hotdogs,
  chipped or corned beef, canned
  beef (Spam), canned fish (tuna,
  sardines, anchovies), pot pies,
  TV dinners, breaded meats, ham

- Packaged mixes (Hamburger Helper,
  macaroni and cheese...), canned
  dinners (Spaghetti O's, Ravioli...)

- Foods from "fast food" restaurants

- American and processed cheeses,
  cheddar, colby, blue cheese,
  Roquefort cheese, cottage cheese,
  and any cheese not listed on the
  other side, cheese spreads and
  cheese sauces

- Swiss*, mozzarella*, ricotta
  cheese*, and low sodium
  cheese (*limit to one ounce
  only three times a week)

- Dry curd, unsalted cottage
  cheese

- Milk, yogurt, tofu

- Fresh and frozen vegetables
  (if you use regular, canned
  vegetables, drain the liquid
  off and rinse the vegetables
  with water)

- Low-sodium soups (or homemade
  soups that are prepared without
  sodium)

- Canned vegetables (unless <u>low</u>
  <u>sodium</u>), sauerkraut, pick<u>les</u>,
  pick<u>le</u> relish, olives, "pickled"
  products, canned soups, dehy-
  drated soups, tomato juice and
  tomato sauce (with salt)

- Fresh, frozen, or canned fruits

- Fruit juices

- Fresh vegetables

- Unsalted popcorn

- Crackers with unsalted tops

- Potato chips, pretzels and
  other salted chips

- Chip dip

- Salted nuts

- Crackers with salted tops

- Allspice, basil, bay leaves,
  chives, cinnamon, dill, onion
  powder, garlic powder, nutmeg,
  paprika, parsley, pepper, sage,
  thyme, lemon juice, vinegar

Seasonings

- Mustard, ketchup, chili sauce,
  barbeque sauce, soy sauce,
  meat tenderizers, Worchestershire
  sauce, steak sauce, salad dressings
  onion salt, garlic salt, celery
  salt, lemon, pepper, MSG

AVOID: SALT

Figure 10.3

*Educational media for nutrition information. Educational materials should be clearly written,
neat, and attractive, and can be made inexpensively. Figure 10.3 is a handout used in a senior citizen's clinic.*

throughout the world—Togo, Dahomey, and many Latin American nations—are using radio forums effectively to improve agricultural production.

Supplemental feeding programs

Provision of free food to supplement the diet of vulnerable groups has long been the most common method used to reduce malnutrition. Found in over 100 countries, supplementary feeding programs represent the largest item in most nutrition budgets. These programs are by far the most expensive and the most controversial form of nutrition intervention.

See Highlight 5-1 for a discussion of U.S. federal food programs

Supplemental feeding programs distribute food to special high-risk groups in order to improve their nutritional status through the provision of additional nutrients. Most programs attempt to reach children, lactating mothers, and pregnant women through school feeding or maternal and child health programs. A smaller number of programs provide food to the entire family. Examples of each type of supplemental feeding are discussed below.

School feeding programs

Because they offer a relatively large captive audience, schools are popular sites for supplementary feeding programs. In the United States, the greatest expenditures on child nutrition are allocated to the National School Lunch Program. Also housed in the school system and similar institutional settings (orphanages, day care centers) are the National School Breakfast and Special Milk Programs, which provide federal subsidies for children's supplementary foods.

School feeding programs are also popular in developing countries. In rural India, 9.5 million children are provided with the major midday meal through school feeding programs. Most supplementary food, typically bulgar or another grain product, is donated by the United States through international charitable organizations or provided from Indian government surpluses.

Distribution of supplementary foods is handled in several ways. Some schools prepare meals on-site, involving students, parents, and other community members. In one Indian school, for example, children take turns preparing the daily meal. Some fetch the fuel, others collect the local condiments and foods added to the bulgar, while still others prepare and distribute the meal. Not only do the children learn how to use foods wisely, but they experience the satisfaction of helping make the midday meal. In other Indian schools, food is prepared in central kitchens and distributed to surrounding schools. This method is particularly practical in urban areas where schools are located nearby. A third method is the distribution of ready-to-eat products to schools. While efficient, this system has several drawbacks. The food often is too dry to be eaten alone, and because beverages are not available, many children take the food rations home. Not only does this delay its consumption until after the school day, but once in the home, the food is shared with the entire family, diluting its impact on the child's nutritional status.

An evaluation of school feeding programs in India (Community Systems Foundation 1979:70) revealed mixed results. The program was criticized because of its failure to meet the children's greatest nutrition needs for nutrients such as vitamin A and B-complex vitamins. Also, most schools had fewer rations than required to feed all the children; as rations were divided to feed larger numbers of children than intended, the amount received by any one person became too small to meet the daily nutritional needs.

Figure 10.4
Supplemental feeding programs. School feeding programs, such as this one in India, allow children to take an active role in preparing meals. They teach food preparation skills and promote feelings of accomplishment, in addition to the primary goal of providing nutritional supplements.
(AID)

Despite these limitations, one controlled study (Devadas and Radharakmani 1965:35–37) found significant improvements in height and weight, hemoglobin levels, clinical signs of malnutrition, and educational achievements of junior high school students participating in the school lunch program.

Maternal and child health programs

Another method of providing supplemental nutrients to women and children is to distribute food through established health centers. In the U.S., women and children are given special food supplements through the WIC program. In Chile, this approach has been used to distribute milk to women and children for over 60 years.

Chile's milk program began in 1924 with the distribution of one-half liter of milk per day to working women with children under two years of age. Initially, only a small number of families received the milk rations. But as the program expanded during the next four decades, significant segments of the population were reached. By the 1970s, milk distribution had risen to 39 million kilograms annually, benefiting approximately 3 million recipients—60 percent of Chile's women and children. Program costs in 1972 were $28.4 million, not including administrative and operational costs absorbed by the health centers. Ninety percent of this cost represents milk purchased from dairies in Chile and other countries. The program's impact is difficult to assess because its effect cannot be separated from other improved health and sanitation conditions taking place during the same period. Nevertheless, Hakim and Solimano (1978) made these observations about the milk distribution program's possible consequences:

kilogram
A metric measure equal to 2.2 pounds

1. From 1937 to 1973, as the program expanded, infant mortality dropped from 200 to 65 per thousand live births. Likewise, during the Allende administration (1970–1973) when the program had its greatest coverage, infant mortality dropped by nearly 18 percent and child mortality by 20 percent. Other malnutrition indicators (the incidence of diarrhea and respiratory infection) also declined dramatically.

2. Public awareness of milk's importance in childrens' diets was increased.

3. Concern for nutrition problems was stimulated among medical professionals, social workers, and even government officials.

4. Research in nutrition and food technology, especially the development of milk expanders and substitutes, was given high-level government attention and support.

The key components in the Chilean program's success are the prior existence of a country-wide clinic network capable of reaching vulnerable groups and the consistent governmental support that allowed experience in program operation to accumulate and improve with time. Many maternal and child health programs in other countries do not benefit from these supporting conditions, and, as a result, often are much less successful.

The major problems noted in the Chilean program were improper milk preparation (too concentrated or diluted), improper storage, and sharing of rations by all family members, which prevented children and women from getting nutritionally adequate supplements.

Distribution programs for families

A successful family supplementary feeding program has been developed in Panama. As described by Julio Sandoval (1978), the Panamanian program was established to assist population groups at high nutritional risk. An assessment of nutrition indicators (e.g., infant mortality, percent of homes without potable water) revealed that 25 percent of the people living in 15 of Panama's 26 districts were in great nutritional need. Five of these districts were selected for a comprehensive pilot food distribution program.

potable water
Clean and healthful for drinking

Food rations were designed in order to cover a family's deficit but not replace foods already consumed: rations would supplement, but not substitute for, a family's regular diet. Because the survey revealed a 25 percent nutrition deficit, food rations were designed to contribute 20 to 30 percent of the daily demand for calories and protein and a slightly higher percentage of other nutrients. Two types of rations were designed, each using local foods to enhance their acceptability: one for young children and another for other family members. The child's mixture contained 60 percent rice, 16 percent whole milk powder, 24% sugar, and a vitamin and mineral concentrate. The other ration included rice (75 grams), skim milk power (10 grams), oil (15 grams) and sugar (10 grams).

By the end of its pilot year, the program had reached over 24,000 people in 224 villages, with the total value of food supplements representing about 50 percent of the average annual income for these families. Although the program encountered problems in

Figure 10.5
Food-for-Work. Food-for-Work programs use food as a wage to pay laborers, providing benefits to communities in developing countries, as well as distributing food to people. (AID)

distribution to remote areas, wastage due to faulty packaging, and co-ordination difficulties at all levels, it proved sufficiently successful to warrant expansion to other districts.

Another supplementary food program that provides rations to the entire family is the Food For Work (FFW) approach. These programs use food as a wage to pay laborers who otherwise would be unemployed. In addition to channeling food into food-scarce areas, FFW projects contribute indirectly to recipients' nutritional and general well-being in several ways. First, they generate employment to poor unskilled laborers when jobs are scarce. Second, they improve the economic position of the poor by providing needed income and creating marketable skills through on-the-job training.

Third, they foster economic development by creating irrigation wells, schools, houses for the poor, or improved agricultural land through clearing and leveling.

Some of India's best FFW projects have served as important catalysts for community organization in which people pooled resources and worked together for the first time on community projects. In an analysis of India's FFW program, the Community Systems Foundation (1979) concluded that FFW projects showed potential for helping the poor, especially when projects stimulated community development. Although food is used essentially as a substitute for cash wages, the long-term nutritional impact may be greater than that of any direct feeding program.

Of course not all FFW projects function equally well. In some cases, FFW programs have built roads from "nowhere in particular to nowhere in general" (Latham 1978:491); while in other instances, they have built farm-to-market roads that doubled the prices farmers received for their crops.

Advantages and disadvantages As described in the examples above, supplementary feeding programs have certain strengths and weaknesses as nutrition intervention methods. Program proponents claim that programs such as WIC and Chiles' milk program are effective in keeping people healthy. The Japanese make similar claims for their school feeding program, noting dramatic evidence in the physical size of students: "The typical Japanese fourth grader no longer fits in the chair his parents occupied a generation ago; twice since the end of the war, desks in Japanese schools have been moved out for larger ones, and architects are now designing doorways for homes and offices six inches higher than before" (Berg 1973:170).

Even when direct nutritional benefits are not demonstrated, advocates claim that supplemental foods act as an important incentive for families to utilize health clinics or send their children to school. Some supplementary feeding programs also offer health screening and nutrition education to recipients (WIC) and raise an awareness of nutritional needs (Chile's milk distribution program).

School feeding programs also are seen as an effective way to improve the learning abilities of poor children. By combating hunger, school feeding reduces childrens' apathy, inability to concentrate, and poor retention. Studies (Berg 1973) in South India suggest that diet supplements have resulted in significantly improved classroom performance.

Finally, public feeding programs are politically attractive because of their high visibility and emotional appeal. Salvador Allende, Fidel Castro, and Indira Gandhi used promises of child feeding programs in their political campaigns. In programs relying on food aid from other countries, supplementary feeding may continue to be supported even when other aid is withdrawn. For example, U.S. food aid to Chile's school feeding program continued during the Allende years when all other types of assistance were withdrawn. Thus, supplementary feeding programs allow food aid to be used in a more sensitive, politically acceptable form than other welfare programs: few people want to deny hungry children food.

As with other forms of nutrition intervention, supplementary feeding programs have their critics. Administrative costs are extensive, so that even when the food is donated, these programs require a sizeable proportion of a country's nutrition budget, tapping funds which critics believe could be better spent on other nutrition programs. Perhaps the most serious objection to supplementary feeding programs is their failure to attack the basic causes of malnutrition: poverty and political inequities. At best, food giveaways are a stopgap measure; at worst, they create dependency on free foods, a potentially dangerous situation when supplies are unstable.

There are other problems too. Often supplementary feeding programs are incompatible with recipient's norms, values, and beliefs. Some food recipients resent being put into what they see as a welfare role that undermines their sense of pride and dignity. Parents in one Indian village resented having their children fed yellow corn and powdered cow's milk when they prided themselves on producing the best rice and buffalo milk in the village. Similarly, program objectives may be misunderstood. Participation in one lunch program dropped dramatically because parents believed its main purpose was to fatten boys for recruitment into the army. Finally, dispersion of free food has been shown to compete with locally grown and manufactured foods and thus depress local prices. Supplementary feeding programs in some areas have discouraged local manufacture of low-cost foods, induced early weaning, fostered black marketeering, and overburdened teachers and health workers responsible for food distribution.

In sum, advocates note the programs' potential for eradicating malnutrition, citing a few successful examples. Opponents point to program failures and note the numerous cultural and economic barriers to the programs' ability to improve nutrition. Evidence available at this point suggests that supplementary feeding programs can be useful as a stopgap method of providing food to high-risk groups. But beyond this "first aid" nutritional role, supplementary feeding must be combined with other program approaches (nutrition education, health and family planning services, public education, and economic development activities) in order to effectively reduce malnutrition. As Hakim and Solimano (1978:69) conclude, "these differences between critics and proponents suggest to us that an assessment of the usefulness of supplementary feeding as a nutrition intervention cannot be made in the abstract but only within the context of a specific nation setting."

Focus 10-4

Nutrient interactions

In distributing supplemental foods it is important to consider *nutrient interactions*—the ways that amounts of one nutrient can affect the body's ability to metabolize other nutrients. Disturbances of nutrient relationships can have a profound effect on health. This is exemplified by the relationship between vitamin A and protein. Animals fed a high-protein diet apparently consume their body stores of vitamin A more rapidly and develop eye lesions more quickly than their slower-growing litter mates fed rations low in protein (McLaren 1952:234). Clinical evidence suggests that human infants behave in a similar fashion (Oomen et al. 1964:271). Thus vitamin A deficiencies may be stimulated by giving protein supplements to children who previously consumed low-protein diets.

After World War II many relief agencies (UNICEF, for example) used nonfat milk powders as a major item in famine relief and distributed separate fat soluble vitamin A capsules along with it. Parents were warned that children might lose their sight if the capsules were not taken as directed. More recently this practice of distributing vitamin A and protein separately has been considered hazardous because information about the importance of taking the vitamin A supplement along with the protein supplement might not be disseminated, understood, or followed. In fact, in some areas such as North East Brazil, increased blindness among children has resulted from separate distribution of nonfortified skim milk powder and vitamin A pills (Bunce 1969). Fortunately, separate distribution is no longer necessary; a stable water-dispersable vitamin A derivative was developed in the 1960s that can be added directly to nonfat milk powder.

Formulated foods

As early as the 1950s, formulated foods were seen as a potential method for reducing malnutrition. In order to combat protein deficiencies found in many underdeveloped countries, nutritionists and food technologists began searching for techniques to manufacture food mixtures from inexpensive vegetable proteins. Their goal was to use low-cost protein foods produced in developing countries in both supplementary feeding programs and commercial products. It was hoped that these mixtures would make protein available at prices within financial reach of the poor (Orr 1977:2).

Efforts to develop formulated foods became even more widespread in the 1960s as the amount of U.S. food aid sent to developing countries declined, leaving supplementary feeding programs without the free grains or milk they had grown dependent upon. Poor countries were not in a position to replace these food supplements and turned to industry and the scientific community for help in developing low-cost substitutes.

The United Nation agencies, in conjunction with local governments, played a major role in developing at least 15 products. Research institutes, universities, and other agencies (Central Food Technological Research Institute, Meals for Millions) interested in formulated foods also carried out extensive research and development in protein-rich foods. One of the most successful early enterprises was *Incaparina,* a mixture of corn and cottonseed flour developed by the Institute of Nutrition of Central America and Panama (INCAP). Private industry soon joined in on the efforts, and by 1972, private sources owned 71 percent of the formulated products (Orr 1972:34).

Today, most formulated products contain a blend of oilseed meal, cereals, sugar, and a vitamin/mineral concentrate. The oilseed meal (a residue left from the soya bean, cottonseed, ground nut or other oilseed) is the key element in these foods. Although certain oilseeds are deficient in one or more amino acids, they usually contain those lacking in the cereals with which the formulated product is combined. (See Chapter 2 for a description of protein complementation.) Also, because the meal is a byproduct, it offers an inexpensive protein source (less than half the cost of nonfat dry milk and more than eight times less expensive than most animal protein sources).

Formulated foods come in a variety of product types. The earliest were designed as food supplements or additives that could be made into soups or incorporated into other dishes intended for the entire family rather than special target groups. Multipurpose supplements such as the *Nutricube,* a small cube full of nutrients that can be dropped into the family cooking pot, and nutrient dense powders that can be sprinkled on cooked foods are common examples. Although some of these products have proven successful, most modern products have abandoned this approach and instead are promoted as separate dietary items. *Colombiharina, Puma,* and *Milpro* are high protein soft drinks; *Nutrovite* and *Protene* are soup and

Figure 10.6
Formulated foods as nutrition intervention. Formulated foods can be effective nutritional supplements when care is taken to make them relevant to the cultures and communities for which they are provided. The CARE soybean processing plant in Costa Rica makes formulated food products such as VITA LECHE *for the nation's supplementary feeding program.*
(AID)

gravy powders, *Kupangi Biscuits* and *Uni-Protein Biscuits* are bakery products used by the entire family; and *Cherish* and *Duryea* baby foods are directed at high-risk groups.

Not all formulated foods have won consumer acceptance. In an analysis of 71 products, Elizabeth Orr (1972, 1977) of the Tropical Products Institute reports that 19 (27 percent) were terminated and another 13 (18 percent) were produced on a special order basis only.

A common obstacle is consumer rejection of a products' taste, color, appearance, smell, or texture. In developing one formulated food, *Peruvita,* The United Nations, Nestle, and the Peruvian government worked together to promote the product. Despite widespread publicity and brisk initial sales, consumers did not return for second purchases. The product's taste, color, and smell had not been adequately tested for consumer acceptability. Similarly, sales of some cottonseed products faltered until their greenish color was changed to give a more appealing appearance.

Formulated foods also fail because potential acceptors view them as incompatible with their beliefs and norms. This is especially true when formulated foods are made into completely new products such as multipurpose food additives or *Nutricubes.* To many people, such products represent an entirely new eating concept. *Ladyloe,* a food used for weaning babies, was introduced into the Sengalese market in 1966. Despite governmental support, production ceased after only six months. Among the many reasons for its rejection was the fact that few women had ever purchased processed weaning foods. Convenience foods did not fit into the cultural pattern and were strongly opposed by male members of the community.

A product's image also affects its acceptability. Some companies have found that overemphasis on the nutritional benefits of formulated foods can backfire. In promoting *AMANA* for instance, malnutrition was depicted as a sickness that this product could eradicate. To the promoters surprise, some women mistook the food for medicine to *treat* marasmus and other forms of frank, acute protein deficiency. They failed to recognize its preventative value and the need for regular use.

Because of these barriers to acceptance, most companies now conduct extensive food habit research and consumer testing before developing a new product. As Orr (1972:56) explains, past experience has shown that "the nutritional value of a product will not guarantee its marketability . . . protein-rich foods must fit into the dietary pattern of the potential consumers and organoleptic acceptability."

organoleptic
Affecting the senses in the evaluation of food; e.g., taste, texture, color, smell

Even though gains are being made in marketing formulated foods, the question must be asked: do they contribute to the reduction of malnutrition? A review of formulated food mixtures (Orr 1977) suggest that they have had little direct impact on low-income groups. Most enterprises have not established significant retail trades. In fact, only Guatemala's *Incaparina* and *Pronutro* in South Africa reach large numbers through retail markets. More commonly, they are distributed by charitable agencies or the government as a part of supplementary feeding programs, reaching a relatively small proportion of those who need supplements.

To make formulated foods effective in reducing malnutrition, distribution will have to be greatly expanded. One movement in this direction is the use of formulated foods in programs that reach large numbers of poor families, such as CARE's school feeding program. The U.S. Agency for International Development also is working to develop inexpensive formulated products that would be sold in retail markets.

Food fortification

fortification
The addition of nutrients to a food, often in amounts much larger than might be found naturally

One of the simplest means of increasing the nutritional value of vulnerable peoples' diets is to add nutrients to the foods they normally eat. This method is used widely to increase the vitamin, mineral, and protein levels of popular foods.

Foods are fortified with synthetic as well as natural nutrients. Vitamin D fortification of cow's milk was first accomplished by feeding cows irradiated yeast and ergosterol, and then by direct irradiation of milk with ultraviolet light. Now synthetic vitamin D is added directly to milk.

Effective fortification schemes rely on the availability of a suitable food carrier—one that is centrally processed, reasonably priced, and consumed by the target population. The most common carriers are flour, salt, margarine, rice, breakfast cereals, confections, cooking oils, and corn products.

enrichment
Now considered synonymous with fortification, but previously referring to the restoration of specific nutrients (lost during the refining process) to breads and cereals in the United States

Food fortification has a long history. The addition of fish oil concentrate to margarine as a source of vitamin A and the addition of iodine to salt as a means of preventing goiter date back almost a century. The fortification of bread in the United States offers an early example of the methods used to improve nutritional status. In the 1930s, medical records revealed widespread beriberi, pellegra, ariboflavinosis, and iron-deficiency anemia. Medical and public health professionals actively searched for a means to combat these deficiencies. Educational approaches were abandoned because attempts to persuade people to eat whole-grain products had failed for years and vitamin pill distribution was considered too costly and impractical. They proposed, therefore, that the needed nutrients be placed back into the white flour from which they had been extracted during milling. Because the average bread consumption at that time was six slices per day, nutrients would be added in quantities that would enable six slices to bring the daily intake up to recommended levels.

The American Medical Association, millers' and bakers' professional organizations, nutritionists, biochemists, and governmental officials gave immediate support to the fortification plan. However, the public and Congress were more skeptical. Many issues were raised: people should use only natural foods, synthetic fortification will create an imbalance of nutrients, the National Institutes of Health is a tool of the drug industry looking for business, and the

Focus 10-5

Defining our terms

A number of terms have been used to describe the process of adding nutrients to foods: fortification, enrichment, and super-enrichment. These terms are often used interchangeably today, but they have had different meanings over the years. *Fortification,* the most general term, involves adding nutrients to foods, "but not necessarily the nutrients that were originally found there" (Whitney and Hamilton 1981:464). The addition of iodine to salt, iron to breakfast cereals, and vitamins A and D to milk are examples of food fortification.

Enrichment, on the other hand, involves restoring nutrients lost during food processing. "With respect to breads and cereals in particular, this term refers to the process by which four specific nutrients lost during refinement are added back to refined grain products at levels specified by law: thiamin, niacin, and iron at levels about equal to those in the original whole grain, riboflavin at a level about twice that in the original whole grain" (Whitney and Hamilton 1981:337).

The term *superenrichment* has been used recently in reference to the proposed addition of iron to flour and bread in amounts three times the currently accepted standards. In this chapter, the word *fortification* is used as an inclusive term for adding nutrients to food.

value of fortification cannot be proved (Berg 1973:109). Despite the controversy, a National Mandatory Enrichment Policy was established during World War II. The United States Food and Drug Administration set legal standards for minimum and maximum thiamine, riboflavin, niacin, and iron levels. Although federal policies and guidelines terminated at the national level after the war, most states continue to enact laws requiring fortification, and today 92 percent of all commercial white bread is enriched. (In 1970, the American Baker's Association and the Millers' National Federation requested that the Food and Drug Administration raise the standard of enriched bread and flour by tripling the amount of iron in the staples. This proposal opened a controversy that continued actively until 1978, when the petition was rejected.)

In general, food fortification continues to be used to improve nutritional status. There are several reasons for the continued popularity of these programs. The addition of nutrients does not alter the food's appearance, taste, or smell so that fortification schemes do not create special packaging or promotional demands. Also food fortification demand little administrative training and outreach. Unlike supplementary feeding programs that require sophisticated coordination at local, regional, or even international levels, a food fortification program involves few decision–makers and other personnel. In fact, it requires less time, less administration, and fewer clearances than other intervention methods (Berg 1973:112–3).

Another advantage is the low cost of food fortification. Even amino acid fortification, which is considerably more expensive than vitamin or mineral supplementation, is cheaper than conventional protein sources or protein-rich formulated foods. Moreover, synthetic nutrient costs decline rapidly as their use increases. The cost of synthetic vitamins A, C, and riboflavin and lysine have decreased dramatically as production uses have increased (see Figure 10.7).

The major shortcomings of food fortification derive from the food carrier's limitations in reaching vulnerable groups. In rural areas this is especially problematic because people rely primarily on subsistence agriculture and purchase few processed food products. In Southeast Asia, for instance, most peasants grow their own rice and have it milled locally. Rice fortification would require tremendous expenditures for special equipment and training in thousands of small units. Fortification is also criticized because it may provide nutrients to those who do not need them as well as those who do. For example, if the proposed iron super-enrichment plan had been implemented, adult men would have received an unnecessary iron supplement in enriched white bread and breakfast cereals, along with the women and children the superenrichment was intended to help. This seemed uneconomical, and opponents feared that it could have created nutritional imbalances—perhaps even toxicity. Finally, fortification of foods high in fat, sugar, and salt, such as presweetened breakfast cereals, has been severely criticized. In this case, fortification helps promote "junk food" and may contribute to a decline rather than an increase in the diet's nutritional quality. As Carol Christopher points out: "The consumer is unwittingly playing a game of 'Let's pretend that Tang is an orange.'" (Christopher 1980:4-5). The consumer loses the orange's nutritional contributions (vitamins, minerals and fiber) and instead drinks a highly processed beverage rich in sugar, additives and colorings.

Despite these drawbacks, food fortification's advantages far outweigh the disadvantages, especially for developing countries, and most government officials support mandatory fortification programs.

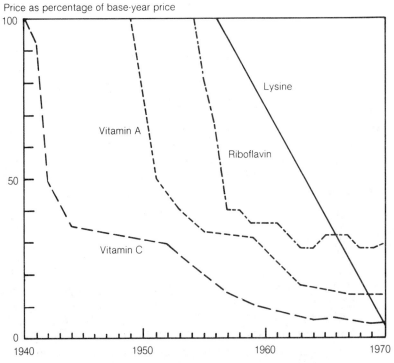

Price as percentage of base-year price

Figure 10.7
Decline in costs of se-
lected synthetic nutri-
ents, 1940–1970.
(Adapted from Alan Berg's
The Nutrition Factor: Its Role
in National Development.
Washington, D.C.: The
Brookings Institute, 1973,
p. 115.)

Source: Based on cost data from Hoffmann-La Roche, Inc., 1972.
Percentages are figured from the following base-year prices: for
vitamin C, $71 per kilogram in 1940; for vitamin A, 30 cents
per million international units in 1949; for riboflavin, $100 per
kilogram in 1952; for lysine, $30 per kilogram in 1956.

Consumer advocacy

When malnutrition results from inaccurate or inadequate nutrition
knowledge, educational programs can be highly effective. More
commonly, however, lack of information is combined with lack of
other resources: money, opportunity, and power. Knowledge of
what is best to eat does little when proper food is unobtainable. As
we saw in Chapter 8, planners and policymakers now recognize that
the basic causes of poor health reflect a synergistic interaction between the inequitable distribution of power, land, and wealth, as
well as lack of access to accurate information. The major constraint
to change is inequality: inequality of wealth, government services,
educational and occupational opportunities, wages, and basic
human rights. "This inequity undermines the capacity and confidence of the poor to control their lives; it conditions them to accom-

modate themselves to the norms of the dominant group which assumes an increasingly paternalistic stand, under which the rural poor become the politically voiceless recipients of the ideas of the dominant classes and of further exploitation" (Kidd 1979:5). Nutrition intervention in this case must move beyond information dissemination designed to change dietary beliefs and practices. It must deal instead with broader issues, teaching people to identify their nutrition needs and giving them skills to participate effectively in the decisions, political or otherwise, that determine their health and well-being.

For these reasons, consumer advocacy has proven increasingly popular and effective as a nutrition intervention strategy. Over the last decade, advocacy groups have been successful in modifying nutrition policies and practices of the U.S. government and many commercial firms. Some U.S. based consumer advocacy groups include the following.

Action For Children's Television (ACT) is an advocacy group devoted to promoting more responsible advertising aimed at children. One example of ACT's advocacy efforts is its petition to the Federal Trade Commission to ban ads for sugary foods that promote cavities. Although the FTC proceedings were largely unsuccessful, the controversy sensitized the U.S. public to the issue and stimulated many television stations to broadcast more public service announcements on nutrition and related issues (Nutrition Action 1981:8).

The Children's Foundation is the oldest and largest antihunger group. The foundation uses lobbying efforts on Capitol Hill as well as political organizing at the community level to promote child nutrition programs (WIC, food stamps, and the school lunch program).

The Food Research and Action Center (FRAC) is a nonprofit law firm that uses litigation and emphasizes client rights in its fight against hunger. FRAC has published a profile of the Federal Food Programs that summarizes food programs available to economically disadvantaged people in the U.S.

The Community Nutrition Institute (CNI) reports on nutrition education, research, and legislative action concerning federal food programs in its *CNI Nutrition Week*.

The Center for Science in the Public Interest (CSPI) "is a nonprofit, tax-exempt organization that investigates and seeks solutions for consumer and environmental problems . . . . CSPI's Nutrition Action Project seeks to provide the public with reliable, interesting information about food, the food industry and the government regulation of foods" (Katz and Goodwin 1976:212).

While advocacy is increasingly popular among some consumer groups, others are critical of their special interest or narrow focus, and the emotional tone that often accompanies their arguments. Perhaps one of the most dramatic examples of both the effectiveness and high-pitched emotions frequently associated with consumer advocacy comes from the recent battle waged against the infant formula companies.

Since World War II, and particularly in the late 1970s and early 1980s, marketing practices used to promote infant formula in developing nations came under attack. The formula companies were criticized, for example, for the use of milk nurses—company employees dressed in nurses uniforms who distributed formula. Other promotional techniques considered unscrupulous included the use of advertising messages that equated infant formula with modernization, prestige, and superior health status; endorsements from medical personnel; the use of health care professionals and health facilities for distribution of free formula samples; and calendars, brochures, and lavishly illustrated baby books prepared by the commercial firms (Jelliffe and Jelliffe 1978:227–30).

Formula companies also were accused of contributing to high rates of infant morbidity and mortality. Critics agreed that misuse of infant formula was inevitable in many developing nations because poor sanitation and unsafe water supplies, illiteracy, and poverty frequently resulted in bacterial contamination and over dilution of formula (Miller 1983:5).

With the 1974 publication of *The Baby Killers,* (Muller 1974) a report blaming high infant mortality in Chile on multinational corporations, and the widespread formula controversy, numerous consumer advocacy groups sprang into action. These groups used three major tactics in their fight against the infant formula companies: shareholder resolutions and litigation, boycotts, and demands for international and national regulation. Fred Miller (1983:5–9) describes how each of these tactics were used in *Out of the Mouths of Babes: The Infant Formula Controversy.*

The first tactic involves the use of resolutions passed by a group of people holding shares of formula company stock to force company leaders to reveal their marketing practices and adapt more "socially responsible" policies. For example, as a result of pressure applied by the Sisters of the Precious Blood, a Roman Catholic Order holding 500 shares of Bristol-Myers (manufacturers of infant formula) stock, that company agreed to distribute a report of its marketing practices to shareholders including information prepared by the Sisters on alleged formula abuse and the need to curtail marketing in Jamaica (Miller 1983:6).

The second tactic, a world-wide boycott of the Swiss formula manufacturer, the Nestle'Company was organized by the Infant Formula Action Coalition (INFACT). Numerous political, religious, civic, and consumer groups around the world quickly endorsed the

Figure 10.8
Consumer advocacy and nutrition education. The international boycott of Nestle *products stopped* Nestle *from continuing its promotional advertising campaign of breastmilk substitutes.* *(INFACT/Nick Allen)*

boycott against Nestle´products, demanding that the company ". . . discontinue mass media advertising, distribution of free samples, milk nurses, and promotion through the medical profession, and that it prevent the use of formula by those without the means to use it safely" (Miller 1983:8).

As a third tactic, industry critics sought legal regulation through the United Nations World Health Organization (WHO) national legislatures. Years of lobbying efforts culminated in the passage of the WHO International Code of Marketing, preventing companies from advertising or promoting commercially manufactured infant formulas to the general public, placing restrictions on labeling and packaging, and prohibiting commercial firms and their representatives from conducting educational activities aimed at pregnant women or mothers. Also, promotional material designed for medical personnel are subject to government regulation. Although the Code is voluntary, legislation to enforce it at the national level currently is being sought (Miller 1983:1). Since its passage, many formula manufacturers have expressed public support for the WHO code and formed committees comprised of clergy, scientists, pediatricians, and/or politicians to monitor their compliance with its regulations.

Nevertheless, controversy still surrounds industry promotional activities and the extent of adherence to code regulations. On one hand, " . . . the Infant Food Action Coalition has documented numerous instances of continued promotion and direct sample dissemination . . . ." (Popkin et al. 1983:18). On the other, direct public advertising appears to have declined and most formula manufacturers appear to have shifted away from materials and messages discouraging breastfeeding and now use a more balanced supportive position (Popkin et al. 1983:18).

Currently, consumer advocates, industry representatives, and other analysts of the infant formula controversy are debating the ethical and philosophical basis of the Code as well as its impact on women and children in developing nations. For example, some analysts question the Code's ban on public advertising, claiming that it is a "disregard of the basic rights such as the freedom of speech . . . ." (Miller 1983:80). Others fear that strict restrictions placed on formula distribution and other marketing practices may make formula more expensive and less accessible to mothers in some parts of the Third World, thus restricting their freedom to choose the feeding method best suited to their needs (Dugdale and Doessel 1980:366).

Because mothers' decisions to breastfeed or bottle feed are influenced by multiple factors, some experts also fear that the focus placed on formula promotional activities may divert attention from other, equally important determinants of breastfeeding: the woman's work roles and daily schedule of activities, family size and child spacing, family income and other economic assets, mother's and health professionals' knowledge and attitudes about infant feeding, hospital facilities, and a host of other biological, ecological, and emotional factors affecting women's ability to lactate (Popkin et al. 1983).

Unfortunately, we do not have reliable data on how formula advertising influences women's decisions to feed their infants. A few studies have shown that formula advertising affects mothers' knowledge and attitudes about infant feeding (Orwell and Murray 1974), but they do not measure its impact on breastfeeding decisions or behavior. Likewise, little reliable data is available on how regulations that restrict advertising affect breastfeeding and bottle feeding practices (Popkin et al. 1983).

Despite the paucity of scientific data, the debate continues. And with high political and economic stakes, people on both sides of the issue have allowed emotion to invade their arguments and cloud their objectivity (Miller 1983: 10–11). In sum, the infant formula controversy illustrates the numerous problems as well as the amazing results that can be achieved through consumer advocacy. It also highlights the importance of maintaining objectivity and relying upon reliable scientific data when intervening as a consumer advocate.

Summary

- Nutrition education programs provide information and skills through person-to-person media or a combination of these strategies. Nutrition education success is enhanced by methods that actually involved the learners (self-discovery, learner participation).

- Educational media are used in both developing and developed countries to promote good nutrition. Television and radio broadcasts, billboards, posters, audio cassettes, brochures, comic books, puppet shows, and folk theater are popular and effective.

- Supplemental feeding programs distribute food to special high-risk groups in order to improve their nutritional status through the provision of additional nutrients. Many of these programs have proven highly effective in promoting good health and well-being. They have been criticized, however, for their failure to attack the underlying causes of malnutrition. If not planned carefully, they may prove incompatible with recipients' food practices and compete with local farmers or manufacturers.

- Formulated foods have been used by many nations and charitable agencies to combat malnutrition. However, problems with distribution and consumer acceptance have hampered their effectiveness.

- Fortification of foods with vitamins, minerals, and protein has been used for almost a century to enhance the nutritional value of vulnerable peoples' diets. Food fortification is technologically simple and inexpensive and requires little program coordination. The major shortcomings of food fortification are its inability to reach many vulnerable groups who do not purchase processed (fortified) foods.

- Consumer advocacy can be a highly effective strategy for intervening in the nutrition policies and practices of governmental agencies and food manufacturers. Consumer advocate groups have influenced federal food policies, television advertising and the infant formula companies' marketing practices in developing nations. These groups have been criticized, however, for their special-interest focus and the emotional tone that often accompanies their arguments.

Highlight 10-1   Program planning

We have seen that no single program approach is effective in solving all nutrition problems; each is more appropriate in some situations than others. But how do nutrition planners decide which program(s) would be best for the community or country they are serving? And how do they recognize areas of resistance to the dietary innovations being introduced?

The first step in the planning cycle is the identification of needs, factors contributing to nutrition problems, and other aspects of the client's culture that influence receptivity to change. Collection of this information, often called *needs assessment* or *community diagnosis,* takes time and money. However, it is critical in the effective planning and development of any nutrition program. Second, this information is used to develop program goals and objectives and to identify appropriate program approaches. Third, as the program is implemented, more specific objectives and methods are constructed. Finally, the program is evaluated, with the results fed back into the next round of the planning cycle.

Needs assessment or community diagnosis

The final results of all program development is to meet needs, satisfy wants, or change existing conditions. It is essential, therefore, at the outset of the planning sequence to develop a clear description of the nutrition needs of a group or population and identify the nutrition problems a program would solve.

The benefits of obtaining information about clients' needs and interests prior to carrying out nutrition activities have been summarized by Gifft et al. (1972:96) in *Nutrition, Behavior and Change.*

"Prior inquiry can prevent an inappropriate approach." This is exemplified by an adult education minicourse (Dagley 1976:79), in which a series of lecture discussions was organized on the following topics: "Assessing Your Food Intake," "Basic Nutrients and Their Functions," "Selecting and Buying Foods," "Food Fads and Fad Diets." "The Nutrition Canada Survey," and "Food as Children See it."

The course was advertised in a local newspaper and class capacity was reached within ten days. Prior to the first class, each participant was interviewed to determine what was expected from classes so that their interests could be incorporated into the curriculum. Interviews showed that participants were not interested in the planned topics, but rather wanted information on the meaning of food labels, the nutritive value of cereals and breads, diet-related disorders, natural foods, and other topics. By changing the series to meet participants' interests, cooperation was obtained and the program succeeded.

"Prior inquiry can identify nutrition needs not previously recognized or show that supposed needs do not really exist"

413

(Gifft et al. 1972:297). Goiter, for example, was believed to be extinct in the United States until the National Nutrition Survey documented its reappearance in some regions. In Mexico, calcium deficiency was assumed from diet histories even though clinical signs were absent. Later it was shown that significant amounts of calcium were obtained through the traditional method of treating corn with lime before preparing tortillas (Gifft et al. 1972:298).

Careful analysis of the nutritional content of local foods as locally prepared should be a routine part of the planning phase of every program contemplating dietary change. An important result of a survey of native nutrition and health in New Guinea, for example, was the discovery that native methods of cooking, however strange to European eyes, were about as good as could be devised from the standpoint of preserving the nutritional value of food. While there were some serious dietary deficiencies, they had nothing to do with cooking methods. Indeed, native practices in this regard were often better from a nutritional point of view than European and American practices.

(Goodenough 1966:467)

"Prior inquiry can pinpoint the most important needs" (Gifft et al. 1972:298). Typically, nutrition interventionists are faced with limited time, money and personnel. Because there are not enough resources to address all problems, the nutritionist must determine which needs are greatest. Should program time be devoted to distributing food, building enthusiasm for nutrition, developing an understanding of other people's eating practices or teaching new cooking and eating habits?

"Prior inquiry can identify leverage points (stimulants) and barriers toward learning" (Gifft et al. 1972:299). John Cassel illustrates this well in his classic study of a health care program serving the Zulu tribe of Africa. Analysis of the

tribespeoples' diet revealed a severe lack of essential nutrients. Yet the Zulu claimed that their ancestors had thrived on the same food, and discredited any relationship between their current diet and ill health. This barrier to the acceptance of nutritional advice was overcome when a search of the literature showed that ancestoral Zulus had eaten a diet containing large quantities of meat, milk, wild greens, and millet. Compared to current food intake based largely on corn and a few other vegetables, the traditional diet provided for more protein and other essential nutrients. Older Zulus confirmed these facts and supported the argument that the present diet was not as traditional as the tribesmen believed. A stimulant to change had been identified.

Finally, prior inquiry can identify existing resources available for nutrition activities. Other health and human resource programs, skilled personnel, technical assistants, and materials that can be incorporated into program planning and implementation may be identified through a planning survey. In some instances administrative support form other agencies and technical assistance from key individuals may prove essential to a program's development. If surveys reveal nutrition or health education activities already being conducted in the area, coordination with these programs might be arranged. For instance, when protein-rich foods are distributed through local mother-infant centers, nutrition education activities may be designed to reinforce the importance of correctly using these formulated foods and other local protein-rich resources.

Nutrition assessment methods

A community or group's needs can be assessed using a wide variety of methods. As seen below, these vary considerably in the amount of time, money, and type of professional expertise required to collect and/or analyze data. Each method also varies in its ability to identify a sound and culturally appropriate approach to nutrition problems.

Analysis of Health and Nutrition Statistics, certainly the easiest and least expensive means of identifying nutrition problems, uses information that already has been collected. Results of nutrition surveys, health studies, and national surveillance systems, for instance, are often used by planners to pinpoint the groups at greatest need and the types of nutrition problems found among the largest number of people.

George Christakis (1973:1) in *Nutritional Assessment in Health Programs* gives an excellent discussion of how to use existing data to "paint a picture of the community, its ecology and the factors influencing the way people live." He reminds us that for most communities, information is available on a wide range of topics that affect the health and nutritional status of the community. This information can be obtained by consulting nutritionists, physicians, directors of local programs and personnel in health agencies such as the Canadian Bureau of Nutrition Scientists, U.S. Department of Health and Human Services, and state and local public health departments. Also, published materials such as the *Assessment of Nutrition Status in Canada* or the *Ten State Nutrition Survey* make excellent sources of data on dietary intake, biochemical values, and anthropometric measurements of large numbers of people.

In the United States, information on nutrition problems and needs and resources can be obtained from the following sources:

1. At the national level.

a. National Center for Health Statistics

Health and Nutrition Examination Survey (HANES)–Vital statistics on infant mortality, low birth weight, cause-specific death rates, and age-adjusted death rates from chronic and degenerative disease.

b. National Institutes of Health

Lipid Clinic Data

National Heart, Lung, and Blood Institute conference data

Multiple Risk Factor Intervention Trial (MRFIT) data

National Institute of Dental Research data

c. U.S. Department of Agriculture (USDA)

National Food Consumption Bank

d. USDA Nutrient Data Bank

Data on food costs and availability

e. Food and Drug Administration–food labeling data

f. Bureau of Labor Statistics

Data on food costs and availability

g. Blue Cross/Blue Shield data

h. National menu surveys (Chicago)

i. United States Census

2. At the state and/or local level.

a. Health Systems Agency information–Health resources, utilization of health facilities, planning goals, and the data upon which these are based

b. Health Department data–Vital statistics, program statistics, environmental conditions

c. Center for Disease Control surveillance data–Incidence of major diseases

d. Early Periodic Screening Diagnosis and Treatment (EPSDT) results

e. City or County Planning Commission information–Demographic and socioeconomic stratification

f. Local service program statistics on housing, transportation, education, dental health, and other community aspects.

g. *University libraries and departments of nutrition, food science, home economics, and agriculture.*

Analysis of existing health and nutrition data is a relatively simple method of assessing a community's needs, requiring little additional staff time or money. There are several limitations, however, that must be recognized. First, national and regional statistics may not accurately document the needs of a specific group or community being assessed. Diabetes, for example, is found in a much higher percentage of Pimas than American Indians in general, and obesity is more prevalent among Samoan Americans than other ethnic groups on the West Coast. Second, most regional surveys and agency records do not include information on clients' perceptions of their needs or the types of nutrition services they would like in their community. And third, because national and local statistics rarely include information on beliefs, values, and attitudes that affect people's receptivity to new nutrition and health programs, they provide little assistance in determining the type of program most effective in solving these problems.

Review of ethnographies, community studies and other documents

Valuable insights into a people's beliefs, practices and responses to change can be obtained from ethnographies, community studies and other publications.

Ethnographies

These documents are detailed descriptions of many aspects of the customary behavior and beliefs of a cultural group. They frequently contain information on food preparation, storage and eating habits, as well as the social and cultural context in which diet practices occur. Community studies focus on social relationships and the norms, beliefs, and values that guide human interaction. Information on more specific topics, including descriptions of a society's diet practices or analyses of a community's receptivity to directed change programs may be found in journal articles, dissertations, and other documents.

As with the use of health and nutrition statistics, the literature may not always portray accurately the needs and interests of the specific audience being served. Puerto Ricans in Dade County, Florida, for instance, may differ in some ways from their counterparts in New York City. And, of course, the needs of both groups in the 1980s may be quite different than those identified by research conducted in the 1960s. With these limitations in mind, however, a literature review offers the nutritionist a quick and inexpensive means of obtaining information about diet practices, and social and cultural factors which may influence nutrition change.

Community and group surveys

The most direct and accurate view of a target community or group's problems can be obtained from a survey of its members. The methods used in these surveys include individual dietary histories (24 hour recall or diaries), family histories, food frequency consumption questionnaires, anthropometry (measurement of the human body), biochemical indicators, and questionnaires to explore food habits and beliefs. In almost all cases, a needs assessment survey is conducted on a sample or portion of the population to be served. For large communities or groups, a sample size of 1 percent of the population may be enough. But for small groups, such as the elderly living in a particular section of town, a larger percentage of the group's members is interviewed. An effort also is made to include representatives of all ages, ethnic groups, income levels, and both sexes.

One nutritionist used a survey of county grocers and farmers as the initial planning step in developing ways to increase consumption of locally grown produce. The survey revealed that the majority of grocers were interested in purchasing more local produce, while a large percentage of farmers would rather sell their wares locally than to their out-of-state markets. Data were gathered regarding the needs and constraints of both groups. With this information in hand, she will work with city officials to develop a centralized warehouse where local farmers and grocers can trade (Courtney 1984).

Unless the nutritionist has special training in research methodology, she may choose to call upon professionals for assistance in selecting a sample, preparing and pilot-testing research instruments (questionnaires or interview schedules), training interviewers, conducting statistical analysis, mechanically processing the data, and interpreting results.

Community or group surveys require more time, money, and personnel than other needs assessment methods. Several advantages make these extra expenses worthwhile. For example, surveys enable the nutritionist to collect information on the clients' perceptions of their problems and identify the issues or questions that they would like addressed. As we have discussed, designing a program to fit the audience's felt needs and interests greatly increases its likelihood of success; people are more likely to accept innovations that relate to issues that they are concerned with than those that replace traditional beliefs they have no desire to change. Surveys also are designed to determine the types of program activities

and methods that a group will respond to best. Some people, especially those with many years of formal education, are accustomed to lectures and classroom teaching techniques and have little trouble being attentive or retaining the material presented. This may not be true, however, for others who learn best from experimental methods, e.g., cooking demonstrations and workshops. And, as mentioned in Chapter 9, participation in certain learning roles may conflict with local norms of pride and dignity.

Finally, surveys are used to identify the best time and place to schedule program activities. In many communities, economic and other constraints limit attendance at special meetings or classes. This is particularly true of agricultural communities in which most activities revolve around seasonal cycles.

Community representatives

Information and advice about a particular community's needs and wants can also be obtained from health care professionals, elected officials, community leaders, and consumers.

Information can be secured through formal or informal means. Using a set of standardized questions and formal interviews enables the nutritionist to compare the responses of individuals to determine the number and type of people providing the information or recommendations obtained. On the other hand, some community representatives are more open and cooperative when interviewed informally. Whether community representatives are approached formally or informally, their assistance is critical in effective program planning. They may suggest ways to introduce new practices and schedule program activities, become active supporters of the program, promote its objectives, and assist with its implementation.

When asking for advice from community representatives the nutritionist frequently needs to be prepared to explain general program goals and ask specific questions about community needs, local resources, and methods for solving local problems; some people are unaccustomed to being asked for advice and need to know the types of information being sought. And not infrequently they need to be reassured that their opinions are valued. This is especially true of consumers who are not used to being considered "experts."

Depending on the situation, community representatives can be organized into ad hoc committees to express views on a specific problem or advisory committees to assist with planning and implementation on a long-term basis. Planners must exercise care and forethought in selecting committee members. To the extent that committee members truly represent the people served by a program, the use of advisory or ad hoc committees is an effective source of planning information. Unfortunately, many planners make the mistake of filling advisory committees with well-known leaders who are too busy with community programs and political activities to keep in touch with the needs and interests of the people they represent. Furthermore, community studies indicate that leaders are often issue-specific. In other words, a leader of one issue may not be an equally effective representative regarding other topics or programs. Also, in communities divided into different, or even competing groups, members should be chosen to represent all segments. Members of factions within a community may resist a nutrition program if they feel its planners have sided with competing groups. This may occur even when the faction center around issues that are totally unrelated to the nutrition program itself. These factors are often overlooked. Membership, then, largely determines the success of a committee or use of representatives as a planning tool.

In summary, each of these needs assessment methods produces a slightly different picture of a community and its problems. Nutrition and health statistics are used to map the distribution of specific nutrition problems; a literature review is done to explore cultural and social factors contributing to nutrition problems and identify barriers to change in groups like the one being served; special surveys are conducted for a closeup view of the needs and interests of the specific population being served; and advisory committees are formed to gain input from select representatives of the professional groups and the target audience. Because each source yields slightly different information, many nutritionists rely on a combination of methods for program planning.

Developing program goals and objectives

Regardless of the source, information obtained in a needs assessment is used to determine program goals and objectives. Program goals are a general statement of what should occur; they are general in scope and set the direction for defining more specific objectives. Goals may be somewhat unreachable and unquantifiable such as "To ensure the nutritional well-being of all community residents." Program objectives are statements of expected outcomes that must be met to reach the goals. They are the heart of program planning, evaluation, and implementation. If objectives are vague, both their evaluation and implementation will be difficult. In addition to meeting community needs and wants, objectives should be realistic and measurable. In other words, they should be achievable within the available time and resources of the program, and they should contain the information required to implement them. The following objectives outline the proper requirements and format.

Target Audience: Employees of Webster, Inc. who have hypertension.

What is to be accomplished: Program participant will be encouraged to alter diet and exercise habits to decrease blood pressure.

To What Extent: 20 percent of participants will reduce blood pressure.

By Whom: Two industrial nurses and one nutrition consultant are required to implement the program.

When: During 1985.

Example: During 1985, 2 industrial nurses and 1 nutrition consultant will encourage program participants to alter diet and exercise habits resulting in reduced blood pressure for 20%.

For detailed information on writing program goals and objectives, consult Frankle and Owen, *Nutrition in the Community: The Art of Delivering Services* (1978).

Program implementation

Even a well-planned program requires careful implementation. Successful implementation usually is attributed to strong leadership, sound organization, and proper training. Equally important is the ability to readjust program objectives and activities to fit recipients' needs. This not only requires flexibility but also a continuous input of information about recipients.

To ensure that program goals and activities are well-received and appropriate, the nutritionist must stay in constant touch with participants' reactions to the program and its staff. All too often, a seemingly successful program receives rejection from large segments of the target population. By the time the reasons for this rejection are identified, it may be too late to convince the community to utilize the program.

This is exactly what happened to a nutrition project in Guatemala sponsored by the Nutritional Institute of Central America and Panama (INCAP) (Adams 1955). The Guatemalan project was part of a larger program to determine which supplemental foods were needed to improve local diet. Each day school children were given supplemental food, and periodically, physical examinations were conducted to evaluate the impact of the supplements on nutritional status. Of particular concern were height, weight, and blood data. To enhance local cooperation INCAP also established a clinic for routine medical cases.

Although villages initially accepted the project, their support was later withdrawn. Some villages even became antagonistic to staff members and threatened to expel the entire project. An anthropologist was brought in to analyze the situation and identify sources of hostility. His investigation revealed several areas of cultural conflict that had arisen between villagers and project staff.

One problem revolved around the village political structure. The village was divided into two opposing factions: one was anti-government, Catholic, and conservative; the other was pro-government, religiously mixed, and more liberal. The INCAP project was identified with the second group, because a staff member had made all her initial village friendships with members of the pro-government faction and so was rejected by the first group.

A related issue pertained to the alignment of the progovernment and Communist forces in Guatemala. The INCAP project was viewed as a government project, hence Communist-oriented. Villagers were worried about the threat of Communism and grew cold and hostile to project personnel, whom they thought were Communists.

Villagers also grew suspicious of clinic activities, particularly the blood tests performed on children. According to local beliefs, blood is not regenerated and its loss weakens the body permanently. As the project progressed, many villagers refused to send their children for the examinations. As a further deterrent, a rumor began that the supplemental food was being used to fatten children so that they could be sent to the United States or Russia for eating. The blood test was used to determine when a child was fat enough for export!

The anthropologist helped staff members combat these misunderstandings, but not before much time and money was lost. Clearly, it would have been far better to stop the conflicts as they arose.

Community participation and feedback throughout all implementation phases are the best means of avoiding this type of calamity. Several methods are used to invoke community involvement. As in the planning phase leaders and other community members may serve on formal advisory committees or function informally as consultants. Surveys can be conducted of program participants and/or nonparticipants on a periodic basis. Even suggestion boxes may yield valuable input from concerned clients in some settings.

Another means of eliciting community involvement is to employ community members in regular staff positions as aides or volunteers. We have already seen in Chapter 9 that many nutrition programs now utilize village-level workers or neighborhood workers to educate, distribute food, and carry out other advocacy roles. The benefits of involving community members in that way are numerous. Community feedback enables the planner to recognize when objectives no longer are relevant to recipient's needs; learn of rumors, growing mistrust, or other misunderstandings about the program or its personnel; identify and utilize local resources such as indigenous communication networks for promoting program activities; and assess recipient's perceptions of novelty characteristics and advocate attributes.

Most importantly, community involvement is necessary if the nutrition program is going to have a lasting impact. In the long run, a program is successful only when it enables people to better control and improve their own health and nutrition.

Occasionally program coordinators fail to realize that their programs can either increase peoples *independence,* enabling them to determine their own lives, or increase their *dependence* on others for advice and resources. Consider, for example, the difference between a program that teaches children which foods contain nutrients and one that enables them to analyze nutrition information and use it in food selection.

The first approach is exemplified by most school nutrition education programs in which the children memorize basic food groups and the foods comprising them. In many cases, the knowledge gained has little or no impact on diet habits. The latter approach is used less often, but with great success, as exemplified by the Center for Science in the Public Interest. The learner is taught to analyze the accuracy and objectivity of educational materials and nutrition messages used by teachers, parents, and advertisers. Evaluation of materials is based on questions like:

- What is the source of the information?

- What do advocates of the information have to gain by its acceptance?

- Is the message promoting good health and social well-being?

- Is this information complete?

- Are statements supported with acceptable evidence, or is the evidence misleading?

Programs that foster dependence usually find that the behavioral changes promoted fail to survive after program incentives, resources, or information is withdrawn. Recipients stop eating the food, forget the food groups, or switch back to traditional practices. This rarely occurs in programs that truly involve clients in program implementation because the skills and information needed to determine nutrition choices are transferred to them to use for their own lasting benefit.

Program evaluation

Nutrition programs, like all health, education and social services, are experiencing increased pressure to determine the extent to which they meet societal needs. Most U.S. funding agencies, for example, are requiring more extensive program evaluation than they did five years ago. Evaluation research uses scientific research procedures to determine the degree of progress made in achieving program objectives. It is a demanding activity, requiring time, money, and special expertise. In fact, many programs employ a specialist trained in evaluation research techniques for this phase of programming.

Why is evaluation so important? Al Loeb (1975) gives five reasons for evaluating nutrition programs.

1. To help make or modify decisions—to expand, to curtail, to continue, or to terminate programs.

2. All organizations using resources should see that the most and best services possible are being rendered, making sure the public programs meet genuine public needs, and that public revenues are spent wisely.

3. The need for a given program may change with the passage of time, and therefore, each program should be analyzed regularly from the standpoint of need, objectives, and alternative ways of accomplishing its objectives.

4. Without program evaluation there is no way of knowing or documenting that public activities are in fact achieving program objectives.

5. Evaluation assists the program administrator to demonstrate (to the legislature, public, client, or press) that the program is achieving its objectives.

The research criteria and methods used to evaluate a program usually are determined during the planning phase: the types of information needed to determine if the criteria are met (number of people attending classes, weight of participants before and after the program); how the information will be collected (diaries, records, surveys, observations); how the information will be analyzed (computer analysis, statistical tests); how the results will be used and shared with others (who will be responsible for making the information accessible to future planners and educators).

A final component in evaluation concerns the recipients' needs and interests. If participants have been involved in the planning and implementation phases, their needs will be incorporated into the objectives and activities evaluated. Therefore, Norge Jerome (1975) has recommended an additional set of parameters for inclusion in evaluation of nutrition programs These are as follows:

1. *Appropriateness to the individual, group, community, culture, and period.* The social, cultural, and economic characteristics of the recipient and community should be considered.

2. *Specificity in relation to program objectives and content.* Objectives and activities that are evaluated should be clear-cut, reflect recipient needs and goals, and be stated

in the form of specific behavioral outcomes.

3. *The amount of time required to achieve behavioral changes.* This should be assessed according to available resources and mechanisms for meeting program goals.

4. *Unintended side effects.* Programs may create beneficial, neutral or harmful effects that were unanticipated. These have important consequences for program control, expansion, and future planning.

In sum, evaluation as with all aspects of programming brings us back to our major theme: the importance of a consumer-oriented, culturally based approach to nutrition intervention. As presented above, the assessment-planning-implementation-evaluation cycle appears to be a set of clear and distinct steps. In practice, however, these activities often overlap in a process that "resembles more the tango—four steps forward, three steps back, with an occasional turn-around" (Berg 1973:234). Objectives, for example, may be dictated by the funding agency long before the needs assessment is conducted. As the program is implemented, community resistance to, or outright rejection of, some innovations necessitate a redefinition of objectives and adjustment of activities. Perhaps, an entirely new program is adopted (nutrition education may be replaced by supplementary feeding) that is more feasible and more culturally appropriate. Throughout a program's course, then, most planners examine and reexamine objectives, adjust and readjust program approaches, and redesign activities to make the program practical and acceptable to the special needs of the cultural group.

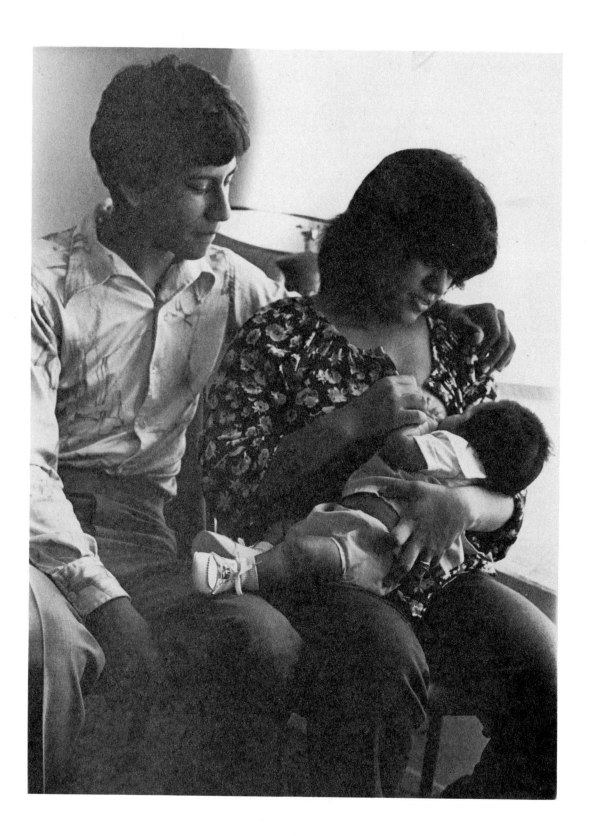

Highlight 10-2   Helping mothers to breastfeed: Program strategies in the United States

Recent research provides unequivocal evidence that breast milk is the superior food for infants. A mother's milk is well adapted to her child's needs and provides nutritional, immunological, and psychosocial benefits that cannot be duplicated by infant formula.

Breastfeeding reached an all-time low in the late 1960s when only 16 percent of American mothers were breastfeeding their infants (Forman 1979). A number of factors contributed to this trend. Manufacturers of infant formulas increased their advertising campaigns through the mass media and distributed free formula samples to hospital patients. New work roles for women, changing norms of modesty, and emphasis on the sexual rather than the nutritional functions of breasts also played a part. Some health professionals also may have contributed to the shift toward bottle feeding through their complacency about the subject (Jelliffe and Jelliffe 1978).

During the 1970s, significant changes in infant feeding practices began. By 1981, 58 percent of infants born in the U.S. were receiving some breast milk, certainly an impressive change from the 1960s. A number of factors account for the increased popularity of breastfeeding (Martinez and Dodd 1982). They include a heightened awareness of nutrition, desire for less mechanized or artificial lifestyles, increased publicity about breastfeeding from groups such as the La Leche League and public health agencies,

and growing support from the medical community. For example, some hospitals now provide *rooming in* as an option for new mothers who wish to breastfeed. This keeps the mother and child together, rather than corridors apart, increasing the chances of successful lactation.

Despite the increase in breastfeeding in the U.S., today women of lower income and educational levels are less likely to breastfeed than middle income women. Poor women that do breastfeed are likely to do so for shorter periods of time. Bottle feeding may be more popular among economically disadvantaged women because until recently it was associated with higher social status.

Programs have been developed to increase the incidence and duration of breastfeeding in economically disadvantaged communities. Many who have worked in such programs have found that successful lactation depends first and foremost on the type of social support and advice the mother receives during the perinatal period (near or about the time of birth).

A review of infant feeding practices in a wide variety of cultural settings shows that " . . . women require a supportive network in order to lactate. At the very least, one other person, a doula (supportive other) must be available to mother the mother at critical moments during the breastfeeding period" (Raphael 1976:3).

A study done in Dade County, Florida, of economically disadvantaged Cuban, Puerto Rican, and Anglo families is described below to show how friends, neighbors, and relatives affect a woman's decision to breastfeed and her success at it.

The Dade County, Florida study

Formal and informal interviews were conducted with 76 families enrolled in the Dade County Maternal, Infant and Children (MIC) Program. In many instances, friends and neighbors were also interviewed. The resulting data clearly show that kin, friend, and neighbor networks influence mothers' decisions in several ways. For one, friends, neighbors, and to a lesser extent relatives are a major source of information. To the extent that they emphasize all the problems associated with lactation, they are likely to discourage women from breastfeeding. The problems mentioned most frequently as reasons for not breastfeeding by women were: public exposure of breasts is embarrassing; a mother's anxiety will spoil her milk and make the baby nervous; a nursing mother has to eat a special diet; breast milk can harm the baby if the mother is not healthy and well-nourished herself; breasts leak between feedings; and breastfeeding will ruin the mother's figure.

The interviews also showed that mothers' decisions are influenced by the attitude of network members towards lactation. Here it is clearly the husband or boyfriend who is most important. Many of the Latin women and a few of the Anglo respondents reported their husband's or boyfriend's disapproval of breastfeeding. According to these women, the men disapproved of lactation because it disrupts sexual relations, is old-fashioned, and because the woman may have to expose her breasts in public. Some men actively discourage their wives from the practice. For

instance, one young Puerto Rican who had planned to breastfeed later did not because

I can't explain it. Maybe it has a lot to do with my husband. He's sort of shy about that, too. You know, I think he's jealous. [When she told him she wanted to breastfeed the baby] he said, "You're going to breastfeed?" But if I had to do it again, I'd try it.

(Bryant 1984:165)

More commonly, however, a woman's knowledge that her husband disapproves of breastfeeding is sufficient motivation to bottle feed. A typical case is an Anglo mother who reported that she fed by bottle because she was afraid her husband would become jealous if she breastfed her baby in front of other people, especially men: "He might think I was doing it just to provoke the other men."

On the other hand, many Anglo women and a few of the Latin respondents said their husbands approved of breastfeeding. In several Anglo families, the husband played a major role in his wife's decision to breastfeed.

A related issue concerns the types of assistance and support that is available from relatives, friends, and neighbors during the perinatal period. This is in keeping with Raphael's finding that at least one other person must be available as a "supportive other" to help feed and care for the mother immediately after birth and at critical periods during the breastfeeding period (1976:41). If this support breaks down, lactation becomes more difficult.

Nine of the women in the Dade County sample who breastfed were studied in sufficient depth to permit an analysis of the types and amount of support provided by kin, friends, and neighbors. With only two exceptions, the presence of a supportive environment was associated with successful lactation while the absence of a supportive person was associated with an unsuccessful experience.

The importance of network support is even more obvious when individual cases are reviewed. Turning first to the women with unsuccessful experiences (i.e., they stopped before they had planned to and were unhappy over their inability to breastfeed longer), all five stopped breastfeeding within one or two weeks. Only one of them, Nancy, received any assistance when she had difficulty lactating. Nancy's mother helped her use a breast pump and transport the milk to the hospital where the baby had to remain after Nancy had returned home. However, after a week in which her milk supply was insufficient to nourish the baby, Nancy stopped breastfeeding. It was later discovered that she had mistakenly been given medication to dry up her milk.

The other four women reported an absence of support from network members. They were neither encouraged to breastfeed nor did they receive assistance from network members in the weeks following birth. Rosa is a fairly typical example. She had successfully breastfed two children in Cuba and was planning to do the same with her third child born in the United States. But her milk failed to appear until after she had begun using an infant formula. No one helped her during this postpartum period nor did anyone support her decision to breastfeed. Moreover, her husband actively discouraged breastfeeding, saying it was old-fashioned. Rosa explained the delay in her milk supply as "possibly something emotional" and said that life is very "agitated" in the United States.

By contrast, three of the four mothers reporting successful breastfeeding experience did receive support from network members during the first few months of lactation. Their husbands approved of breastfeeding; and friends, relatives, and/or neighbors offered advice and assistance with many of their household duties. For one Anglo mother, the major source of support came from her husband, who had acquired his knowledge from his first wife, who nursed five children. The husband convinced her to breastfeed, assumed responsibility for much of the cooking and cleaning for almost three months, and also taught her to use a breast pump when she got "milk fever."

Only one woman breastfed successfully without receiving support from a friend or relative. Mercy, who was from Cuba, bottle fed two children before deciding to breastfeed "to see what it was like." Initially, she obtained information about lactation from the WIC program. Her mother, who has had experience with breastfeeding, was also available; but Mercy is quick to note that while the information was available, she rarely asked her mother's advice. None of Mercy's friends were breastfeeding at the time, and her husband had "not said much about it, but he sits and watches and he smiles, so I know that he likes it." Also, although no one offered to help with her household chores right after her baby's birth, Mercy hired a catering service, which partially reduced her workload during the period she was breasfeeding.

The value of supportive networks was well-known to the Cuban, Puerto Rican, and Anglo residents. In fact, a majority of the women in the study complained about not receiving enough assistance during the postpartum period. Some of the Latin women definitely attributed their decision to bottle feed to the absence of support from other persons. In the words of one 38-year-old Cuban woman,

If I had someone to take care of me, like my sister or my mother, then I could do it [breastfeed]. But with me here alone it would be like this [panting] with me running around trying to do this and that. No, it wouldn't be good for me.

(Bryant 1984:169)

In sum, kin, friends, and neighbors do have significant impact on mothers' decisions to breast or bottle feed. Moreover, the support and assistance from such networks contribute greatly to the success of breastfeeding. Understanding this phenomenon is important in the development of programs designed to promote breastfeeding.

Community advisors for breastfeeding mothers (CAB)

When natural supportive networks of kin, friends, or neighbors are absent, it may be possible to develop other kinds of supportive social networks. A good example is La Leche League International, which is comprised of experienced breastfeeding mothers who provide information and support through telephone counseling, informal group meetings and literature. However, although the League has been popular and highly successful with well-educated middle-income women, it has not met the special needs of economically and educationally disadvantaged groups. The league does not intentionally exclude such groups. In fact, the contrary is true; the League leaders have launched a number of outreach programs. But the fact remains that La Leche attracts mainly white, married, affluent, and formally educated women.

Recognizing the need for an alternative network of similar services for minorities, working women, single parents, and economically disadvantaged families, the Lexington-Fayette County Health Department began to organize Community Advisors for Breastfeeding Mothers (CAB) early in 1977. CAB is essentially an association of women with lactation experience who advise and encourage other mothers interested in breastfeeding. Two Anglos, six black women, and six of their husbands have participated during the eight years CAB has engaged in these outreach and counseling activities.

The organization began after inquiries through the local Community Action Program turned up a group of friends who had already been sharing knowledge, books, and experiences about breastfeeding for several years. They in turn recruited other advisors into the program. Following several formative meetings with Health Department educators, plans were made for a formal training session.

The initial training took place in a six-hour session led by a health educator and a La Leche League leader. CAB mothers are trained in counseling techniques, the advantages of breastfeeding, solutions to common breastfeeding problems, and other aspects of lactation. Each CAB mother also has a reference manual containing program policies and a variety of La Leche League information sheets on problems associated with breastfeeding.

In addition, a referral system has been established with several local agencies, including the obstetrical outpatient clinic and the University of Kentucky Medical Center, a private hospital maternity program, a private birthing clinic, and a health maintenance organization. The majority of referrals, however, still come from the WIC and maternity programs at the Lexington-Fayette County Health Department.

In some cases mothers call the CAB counselors for specific technical information, but most are searching for general information and encouragement to breastfeed. In addition to telephone counseling, CAB members mail written materials or make visits to the homes of interested families. They also have appeared on television and radio shows, staffed displays at health fairs, and led discussion groups at community agencies such as the Florence Crittenton Home for Unwed Mothers and in high school home economics classes.

CAB organized a one-day workshop that attracted about 60 pregnant women (ten of them teenagers) and three husbands. The agenda included audience participation, discussions of the benefits and techniques of breastfeeding and special concerns such as Caesarean sections and premature births. One unique feature of the workshop was a panel of men discussing ways fathers can support the lactating mother. In the course of their efforts to reach potential breastfeeders, CAB advisors have discovered several strategies and guiding principles. First, they recognize that knowledge about the benefits of breastfeeding is not enough. Even highly motivated women may find that they are unable to breastfeed. Opposition from friends, relatives, especially the husband or boyfriend, can create doubts about the desirability of the practice and may actually interfere with the let-down response needed to start lactation. (The let-down response is a hormonally controlled signal that allows milk to flow from the breast ducts.) Advisors need to assess the relative amounts of antagonism and support that a woman who decides to breastfeed will encounter. They can use this information to help the woman decide whether breastfeeding or bottle feeding is the better method in her particular situation. In some cases, encouragement from friends or a CAB member is sufficient to overcome criticism, skepticism, and hostility from other network members. Sometimes it is not, and CAB advisors have learned to be especially cautious about promoting breastfeeding when the husband or boyfriend expresses unyielding opposition. CAB advisors always present bottle feeding as a viable alternative so that a mother who finds lactation intolerable for whatever reason need not be left with feelings of guilt or failure.

Second, where other programs often overlook the importance of the male role in the lactation experience, male advisors have been a valuable asset in the CAB program.

They have served principally as counselors to men, discussing with them the benefits of lactation, methods of supporting the woman who chooses to breastfeed, and generally, dispelling whatever reservations the men may have about breastfeeding (e.g., its impact on sexual relations). The male members of CAB have also participated in television shows and other promotional activities. By addressing men's concerns, they transmit the message that men can support breastfeeding.

Third, the CAB advisors came to realize the need to make use of the mass media if they were to reach large numbers of individuals. Television, newspapers, and radio all offer highly influential and relatively inexpensive means to reach many people in a short time. Unfortunately, the media tend to be unreceptive to topics such as breastfeeding, which may offend some conservative attitudes; but more so because the topic is not "newsworthy" in the way a special event might be (Greist and Markesbery 1979). But it is possible to seek invitations to talk shows to discuss nutrition, infant feeding, and parenting in ways that include breastfeeding.

Fourth, it is clear that for maximum effectiveness, the mother's breastfeeding education should begin long before the final trimester of her pregnancy. Ideally, a close friend or relative will just have had a successful breastfeeding experience. Most often this is not the case. Even the most committed health professionals, however, may find it difficult to devote much time to breastfeeding during the initial prenatal visits that are so full of other tasks. Therefore, to provide this early promotion of nursing that may not be available in family or clinic, CAB has attempted to establish referral networks that put an advisor in touch with a woman as early in her pregnancy as possible.

What's so special about mother's milk?

Each mammalian species produces milk uniquely suited to support the growth of infants of that species. Since no two species have exactly the same needs, no animal's milk is exactly like that of any other. A calf's needs are quite different from a human baby's. Calves grow quickly, developing lots of muscle and increasing bone size to allow for early independence from their mothers. Humans, on the other hand, do not reach their full size for over 15 years. But while the body grows slowly, the brain and central nervous system develops quickly and extensively.

The makeup of cow's and human milk reflect these developmental differences. For example, cow's milk has four times as much protein as human milk, and a different amino acid composition. Cow's milk protein is very low in the amino acid, cystine, which human infants require in their diet. It is high in the amino acid phenylalanine, which the human infant has a limited ability to metabolize (Forman 1979). Also, compared to cow's milk, more lactalbumin is found in human milk. Lactalbumin is easier for infants to digest than casein, the major protein in cow's milk (Jelliffe and Jelliffe 1977).

The fats in cow's milk are also different from the fats in human milk. Saturated fats predominate in cow's milk, while human milk has mostly unsaturated fat. Human milk is rich in lipase, an enzyme that predigests the fats before they reach the baby's intestine. Cow's milk has very little lipase (Jelliffe and Jelliffe 1977).

Human milk contains less calcium than cow's milk, but because it is more easily absorbed, breastfed infants have higher levels of calcium in their blood than those who are bottle fed. Both cow's milk and human milk contain small amounts of iron, but the iron in human's milk is absorbed more effectively by the infant, hence totally breastfed babies do not require iron supplements until about six months of age, when infant liver stores become depleted (Nicholas and Nicholas 1981).

Infant formulas are not replicas of breast milk. They are made of cow's milk and processed in such a way that makes them nutritionally closer to "the real thing" than cow's milk.

Protection against infection

Breastfed babies have fewer infections than those that are bottle fed. For years, it was reasoned that this was because bottles were more likely to be contaminated. While this is an important factor, it is not the only one. Breast milk is now known to contain as many infection-fighting white blood cells as are found in blood; and those in milk are even more effective in destroying bacteria. Recent studies show that the nursing mother, who necessarily maintains close contact with her baby, produces antibodies to disease-causing organisms in the baby's environment. The mother then passes these antibodies through the milk to her baby. The nursing mother, in other words, acts as an "antibody factory," making the specific antibodies the baby needs to stay healthy. An antibody is a body globulin that is produced to respond specifically with an antigen (usually a foreign protein) to reduce the toxic side effects. Human milk also contains a type of antibody that helps to protect the gut from foreign organisms and potentially allergenic proteins. This is one reason breastfed infants are less likely to have allergies than those fed formulas (Jelliffe and Jelliffe 1977).

Mother and child bonding

A special relationship develops between the breastfeeding mother and her child. The continuous give and take between the nursing pair gives each a great deal of emotional satisfaction. While bonding also takes place between bottle feeding pairs, breastfeeding mothers derive special pleasure due to the release of certain hormones stimulated by suckling, and the infant gets the pleasure of skin-on-skin contact.

Other advantages of breastfeeding for the mother

Women who nurse have an easier time losing the excess fat that accumulated during pregnancy. The average woman adds an extra ten pounds of fat, thought to be provided to support milk production. When breast feedings are frequent—at least six or more times per day—the hormone prolactin is produced, which prevents the formation of fat and diverts the mother's fat as well as dietary fat into breast milk production (Quandt 1984). Many women who do not breastfeed find weight loss quite difficult. The hormones produced by the nursing mother also help the uterus to contract and return quickly to the nonpregnant state.

Highlight 10-3   The ethics of directed change

Interventionists are dedicated to improving the human condition by managing the direction of change. The goal of directed dietary change is to improve the ability of people to protect and promote their health and nutritional well-being through food choices and availability. We must realize, however, that neither altruistic motives nor specialized training can ensure success as an architect of change. Good intentions do not always result in good deeds.

Any human community can fail to maintain its integration through too little intervention, or none at all, or through too much intervention or the wrong kind. The world abounds with examples of interventionists who have charted courses that destroyed the very friends they sought to help.

(Gallaber 1973:478)

If any attempt to change the way of life of people carries moral and ethical implications, what, then, are the ethical responsibilities of the nutrition interventionist?

First, nutrition interventionists must protect their clients' rights and well-being. Whether counseling individual clients or designing programs for entire communities, nutritionists gain access to information about many aspects of people's lives, including their health problems, economic status, and religious beliefs, as well as their food practices. All client information, regardless of its apparent public or private nature, must be regarded as confidential. Most health clinics and programs have formed policies that protect client records from unwarranted exposure: only authorized personnel may review the information they contain, security is strictly enforced, and regulations dictate when and how they may be destroyed. Research data—questionnaires, interview notes and tapes—are protected in a similar fashion. However, despite this protection, records can be lost or stolen and the information abused. The professional, therefore, should record information only if it is required for intervention purposes. Confidentiality is of equal concern in preparing reports. Client or respondent names should never be used, and care should be taken to eliminate all information which might reveal the clients' identity. This may be difficult when summarizing research findings on small communities, groups or programs in which there is only one mayor, one nurse, or one diabetic teenager, for example, but especially important. Confidentiality is a cornerstone of codes of ethics of the American Dietetics Association, Society of Applied Anthropology, and most scientific and health care professional societies.

A second responsibility entails the use of scientific data rather than personal bias to advise clients and interpret conflicting or controversial information. For example, when someone asks for advice about low-sodium diets and their ability to prevent hypertension, the nutritionist should give a clear and balanced summary of nutrition knowledge currently available on the topic.

An appropriate answer might include a discussion of the statistical association found between salt intake and prevalence of hypertension in certain populations. The nutritionist might advise the client to reduce salt as a way of decreasing the *risks* of developing hypertension. However, it would be unethical to imply that a low-sodium diet will unequivocally prevent hypertension or claim that failure to reduce salt will necessarily cause high blood pressure. Such promises and overstatements are clear violations of the American Dietetics Association's Code of Ethics.

Because nutrition science is expanding rapidly, the interventionist has a responsibility to maintain current knowledge and skills through literature review and other continuing education activities. Most health professional societies now require members to participate in a specified number of hours of continuing education each year, thus encouraging them to assume their responsibility for professional competence.

A fourth area of knowledge for which the nutrition interventionist is held responsible concerns the clients needs, values, beliefs, and practices. In diet counseling, this may take the form of intake interviews and attentive listening, especially during initial sessions. Many dietitians ask their patients to bring a food diary and other basic information with them to the first counseling sessions. For some, the first session is devoted primarily to exploring patients' needs and expectations. We have noted, for example, that information on a person's typical diet patterns can be explored for insight into food preferences, meal patterns, and the social context of eating. Also valuable is an examination of the patient's perceptions of the new diet plan. Does the patient believe the diet is necessary? What difficulties are anticipated in following it? How could the diet be modified to overcome these problems?

Answers to these questions enable the dietitian to identify felt needs, benefits, and penalties associated with a diet plan and areas of incompatibility with existing beliefs and values and assists in making modifications and overcoming barriers to acceptance. Because this is a critical step in the counseling process, nutritionists must allocate the time and effort required to understand clients' special needs. Even if a large proportion of the counseling session is required to understand a patient, it is well worthwhile. Community nutrition programs may require even more extensive knowledge of potential adopters, including an understanding of local family structure, economic organization, political structure and religious beliefs and activities. As we have seen in Chapters 9 and 10, this information is essential for success in directing dietary change responsibly.

In addition to knowledge of client's needs, nutrition interventionists are responsible for respecting the ideas and values of the people they hope to change. Recipients of dietary advice are not "empty vessels" into which new information and advice is poured. All people have thoughts about what behaviors and attitudes they would and would not like to change.

We are reminded of the need to respect clients beliefs each time that science discovers the biochemical or physiological basis for a folk belief or remedy. For example, the traditional notion of fish as a "brain food" recently gained support when researchers at the Massachusetts Institute of Technology determined that choline, found in high levels in fish, stimulates the formation of acetylcholine in the brain, thus enhancing recall and improved memory in some individuals. Perhaps we should recall Foster's (1962:268) advice:

Uneducated peoples may be wrong on technical matters; they often are. But until we are sure they are wrong on a particular point, it is unwise and morally wrong to try to "improve" them. It is wrong to assume that a way, because it is modern, scientific and Western, is better than a traditional method.

The type of knowledge and respect for client's needs and interests referred to here prevents the enthusiastic interventionist from trying to change others without first considering their special problems, needs, and interests. As Art Gallaher (1973:437) reminds us: "It is indeed frustrating to be presented with solutions to problems of which one is not aware; more so to be presented with answers to questions that are not yet asked. Both are mistakes common to interventionists; in either case, the likelihood of confused and misinterpreted motives, and hence conflict is great. It follows that those who intervene to reduce tensions should be especially careful that by their actions they do not add to waters already troubled."

Because interventionists often have access to knowledge about the long-term and unintended consequences of change, they are responsible for assisting their clients in weighing the advantages and disadvantages of adopting new ideas or practices. Many innovations bring great short-term advantages but lead to other changes that cannot be avoided. Everywhere industrialization has had widespread effects on family structure and other societal patterns; it is not possible to reap the economic benefits without affecting social and political structures as well. Likewise, a shift from subsistence agriculture to a cash economy typically leads to increased consumption of nonnutritous, highly processed foods.

Additionally, nutrition interventionists often can anticipate the unintended consequences of change. Pesticide use in rice fields in the Philippines has increased yields but also has killed some of the wild greens and small animals that lived in the rice paddies and that people used for food. Interventionists in other communities considering the use of pesticides in rice production have a responsibility to inform people of the possible negative consequences.

Here, the duty of the nutrition interventionist is to determine the available alternatives and advise the people of *all* the consequences of their choices (Foster 1962:265). Once these duties are met responsibly, the interventionist must then respect the peoples' right to decide how they want to live. And at this point in the intervention process it is helpful to remember a segment from *Alice in Wonderland*: When Alice asked "would you tell me please, which way I might go from here?", the Cheshire Cat replied, "that depends on where you want to get to." The client, not the interventionist, should chart the course.

References

Acosta, P. B. and R. Aranda
>
> 1972 Cultural Determinants of Food Habits in Children of Mexican Descent in California. *In* Practices of Low-Income Families in Feeding Infants and Small Children. HEW Publication (HSA) 75–5605. Washington, D.C.: Government Printing Office; issued 1972, reprinted 1975.

Adams, David B., Phillip J. Michels, and David L. Keisler
>
> 1981 Intervention Strategies—Management of Obesity. *Journal of Family Practice* 12(6): 1063.

Adams, Richard N.
>
> 1955 A nutritional research program in Guatemala. *In* Benjamin D. Paul (ed.), Health, Culture, and Community, N.Y.: Russell Sage Foundation.

Alford, B. B. and E. B. Nance
>
> 1976 Customary Foods in the Navajo Diet. *Journal of the American Dietetic Association* 69: 5.

Allaby, Michael
>
> 1977 *World Food Resources: Actual and Potential.* London: Applied Science Publishers.

Altman, Nathaniel
>
> 1984 Vegetarian Basics. *Vegetarian Voice,* Dodgeville, N.Y., p. 1.

American Dietetic Association
>
> 1980 Cultural Food Patterns in the U.S.A. *In* Alice L. Tobias and Patricia J. Thompson (eds.), Issues in Nutrition for the 1980's: An Ecological Perspective, Monterey, CA.: Wadsworth Health Sciences Division, p. 244.

Ames, Bruce N.
>
> 1983 Dietary Carcinogens and Anticarcinogens. *Science* 221:1256.

Angier, Bradford
1974   *Field Guide to Edible Wild Plants.* Harrisburg, PA: Stackpole Books.

Apodaca, Anacelto
1952   Introduction of Hybrid Corn to Spanish American Farmers in New Mexico. *In* Edward Spicer (ed.), Human Problems in Technological Change: A Casebook. New York: Russell Sage Foundation.

Armelagos, George and J. R. Dewey
1970   Evolutionary Response to Human Infectious Diseases. *Bioscience* 157:638.

Atwater, W. O. and Charles Wood
1897   *1895–96 Food of the Negro in Alabama.* Alabama Agricultural Experimental Station Bulletin No. 3:15.

Barlow D.
1976   *Self-Report Measures.* Paper presented at the High Blood Pressure Education Research Program, New Orleans, Louisiana.

Barnett, H. G.
1953   *Innovation: The Basis of Cultural Change.* New York: McGraw-Hill Book Co.

Barth, Frederick
1969   *Ethnic Groups and Boundaries, the Social Organization of Cultural Difference.* Boston: Little, Brown, Co.

Bass, M. A. and Wakefield, L. M.
1974   Nutrient Intake and Food Patterns of Indians on Standing Rolls Reservation. *Journal of the American Dietetic Association* 64:36.

Bauwens, Eleanor E.
1978   *The Anthropology of Health.* St. Louis: C. V. Mosby Co.

Bengoa, J. M.
1964   Nutritional Rehabilitation Programs. *Journal of Tropical Pediatrics* 10:63.

Bentz, L. and D. Sanjur
1981   The Effects of Environmental Changes on Nutrient Intake Among Puerto Rican Families. *Federation Proceedings* 40(3).

Berg, Alan
1973   *The Nutrition Factor: Its Role in National Development.* Washington, D.C.: The Brookings Institution.

Bitar, K. and J. G. Reinbold
1972   Phytase and Alkaline Phosphotase Activities in Intestinal Mucosae of Rat, Chicken, Calf and Man. *Biochemica et Biophysica Acta* 268:442.

Black, Frances et al.
1974   Evidence for Persistence of Infectious Agents in Isolated Human Populations. *American Journal of Epidemiology* 100:230.

Blakkan, Renee
1983   To Know "What's Cooking," Ask a Teenager. *Advertising Age,* August 1, 1983: M–38 and M–39.

Blumberg, Roe Lesser
1981   Females, Farming and Food: Rural Development and Womens' Participation in Agricultural Production Systems. *In* Barbara C. Lewis (ed.) *Invisible Farmers: Women and the Crisis in Agriculture.* Washington, D.C., Office of Women in Development, Agency for International Development.

Black, Francis, et al.
1974   Evidence for Persistence of Infectious Agents in Isolated Human Populations. *American Journal of Epidemiology* 100:230.

Bondar, Barry and P. J. Bobey
1978   Should We Eat Krill? *In* Joan Gussow (ed.), *The Feeding Web: Issues in Nutritional Ecology.* Palo Alto, CA: Bull Publishing Co.

Borlaug, Norman
1983   Contributions of Conventional Plant Breeding to Food Production. *Science* 219:689.

Bowden, S.
1968   *Nutritional Beliefs on Food Practices of Mexican-American Mothers.* Thesis, Department of Home Economics, Fresno State College.

Bradfield, R. B. and T. Brun
1970   Nutritional Status of California Mexican-Americans. *American Journal of Clinical Nutrition* 23:798.

Bradfield, R. B. and D. Coltrin
1970   Some Characteristics of the Health and Nutritional Status of California Negroes. *American Journal of Clinical Nutrition* 23:420.

Brady, Nyle C.
1982   Chemistry and World Food Supplies. *Science* 218(4515):847.

Bressani, Richardo and Nevin Schrimshaw
1958   Effect of Lime Treatment on In Vitro Availability of Essential Amino Acids and Solubility of Protein Fractions in Corn. *Journal of Agricultural and Food Chemistry* 6:744.

Brody, Jane E.
1981   *Jane Brody's Nutrition Book.* New York: W. A. Norton and Company.

Brown, Antoinette B.

1981   Assessment of Paleonutrition from Skeletal Remains: The Research Potential of Anthropological Museum Collections. *In* Anne-Marie Cantrell, James B. Griffin and Nan Rothschild (eds.) Annals of the New York Academy of Sciences 376:405. New York: New York Academy of Sciences.

Brown, Lester R. and Gail W. Finsterbusch

1972   *Man and His Environment: Food.* New York: Harper and Row.

Brown, M. L. and C. H. Ho

1975   Low-Income Groups in Hawaii. *In* Practices of Low Income Families in Feeding Infants and Children with Particular Attention to Cultural Subgroups. Washington, D.C.: HEW Publication 75.

Brown, M. L. and S. F. Adelson

1969   Infant Feeding Practices Among Low and Middle-Income Families in Honolulu. *Tropical and Geographic Medicine* 21:63.

Brownell, Kelly D. and Albert J. Stunkard

1981   Couples Training, Pharmacotherapy, and Behavior Therapy in the Treatment of Obesity. *Archives of General Psychiatry* 38:1224.

Brownell, Kelly D., Carol L. Heckerman, Robert J. Westlake, Steven C. Hayes, and Peter M. Monti

1978   The Effects of Couples Training and Partner Cooperatives in the Behavioral Treatment of Obesity. *Behavioral Research and Therapy* 16:323.

Brownell, Kelly D., Jane H. Kelmar, and Albert J. Stunkard

1983   Treatment of Obese Children With and Without Their Mothers: Changes in Weight and Blood Pressure. *Pediatrics* 71(4)515.

Brownlee, Ann T.

1978   *Community, Culture and Care—A Cross-Cultural Guide for Health Workers.* St. Louis: C. V. Mosby.

Bruhn, C. M. and R. M. Pangborn

1971   Food Habits of Migrant Farm Workers in California. *Journal of the American Dietetic Association* 59:347.

Brunson, R. T.

1962   Socialization Experiences and Socioeconomic Characteristics of Urban Negroes as Related to Use of Selected Southern Foods and Medical Remedies. *Dissertation Abstracts* 23:1824.

Bryant, Carol A.

1984   Implication of Support Networks on Breastfeeding Practices: Implications for Program Development. *In* Judith D. Gussler and Carol A. Bryant (eds.) Helping Mothers to

Breastfeed: Program Strategies for Minority Communities. *Health Action Papers No. 1* Lexington, Kentucky, Lexington-Fayette County Health Department and Department of Behavioral Science College of Medicine, University of Kentucky.

Bryant, Carol A.
1982   Impact of Kin, Friend and Neighbor Networks on Infant Feeding Practices. *Social Science and Medicine* 16:1757.
1981   *Nutrition Change of the Month Program Report.* Unpublished Report Submitted to the Kentucky State Department of Education.
1978   *The Impact of Kin, Friend and Neighbor Networks on Infantile Obesity.* University of Kentucky, Lexington, KY, unpublished dissertation.
1975   The Puerto Rican Mental Health Unit. Psychiatric Annals 5:8.
1974   *The Practicum: My Experience as Consultant to the Child Development Services of Dade County, Florida, Summer 1974.* Unpublished manuscript available from author.

Bryant, Carol A. and Cathy Peterjohn
1978   *Nutrition Education as Culture Change.* Paper presented at the Eleventh Annual Meeting of the Society for Nutrition Education. Minneapolis, Minnesota, July 16–19.

Bryant, Carol A., Lynn Johnson, and John van Willigen
1981   *Nutrition Component Report.* Report submitted to the National Institute on Aging.

Bryant V. M., Jr. and G. Williams-Dean
1976   The Coprolites of Man. *Avenues of Antiquity: Readings from Scientific American.* San Francisco: W. H. Freeman and Co.

Burroughs, A. L. and R. L. Huenemann
1970   Iron Deficiency in Rural Infants and Children. *Journal of the American Dietetic Association* 57:122.

Bunce, G. Edwin
1969   Milk and Blindness in Brazil. *Natural History* 78(2):52.

Burma, John H., ed.
1970   *Mexican-Americans in the United States.* Cambridge, MA.: Schenkman.

Busse, C. D.
1977   Chimpanzee Predation as a Possible Factor in the Evolution of Red Colobus Monkey Social Organization. *Evolution* 31:907.

Caliendo, Mary Alice
1979   *Nutrition and the World Food Crisis.* New York: MacMillan Publishing Co.

Campbell, K. O.
1975   *Food for the Future.* Lincoln, NB: University of Nebraska Press.

Cardenas, Jose, et al.
1976   Nutritional Beliefs and Practices in Primagravida Mexican-American Women. *Journal of the American Dietetic Association* 69:262.

Carlile, W. K., et al.
1972   Contemporary Nutritional Status of North American Indian Children. *In* W. M. Moore, M. M. Silverberg, and M. S. Read (eds.), Nutrition, Growth and Development of North American Indian Children. Washington, D.C.: HEW Publication (NIH) 72.

Casey, P. and I. Harrill
1977   Nutrient Intake of Vietnamese Women Relocated in Colorado. *Nutrition Reports International* 16:687.

Cassel, John
1957   Social and Cultural Implications of Food and Food Habits. *American Journal of Public Health* 47:732.

Cassidy, C. M.
1982   Subcultural Prenatal Diets of Americans. *In* Alternative Dietary Practices and Nutritional Abuses in Pregnancy. Proceedings of a Workshop. Washington, D.C.: National Academy Press, p. 25.
1980   Nutrition and Health in Agriculturalists and Hunters and Gatherers. *In* Norge Jerome, Randy Kandel, Gretel Pelto (eds.), Nutritional Anthropology. New York: Redgrave Publishing Co.

Chan, Michelle
1977   *A Preliminary Survey of the Food Habits of Chinese in Manhattan, New York.* Cornell University, Ithaca, New York, Senior Honors Thesis.

Chang, B.
1974   Some Dietary Beliefs in Chinese Folk Culture. *Journal of the American Dietetics Association* 65(4):436.

Chang, K. C., ed.
1978   *Food in Chinese Culture: Anthropological and Historical Perspectives.* New Haven, CN: Yale University Press.

Chrispeels, Maarten J. and David Sadava
1977   *Plants, Food, and People.* San Francisco: W. H. Freeman.

Christakis, George (ed.)
1973   Nutritional Assessment in Health Programs. *American Journal of Public Health* 63, Part II.

Christopher, Carol
1980   The Case Against Fortifying Foods. *CNI Weekly* 10(28):4.

Chou, Marilyn and David P. Harmon
1979   *Critical Food Issues of the Eighties.* New York: Pergamon Press.

Clark, M.
    1959   *Health in the Mexican American Culture: A Community Study.* Berkeley, CA: University of California Press.
Clark, Margaret and L. M. Wakefield
    1975   Food Choices of Institutionalized and Independent-Living Elderly. *Journal of the American Dietetic Association* 66:600.
Clark, Sir W. E. LeGros
    1960   *Antecedants of Man: An Introduction to the Evolution of Primates.* Chicago: Quadrangle Books.
Cloud, Kathleen
    1978   *Sex Roles in Food Production and Distribution Systems in the Sahel.* Paper presented at the International Conference on Women and Food. University of Arizona, Tucson.
Coale, M. S.
    1971   *Factors Influencing the Food Habits of Negro Preschool Children in the Inner City.* Cornell University, Ithaca, New York, M.S. thesis.
Cohn, Theodore
    1979   *Canadian Food Aid: Domestic and Foreign Policy Implications.* Monograph Series in World Affairs. Denver, CO: University of Denver.
Colon, Mirta
    1981   *Home Food Production and Household Income as Predictors of Nutritional Status of Puerto Rican Preschool Children and Their Mothers.* University of Puerto Rico Medical Campus, Rio Piedrus, M.S. Thesis.
Community Nutrition Institute
    1979   *CNI Weekly Report* May 24, 1979; p. 4.
Community Systems Foundation
    1979   *An Evaluation Report of the P.L. 480, Title II, Program in India.* Report submitted to Office of Food for Peace, Agency for International Development.

Cooley, M. J. E.
    1978   Design, Technology and Production for Social Needs. *In* Ken Coates (ed.), The Right to Useful Work. Nottingham, England: Spokesman Books.

Connelly, Debra and Joel Hanna
    1978   *Cultural Perceptions of Obesity Among A Samoan Migrant Population: A Preliminary Report.* A paper presented at the 77th Annual Meetings of the American Anthropological Association, 1978, Los Angeles, California.

Cornely, P. B., and S. K. Bigman
    1961   Cultural Considerations in Changing Health Attitudes. *Medical Annals of the District of Columbia* 30:191.

Cornucopia Project
1981   *Organic Paths to Food Security.* Emmaus, PA.: Rodale Press.

Council on Environmental Quality and the Department of State
1980   *Global 2000 Report to the President of the U.S.: Entering the 21st Century.* Volume Two: The Technical Report. Washington, D.C.: Government Printing Office, 1980–1981.

Courtney, Anita
1984   Status and Potential of Fruit and Vegetable Production in the Kentucky Bluegrass Region. Lexington-Fayette County Health Department, Lexington, Kentucky.
1983a   Cooking for Health. *The Community Nutritionist* II (1):1.
1983b   *Eat Better for Less.* Brochure published by Lexington-Fayette County Health Department, Lexington, Kentucky.

Courtney, Anita and Barbara A. Markesbery
1983   Food Co-ops: Windows to the Community. *The Community Nutritionist* 11(5):19.

Cosminsky, Sheila
1975   Changing Food and Medical Beliefs and Practices in a Guatemalan Community. *Ecology of Food and Nutrition* 4(3):183.

Crittenden, Ann
1981   Food and Hunger Statistics Questioned. New York Times, Oct. 5, 1981: p. 10.

Crosson, Pierre R.
1975   Institutional Obstacles to Expansion of World Food Production. *Science* 188:519.

Crosswell, Michael
1981   *Growth, Poverty Alleviation, and Foreign Assistance.* AID Discussion Paper No. 39 (August).

Cussler, M. and M. deGive
1952   *Twixt the Cup and the Lip.* New York: Twayne.

Czajkowski, J. M.
1971   Puerto Rican Foods and Traditions. Storrs, CT: Cooperative Extension Service, University of Connecticut.
1964   Mexican Foods and Traditions. Storrs, CT: Connecticut Agricultural Extension Service.

Dagley, Beverly D.
1976   Adult Education Minicourse in Nutrition Involves Groups. *Journal of Nutrition Education* 8(2)79.

Darby, W. J., C. G. Salsbury, W. J. McGanity, H. F. Johnson, E. B. Bridgforth and H. R. Sanstead
1960   Study of the Dietary Background and Nutrition of the Navajo Indian. *Journal of Nutrition* 60 (Supplement 2).

deLumley, Henry

1969   A Paleolithic Camp of Nice. *Scientific American* 220(5):42.

1975   *Nutrition Canada: The Ontario Survey Report*. Report from Nutrition Canada by the Bureau of Nutritional Sciences.

Devadas, R. P. and A. Radharukmani

1965   The Effects of a Balanced Lunch Program on the Growth and Nutritional Status of School Children. *Nutrition Reviews* 23(2):35.

DeWalt, Billie

1984   *The Cultural Ecology of Development: Ten Precepts for Survival*. Lexington: University of Kentucky, unpublished manuscript.

1983a   The Cattle Are Eating The Forest. *Bulletin of the Atomic Scientists* 39:18.

1983b   *Mexico's Second Green Revolution: Food for Feed*. Mexican Studies/Estudios Mexicanos 1:25.

DeWalt, Kathleen Musante

1983   *Nutritional Strategies and Agricultural Change in a Mexican Community*. Ann Arbor: UMI Research Press.

Dickins, Dorothy

1928   A Nutrition Investigation of Negro Tenants in the Yazoo Mississippi Delta. *Mississippi Agricultural Experimental Station Bulletin* No. 254:5.

Division de Nutricion del Instituto Nacional de la Nutricion

1969   Habitos de Alimentacion en una Region Fronteriza. *Salud Publica de Mexico,* No. 11.

Dube, S. C.

1958   *India's Changing Villages: Human Factors in Community Development*. Bombay: Allied Publishers Private Limited.

Dubos, Rene

1980   *Man Adapting*. New Haven, CT: Yale University.

Dugdale, A. E. and D. P. Doessel

1980   A Simulation Model of Infant Feeding and Family Economics in Developing Countries. *Journal of Policy Modeling* 2:345.

Dunbar, Jacqueline M. and Albert J. Stunkard

1979   Adherence to Diet and Drug Regimen. *In* R. Levy, B. Rifkind, B. Dennis and N. Ernst (eds.), Nutrition, Lipids and Coronary Heart Disease. New York: Raven Press.

Dunbar, Jacqueline, Gary D. Marshall, and Mel F. Hovell

1979   Behavioral Strategies for Improving Compliance. *In* R. B. Haynes, D. W. Taylor, and D. L. Sackett (eds.), Compliance in Health Care. Baltimore, MD: Johns Hopkins Press.

Duncan, E. R., ed.

1977   *Dimensions of World Food Problems.* Ames: Iowa State University Press.

Dunn, Frederick

1968   Epidemiologic factors: Health and Disease in Hunter-Gatherers. *In* R. B. Lee and I. DeVore (eds.), Man the Hunter. Chicago: Aldine Press.

Duyff, R. L., D. Sanjur, and H. Y. Nelson

1975   Food Behavior and Related Factors of Puerto Rican-American Teenagers. *Journal of Nutrition Education* 7(3).

Eckholm, Erik

1978   Vanishing Firewood. *Human Nature* May, 1978, p. 58.

Ehrlich, Paul, Anne H. Ehrlich, and John P. Holdren

1977   *Ecoscience:* Population, Resources, Environment. San Francisco: W. H. Freeman and Company.

Etkin, Nina L. and Paul J. Ross

1983   Malaria, Medicine, and Meals: Plant Use Among the Hausa and Its Impact on Disease. *In* Romanucci, Ross et al. (eds.) *The Anthropology of Medicine: From Culture to Method.* New York: Praeger Publisher.

Epstein, Emanuel, Jack D. Norlyn, Dale W. Rush, Ralph W. Kingsbury, David B. Kelley, Glen A. Cunningham, and Anne F. Wrona.

1980   Saline Culture of Crops: A Genetic Approach. *Science* 210(24):399.

Fagen, Richard R.

1978   Equity in the South in the Context of North-South Relations. *In* Albert Fishlow, et al. (eds.), Rich and Poor Nations in the World Economy. New York: McGraw-Hill.

FAO

1982   *Malnutrition: Its Nature, Magnitude and Policy Implications.* COAG/83/6, December, 1982.

1968   *The State of Food and Agriculture 1968.* Rome: United Nations Food and Agriculture Organization.

Farb, Peter and George Armelagos

1980   *Consuming Passions: The Anthropology of Eating.* Boston: Houghton Mifflin Co.

Fathauer, George H.

1960   Food Habits—an anthropologist's view. *Journal of the American Dietetic Association* 37:335.

Fenichel, Allen and Azfa Kahn

1981   The Burmese Way to "Socialism." *World Development* 9:813.

Fernandez, N., et al.

1968   *A Nutrition Survey of Five Rural Puerto Rican Communities.* University of Puerto Rico, Rio Piedras, School of Medicine, mimeo.

Fernandez, N., et al.

1965   Nutritional Status of People in Isolated Areas of Puerto Rico. Survey of Barrio Mavilla, Vega Alta, Puerto Rico. *American Journal of Clinical Nutrition* 17:305.

Fernandez, Nelson A.

1975   Nutrition in Puerto Rico. *Cancer Research* 35(3272).

Filer, L. J. and E. F. Colesa

1978   Multimedia Education About Infant Nutrition for Physicians. *Journal of the American Dietetic Association* 72:404.

Fitzgerald, Thomas K.

1979   Southern Folk's Eating Habits Ain't What They Used To Be . . . If They Ever Were. *Nutrition Today* July/August, 16.

Fitzpatrick-Nietschmann, Judith

1983   Pacific Islanders—Migration and Health. *The Western Journal of Medicine* 139(6):848.

Flannery, Kent V.

1971   Archeological Systems Theory and Early Mesoamerica. *In* Stuart Streuven (ed.), Prehistoric Agriculture. New York: The Natural History Press.

Flatz, G. and H. W. Rotthauwe

1973   Lactose Nutrition and Natural Selection *Lancet.* 2:16.

Forman, M. R.

1979   *Breast and Bottle Feeding in the U.S.: 1979 National Natality Survey.* Unpublished manuscript.

Foster, George M.

1979   Humoral Traces in United States Folk Medicine, *Medical Anthropology Newsletter* 10(2):17.

1962   *Traditional Cultures and the Impact of Technological Change.* New York: Harper and Row.

Foster, George and B. G. Anderson

1978   *Medical Anthropology.* New York: John Wiley & Sons.

Franke, Robert G. and Dorothy N. Franke

1975   *Man and the Changing Environment.* New York: Holt, Rinehart and Winston.

Frankle, Revat and Anita Yanuchik Owen

1978   *Nutrition in the Community: The Art of Delivering Services.* St. Louis: The C. V. Mosby Company.

Fremouw, W. J., and R. E. Zilter

1980   Individual and Couple Behavioral Contracting for Weight Reduction and Maintenance, *Behavioral Therapist* 3:15.

French, J. G.

1967   Relationship of Morbidity to the Feeding Patterns of Navajo Children from Birth Through Twenty-Four Months. *American Journal of Clinical Nutrition* 20:375.

Freeman, L. G.

1975 "Acheulian Sites and Stratigraphy in Iberia and the Maghreb." *In* K. W. Butor and G. L. L. Isaac (eds.), After the Australopithecines. The Hague: Mouton.

Frisancho, Robert A.

1981 *Human Adaptation: A Functional Interpretation.* Ann Arbor: University of Michigan Press.

Gallaher, Art

1973 Intervention: Changing the System. *In* Thomas Weaver's To See Ourselves: Anthropology and Modern Social Issues. Scott, Foresman and Company, Glenview, Illinois.

1961 *Plainville Fifteen Years Later.* New York: Columbia University Press.

Gallup Poll

1979 Gardens for All News. Burlington, Vermont.

Gandhi, Mohandas K.

1954 *How To Serve the Cow.* Ahmedabad. Navajivan Publishing House.

Gaisford, John (ed)

1978 *Atlas of Man.* New York: St. Martin's Press.

Garrity, Thomas F.

1981 Medical Compliance and the Clinician-Patient Relationship: A Review *Social Science and Medicine* 158:215.

Gaulin, Steven J. C. and Melvin Konner

1977 On the Natural Diet of Primates, Including Humans. *In* R. J. Wurtman and J. J. Wurtman (eds.), Nutrition and the Brain, vol. 1. New York: Raven Press.

Geertz, Clifford

1965 Religion as a Cultural Symbol. *In* W. A. Lessa and E. Z. Vogt (eds.), Reader in Comparative Religion (2nd ed.) New York: Harper and Row.

Geile, Janet Zollinger

1979 Changing Sex Roles and Family Structure. *Social Policy* 9(4):32.

Gibbons, Euell and Gordon Tucker

1979 *Euell Gibbons' Handbook of Wild Plants.* Virginia Beach, VA: The Donning Company.

Gifft, Helen H., M. B. Washban, Gail G. Harrison

1972 *Nutrition, Behavior and Change.* Englewood Cliffs, N.J.: Prentice Hall, Inc.

Gillin, John

1972 Variety in Food Customs. *In* Charles C. Hughes (ed.) *Make Men of Them: Introductory Readings for Cultural Anthropology.* Chicago: Rand McNally and Company.

The Global 2000 Report to the President:

1980 *Entering the 21st Century. Volume 2: The Technical Report Washington, D.C.:* Prepared by the Council on Environment Quality and the Department of State. Gerald Barney, Study Director 1980-81.

Goldberger, J. and G. A. Wheeler
1915   Experimental pellagra in human subjects brought about by restricted diet. *Public Health Reports* 30:3336.
1928   Experimental black tongue in dogs and its relation to pellagra. *Public Health Reports* 43:172.

Goldblait, Phillip B., Mary E. Moore and Albert J. Stunkard
1965   Social Factors in Obesity. *Journal of American Medical Association* 192:1042.

Goldschmidt, Walter
1968   Theory and Strategy in the Study of Cultural Adaptability. *In* Yehudi, Cohen (ed.), Man in Adaptation: The Cultural Present. Chicago:Aldine.

Goodenough, Ward Hunt
1966   *Cooperation in Change: An Anthropological Approach to Community Development.* New York:John Wiley and Sons, Inc.

Gordon, Bertram M.
1983   "Why We Choose the Foods We Do." *Nutrition Today.* March/April:17.

Greist, Ellen and Barbara Markesbery
1979   Making News: A Nutrition Education Happening. *Journal of Nutrition Education* 11(2): p. 90.

Griffin, Keith
1974   *The Political Economy of Agrarian Change: An Essay on the Green Revolution.* Cambridge Harvard University Press.

Gross, Daniel and B. Underwood
1971   Technological Change and Calorie Costs. *American Anthropologist* 73:725.

Gussow, Joan Dye
1978   Whatever Happened to Food or Does it Pay to Fool Mother Nature? *In* Joan Gussow (ed.) *The Feeding Web.* Palo Alto, California: Bull Publishing Company.

Haas, Jane D. and Gail G. Harrison
1977   Nutritional Anthropology and Biological Adaptation. *Annual Review of Anthropology.* 6:69.

Hakim, Perer and Giorgio Soliman
1978   *Development, Reform and Nutrition in Chile.* Cambridge, Massachussets: The MIT Press.

Hamilton, Eva May and Eleanor Whitney
1982   *Nutrition: Concepts and Controversies,* 2nd ed. St. Paul, Minnesota: West Publishing Company.

Hampton, M. C., R. L. Huenemann, L. R. Shapiro, and B. W. Mitchell
1967   Caloric and Nutrient Intakes of Teenagers. *Journal of the American Dietetic Association* 50:385.

Harding, Robert S. O. and Geza Teleki

1981 *Omnivorous Primates: Gathering and Hunting in Human Evolution.* New York: Columbia University Press.

Harrill I., C. Ervers, and C. Schwartz

1976 Observations on Food Acceptance by Elderly Women. *Gerontologist* 16(4): 349.

Harlan, Jack R.

1975 *Crops and Man.* Madison, WI: American Society of Agronomy, Crop Science Society of America.

Harris, Ben Charles

1973 *Eat the Weeds.* New Caanan, CT: Keats Publishing Co.

Harris, La Donna

1972 The Heritage of North American Indians. *In* W. M. Moore, et al. (eds.), Nutrition, Growth and Development of North American Indian Children. Washington, D.C.: HEW Publication (NIH).

Harris, Marvin

1980 *Culture, People and Nature: An Introduction to General Anthropology,* 3rd ed. New York: Harper & Row Publishers.

1975 *Culture, People, Nature: An Introduction to General Anthropology,* 2nd ed. New York: Thomas Crowell.

Harris, Robert and Harry von Loesecke (eds.)

1975 *Nutritional Evaluation of Food Processing,* 2nd ed. Westport, CT: AVI Publishing Co.

Harris, Robert T.

1983 Bulimarexia and Related Serious Eating Disorders with Medical Complications. *Annals of Internal Medicine* 99:800.

Harwood, Alan

1971 The Hot-Cold Theory of Disease: Implications for Treatment of Puerto Rican Patients. *Journal of the American Medical Association.* 216(7):1153.

Harwood, Alan, ed.

1981 *Ethnicity and Medical Care.* Cambridge, MA: Harvard University Press.

Haynes, R. B.

1976 A Critical Review of the Determinants of Patient Compliance with Therapeutic Regimens. *In* D. L. Sackett and R. B. Haynes (eds.), Compliance With Therapeutic Regimens. Baltimore: Johns Hopkins University Press.

Henricksen, B. and H. D. Cate

1971 Nutrient Content of Food Served versus Food Eaten in Nursing Homes. *Journal of American Dietetic Association* 59:126.

Hetzel, Basil

1978 The Changing Nutrition of Aborigines in the Ecosystem

of Central Australia. *In* B. S. Hetzel and H. J. Firth, The Nutrition of Aborigines in Relation to the Ecosystem of Central Australia. Melbourne, Australia: Commonwealth Scientific and Industrial Research Organization.

Heyneman, Donald

1971 Mis-aid to the Third World: Disease Repercussions Caused by Ecological Ignorance. *Canadian Journal of Public Health* 62:303.

Hoebel, E. Adamson and Everett Frost

1976 *Cultural and Social Anthropology.* New York: McGraw Hill Book Co.

Hogbin, Herbert I.

1958 *Social Change.* London: Watts.

Honigmann, John J.

1959 *The World of Man.* New York: Harper & Row.

International Bank for Reconstruction and Development

1982 *World Report.* Washington, D.C.: International Bank for Reconstruction and Development.

Innis, Donald Q.

1980 The Future for Traditional Agriculture. *Focus* (a publication of the American Geographical Society) 30(3):1.

International Society for Krishna Consciousness

1983 *Higher Taste: A Guide to Gourmet Vegetarian Cooking and a Karma-Free Diet.* Los Angeles: The Bhaktivedanta Book Trust.

Jackson, Jacqueline J.

1981 *Urban Black Americans.* In Alan Harwood (ed.), Ethnicity and Medical Care. Cambridge: Harvard University Press.

Jackson, Tony and Deborah Eade

1982 *Against the Grain: The Dilemma of Project Food Aid.* Oxfam: Oxford. Oxford, England: Oxfam.

Jacobson, N. L. and G. N. Jacobson

1977 Animals—Potentials and Limitations for Human Food. *In* E. R. Duncan (ed.), Dimensions of World Food Problems. Ames, IA: Iowa State University Press.

Jelliffe, D. B.

1957 Social Culture and Nutrition: Cultural Blocks and Protein Malnutrition in Early Childhood in Rural West Bengal. *Pediatrics* 20:128.

Jelliffe, D. B. and E. F. P. Jelliffe

1978 *Human Milk in the Modern World: Psychosocial, Nutritional and Economic Significance.* New York: Oxford Press.

1977 Breast is Best. Modern Meaning. *New England Journal of Medicine* 297(17):912.

Jenkins, David J. A.
1981 Dietary Fiber and Other Antinutrients: Metabolic Effects and Therapeutic Implications. *In* Gene Spiller (ed.), Nutritional Pharmacology. New York: Alan R. Liss, Inc.

Jerome, N. W.
1981 The U.S. Dietary Pattern From An Anthropological Perspective. *Food Technology* (February):37.
1980 Diet and Acculturation—The Case of Black American In-Migrants. *In* N. W. Jerome, R. F. Kandel, and G. H. Pelto (eds.), Nutritional Anthropology. Pleasantville, NY: Redgrave.
1979 Changing Nutritional Styles Within the Context of the Modern Family. *In* D. P. Hymovich and M. A. Barnard (eds.), Family Health Care, 2nd ed. New York: McGraw Hill.
1975 On Determining the Food Patterns of Urban Dwellers in Contemporary United States Society. *In* Margaret L. Arnott (ed.), Gastronomy: The Anthropology of Food and Food Habits. The Hague: Mouton Publishers.
1970 American Culture and Food Habits. *In* J. Dupont (ed.), Dimensions of Nutrition. Boulder: Colorado University Press, p. 223.
1969 Northern Urbanization and Food Consumption Patterns of Southern-Born Negroes. *American Journal of Clinical Nutrition* 22:12.

Jerome, N. W., G. H. Pelto and R. F. Kandel
1980 An Ecological Approach to Nutritional Anthropology. *In* N. Jerome, R. Kandel, and G. H. Pelto (eds.), Nutritional Anthropology: Contemporary Approaches to Diet and Culture. Pleasantville, NJ: Redgrave Publishing Company.

Johnston, Francis E.
1982 *Physical Anthropology*. Wm. C. Brown Co. Publishers.

Jones, R. E. and H. Schendel
1966 Nutritional Status of Selected Negro Infants in Greenville County, South Carolina. *American Journal of Clinical Nutrition* 18:407.

Kahn, P.
1976 One and Two-Member Household Feeding Patterns. *Food Product Development* 10(8):22.

Kaplan, Laurence
1971 Archaeology and Domestication in American Phaseolus (Beans). *In* Stuart Struever (ed.), Prehistoric Agriculture. New York: Natural History Press.

Kart, C. S., et al.
1978 *Aging and Health: Biologic and Social Perspectives*. Reading, Massachussets: Addison-Wesley Publishing Co.

Katz, D. and M. T. Goodwin

1980 The Food System: From Field to Table. *In* Alice L. Tobias and Patricia J. Thompson (eds.), Issues in Nutrition for the 1980's. Belmont, CA: Wadsworth, Inc.

1976 *Food: Where Nutrition Politics and Culture Meet: An Activities Guide for Teachers.* Washington, D.C.: Center for Science in the Public Interest.

Katz, S. H., M. L. Heidger, and L. A. Valleray

1974 Traditional Maize Processing Techniques in the New World. *Science* 184:765.

Katz, Solomon H.

1983 Food, Behavior and Biocultural Evolution. *In* Lewis M. Barker (ed.), The Psychobiology of Human Food Selection, Westport, CT: AVI Publishing Co.

Katz, Solomon H. and J. Schall

1979 Fava Bean Consumption. *Medical Anthropology,* Fall:459.

Keys, Thomas, et al.

1950 *The Biology of Human Starvation.* Minneapolis, MN: University of Minnesota Press.

Keys, Thomas, et al.

1983 Geophagia as a cause of maternal death. *Obstetrics and Gynecology* 6(4)525.

Kidd, Ross

1979 Folk Theater: One Way or Two Way Communication? *Development Communication Report.* No. 28, October.

King, Clarence

1965 *Working with People in Community Action: An International Casebook for Trained Community Workers and Volunteer Community Leaders.* New York: Associated Press.

King, Kendall W.

1971 Mother Craft Centers Combine Nutrition and Social Sciences. *Journal of Nutrition Education* 3(Summer):9.

Kluckholn, Clyde

1968 *Mirror for Man: A Survey of Human Behavior and Social Attitudes.* Greenwich, CT: Fawcett Publications.

Knapp, Thomas R.

1983 A Methodological Critique of the "Ideal Weight" Concept. *Journal of the American Medical Association* 250(4)506.

Knight, Mary Ann, et al.

1969 Nutritional Influence of Mexican American Foods in Arizona. *Journal of American Dietetic Association* 55:557.

Knutson, Ronald D., J. B. Penn, and William T. Boehn

1983 *Agricultural and Food Policy.* Englewood Cliffs, NJ: Prentice-Hall, Inc.

Kodicek, E. and P. W. Wilson
1959   The Availability of Bound Nicotinic Acid to the Rat. I. Effect of Limestone Treatment of Maize and Subsequent Baking into Tortilla. *The British Journal of Nutrition* 13:418.

Kolars, Joseph, Michael Levih, Aonji Mostafa, Dennis Savaiano
1984   Yogurt—An Autodigesting Source of Lactose. *New England Journal of Medicine* 310(1):1.

Kottak, Conrad Phillip
1982   *Anthropology: The Exploration of Human Diversity,* 3rd ed. New York: Random House.

Kotz, Nick
1970   *Let Them Eat Promises: The Politics of Hunger in America.* Garden City, New York: Doubleday Anchor Books.

Kuhnlein, H. V., and D. H. Calloway
1977   Contemporary Hopi Food Intake Patterns. *Ecology of Food and Nutrition* 6:159.

Kusum, Nair
1962   Blossoms in the Dust: The Human Factor in Indian Development. New York: Praeger Publishing.

Lackey, Carolyn
1983   Pica During Pregnancy. *Contemporary Nutrition* 8(11).

Langlois, J.
1972   Mooncake in Chinatown, New York City: Continuity and Change. *New York Folklore Quarterly* 28:83.

Lantz, E. M. and P. Wood
1958   Nutrition of New Mexican, Spanish-American, and Anglo Adolescents. I. Food Habits and Nutrient Intakes. *Journal of the American Dietetic Association* 34:138. II. Blood Findings, Height and Weight Data and Physical Condition. *Journal of the American Dietetic Association* 34:145.

Lappé, Frances Moore
1982   *Diet for a Small Planet.* New York: Ballantine Books.

Lathan, Michael
1978   Nutrition and Culture. *In* Beverly Winikoffs (ed.), Nutrition and National Policy. Cambridge, MA: The MIT Press.

Learner, R. and V. R. Kivett
1981   Discriminators of Perceived Dietary Adequacy and the Rural Elderly. *Journal of the American Dietetic Association* 78:330.

Lee, Richard B.
1968   What Hunters Do For a Living, or How to Make Out on Scarce Resources. *In* Richard B. Lee and I. deVore (eds.), Man The Hunter, Chicago: Aldine.

Leininger, Madeline

1970   Some Cross Cultural Universal and Non-Universal Functions, Beliefs, and Practices of Food. *In* J. Dupont (ed.) Dimensions of Nutrition. Boulder: Colorado University Press.

Lenski, Gerhard Emmanuel

1970   *Human Societies: A Macrolevel Introduction to Sociology.* New York: McGraw-Hill.

Lewin, K.

1958   Group Decision and Social Change. *In* E. Maccoby, T. M. Newcomb, E. L. Hartley (eds.), Readings in Social Psychology. New York: Holt, Rinehart and Winston.

Lewis, Jane S. and Maria Fe Glaspy

1975   Food Habits and Nutrient Intakes of Filipino Women in Los Angeles. *Journal of the American Dietetic Association* 67:122.

Lewis, Oscar

1958   *Village Life in Northern India: Studies in a Delhi Village.* New York: Vintage Books.

Ley, P., et al.

1977   Psychological Studies of Doctor-Patient Communication. *In* S. Rachman (ed.), Contributions to Medical Psychology. Oxford, England: Pergamon.

1976   Improving Doctor-Patient Communication in General Practice. *Journal of the Royal College of General Practitioners* 26:720.

Livingstone, F. B.

1958   Anthropological Implications of Sickle-Cell Gene Distribution in West Africa. *American Anthropologist* 60:533.

Loeb, Al

1975   Evolution of Nutrition Programs. School of Public Health Social Work, University of California at Berkeley. Cited in R. T. Frankle and A. Y. Owen, *Nutrition in the Community: The Art of Delivery Services.* St. Louis: C. V. Mosby Co. (1978), p. 257.

Lynch, G. W.

1970   Food and Cultism in Modern Western Society. *In* G. Blix (ed.), Food Cultism and Nutrition Quackery, Symposia of the Swedish Nutrition Foundation. Uppsala: Almquist and Wiksells.

Mann, Alan E.

1981   Diet and Human Evolution. *In* Robert Harding and Geza Teleki (eds.), Omnivorous Primates. New York: Columbia University.

Mann, George V., Ann Spoerry, Jarasha W. Gray
1971 Atherosclerosis in the Masai. *American Journal of Epidemiology* 96:26.

Mann, N. S. and S. K. Mann
1983 Lactose Malabsorption. *American Journal of Proctology Gastroenterology and Colon and Rectal Surgery,* Dec. 10:28.

Mann, V. R.
1966 Food Practices of the Mexican-American in Los Angeles County, including a Method for Evaluating the Diet (revised). Los Angeles: Los Angeles County Health Department.

Manoff, Richard
1973 Potential Uses of Mass Media in Nutrition Programs. *Journal of Nutrition Education* 5(2):125.

Marei, Sayed Ahmed
1978 *The World Food Crisis.* London: Longman.

Margen, S., et al.
1974 Studies in Calcium Metabolism. The Calciuretia Effect of Dietary Protein. *American Journal of Clinical Nutrition* 27:584–89.

Marquess, Carriemae
1977 *Food Habits of Black Americans.* Ithaca, New York: Cornell University, unpublished paper, Division of Nutritional Sciences.

Marshall, Lorna
1976 *The !Kung of Nyae Nyae.* Cambridge, MA: Harvard University Press.

Martin, E. A. and A. A. Coolidge.
1978 *Nutrition in Action.* New York: Holt, Rinehart and Winston.

Martin, Norman
1980 *News release.* College Station, TX: Texas A & M University, Office of Public Information.

Martinez, G. S. and D. A. Dodd
1983 1981 Milk Feeding Practices in the U.S. during the First Twelve Months of Life. *Pediatrics* (71)2:166.

Massara, E. B. and S. J. Stunkard
1979 A Method of Quantifying Cultural Ideals of Beauty and the Obese. *International Journal of Obesity* 3(2):149.

Masur, Frank T.
1981 Adherence to Health Care Regimens. *Medical Psychology Contributions to Behavioral Medicine* New York: Academic Press.

May, Jacques and Donna McClellan
1972 *The Ecology of Malnutrition in Mexico and Central America.* New York: Hafner Publishing Co.

Mayer, J.
1965   The Nutritional Status of American Negroes. *Nutrition Reviews* (23) 161.

McCracken, R.
1971   Lactase deficiency: An Example of Dietary Evolution. *Current Anthropology* 12:479.

McDonald, B.
1965   *Nutrition of the Navajo,* 2nd ed. Window Rock, AZ: U.S. Public Health Services, Division of Indian Health, Window Rock Field Office.

McIntosh, William Alex and Peggy A. Shiffleet
1984   The Impact of Religious Social Support on the Dietary Behavior and Dietary Adequacy of the Aged. *Review of Religious Research,* in press.

McLaren, D. S.
1952   Influence of Protein Deficiency and Sex on the Development of Ocular Lesions and Survival Time of the Vitamin A Deficient Rat. *British Journal of Opthalmology* 43:234.

McNamara, Robert
1977   *Accelerating Population Stabilization through Sound and Economic Progress.* Washington, D.C.: Overseas Development Council Development Paper No. 24.
1973   *One Hundred Countries, Two Billion People: The Dimensions of Development.* New York: Praeger Publishers.

McRobie, George
1981   *Small is Possible.* New York: Harper & Row.

Mesteri, Mahmoud
1979   Speech, U.N. Assembly. Quoted *in* W. W. Murdoch, The Poverty of Nations. Baltimore: Johns Hopkins University Press, 1980, p. 319.

Meyer-Rochow, V. B.
1973   Edible Insects in Three Different Ethnic Groups of Papua and New Guinea. *American Journal of Clinical Nutrition* 26:673–77.

Meyerhoff, Eleanor and Alice Tobias
1980   The Technological Impact on the Food Supply. *In* Alice Tobias and Patricia J. Thompson (eds.), Issues in Nutrition for the 1980's. Belmont, CA: Wadsworth, Inc.

Miller, Fred D.
1983   *Out of the Mouths of Babes: The Infant Formula Controversy.* Bowling Green, Ohio: The Social Philosophy and Policy Center.

Minear, Larry
1975   *New Hope for the Hungry?: The Challenge of the World Food Crisis.* New York: Friendship Press.

Molina, Sergio
1983   Comments on Economic Growth, Income Distribution and Hunger and Social Development in Latin America. *In* Barbara Underwood (ed.), Nutritional Intervention Strategies in National Development. New York: Academic Press.

Monckeberg, Fernando
1983   Nutrition Intervention: Basic Concepts. *In* Barbara Underwood (ed.), Nutrition In Intervention Strategies in National Development. New York: Academic Press.

Moore, Carl V., Robert S. Goodhart and Maurice E. Shils
1973   Iron. *In* Carl V. Moore, Robert S. Goodhart and Maurice E. Shils (eds.), Modern Nutrition in Health and Disease. Philadelphia: Lea and Febiger pp. 300.

Moore, W. M., M. M. Silverberg, and M. S. Read, eds.
1972   *Nutrition, Growth, and Development of North American Indian Children.* Washington, D.C.: HEW Publication (NIH) 72.

Moragne, Lenora
1969   *Influence of Household Differentiation on Food Habits Among Low Income Urban Negro Families.* Ithaca, New York: Cornell University, Ph.D. Dissertation.

Moran, Emilio F.
1982   *Human Adaptability: An Introduction to Ecological Anthropology.* Boulder, CO: Westview Press.

Murai, Mary M.
1975   Discussion Section—Low Income Groups in Hawaii. *In* Practices of Low-Income Families in Feeding Infants and Small Children with Particular Attention to Cultural Subgroups. Washington, D.C.: HEW Publication 75–5605.

Murdoch, William W.
1982   *The Poverty of Nations: The Political Economy of Hunger and Population.* Baltimore, MD: Johns Hopkins University Press.

Muller, M.
1974   *The Baby Killers.* War on Want Coalition, London, England.

Nance, E. B.
1972   Food Consumption of 200 Navajo Adults Receiving USDA Donated Foods. Denton, Texas: Texas Women's University, M.S. Thesis.

National Research Council
1982   *Diet, Nutrition and Cancer.* Washington, D.C.: National Academy Press.

National Research Council
1977   *World Food and Nutrition Study: Potential Contributions of Research.* Washington, D.C.: National Academy of Sciences.

Nelli, Humbert S.

1976   *The Business of Crime*. Oxford University Press.

Nelson, Harry and Robert Jurmain

1979   *Introduction to Physical Anthropology*. St. Paul, MN: West Publishing Company.

Newark, Stephen and Beverly Williamson

1983   Survey of Very-Low Calorie Weight Reduction Diets. *Archives of Internal Medicine* 143:1423.

Newcomer, A. D., H. S. Park, D. C. O'Brien, D. B. McGill

1983   Response of Patients with Irritable Bowel Syndrome and Lactase Deficiency Using Unfermented Acidophilus Milk. *American Journal of Clinical Nutrition* 38:257.

Newcomer, Albert D. and Douglas B. McGill

1984   Clinical Importance of Lactase Deficiency. *The New England Journal of Medicine* 310(1):42.

Nichols, B. L. and V. N. Nichols

1981   Human Milk: Nutritional Resource. *In* R. C. Tsang and B. L. Nichols (eds.), *Nutrition and Child Health*. New York: Alan R. Liss, Inc.

Nicholson, Heather Johnson, and Ralph L. Nicholson

1979   *Distant Hunger: Agriculture, Food, and Human Values*. West Lafayette, IN: Purdue University.

Nong The Anh, Tran Kiem Thuc, and Jack D. Welsh

1977   Lactose Malabsorption in Adult Vietnamese. *American Journal of Clinical Nutrition* 30:468.

Nutrition Action

1981   Peggy Charren: The 'Kid Vid' Crusader. *Nutrition Action* 8(3):8.

Nutrition Week

1983   Vol. XIII, No. 36.

Ogg, Clayton and Arnold Miller

1981   *Minimizing Erosion on Cultivated Land: Concentration of Erosion Problems and the Effectiveness of Conservation Practices*. Washington, D. C.: USDA.

Oomen, HAPC, et al.

1964   A Global Survey of Xerophthalmia, Epidemiology and Public Health Aspects of Hypervitaminosis A. *Tropical and Geographical Medicine* 16:271.

Orr, Elizabeth

1977   The Contribution of New Food Mixtures to the Relief of Malnutrition. *Food and Nutrition* 3(2):2.

1972   *The Use of Protein-Rich Foods for the Relief of Malnutrition in Developing Countries: An Analysis of Experience*. London: Tropical Products Institute.

O'Rourke, A. Desmond

1981   *The Changing Market for Food Away from Home and Its Implications for Washington Producers and Processors*.

Pullman, Washington: Washington State University College of Agriculture Research Center Bulletin 0894.

Orwell, S. and J. Murray
1974   Infant Feeding and Health in Ibandan. *Journal of Tropical Pediatrics and Environmental Child Health* 20:205.

Owen, G. M., et al.
1972   Nutrition Survey of White Mountain Apache Preschool Children. *In* W. M. Moore, M. Silverberg, and M. S. Read (eds.), Nutrition, Growth, and Development of North American Indian Children. Washington, D.C.: HEW Publication (NIH) 72–26.

Paddock, William and Paul Paddock
1967   *Famine, 1975! America's Decision: Who Will Survive?* Boston: Little, Brown.

Parker, S. L., and J. Bowering
1976   Folacin in Diets of Puerto Rican and Black Women in Relation to Food Practices. *Journal of Nutrition Education* 8(2).

Pelto, Gretel
1981   Anthropological Contributions to Nutrition Education Research. *Journal of Nutrition Education* 13(1):52.

Pelto, Gretel and Pertti Pelto
1976   *Food and Culture in Contemporary Society.* Paper presented at the workshop: Our Daily Bread: Changing Priorities and Human Concerns.

Perelman, Michael
1976   Efficiency in Agriculture: The Economics of Energy. *In* Richard Mervill (ed.), Radical Agriculture. New York: Harper & Row.

Perrett, Heli, E. Sagasti
1977   *Nutrition Education In Bolivia: Guidelines For Planning At the National Level and A Mass Media Pilot Research Design.* Washington, D.C.: Academy for Educational Development, S2–S8.

Peterson, Mary A.
1975   Indian and Alaska Native Low-Income Groups. *In* Practices of Low-Income Families in Feeding Infants and Small Children With Particular Attention to Cultural Subgroups. Rockville, MD: HEW Publication (HSA) 75–5605.

Pilbeam, David
1984   The Descent of Hominoids and Hominids. *Scientific American* 250(3):84.

Pimentel, Carmencita
1976   *An Evaluation of Food Habits of a Selected Group of Filipinos of Preschool Age in the Washington, D.C. Metropolitan Area.* Washington, D.C.: Howard University, M.S. thesis.

Pimentel, David and Marcia Pimentel
1979   *Food, Energy and Society.* London: Arnold.

Pimentel, David, P. A. Olteracu, M. C. Nesheim, John Krummel, M. S. Allen, and Sterling Chick
1980   The Potential for Grain-Fed Livestock: Resource Constraints. *Science* 27:843.
1980   Counting Kilocalories. *American Geographical Society,* 30(3):9.

Plucknett, Donald and Nigel J. H. Smith
1982   Agricultural Research and Third World Food Production. *Science* 217:215.

Poleman, Thomas
1981   A Reappraisal of the Extent of World Hunger. Food Policy. November 1981:236–52.

Poleman, Thomas T.
1975   World Food: A Perspective. *In* Philip H. Abelson, (ed.) Food: Economics, Politics, Nutrition and Research. Washington, DC: American Association for the Advancement of Science (AAAS).

Popkin, Barry M., Richard E. Bilsborro, John S. Akin, and Monica E. Yamatuoto
1983   Breastfeeding Determinants in Low-Income Countries. *Medical Anthropology* (Winter):1.

Presidential Commission on World Hunger (PCWH)
1980   *Overcoming World Hunger: The Challenge Ahead. Report of the Presidential Commission on World Hunger.* Washington, D.C.: Superintendent of Documents.

Public Health Service
1982   *Prevention 82.* Washington D.C.: U.S. Department of Health and Human Resources, PHS, Office of Disease Prevention and Health Promotion, DHS No. 82–50157.

Quandt, Sara A.
1984   Nutritional Thriftiness and Human Reproduction: Beyond The Critical Body Composition Hypothesis. *Social Science and Medicine* 19:177.

Rabinowicz, H.
1971   Modern Views Of The Dietary Laws. *Encyclopedia Judaica Jerusalem* 6:26.

Raphael, Dana
1976   *A Design For Improving Infant Feeding Practices In Third World Countries With Special References To Breastfeeding.* Westpont, CT: Human Lactation Center, unpublished manuscript.

Rappaport, Roy
1968   *Pigs For The Ancestors: Ritual In The Ecology Of A New Guinea People.* New Haven: Yale University Press.

Rawlins, N. Omri
1980   *Introduction To Agribusiness.* Englewood Cliffs, NJ: Prentice-Hall, Inc.

Read, Margaret
1966   *Culture, Health and Disease.* London: Tavistock Publishing, J. B. Lippincott Co.

Redclift, Michael
1981   *Development Policymaking in Mexico: The Sistema Alimentario Mexicano (SAM).* Program in United States-Mexican Studies, working paper in U.S.-Mexican Studies, 24. San Diego: University of California.

Regelson, Stanley
1976   The Bagel: Symbol and Ritual At The Breakfast Table. *In The American Dimension: Cultural Myths and Social Realities.* W. Arens and Susan P. Montague (eds.). Port Washington, NY: Alfred Publishing Co., Inc., pp. 124.

Reichel-Dolmatoff, Geraldo and Alicia Reichel-Dolmatoff
1961   *The People of Aritama: The Cultural Personality of a Colombian Mestizo Village.* Chicago: University of Chicago Press.

Richards, Cara E.
1972   *Man In Perspective: An Introduction to Cultural Anthropology.* New York: Random House.

Ritenbaugh, Cheryl
1978   Human Foodways: A Window on Evolution. *In* Eleanor Bauwens (ed.), Anthropology of Health. St. Louis: C. V. Mosby Co.

Roberts, L. J., and R. Stefani
1949   *Patterns of Living in Puerto Rican Families.* Rio Piedras, Puerto Rico: University of Puerto Rico Press.

Robinson, Corinne H. and Marilyn R. Lawler
1977   *Normal and Therapeutic Nutrition.* 15th Edition. New York MacMillan Publishing Co.

Rodale, Robert
1982   *The Cornucopia Papers.* Emmaus, PA: Rodale Press.

Rody, Nancy
1978   Things Go Better With Coconuts—Program Strategies in Micronesia. *Journal of Nutrition Education* 10(1):19 (Jan-Mar).

Rogers, Everett and F. Floyd Shoemaker
1971   *Communication of Innovations.* New York: Free Press.

Root, Waverly and Richard de Rochemont
1976   *Eating In America/A History.* New York: William Morrow and Co.

Rosenthal B., G. J. Allen and C. Winter
1980   Husband Involvement in the Behavioral Treatment of Overweight Women: Initial Effects and Long-Term Follow-Up. *International Journal of Obesity* 4:165.

Royce, William
1975   Food From The Waters. *In* Business Communication Co., Can Business Help Solve the World Food Problems? BCC First Annual Food Conference, New York, March 19.

Rozovski, S. Jaime
1983   Nutrition for Older Americans, *Nutrition and Health,* 5(3):1.

Sanderson, F.
1975   The Great Food Fumble. *In* Philip H. Abelson, Food: Politics, Economics, Nutrition and Research. Washington, D.C.: American Association for the Advancement of Science (AAAS).

Sandoval, Julio
1978   Supplementary Feeding Intervention: A Program to Protect Population Groups at High Nutritional Risk in the Republic of Panama. *In* Beverly Winikoff (ed.), Nutrition and National Policy. Cambridge, MA: MIT Press.

Sanjur, D., et al.
1972   *A Community Study of Food Habits and Socio-Cultural Factors of Families Participating in the East Harlem Nutrition Education Program.* Ithaca, New York: Cornell University, New York State College of Human Ecology Research Report. Cornell University.
1970   Infant Feeding and Weaning Practices in a Rural Pre-Industrial Setting. *Acta Pediatrica Scandinavica Supplement* 200.

Sanjur, Diva
1982a   *Social and Cultural Perspectives in Nutrition.* Englewood Cliffs, NJ: Prentice-Hall, Inc.
1982b   Ethnicity and Food Habits. *In* Social and Cultural Perspectives in Nutrition. Englewood Cliffs, NJ: Prentice-Hall, Inc.
1970   *Puerto Rican Food Habits.* Ithaca, NY: Cornell University.

Sanjur, D., J. Cravioto and A. Van Veer
1970   Infant Nutrition and Socio-Cultural Influences in a Village in Central Mexico. *Journal of Tropical and Geographical Medicine* 22:443.

Sanjur, D., E. Romero, and M. Kira
1971   Milk Consumption Patterns of Puerto Rican Pre-School Children in Rural New York. *American Journal of Clinical Nutrition* 24:1320.

Saynor, R., D. Verel and T. Gillott
1984   The Long-Term Effect of Dietary Supplementation With Fish Lipid Concentrate on Serum Lipids, Bleeding Time, Platelets and Angina. *Atherosclerosis* 50:3.

Schumacher, E. F.
1977   Technology for a Democratic Society. Speech given at

International Conference at Caux, Switzerland. *In* George McRobie, Small is Possible. New York: Harper & Row (1981).

Schwartz, Barton M. and Robert H. Ewald

1968   *Culture and Society: An Introduction to Cultural Anthropology.* New York: The Ronald Press Co.

Scott, E. M.

1956   Nutrition of Alaskan Eskimos. *Nutrition Reviews.* 14:1.

Scrimshaw, Nevin and Vernon Young

1980   The Requirements of Human Nutrition. *In* Alice L. Tobias and Patricia J. Thompson (eds.), Issues in Nutrition for the 1980s. Monterey, CA: Wadsworth Health Sciences Division.

Segal, I., et al.

1983   Lactase deficiency in the South African Black Population. *American Journal of Clinical Nutrition* 38(6):901.

Senyas, C. T., N. E. Johnson, P. J. Elmer, J. K. Allington, and M. E. Matthews

1982   A Dietary Survey of 14 Wisconsin Nursing Homes. *Journal of the American Dietetic Association* 81:35.

Serrin, William

1980   Let Them Eat Junk. *Saturday Review,* Feb. 2, pp. 17.

Sheils, Merrill

1983   A Portrait of America. *Newsweek* 101:20 (Jan.17).

Shostak, Marjorie

1981   *Nisa: The Life and Words of a !Kung Woman.* Cambridge, MA: Harvard University Press.

Shapiro, L. R., R. L. Huenemann, and M. C. Hampton

1962   Dietary Survey for Planning a Local Nutrition Program. *Public Health Reports* 77:257.

Silverberg, M. M.

1972   The Future of Native Americans. *In* W. M. Moore, et al. (eds.), Nutrition, Growth and Development of North American Indian Children. Washington, D.C.: HEW Publication (NIH) 72–26.

Simon, Julian

1981   *The Ultimate Resource.* Princeton, NJ: Princeton University Press.

1980   Resources, Population, Environment: An Oversupply of False Bad News. *Science* 208(4451):1431.

Simons, Lewis W.

1981   From Quinto to Delphin, the World Bank is More Than a Global Money Store. *Smithsonian* 12(3):60.

Simoons, F. J.

1983   Geography and Genetics as Factors in the Psychobiology of Human Food Selection. *In* Lewis M. Barker (ed.), The Psychobiology of Human Food Selection. Westport, CT: AVI Co.

1971   The Antiquity of Dairying in Asia and Africa. *Geographical Review.* 61:431.

1970a   Primary Adult Lactose Intolerance and the Milking Habit: A Problem in Biological and Cultural Interrelations II: A Culture Historical Hypothesis. *American Journal of Digestive Diseases* 15:695.

1970b   The Traditional Limits of Milking and Milk Use in Southern Asia. *Anthropos* 65:547.

1961   Eat Not This Flesh. Madison, WI: University of Wisconsin Press.

Sinha, Radha

1976   *Food and Poverty: The Political Economy of Confrontation.* New York: Holmes and Meier Publishers.

Smith, D. S. and M. L. Brown

1970   Anthropology in Preschool Children in Hawaii. *American Journal of Clinical Nutrition* 23:932.

Spencer, Robert F.

1959   *The North Alaskan Eskimo: A Study in Ecology and Society.* Washington, D.C.: Bureau of American Ethnology Bulletin 1971.

Stahl, Ann B.

1984   Hominid Dietary Selection Before Fire. *Current Anthropology* 25(2):151.

Steinhart, John and Carol Steinhart

1978   Energy Use in the U.S. Food System. *In* Joan Gussow (ed.), The Feeding Web. Palo Alto, CA: Bull Publishing Co.

Stini, William A.

1975   Adaptive Strategies of Human Populations Under Nutritional Stress. *In* Elizabeth S. Watts, Frances E. Johnston, and Gabriel W. Lasker (eds.), Biosocial Interrelations in Population Adaptation. The Hague: Mouton Publishers.

Stunkard, Albert J.

1981   Adherence to Medical Treatment: Overview and Lessons from Behavioral Weight Control. *Journal of Psychosomatic Research* 25(3):187.

Svarstad, B.

1974   *The Doctor-Patient Encounter: An Observational Study of Communication and Outcome.* Madison, Wisconsin: University of Wisconsin, Ph.d. dissertation.

Szalai, Alexander

1973   *The Quality of Family Life—Traditional and Modern: A Review of Sociological Findings in Contemporary Family Organization and Role Differentiation in the Family.* Paper presented at the U.N.'s Interregional Seminar on the Family in a Changing Society: Problems and Responsibilities of Its Members. London, July 18–31.

Tannahill, Reay

1973   *Food in History*. New York: Stein and Day.

Taylor, Lawrence

1976   Coffee: The Bottomless Cup. *In* W. Arens and Susan P. Montague (eds.), The American Dimension. Port Washington, NY: Alfred Publishing.

Taylor, Theodore W.

1970   *The States and Their Indian Citizens*. Washington, D.C.:, Government Printing.

Teleki, Geza

1981   The Omnivorous Diet and Eclectic Feeding Habits of Chimpanzees in Gombe National Park, Tanzania. *In* Robert S. O. Harding and Geza Teleki (eds.), Omnivorous Primates: Gathering and Hunting in Human Evolution. New York: Columbia Press.

Tillotson, J. L., et al.

1973   Epidemiology of Coronary Heart Disease and Stroke in Japanese Men Living in Japan, Hawaii, and California: Methodology for Comparison of Diets. *American Journal of Clinical Nutrition* 26:177.

Tirado, Nilda

1978   *The Changing Puerto Rican Diet: Implication for Nutrition Education*. Paper presented at the Ethnic Foods Symposium, New York Medical College.

Underwood, Jane

1979   *Human Variation and Human Micro-Evolution. Englewood Cliffs, N.J.:* Prentice Hall.

UNICEF (United Nations Children's Fund)

1983   *The State of the World's Children 1982–83*. Executive Director of the United Nations Children's Fund. United Nations.

United States Department of Agriculture (USDA)

1980   *Report and Recommendations on Organic Farming*. Washington, D.C.

1976   Agricultural Outlook. *Research Service,* AO-16. Washington, D.C.

1961   Livestock Production Units, 1910–1961. *Statistical Bulletin* No. 325.

Valverde, Victor, Reynaldo Marlorell, Victor Mejia-Pivaral, Hernan Delgado, Aaron Lechtiq, Charles Teller, and Robert Klein

1977   Relationship Between Land Availability and Nutritional Status. *Ecology of Food and Nutrition* 6:1.

Vander, Arthur J.

1981   *Nutrition, Stress and Toxic Chemicals*. Ann Arbor: University of Michigan Press.

Van Duzen, J., J. P. Carter, J. Secondi, and C. Federspiel
1969 Protein and Calorie Malnutrition Among Preschool Navajo Indian Children. *American Journal of Clinical Nutrition* 22:1362.

van Willigen, John v., Carol A. Bryant, James S. Boster, and Thomas Arcury
1984 *Doin' the Hogwork: An Ethnohistorical Study of the Domain of Food Preservation in the Hills of the Bluegrass Region of Kentucky.* Unpublished manuscript.

Waldmann, E.
1980 The Ecology of the Nutrition of the Bapedi, Sekhukuniland. *In* Robson, J. R. K. (ed.), Food, Ecology and Culture. London: Gordon and Breach Science Publishers.

Waldram, James B.
n.d. *Hydro-Elective Development and Dietary De-localization in Northern Manitoba, Canada:* Human Organization, in press.

Walker, Alan, Henduch N. Holch, and Linda Perez
1978 Microwear of Mammalian Teeth as An Indicator of Diet. *Science* 210(8):908–10.

Walker, Burnese
1975 *Selected Factors Influencing the Food Habits of Black American Females in Ithaca, New York.* Ithaca, New York: Cornell University, M.S. Thesis.

Wallace, Anthony F. C.
1966 *Religion: An Anthropological View.* New York: Random House.

Wallace, H. M.
1973 The Health of American Indian Children. *Clinical Pediatrics* 12–83.

Walsh, John
1975 U.S. Agribusiness and Agricultural Trends. *Science* 188:531–34.

Wang, David W.
1983 *Pediatric Care in a Multiethnic Indochinese Community.* Paper presented at the Care and Counseling of Ethnic Minorities, Patients' Conference sponsored by Ross Laboratories, Washington, D.C., June 13.

Ward, Gerald M., Thomas M. Sutherland, and Jean M. Sutherland
1980 Animals as an Energy Source in Third World Agriculture. *Science* 208 (May 9).

Weidman, Hazel H.
1978 *Miami Health Ecology Project Report, Vol. 1.* Miami: Department of Psychiatry and Department of Pediatrics, University of Miami School of Medicine.

Weiss, B.

1980 Nutrition Adaptation and Cultural Maladaption: An Evolutionary View. *In* N. W. Jerome, R. F. Kandel, and G. H. Pelto (eds.), Nutritional Anthropology: Contemporary Approaches to Diet and Culture. Pleasantville, NY: Redgrave Publishing Co.

Wellhausen, Edwin J.

1976 The Agriculture of Mexico. *Scientific American* 235:128.

Wenkam, Nao S. and Robert J. Wolff

1970 A Half Century of Changing Food Habits Among Japanese in Hawaii. *Journal of the American Dietetic Association* 57:29.

Werner, David and Bill Bower

1982 *Helping Health Workers Learn.* Palo Alto, CA: Hesparian Foundation.

West, Donald

1978 Food Expenditures by Food Stamp Participants and Non-Participants. *In* National Food Review, United States Department of Agriculture.

West, Kelly, M.

1973 Diet Therapy of Diabetics: An Analysis of Failure. *Internal Medicine* 79:425.

1977 Diabetes in American Indians. *In* H. Bennet and M. Miller (eds.) Epidemiology of Diabetes, Advances in Metabolic Diseases New York: Academic Press.

White House Conference on Food, Nutrition, and Health

1970 *Report of Subpanel on American Indians and Alaska Natives: Eskimos, Indians and Aleuts.* Final Report, Washington, D.C.

Whiteman, J.

1966 The Function of Food in Society. *Nutrition* 20:4.

Whitney, Eleanor and Eva May Hamilton

1981 *Understanding Nutrition,* 2nd ed. St. Paul, MN: West Publishing Co.

1977 *Understanding Nutrition.* St. Paul, MN: West Publishing Co.

Willet, Joseph W.

1983 *Recent Developments in The World Food Situation.* Lexington: University of Kentucky Department of Agricultural Economics, Staff paper #152.

Wilson, C. Anne

1973 *Food and Drink in Britain From the Stone Age to Recent Times.* London: Constable.

Wilson, Christine S.

1973 Food Taboos of Childbirth: The Malay Example. *Ecology of Food and Nutrition* 2(4), 267.

Winikoff, Beverly
    1978   Nutrition and National Policy. Cambridge, MA: MIT Press.
Witschi, Jelia, Martha Singer, Marion Wu-Lee, and Frederick J. Stare
    1978   Family Cooperation and Effectiveness in a Cholesterol-Lowering Diet. *Journal of American Dietetic Association* 72:384.
Wolf, Eric
    1956   San Jose: A Traditional Coffee Plantation. *In* Julian H. Stewart (ed.), The People of Puerto Rico: A Study in Social Anthropology. Urbana, IL: University of Illinois Press.
Wood, Corinne Shear
    1979   *Human Sickness and Health: A Biocultural View.* Palo Alto, CA: Mayfield Publishing Co.
Woodcock, B. E., W. H. Lambert, W. M. Jones, J. H. Galloway, M. Greaves, and F. E. Preston
    1984   Beneficial Effect of Fish Oil on Blood Viscosity in Peripheral Vascular Disease. *British Medical Journal* 288(6417):592.
World Bank
    1978   *World Development Report.* Washington, D.C.: World Bank.
World Bank
    1980   *World Bank Annual Report.* Washington, D.C. World Bank.
Yanochik, A. V., et al.
    1976   The Comprehensive Nutrition Action Program in Arizona. *Journal of the American Dietetic Association* 69:37.
Young, James Harvey
    1970   Historical Aspects of Food Cultism and Nutrition Quackery. *In* Gunnar Blix (ed.), Food Cultism and Nutrition Quackery. Symposium of the Swedish Nutrition Foundation, VIII. Uppsala: Almquist and Wiksell.
Zborowski, Mark and Elizabeth Herzog
    1962   *Life is With People: The Culture of the Shtetl.* New York: Schocken.

Index

Boldfacing indicates the page on which the term is defined in the margin.

Acclimatization, **221**
Acid rain, **248**
Acre-foot, **263**
Action for Children's Television (ACT), 406
Adaptation to environment:
  by humans, 7-16
    behavioral, 7-9, 13-16
    cultural, 8-9, 13-16. *See also*
      Food technologies
    culture as, 79-87
    Eskimo, 30
    genetic, 7, 11-16, 35-38
    physiological, 7, 9-11, 13-16, 30
    in response to scientific revolution, 62-64
  by primates, 17-21
    dietary, 19-21
  See also Human evolution
Additives, 59-60, 144-145
Adolescence, food in, 163-166
Adopters of change, potential, in dietary change process, 334-343, 346-348
Adulteration of food, 59-60
Advertising campaigns for nutritional programs, 382-387
Advertising of foods, 388-389
Advocacy, consumer, as nutrition strategy, 405-409
Advocates for change in dietary change process, 334-335, 343-348
Aerobic, defined, **264**

Aged. *See* Elderly
Agrarian reform in world food crisis, 298-300. *See also entries beginning with* Land
Agricultural productivity in food production, 259-263. *See also* Food production
Agricultural revolution, 41-53. *See also* Green Revolution
Agricultural technology. *See* Agricultural revolution; Green Revolution
Agriculture:
  defined, 115
  and horticulture, continuum between, 115n. *See also* Horticulture
  in Tehuacan Valley, Mexico, 42-44, 46-47
  types of:
    industrialized. *See* Industrialized agriculture
    intensive, 115-121
    mechanized, in developing countries, 260-261
    peasant (traditional), 116-119, 261-263. *See also* Peasant societies
    slash-and-burn, 109, 231-233
  See also Food production; Food technology(ies)
Ague, **221**
Alcohol and Prohibition, 90
Alkali, **46**
Allergies to food, 360, 361
Alum, **59**
AMANA, 401
American Dietetics Association's

Diabetic Exchange system, 350-357
Amino acids, 45-46
Amulets, **105**
Anchovy industry in Peru, 271
Anemia:
  and Glucose–6–Phosphate Dehydrogenase deficiency, 14-15
  iron deficiency, 169, 290
Animals:
  domestication of, 42-44
  ruminant, **112**
  See also Beef; Livestock production; Meat eating
Anorexia nervosa, 95
Anthropologists, biological, **6**
Antibodies, 430
Antihelminthic agents, **223**
Appetites, influences on, 78
Appropriate (intermediate) technologies, 327-330
Aquaculture in food production, 274
Artifacts, **84-85**
Ashanti of West Africa, 151
Asian American food practices, 199-200
Assets, **296**
Atherosclerosis, 115
Australian aborigines, 213, 214
Australopithecines in human evolution, 25
Authority dependence of potential adopters of change, 336-337
Awls, **29**

Balance of trade, 316-317

Bands in foraging societies, 105
Bantu and Pygmy food trade, 156
Beans in agricultural development,
    44-47
Beauty and culture, 93-95
Beef:
    consumption of, 78, 134-135,
        218-291. *See also* Meat
        eating
    raising, history of, 133-134. *See
        also* Livestock production
    slaughter of, Hindus forbidden,
        218-219
Before Present (B.P.), **25**
Behavior:
    cultural versus individual, 8
    culture as guide for, 82-84
    culture expressed through, 84-85
Behavioral adaptation to
    environment, 7-9, 13-16
Beliefs:
    cultural, 83-84
    current, and dietary innovations,
        357-358
    about food, in dietary change,
        341. *See also* Food taboos
    health, systems of, 220-231
        alternative, 229-231
    See also Ideological basis of food
        practices
Beriberi (vitamin B$_1$ deficiency) 61,
    111
Bering Strait, **43**
Bilateral economic development
    assistance, 305
Biological anthropologists, **6**
Biological influences on diets,
    76-78, 172, 174-175
Biomedical concepts in Puerto
    Rico, 228-229
Biomedical health model, **220**
Birth rates and family planning
    programs, 253-257
Black Americans, food practices of,
    198-199
Blood, pastoralist reliance on, 114,
    115
Body image:
    and culture, 93-98
    and health, 95-96
Body size in physiological
    adaptation, 10-11
Body weight:

cultural ideas about, 96-98
    and obesity, 63-64, 94-95
    during pregnancy, 166
Bonding of mothers and infants, 431
Bootlegging, **90**
Boundary maintenance in ethnicity,
    183
B.P. (Before Present), **25**
Bread, white, 60. *See also* Grains;
    Semidwarf wheat
Bread-starchy vegetable exchange
    for diabetics, 353-354
Breakfast and lunch programs for
    schools, 191-192, 391-393,
    396-397
Breastfeeding, 347-348, 425-431.
    See also La Leche League
Bretton Woods Agreement, 316
Britain, enclosure in, 54
Bulimia, 95-96
Buying clubs, 132, 135

CAB (Community Advisors for
    Breastfeeding Mothers),
    347-348, 428-429
Calcium:
    in physiological adaptation, 9-10
    in vegetarian diets, 70
Calories:
    empty, **164**
    in fast foods, 165
    in physiological adaptation, 10-11
    See also Protein/calorie
        malnutrition (PCM)
Cambridge Diet, 93
Canning, effects of, 58-59. *See
    also* Food(s), preservation
    of
Capital-intensive technologies, 328
Carcinogens, **16**
Caribou, **107**
Carnassials, **22**
Carnivores, 21, 22. *See also*
    Beef, consumption of; Meat
    eating
Cash crops, 119-121
Castes and food, 179-181
Cattle. *See* Beef; Livestock
    production; Meat eating
Center for Science in the Public
    Interest (CSPI), 406
Centrifuging, **23**

Century plants, **43**
Cesarean birth, **167**
Ceviche, **78**
    CGIAR (Consultative Group on
        International Agricultural
        Research), 310
Change. *See* Dietary change process;
    Directed change
Chemical fertilizers, 124, 264-265,
    280, 281
Chemical pesticides and herbicides,
    124, 265-267, 281
Child Nutrition Act of 1966, 191
Children:
    consumer advocacy groups for,
        406
    in developing countries,
        malnourishment of, 286-288
    food for, 162-163
    food programs for, 190-193, 364,
        393-394, 426-428
    mortality rates of, 290-291, 293,
        296
    nutrition newsletter for, 389
    See also Infants, feeding; *entries
        beginning with* Infant
Children's Foundation, The, 406
Chilean milk distribution program,
    393-394
Chitlings, **350**
Chutney, **76**
CIMMYT (International Maize
    and Wheat Improvement
    Center), 279-281, 310
Clay eating (geophagia), 168-170
Clients in diet counseling, 372-377
Climate in food production, 267
CNI (Community Nutrition
    Institute), 406
Colonial foods, 52-53
Colonization in developing
    countries, 291-293
Commodity assistance in economic
    development, 305-309
Commodity food distribution, 193
Commodities, **303**
Communication in nutrition
    education, 237-241, 382-391
Community Advisors for Breast-
    feeding Mothers (CAB),
    347-348, 428-429
Community Nutrition Institute
    (CNI), 406

Communities:
  dietary innovation reactions of,
    366
  in nutrition programs:
    diagnosis by, 413-418
    representatives from, 417-418,
      420
    responses to hunger by, 193-194
Condensed milk, 60
Confidentiality in ethics, 433
Consultative Group on International
    Agricultural Research (CGIAR),
    310
Consumer advocacy as nutrition
    strategy, 405-409
Contracts with clients in diet
    counseling, 374
Co-ops, food, 132, 135
Coprolite analysis, 23-24
Corn:
  in agricultural development,
    44-47
  high-yield varieties of, 280
  in United States, yields of, 261
  See also CIMMYT (International
    Maize and Wheat
    Improvement Center)
Cornucopia Project, 132
Coronary heart disease, 115
Corporations in farming, 125-126
Counseling in dietary change
    process, 371-377
Cow's milk versus breastfeeding,
    430. See also Beef; Meat
    eating
Credibility of advocates for change,
    348
Credit in resource distribution,
    301-303
Crops:
  cash, 119-121
  diversity of, loss of, 281
  genetic uniformity of, 122-123,
    301, 303
  intercropping of, 118, 261, 262
  mixed cropping of, 118-119
  monocropping of (monoculture),
    122-123, 261
  multiple, 124
  See also specific entries, for
    example: Corn;
    Semidwarf wheat
C-sections, 167

CSPI (Center for Science in the
    Public Interest), 406
Cuarentena, la, 170-171
Cuisines, national, 55-56. See also
    Ethnicity and food
Cultural adaptations to environment,
    8-9, 13-16. See also Food
    technologies
Cultural behavior, 8
Cultural beliefs, 83-84
Cultural norms, 82-83
Cultural relativity, 88-89, 91. See
    also Ethnocentrism
Cultural values, 84
Culture(s):
  as adaptation to environment,
    79-87
  adaptive mechanisms of, 79-80
  and beauty, 93-95
  as behavior guide, 82-84
  and body image, 93-98
    and obesity, 94-95
    and weight, 96-98
  defined, 77, 79
  expressions of, behavior and
    artifacts in, 84-85
  and food, 75-91
    and diets, 76-79, 86-87
    of elderly, 172-175
  as functionally integrated system,
    85-86
  implications about, for health care
    providers, 89-91
  learning of (enculturation), 80-82
  and social organization, 150
  technology of. See
    Technology(ies)
  See also Societies; Subcultures
Curanderos in Puerto Rico, 229
Curative practices in health belief
    systems, 221-224
Curers as health care providers,
    224-226, 229

Dade County, Florida:
  breastfeeding program in,
    426-428
  day care center and lunch
    program for, 342
  dietary change acceptance in, 346
  Maternal, Infant and Children
    (MIC) Program in, 426-428

Dairy (milkhk) foods in Jewish
    dietary law, 217. See also Milk
Darwin, Charles, 279
Death and food rituals, 175-176
Demonstrations in nutrition
    education, 380
Developed countries:
  agricultural productivity in,
    259-263
  appropriate technologies in, 329,
    330
  classifications of, 293
  versus developing countries,
    286-295
Developing countries:
  appropriate technologies in,
    327-330
  classifications of, 293
  versus developed countries,
    286-295
  malnutrition and hunger in,
    286-291
  mechanized agriculture in,
    260-261
  wealth redistribution in, 318-322
  See also Less-developed countries
    (LDCs)
Development. See entries beginning
    with Economic development
Diabetics, food exchange system for,
    350-357
Diet(s):
  changes in. See Dietary change
    process of elderly. See
    Elderly, foods of, influences on
  influences on:
    biological, 76-78, 172, 174-175
    cultural. See Culture(s), and
      food
    environmental, 76-78
    family, 153-154
  and health, 361
  in forager food technologies,
    105, 107-109
  in horticultural food
    technologies, 111-112
  in industrialized agricultural
    food technologies,
    131-138
  in intensive agricultural food
    technologies, 119, 121
  in pastoral food technologies,
    114-115

Diet(s): (cont.)
  in human evolution
      reconstruction, 21-25
  recommended, 64
  self-monitoring of, 374, 375
  types of:
      macrobiotic, **159**
      protein-sparing, **360**
      therapeutic. *See* Therapeutic
          diets
      vegetarian. *See* Vegetarian diets
  in United States, changes in, 135
  See also Food(s)
Dietary adaptation to environment,
    19-21
Dietary allowances, recommended
    (RDA), **163**-164
Dietary change process, 333-367,
    371-377
  advocates for change in, 334-335,
      343-348
  counseling in, 371-377
  dietary innovations in, 335,
      349-367
      advantages of, 358-359,
          364-365
      compatibility with current
          beliefs of, 357-358
      complexity of, 349-357
      cost of, 363-364
      disadvantages of, 365-367
      efficiency of, 359-361
      enjoyability of, 362
      health effects of, 361
      legal sanctions against, 366
      profits from, 364
      public reaction to, 366
      religious concerns about, 367
  potential adopters of change in,
      334-343, 346-348
Dietary intakes, estimated safe and
    adequate daily (ESA), 136
Dietary laws in religion, 215-219.
    See also Food taboos
Dietary revolutions, 41-64
  agricultural, 41-53. *See also*
      Green Revolution
  industrial, 53-59. *See also*
      Industrial Revolution
  scientific, 59-64
Dieting, cultural aspects of, 93-96
Diet therapy. *See* Therapeutic diets
Dignity of potential adopters of
    change, 340-343

Directed change:
  in diet. *See* Dietary change
      process
  ethics of, 433-435
Discussion approaches to nutrition
    education, 380
Disease. *See* Illness
Distribution programs, family, for
    supplemental food, 394-397
Domestication of plants and
    animals, 42-44. *See also*
    Agriculture; Beef;
    Livestock production
Doubling times of populations, 251

EAAs (essential amino acids), 45-46
Ecological pressures of modern
    technology, 246, 248
Ecology, **244**
Economic alliances, food in,
    155-157
Economic development and under-
    development in world food
    crisis, 286-295
Economic development assistance
    in world food crisis, 304-315
Economic growth, self-sufficiency
    in, 321-322
Economic influences on foods of
    elderly, 172-175
Economic order. *See* International
    economic order in world food
    crisis
Education:
  in diet therapy counseling,
      372-373
  about nutrition:
      communication in, 237-241,
          382-391
      educational media in, 382-391
      as nutrition strategy, 380-391
      person-to-person approaches
          in, 387-391
Efficiency of dietary innovations,
    359-361
Eicosapentenoic acid (EPA), 30
Eijkman, Dr. Christian, 61
Elderly:
  foods of, influences on, 171-175
      biological, 172, 174-175
      religious, 215
      social, cultural, and economic,

    172-175
  nutrition programs for, 190, 193
Embargoes, **314**
Empacho, treatment of, 229
Employment in resource
    distribution, 304
Empty calories, **164**
Enclosure in Britain, 54
Encouragement in diet counseling,
    374, 376-377
Enculturation, 80-82. *See also*
    Culture(s)
Endemic, defined, **112**
Energy use in industrialized
    agriculture, 128-129
Enrichment of foods, **402,** 403.
      See also Food(s), fortification
  of
Entomophagy (insect-eating),
    75-76, 78
Environment:
  adaptation to. *See* Adaptation to
      environment
  diets influenced by, 76-78
EPA (eicosapentenoic acid), 30
Epidemiology, 6
Equity, self-sufficiency in, 321-322
Erosion of soils, 129-130, **248**
ESA (estimated safe and
    adequate daily dietary
    intakes), **136**
Eskimos adapting to environment,
    30
Essential amino acids (EAAs), 45-46
Essential nutrients in human
    evolution, 16-17
Estimated safe and adequate daily
    dietary intakes (ESA), **136**
Ethics of directed change, 433-435
Ethnicity and food, 55-56, 183-185,
    197-203
Ethnocentrism, 87-89. *See also*
    Cultural relativity
Ethnography, **47,** 84, 416
Etiquette of food, 151
Evolution:
  human. *See* Human evolution
  primate, 17-21
  See also Adaptation to
      environment; Natural
      selection
Exchange systems for food,
    350-357

Exercise, recommended, 64
Expectation of change of potential
    adopters of change, 337-340
Exponential growth in population,
    250-252
Exports and imports, 315-317
Export taxes, **316**
Extended families, 151

Families:
    alliances of, food in, 139,
        150-154
    diet influenced by, 153-154
    structures of, 151-154
Family distribution programs as
    supplemental food programs,
    394-397
Family farms, 124-126, 130-131
Family planning programs, 253-257
Farmers' markets, 132
Farming:
    corporations in, 125-126
    family, 124-126, 130-131
    livestock, 133-134, 268-270
    organic (sustainable), 131. *See
        also* Organic gardening
Farming Systems Research and
    Extension (FSR/E), 282
Fast foods, content of, 165
Fatalism in peasant world view, 210
Fat exchange for diabetics, 355-356
Fat in fast foods, 165
Favism and adaptation to
    environment, 14-15
Fecal remains of humans, analysis
    of,
    23-24
Federal government, food programs
    of. *See* Food programs, of U.S.
    federal government
Feeding programs. *See* Food
    programs
Feedlots for cattle, 134
Fermentation:
    of milk, 37
    nutritional benefits of, 144
Fertilizers, chemical, 124,
    264-265, 280, 281
FFW (Food-For-Work) programs,
    395-396
First World countries, 293
Fish in food production, 270-274

Fish protein concentrate (FPC),
    271-273
Fixation of nitrogen, **264**
Fleyshik (meat) foods in Jewish
    dietary law, 217
Fodder, **113**
Food(s):
    adulteration of, 59-60
    of colonists, 52-53
    cultural aspects of, 75-91
    of elderly. *See* Elderly, foods of,
        influences on
    enrichment of, **402**, 403
    and ethnicity, 55-56, 183-185,
        197-203
    exchanges of, between old and
        new worlds, 52-53
    fortification of, **402**-405
    functions of, 85-86
    and gender, 159-161. *See also*
        Women, in agricultural
        productivity
    as gift, 156-157
    historical influences on. *See*
        Dietary revolutions
    for infants. *See* Infants, feeding
    in life cycle. *See* Life cycle, food
        in
    of native Americans (Indians),
        52-53, 201-202
    preparation of, cultural
        influences on, 78
    preservation of, 60-61
    as prestige symbol, 181-182
    restrictions on, postpartum,
        170-171. *See also* Food
        taboos
    and social class, 176-181
        and castes, 179-181
    social context of, 149-194, *See
        also entries beginning with*
        Social
    superenrichment of, 403
    trade in, 155-156
    transportation of, 56-57, 101-102
    types of:
        alternate, for world food
            supplies, 273-275
        fast, 165
        formulated, as nutrition
            strategy, 398-402
        Kosher, 216-217
        natural or less processed,
            145-146

Shokori, 162
    See also Diet(s)
Food additives, 59-60, 144-145
Food advertising, 388-389
Food aid, 193, 305-309
Food allergies, 360, 361
Food co-ops, 132, 135
Food cravings during pregnancy,
    167-170
Food crisis. *See* World food crisis
Food etiquette, 151
Food exchange systems, 350-357
Food for Peace Act, 306-307
Food-For-Work (FFW) programs,
    395-396
Food-getting (subsistence)
    activities. *See* Food
    technologies
Food groups:
    in food exchange systems,
        350-357
    for vegetarian diets, 71-72
Food practices:
    ideological basis of. *See*
        Ideological basis of food
        practices
    regional and ethnic, 197-203
Food processing, nutritional
    changes in, 143-146
Food production:
    women in, 311-313
    and world food supplies,
        257-276, 279-282
    alternate foods in, 273-275
    aquaculture in, 274
    climate in, 267
    of developed countries,
        agricultural productivity
        in, 259-263
    fish in, 270-274
    Green Revolution in, 260,
        279-282, 363-364
    land cultivation in, 258-259
    livestock production and meat
        consumption in, 268-270
    pesticides in, 124, 265-267,
        281
    research on, 275-276
    soil nutrients and chemical
        fertilizers in, 124, 264-265
        280, 281
    water (irrigation) in, 263-264,
        274

Food programs:
in Chile, 393-394
of U.S. federal government, 177,
189-194
food stamp, 189-191, 303
supplemental, 190, 192-193,
364, 387, 391-398,
426-428
thrifty, 177
Food Research and Action Center,
(FRAC), 406
Food rituals, 212-213
Food security, world, in resource
distribution, 314-315
Food Security Wheat Reserve Act,
314
Food Stamp Act of 1977, 191
Food stamp programs, 189-191,
303
Food supplies. *See* World food
supplies
Food systems:
local (farmers' markets), 132
in Mexico (Sistema Alimentario
Mexico), 302-303
Food taboos:
in dietary change, 341
postpartum, 171
during pregnancy, 167, 170
in religion, 215-219
Food technologies, 101-140
agricultural:
industrialized. *See*
Industrialized agriculture
intensive, 115-121
changing, 138-140
forager, 103-109. *See also*
Foragers; Foraging
horticultural, 109-112. *See also*
Horticulture
pastoral, 112-115
See also Agriculture
Forager food technologies, 103-109
Foragers, 6
Foraging, **42**, 103
Foreign aid in world food crisis,
304-315
Formulated foods as nutrition
strategy, 398-402
Fortification of foods, **402-405**
Fossil teeth, studies of, 21-23
FPC (fish protein concentrate),
271-273

FRAC (Food Research and Action
Center), 406
Friends, relationships of, food in,
154-155
Fruit exchange for diabetics, 352
FSR/E (Farming Systems Research
and Extension), 282

Gardening, organic, 329. *See also*
Organic farming
GATT (General Agreement on
Tariffs and Trade), 316
Gender and food, 159-161. *See also*
Women, in agricultural
production
General Agreement on Tariffs and
Trade (GATT), 316
Generation gap, 82
Genetic adaptation to environment,
7, 11-16, 35-38
Genetic diversity, loss of, 281
Genetic uniformity, 122-123, **301,**
303
Geophagia (clay eating), 168-170
Germ plasm banks, 281
Gibbons, Euell, 106-107
Gifts of food, 156-157
Glucose–6–Phosphate Dehydro-
genase (G6PD) deficiency,
13-15
GNP (gross national product) in
development, 286
Goiters, **220**
Goodall, Jane, 20-21
Grains:
lodging of, 280
semidwarf, 279-280
supplies of, and livestock
production, 268-269
See also Corn; Rice; Semidwarf
wheat
Green Revolution, 260, 279-282,
363-364. *See also*
Agricultural revolution
Gross national product (GNP) in
in development, 286
Groups, specific identifiable, 79.
See also Culture(s)
Group surveys in nutrition program
assessment, 416-417
Grubs, **214**

G6PD (Glucose–6–Phosphate
Dehydrogenase) deficiency,
13-15
Guatemala:
INCAP project in, 419-420
Maya Indian community in, 211

Hardin Village in Kentucky, 48-49
Hare Krishna devotees, **84,** 159
Health:
and body image, 95-96
and diet. *See* Diet(s), and health
holistic, 230
Health belief systems, 220-231
alternative, 229-231
Health care providers:
cultural implications for, 89-91
in diet counseling, 371-377
in health belief systems,
224-226, 229
in ideal weight determination,
96-98
Health care systems, appropriate
technologies in, 329-330
Heart disease, 115
Height and weight tables, 97
Hemlock, **59**
Herbal remedies for illness,
223-224, 229
Herbicides, chemical, 124. *See also*
Pesticides, chemical
Herbivores, teeth of, 23. *See also*
Vegetarian diets
High-yield varieties of seeds
(HYV), 279-281
Hindus of India, 180-181, 218-219
Holistic health movement, 230
Hominids. *See* Humans; *entries
beginning with* Human
Homo erectus in human evolution,
26-29
Homo sapiens in human evolution,
29-31
Homophily of potential adopters of
change and advocates for
change, 347-348
Honduras, grain supplies in,
268, 269
Horticultural food technologies,
109-112
Horticulture:
and agriculture, continuum

Horticulture: (cont.)
    between, 115*n. See also*
        Agriculture
    defined, 109
    slash-and-burn, 109, 231-233
Hot/cold humoral model of illness,
    221-224, 227-228
Human evolution, 21-31
    essential nutrients in, 16-17
    reconstructing, diet in, 21-25
    scenarios of, 25-31
        australopithecines in, 25
        Homo erectus in, 26-29
        Homo sapiens in, 29-31
    See also Adaptation to
        environment: Evolution
Human fecal remains, analysis of,
    23-24
Humans:
    adaptation to environment by. *See*
        Adaptation to environment,
        by humans
    skeletal analyses of, 24-25
    teeth of, 22
Humoral model of illness, hot/cold,
    221-224, 227-228
Hunger:
    community responses to,
        193-194. *See also*
        Food programs
    defined, 289
    in developing countries, 286-291
    world, politics of, 318-323
    See also Malnutrition; World food
        supplies
Hunting and gathering. *See* Forager
    food technologies; Foragers;
    Foraging
Hydraulic, defined **264**
HYV (high-yield varieties of
    seeds), 279-281

Ideal weight, determining, 96-98
Identifiable groups, specific, 79.
    See also Culture(s)
Ideological basis of food practices,
    205-233
    health belief systems in, 220-231
        alternative, 229-231
        religion in, 212-219, 231-233
    technology and social
        organization related
        to, 231-233

world view in, 206-211
    in peasant societies, 209-211
    in United States, 207-208
    See also Social, political, and
        ideological features of food
        technologies
Ideologies, **206**
    as adaptive mechanism, 80
    See also Beliefs
Illness:
    herbal remedies for, 223-224,
        229
    models of, 221-224, 227-228
    *See also specific entries, for
        example:* Heart disease,
        Malaria
Imports and exports, 315-317
Inborn errors of metabolism, **14**
INCAP (Nutritional Institute of
    Central America and Panama)
    project, 419-420
Incaparina, 399, 401
India, Hindus of, 180-181, 218-219
Indian Knoll in Kentucky, 48-49
Indian (native American) foods,
    52-53, 201-202
Indigenous, defined, **289**
Individual behavior, **8**
Individualism in U.S. world view,
    207-208
Industrialization:
    defined, 53
    in resource distribution, 304
Industrialized agriculture, 121-138
    alternatives to, 131-138
    chemical fertilizers in, 124,
        264-265, 280, 281
    chemical pesticides and
        herbicides in, 124,
        265-267, 281
    defined, 121
    diet and health in, 134-138
    energy use in, 128-129
    versus peasant agriculture,
        261-263
    people in, 130-131
    soil erosion in, 129-130
    water supplies in, 130
Industrialized societies:
    First World countries as, 293
    obesity in, 63-64
Industrial Revolution, 53-59,
    291-293

Infant-child mortality rates,
    290-291, 293, 296. *See also*
    Life expectancy by
    development of country
Infant-mother bonding in breast-
    feeding, 431
Infants, feeding, 162-163
    cultural influences on, 82
    by breast, 347-348, 425-431. *See
        also* La Lache League
    formulas for, 407-409, 430
    vegetarian diets in, 71
    WIC food program in, 190,
        192-193, 364, 393
Infections, breastfeeding as
    protection against, 430-431
Infiltration into tissues, **290**
Innovations, dietary. *See* Dietary
    change process, dietary
    innovations in
Insect-eating (entomophagy),
    75-76, 78
Institution development in
    economic development
    assistance, 309
Intensive agriculture, 115-121
Intercropping, 118, **261,** 262. *See
    also* Mixed cropping;
    Monocropping; Multiple
    cropping
Intermediate (appropriate)
    technologies, 327-330
International economic order in
    world food crisis:
    new, 320-321
    trade in, 315-317
International Maize and Wheat
    Improvement Center
    (CIMMYT), 279-281, 310
International Rice Research
    Institute (IRRI), 279-281, 310
International wealth redistribution,
    320-322
Intracultural variations in diet,
    86-87
Iron deficiency anemia, 169, 290
Iron in vegetarian diets, 70-71
IRRI (International Rice Research
    Institute), 279-281, 310
Irrigation, 124, 130, **244, 263-**264.
    See also Water
Italian-American food patterns,
    184-185

Japan, rice yields, in, 260
J-curve of population growth,
    250-252
Jewish dietary laws, 216-217
Jute, **120**
Kaiko in Tsembaga food practices,
    233
Kayapo in Brazil, 111
KIDSFOODS (nutrition newsletter),
    389
Kilograms, **393**
Kinship ties and food, 139,
    150-154
Kosher foods, 216-217
Krishna devotees, **84,** 159
Kula network in Trobriand Islands,
    155-156
!Kung Bushmen, **76,** 104, 105, 109
Kwashiorkor, **111,** 289, 290

Labor-intensive technologies, 328
Lactase deficiency (lactose
    intolerance), 35-38
Lacto-vegetarians, 68. *See also*
    Vegetarian diets
La cuarentena, 170-171
Ladyloe, 401
La Leche League, **82,** 428
Land cultivation in food
    production, 258-259
Land distribution in world food
    crisis, 296-298
    and agrarian reform, 298-300
Land tenure policies, **298-300**
LDCs (less-developed countries),
    293, 294. *See also*
    Developing countries
Leaf protein, 274-275
Learning, malnutrition related to,
    291
Lecture-discussion approach to
    nutrition education, 380
Legal sanctions against dietary
    innovations, 366
Less-developed countries (LDCs),
    293, 294. *See also* Developing
    countries
Let-down response in breastfeeding,
    429
Life cycle, food in, 161-176
    in adolescence, 163-166
    at death, 175-176

in infancy and childhood,
    162-163
in old age, 171-175
in pregnancy, 166-171
Life expectancy by development of
    country, 295. *See also* Infant-
    child mortality rates
Lifestyle of clients in diet therapy
    counseling, 373
Limited good notion in peasant
    world view, 210-211
Livestock production, 133-134,
    268-270. *See also* Beef; Meat
    eating
Local food systems, 132
Lodging of grain, 280
Lunch and breakfast programs for
    schools, 191-192, 391-393,
    396-397
Lying fallow, **109**

Macrobiotic diet, **159**
Maize. *See* Corn
Malanga, **350**
Malaria, 13-15, 220-221, 224
Malnutrition:
    defined, 289
    in developing countries, 286-291
    in infant-child mortality rates,
        290-291
    protein/calorie, 289-291
        kwashiorkor, **111,** 289, 290
        marasmus, 289, 290
    See also Hunger
Malthus, Thomas, 244, 249-250
Manioc, **111**
Manoff International Project in the
    Philippines, 383-384, 386
Marasmus, 289, 290. *See also*
    Kwashiorkor
Market economies, transition to,
    119-121
Markets:
    farmers', 132
    in resource distribution, 301-303
Marshall plan, 305
Masai of Africa, 114, 115
Mass media in nutrition, 382-391
Mastodons, **43**
Maternal and child food programs.
    See Food programs, of U.S.
    federal government

Maternal, Infant and Children
    (MIC) Program of Dade
    County, 426-428
Maya Indian community in
    Guatemala, 211
Meat eating:
    of beef, 78, 134-135, 218-219
    in food production, 268-270
    by humans, 21-23
    of pigs, by Tsembaga, 232-233
    by primates, 20-21
    See also Animals; Livestock
        production
Meat exchange for diabetics,
    354-355
Meat (fleyshik) foods in Jewish
    dietary law, 217
Mechanized agriculture in
    developing countries, 260-261.
    See also Technology(ies)
Media in nutrition, 382-391
Medicinal herbs, 223-224
Mendel, Gregor, 279
Mental development and
    malnutrition, 291
Metabolism, inborn errors of, **14**
Metaphysical, defined, **80**
Metates (querns), **46,** 47
Mexican American food practices,
    198
Mexico:
    agricultural development in,
        42-44, 46-47
    grain supplies in, 268-269
    Green Revolution in, 281-282,
        363-364
    Sistema Alimentario Mexico food
        system in, 302-303
MIC (Maternal, Infant and
    Children) Program of Dade
    County, 426-428
Milk:
    aversion to (lactase deficiency),
        35-38
    for children, government
        program for, 391
    Chilean distribution of, 393-394
    for infants, 347-348, 425-431.
        See also Infants, feeding
    as food taboo, 341
    pastoralist reliance on, 114, 115
    types of:
        condensed, 60

Milk: (cont.)
    cow's versus human, 430. *See
        also* for infants, *above*
    fermented, 37
Milk exchange for diabetics, 351
Milkhk (dairy) foods in Jewish
    dietary law, 217
Milk nurses in infant formula
    marketing, 407
Mineral deficiencies, 290
Miskito Indians of Nicaragua,
    138-140
Mixed cropping, 118-119. *See also*
    Intercropping; Monocropping
    (monoculture); Multiple
    cropping
Modern technology versus
    appropriate technology, 328.
    See also Technology(ies)
Monocropping (monoculture),
    122-123, **261**. *See also*
    Intercropping; Mixed cropping;
    Multiple cropping
Mortality rates, infant-child,
    290-291, 293, 296. *See also*
    Life expectancy by
    development of country
Mother-child bonding, 431
Mothercraft Centers, 281
Mukhe bhat (rice-feeding
    ceremony), 162, 213
Multilateral economic development
    assistance, 305
Multiple cropping, 124. *See also*
    Intercroping; Monocropping
    (monoculture); Mixed
    cropping
Mutations, **17**
Myocardial infarction, **115**
Myths, **214**

National cuisines, 55-56. *See also*
    Ethnicity and food
National School Breakfast Program,
    191, 391. *See also* Breakfast
    and lunch programs for
    schools
National School Lunch Program,
    191, 391. *See also* Breakfast
    and lunch programs for
    schools
Native Americans (Indians), foods
    of, 52-53, 201-202

Natural or less processed foods,
    145-146
Natural selection, 8, 11-12. *See
    also* Evolution: Genetic
    adaptation to environment
Nitrogen balance, **232**
Nitrogen fixation, **264**
Needs assessment in nutrition
    program planning, 413-418
Neighbors, relationships of, food in,
    154-155
Nephritis, **230**
Nestlé Company marketing of
    infant formulas, 407-408
New World and old world, food
    exchanges between, 52-53
Nomadism in pastoralism, 112-113
Nonshivering thermogenesis, 30
Norms, cultural, 82-83
Nuclear families, **151**, 152
Nursing homes, foods in, 172-174
Nutricube, 399, 401
Nutrients:
    essential, in human evolution,
        16-17
    interactions of, in government
        food programs, 398
    soil, 264-265, 280, 281
    in vegetarian diets, 69-72
Nutrition:
    assessment of, methods of,
        414-416
    controversies about, 86
    education about. *See* Education,
        about nutrition
    effects on:
        of agricultural revolution,
            47-49
        of food processing, 143-146
        of pica, 169-170
    information about, sources of,
        415-416
Nutrition Institute of Central
    America and Panana (INCAP)
    project in Guatemala, 419-420
Nutrition Change of the Month
    Project, 387, 391
Nutrition newsletter for children,
    389
Nutrition programs and strategies,
    379-409, 413-422, 425-431,
    433-435
    directed change ethics in,
        433-435
    for elderly, 190, 193

program planning in, 413-422
    evaluation in, 421-422
    goal and objective
        development in,
        418-419
    implementation in, 419-421
    needs assessment (community
        diagnosis) in, 413-418
    types of:
        breastfeeding, 425-431
        consumer advocacy, 405-409
        food fortification, 402-405
        formulated foods, 398-402
        nutrition education, 380-391
        supplemental food, 391-398

Obesity, 63-64, 94-95
Old age. *See* Elderly
Old world and new world, food
    exchanges between, 52-53
Omnivores, **20**
Omnivorousness:
    of humans, 21-24
    of primates, 20-21
    See also Meat eating; Vegetarian
        diets
Opposable thumbs, **18**
Organic farming, 131. *See also*
    Farming
Organic gardening, 329
Organoleptic, defined, **401**
Osteomalacia, 144*n*
Ovo-lacto-vegetarians, 68. *See also*
    Vegetarian diets

Palaua, **346**-347
Paleontologists, **24**
Panama:
    family food program in, 394-395
    in INCAP, 419-420
Panel discussions in nutrition
    education, 380
Parasites, **108**
Pareve foods, 217
Pasteur, Louis, 344-345
Pasteurization, **60**
Pastoral food technologies, 112-115
Pathogens, **265**
Patients in diet counseling,
    372-377
PCM (protein/calorie
    malnutrition), 289-291. *See
    also* Kwashiorkor

Peasant agriculturalists, 116-119, 261-263
Peasant societies, 117-119, 209-211
Pellagra, 44, 46, 241
Personalities of advocates for change, 344-345
Person-to-person nutrition education, 380-382
    with mass media approach, 387-391
Peruvian anchovy industry, 271
Peruvita, 400-401
Pesticides, chemical, 124, 265-267, 281
Pestles, **29**
Philippines, Manoff International Project in, 383-384, 386
Photosynthesis research, 275-276
Physical environment, cultural adaptations to. *See* Food technology(ies)
Physiological adaptation to environment, 7, 9-11, 13-16, 30
Phytic acid (phytate), 144
Pica during pregnancy, 168-170
Pigs in Tsembaga food practices, 232-233
Pinta (spirochetosis), 220
Plantain, **111**
Plants, domestication of, 42-44. *See also* Grains; Herbivores, teeth of; Vegetarian diets
Political alliances, food in, 155, 157-159
Political consequences of agricultural revolution, 49-50. *See also* Social, political, and ideological features of food technologies
Politics of world hunger, 318-323
Populations:
    doubling times of, 251
    growth of, and world food supplies, 249-257
    See also Infant-child mortality rates; Life expectancy by development of country
Postpartum food restrictions, 170-171
Potable water, **394**
Potential adopters of change in dietary change process, 334-343, 346-348

Potlatch, functions of, 157
Poverty lines (indexes), 176-178
Pragmatism, **207**, 208
Prasadam of Krishna devotees, 159
Pregnancy:
    food in, 166-171
    toxemia of, **363**
    weight gains during, 166
Preservation of food, 60-61
Prestige:
    of advocates for change, 345-346
    food symbolizing, 181-182
Preventative practices in health belief systems, 221-224
Price ceilings, 303
Price policies in resource distribution, 302-304, 316
Price supports, 303
Pride of potential adopters of change, 340-343
Primate adaptation to environment, 17-21
    dietary, 19-21
    See also Human evolution
Primordial, defined, **16**
Problem solving approaches to nutrition education, 380
Profits from dietary innovations, 364
Prohibition, consequences of, 90
Protein:
    fish, 271-273
    leaf, 274-275
    single-cell, 273-274
    in vegetarian diets, 69-70
Protein/calorie malnutrition (PCM), 289-291. *See also* Kwashiorkor
Protein complementation, 45-47
Protein deficiency, 45
Protein-sparing diets, **360**
Protein supplements and vitamin A deficiencies, 398
Protestant ethic, myth of, 292
PSAs (public service announcements), 385-386
Public. *See* Communities
Public Law 480 (Food for Peace Act), 306-307
Puerto Rico:
    food practices of, 200-201
    health belief systems of, 226-229
Pulque, 144
Pure Food and Drug Act of 1906, 60

Pygmies of Ituri forest, 156

Querns (metates), **46,** 47

Rain, acid, **248.** *See also* Water
Rampur, India, rules of service for castes, 180-181
Rationalism in U.S. world view, 208
Raw materials in balance of trade, 317
Recommended Dietary Allowances (RDA), **163**-164
Red Dye No. 2, 145
Reformist approaches to wealth redistribution, 318-322
Refrigeration, effects on food of 57-58
Regional food practices, 197-203. *See also* Ethnicity and food
Religion:
    defined, 212
    and dietary innovation, 367
    and diets of elderly, 215
    food taboos in, 215-219. *See also* Food taboos
    food rituals in, 212-213
    Hare Krishna, 84, 159
    in ideological basis of food practices, 212-219, 231-233
    Jewish, 216-217
    See also Shamans
Reproduction. *See* Pregnancy
Resource distribution in world food crisis, 295-315, 318-322
Revolutionary approaches to wealth redistribution, 318-322
Revolutions. *See* Dietary revolutions
Rice:
    in Japan, yields of, 260
    semidwarf, 279-280
    See also International Rice Research Institute (IRRI)
Rice-feeding ceremony *(mukhe bhat),* 162, 213
Rickets, **107**
Rites (rituals):
    food, 212-213
    of passage, 161
    Tsembaga, 232-233
Riverine, defined, **43**

Rumbin in Tsembaga rituals, 232-233
Ruminant animals, **112**

Salt. *See* Sodium
Sanctions, **207**
Sashimi, **78**
Scanning electron microscopy, 23
School breakfast and lunch programs, 191-192, 391-393, 396-397
Scientific revolution, 59-64
SCP (single-cell protein), 273-274
Scurvy, **107**
Second Harvest food program, 194
Second World countries, 293
Seeds:
    high-yield varieties of (HYV), 279-281
    storage of, 281
Self-monitoring of diets, 374, 375
Self-sufficiency as route to equity and growth, 321-322
Shamans, **224**-226
Shokhets, **216**
Shokori food, 162
Shoshone Indian rites of passage, 163
Single-cell protein (SCP), 273-274
Single-parent families, 152
Sisal plants, 120
Sistema Alimentario Mexico (SAM), 302-303
Skeletal analyses of humans, 24-25
Slash-and-burn agriculture, 109, 231-233
Social, political and ideological features of food technologies:
    forager, 104-105
    horticultural, 110-111
    intensive agricultural, 115-117
    pastoral, 113-114
    See also Ideological basis of food practices
Social class and food, 176-181
    and castes, 179-181
Social consequences:
    of agricultural revolution, 49-50
    of dietary innovations, 364-365
    of Green Revolution, 279-282
Social influences on foods of elderly, 172-175
Social interaction, 149-150

Socialism, problems of, 319-320
Social organization:
    as adaptive mechanism of culture, 80
    defined, 150
    and food, 149-194, 231-233
    in foraging societies (bands), 105
Social status and food, 159-161
Social stratification and agricultural development, 50
Social support. *See* Support groups
Social ties, food in solidifying, 139, 150-159
Societies:
    defined, 79
    industrialized. *See* Industralized societies
    peasant, 117-119, 209-211. *See also* Peasant agriculturalists
    See also Culture(s)
Sodium:
    in adaptation to environment, 13
    in fast foods, 165
    U.S. consumption of, 136
Soils:
    erosion of, 129-130, **248**
    nutrients in, 264-265, 280, 281
    waterlogged, 264
    See also Irrigation; Water
Soviet bloc countries, 293
Specific identifiable groups, 79. *See also* Culture(s)
Spice-seeking in agricultural revolution, 50-52
Spiritist theories of illness, 228
Spirochetes, **220**
Spirochetosis (pinta), 220
Sri Lankan birth rates, 256
Starchy vegetable-bread exchange for diabetics, 353-354
Status and food, 159-161. *See also* entries beginning *with* Social
Steak tartare, **78**
Steppes, **114**
Stones flakes, **26**
Subcultures, 79, 87. *See also* Culture(s)
Subsidies, **303**, 316
Subsistence activities. *See* Food technologies
Subsistence agriculture. *See* Peasant agriculture; Peasant societies
Sugar consumption in United States, 136

Superenrichment of foods, 403
Supplemental food programs, 190, 192-193, 364, 387, 391-398, 426-428. *See also* Food programs
Support groups:
    for breastfeeding, 426-429
    in diet counseling, 374, 376-377
Surplus (commodity) food distribution, 193
Surveys in nutrition program assessment, 416-417
Suspiciousness in peasant world view, 209-210
Sustainable (organic) farming, 131. *See also* Farming; Organic gardening
Susto, **227**
Synergy, **231**

Taboos. *See* Food taboos
Tactile pads, **18**
Tapirs, **43**
Tariffs, **316**, 317
Taro, **110**
Taste preferences, influences on, 78
Taxes, export, **316**
Technical assistance in economic development, 309-310
Technology(ies):
    as adaptive mechanism of culture, 79-80
    agricultural. *See* Agricultural revolution; Green Revolution
    appropriate (intermediate), 327-330
    capital-intensive versus labor-intensive, 328
    defined, 103
    food (subsistence). *See* Food technologies
    ideological basis of food practices related to, 231-233
    modern:
        versus appropriate, 328
        ecological pressures of, 246, 248
Teen years, food in, 163-166
Teeth, fossil, studies of, 21-23
Tehuacan Valley, Mexico, agriculture, 42-44, 46-47
Teratogenic, defined, **62**

Terracing, **109**
Therapeutic diets:
   counseling in, 371-377
   food exchanges for, 350-357
Third World countries, 293. *See
   also* Developing countries;
   Less-developed countries;
   (LDCs)
Thrifty food plan, 177
Thumbs, opposable, **18**
Tithing, **216**
Title III and Title VII nutrition
   program for elderly, 190, 193
Totemism, 213-214
Toxemia of pregnancy, **363**
Trade:
   balance of, 316-317
   in food, 155-156
   in international economic order,
     315-317
Trade barriers, 316
Traditional (peasant) agriculture,
   116-119, 261-263. *See also*
   Peasant societies
Transportation of food, 56-57,
   101-102
Trobriand Islands, 154-156, 182
Tsembaga of New Guinea, 111,
   176, 231-233
Tubewells, **263**

United Nations World Health
   Organization (WHO)
   International Code of
   Marketing, 408-409
United States:
   corn yields in, 261
   dietary changes in, 135
   family structure in, changing,
     152-154
   food programs in. *See* Food
     programs, of U.S. federal
     government
   sodium consumption in, 165
   sugar consumption in, 136
   world view in, 207-208

Vegans, 68, 72. *See also*
   Vegetarian diets
Vegetable exchange for diabetics,
   351-354
Vegetarian diets:
   benefits of, 67-68
   nutrients in, 69-72
   political aspects of, 159
   of primates, 19-20
   types of, 68, 159
   See also Herbivores, teeth of
Viruses, Puerto Rican view of, 228
Vitamin deficiencies, 61, 107, 111,
   290-291, 398
Vitamins:
   discoveries of, 61-62
   specific:
     A, 290, 398
     B_1, 61, 111
     B-12, 70
     C, 17, 107
     D, 70

Wallabies, **214**
Water:
   in food production, 263-264,
     274
   in industrialized agriculture, 130
   potable, **394**
   See also Acid rain; Irrigation
Waterlogging of soils, 264
Wealth, redistribution of, 318-322
Weight. *See* Body weight
Wheat, semidwarf, 279-280. *See
   also* Food Security Wheat
   Reserve Act; Grains;
   International Maize and Wheat
   Improvement Center
   (CIMMYT)
White bread, 60
WHO (World Health Organization)
   International Code of
   Marketing, 408-409
WIC food program (Supplemental
   Food Program for Women,

Infants, and Children), 190,
   192-193, 364, 393
Women:
   in agricultural production,
     311-313
   hunger and malnutrition among,
     286-288
   supplemental food program for,
     190, 192-193, 364, 393,
     426-428
World food crisis, 285-323
   economic development and
     underdevelopment in,
     286-295
   international economic order
     in, 315-317, 320-321
   politics of world hunger in,
     318-323
   resource distribution in, 295-315
World food security, 314-315
World food supplies, 243-282
   and food production. *See* Food
     production, and world food
     supplies
   and population growth, 249-257
   predictions about, background
     on, 244-249
World Health Organization (WHO)
   International Code of
   Marketing, 408-409
World hunger, politics of, 318-323
World view in ideological basis of
   food practices, 206-211
   in peasant societies, 209-211
   in United States, 207-208
Wormwood, **223**

Yaks, **114**
Yap dietary change, 343, 345

Zinc in vegetarian diets, 70
Zulu tribe of Africa, 414